This book analyzes the relationship between literature and religious conflict in seventeenth-century England, showing how literary texts grew out of and addressed the contemporary controversy over ceremonial worship. Examining the meaning and function of religion in seventeenth-century England, the book shows that the controversies over religious ceremony which were central to the English Revolution had broad cultural significance; they involved not only conflicting attitudes towards art and the body, but a clash between different ways of constructing social relations, human identity, and the relation of the Protestant present to the Jewish, pagan, and Catholic past. Achsah Guibbory's new and original readings of Herbert, Herrick, Browne, and Milton explain how their writings show what was at stake in the struggle over ceremonial worship, and how different ideas of community turned on that conflict.

CEREMONY AND COMMUNITY FROM HERBERT TO MILTON

"Religion Endangered," engraved half-title by William Marshall, in Francis Quarles, *The Shepherds Oracles* (London, 1646). Reproduced by permission of the University of Illinois Rare Book Room (original is approximately 16.7 by 12.2 centimeters).

CEREMONY AND COMMUNITY FROM HERBERT TO MILTON

Literature, religion, and cultural conflict
in seventeenth-century England

ACHSAH GUIBBORY

University of Illinois

CAMBRIDGE
UNIVERSITY PRESS

PUBLISHED BY THE PRESS SYNDICATE OF THE UNIVERSITY OF CAMBRIDGE
The Pitt Building, Trumpington Street, Cambridge, United Kingdom

CAMBRIDGE UNIVERSITY PRESS
The Edinburgh Building, Cambridge CB2 2RU, UK   http://www.cup.cam.ac.uk
40 West 20th Street, New York, NY 10011–4211, USA   http://www.cup.org
10 Stamford Road, Oakleigh, Melbourne 3166, Australia
Ruiz de Alarcón 13, 28014 Madrid, Spain

First published 1998
Reprinted 1999

Printed in the United Kingdom at the University Press, Cambridge

Typeset in Baskerville 11/12½ pt   [CE]

A catalogue record for this book is available from the British Library

Library of Congress Cataloguing in Publication data
Guibbory, Achsah, 1945–
Ceremony and Community from Herbert to Milton: Literature, religion
and cultural conflict in seventeenth-century England
p.   cm.
ISBN 0 521 59355 7 (hardback)
1. English literature – Early modern, 1500–1700 – History and criticism.
2. Christianity and literature–England–History – 17th century.
3. Religion and literature – History – 17th century.
4. Browne, Thomas, Sir, 1605–1682 – Religion.
5. Herrick, Robert, 1591–1675. Hesperides.   6. England – Church history – 17th century.
7. Herbert, George, 1593–1633 – Religion.   8. Rites and ceremonies in literature.
9. Milton, John, 1608–1674 – Religion.   10. Cultural conflict in literature.
11. Community in literature.   12. Ritual in literature.   I. Title.
PR438.R45G85   1998
820.9′3823 – dc21   97–10269 CIP

ISBN 0 521 59355 7 hardback

To my friends and family, whose
love is a blessing

Contents

Acknowledgments

In the process of completing what has turned out to be a ten-year project, I have accumulated debts which are a pleasure to acknowledge, since they are marks of personal as well as professional bonds. My father, who always encouraged my scholarly life, first got me thinking about religion, though I long resisted writing about the subject. A fellowship from the Huntington Library in 1987 allowed me to begin my research in an ideal setting that provided not only books but a beautiful place and a wonderful community of scholars, whose conversation was a real pleasure. Among that community, Paul Christianson encouraged me to believe that I was on the right track and that my project might interest historians. Over the years, I have had ongoing conversations about literature and religion with Dayton Haskin, Claude Summers, Susan Schibanoff, and Tom Hester. All are very special people who have deeply affected my thinking.

Several people read and responded to various parts of the manuscript. I was fortunate to have the opportunity to present an earlier version of chapter 6 to the Newberry Library Milton Seminar. I am grateful to the participants of that seminar, especially to Michael Lieb, David Loewenstein, Helen Marlborough, Michael Murrin, Regina Schwartz, Janel Mueller, Stella Revard, Stephen Honeygosky, Rick Mallette, and Al Labriola for helpful comments on this Milton material. Tom Hester gave a characteristically rigorous reading of an early version of the Herbert chapter; Helen Wilcox read a later version, offering encouragement at a critical time. Noralyn Masselink read the Herrick essay, and Michael Lieb heroically took on both Milton chapters. For all their suggestions, insight, and generosity, I am deeply grateful.

The two readers for Cambridge University Press offered useful, sympathetic, and amazingly speedy reports. I could not have asked for better readers. Josie Dixon has been the kind of editor a scholarly writer dreams of having but does not expect to find. Her combination of intellectual acuity, efficiency, and kindness is rare. I am deeply indebted to her for supporting this project and for moving it so quickly into print.

Some of my debts are nearer home. I am grateful to the University of Illinois for a sabbatical leave, to its Research Board for granting me a research assistant and released time at a crucial moment, and to my department head, Richard Wheeler, for support that allowed me to complete this book in timely fashion. Robin Maier was an exemplary research assistant. Joan Klein, Marianne Kalinke, Dale Kramer, Caroline Hibbard, and, most recently, Lori Newcomb have encouraged the project in various ways, while weekly lunches with Sonia Carringer helped keep me sane.

The Rare Book Room of the University of Illinois has long been a wonderful resource for my research; the Beineke Library of Yale University was useful at a late stage in the work. I thank the staffs of these two rare book libraries, but especially Fred Nash at the University of Illinois, who has gone out of his way for me so many times.

Last but hardly least, thanks and apologies must go to my husband, Tony Kaufman, and my son Gabe, who have suffered my obsession and are probably even more relieved than I to see this project come to a conclusion.

The book is dedicated to my special community of friends and family (many more than can be named here), without whom it would not have been written.

Parts of several chapters appeared in earlier, different versions, and I am grateful for permission to reprint this material.

Chapter 4 includes material from my two essays: "The Temple of *Hesperides* and Anglican-Puritan Controversy." Reprinted from *The Muses Commonweale: Poetry and Politics in Seventeenth-century England* edited by Claude J. Summers and Ted-Larry Pebworth, by permission of the University of Missouri Press. Copyright © 1988 by the Curators of the University of Missouri.
"Enlarging the Limits of the Religious Lyric: the Case of Herrick's *Hesperides*." Reprinted from *New Perspectives on the*

Seventeenth-century Religious Lyric edited by John R. Roberts, by permission of the University of Missouri Press. Copyright © 1994 by the Curators of the University of Missouri.

A section of Chapter 5 reprints material from " 'A rationall of old rites': Sir Thomas Browne's *Urn Buriall* and the Conflict over Ceremony," *Yearbook of English Studies*, volume 21. Copyright © 1991 by The Modern Humanities Research Association.

Chapter 7 includes an excerpt from "Donne, Milton, and Holy Sex" from *Milton Studies*, volume 32, edited by Albert C. Labriola. Copyright © 1995 by the University of Pittsburgh Press. Reprinted by permission of the publisher.

Note on the text: I have followed old spelling but modernized i/j and u/v in titles and quotations. For seventeenth-century texts, the place of publication is presumed to be London unless otherwise noted.

CHAPTER I

Introduction

This book attempts to understand the religious conflicts of the English Revolution. How could people feel so strongly about religious ceremonies that now seem insignificant? Sir Thomas Browne remarked at the outbreak of civil war, "I would not perish upon a Ceremony, Politick point or indifferency,"[1] and we might share his bewilderment at those who would risk martyrdom rather than perform the contested ceremonies, or those who, on the other side, would fight to preserve them. In order to understand the larger human and cultural (rather than more narrow theological or political) significance of these religious conflicts, we need a better grasp of the symbolic meanings of the conflict over worship – and of what religion meant to people in early modern England. A revaluation of seventeenth-century religious conflict demands a reinterpretation of seventeenth-century literature, so much of which is concerned with religion.

Revisionist historians stress continuities in seventeenth-century England rather than revolutionary change, but there persists a sense that the seventeenth century constitutes a crucial period in the emergence of the modern world. Many have felt compelled to understand the transformations that have left their mark on Western culture. The seventeenth-century conflict over religious worship provides insight into the process and significance of these cultural transformations, for it involved a struggle between competing ideas of order. As we shall see, the religious beliefs that collided in the battles over ceremonial worship comprised two different ways of ordering experience: one based on notions of unity, wholeness, and hierarchical integration; the other based on a principle of division, opposition, and difference. I wish to untangle the human and ethical implications of these cultural conflicts, whose legacy continues to define cultural conflicts in our own time.

In the current era of literary and cultural studies that looks to material explanations of experience and behavior as well as phenomena – when it does not discount the possibility of coherent causative explanations – "religion" has been understood in terms of power politics, when it has not been discarded as an outmoded, uninteresting subject of inquiry. I want to argue for a new attention to the function of religion in seventeenth-century England, where religious beliefs, values, and institutions were interwoven with most aspects of society and experience. In spite of gradual secularization, religion was a powerful and pervasive determinant of social and political relations, as well as of the material experience of individuals, some of whom were corporeally and financially punished for voicing or openly practicing their religious beliefs. In the conflict over worship, we see how deeply religion determined texts and experience in seventeenth-century England, shaping cultural as well as individual values and identity.[2]

Religion was not, of course, the sole cause of either the English Revolution or the broader cultural upheaval of the seventeenth century. The issues involved in England's civil war are multiple and complex. Historians have debated what causes or explanations of the Revolution are most compelling, and consensus seems impossible. Surely political and socioeconomic factors are undeniable.[3] Nevertheless, many historians see religion as an important cause of the war. John Morrill has emphasized the mobilizing power of religious conviction. The debates in Parliament in the early 1640s about religious reform show the power of religious motivations. Conrad Russell observes that, though religion did not "cause" the war, "the parties were divided by religion."[4] Without denying interrelations among religious, political, and socioeconomic matters, I focus attention on the role of religion in the belief that conflicts over worship were an integral part of, and an important index to, the cultural disruptions of seventeenth-century England.

The period of the mid-century revolution and the years surrounding it has seen considerable interest recently among historians and literary scholars. Historians have been reexamining the early Stuart church and the emergence of Laudianism. Religious conformity is finally receiving serious attention.[5] But the discipline of history does not address the kinds of broad cultural questions that interest me. The new historicism of seventeenth-century literary studies has explored the political and cultural engagement of literary texts, showing how they are rooted in their particular historical moment. Religion, however, has been largely neglected, though there are signs of change.[6] Still, even when religion has been the object of attention, the emphasis has been on politics when it was not on theology. Radical religion and puritanism have been of most interest as they are believed to counter traditional hierarchies and a repressive dominant ideology, and as they seem precursors for modern political activism. This interest perhaps reflects not just a secular but a Protestant bias – evident in Christopher Hill's ground-breaking books and even in Keith Thomas's monumental *Religion and the Decline of Magic*, which relegates Catholic thinking to superstition. As Christopher Haigh has observed, much of the "history" of religion in England has been written from a perspective that assigns a questionable inevitability and progressivism to Protestantism.[7] Such a bias has also affected the interpretation of seventeenth-century devotional literature. Reacting against earlier twentieth-century readings which privileged Anglo-Catholic traditions, present critical fashions have preferred reformist to high-church poetry, Milton to Donne, and have even reread Herbert or Donne as vigorously Protestant. Assessments of seventeenth-century "religious literature" have often seemed to reflect scholars' commitment to one version or another of Christianity, or to a modern, rationalist secularism.

I seek to reexamine religion and literature in seventeenth-century England without privileging either an anti-ritual or a ritualist ideology, exploring how *both* ideologies could be variously empowering and repressive. Puritan ideology and the ideology that privileged ritual and ceremony need to be understood in relation to each other, as both had a significant place within the established church, and as each defined itself in contrast to the other. In order to understand the full import of the religious conflicts, we need a better understanding of the function and significance of religious thinking, but first we must think about religion in broader, less exclusively political or narrowly theological terms.

I understand religion to be a cultural system expressing the symbolic logic of a society. Religion defines not only a world view but society's construction of human identity and of social relations.[8] Though religion was inseparable from politics in the seventeenth century, its significance cannot be comprehended by narrowly political terms of analysis. Some of the contested issues – such as whether the priest should make the sign of the cross in baptism – may look trivial to us, but they were symbolic of conflicts over some of the most fundamental issues that shape human experience. Conflicting ideas about "true worship" involved not simply rival conceptions of God, but conflicting constructions of human (and Christian) identity and of personal, social, and political relations. That these ideas about worship affected practices and material aspects of life is evidenced by the "puritan" desire to limit Communion to the "godly" (thus restricting what really counted as "humanity"), as well as by the efforts of Archbishop William Laud and others to enforce conformity through fines and corporal punishment. My interest is not in how they imagined God, or what they believed about the afterlife, but in religion as an ideology and practice involving human beings in relationship with each other.[9]

In the controversy over ceremonial worship, we see two different conceptions of the "order of existence" – what I call "puritan" and "ceremonialist" ideologies. Though a broad spectrum of opinion existed in the early seventeenth-century English church and a shared faith united English Protestants,[10] sharp disagreements over worship brought to the surface fissures within English Protestantism. These religious conflicts reveal different structures of thought, feeling, and behavior which signify not only divisions within the church, but conflicts and discontinuities within seventeenth-century English culture and society so profound that they could not be settled by war or legislation.

Historians have discredited the older view that religious problems in the period were caused by a "puritan" opposition to an "Anglican" establishment, pointing out that at least through James's reign many puritans were part of the establishment, that Calvinism had been the dominant theology, and that there was a range of acceptable religious views within the English church. Allegiances in this period were flexible and shifting.[11] It has been argued that "puritanism" was simply a more enthusiastic kind of Protestantism, hardly alien to the church and, for some historians, the most vital part of it. It has become a new orthodoxy to downplay the differences between "puritan" and what formerly was called "Anglican" Protestantism. Nevertheless, recent work has qualified the notion that the early Stuart church was characterized by harmony and consensus, and shown increasing tensions within the English church.[12] I argue that close examination of the texts of the escalating controversy over ceremonial worship reveals radically divergent constructions of experience. As it was the ceremonies rather than theology that divided the church, the controversy over ceremonies most clearly reveals these differences. So long as ceremonial conformity was laxly enforced, ideological differences could coexist within the church. But once conformity was rigorously insisted on under Charles I, those differences were intensified. Generalization and categorization perhaps inevitably involve oversimplification, yet a markedly different set of assumptions separates those defending ceremonial worship from those attacking it.

I use the terms "puritan" and "ceremonialist," recognizing their limitations, but with a sense of their usefulness in designating different religious ideologies. Historians recognize the existence of increasingly polarized religious positions in the late 1620s and 30s, but do not agree on what to call them. I use these terms to refer not so much to distinct parties as to distinctive ways of understanding experience. Neither the "puritan" nor the "ceremonialist" ideology is unitary – articulated by multiple voices, they could encompass a range of emphases. Moreover, a person could be divided between ceremonialist and puritan impulses, as we shall see.

Peter Lake suggests that "puritan" distinguishes "relative religious zeal," and refers to "those advanced protestants who regarded themselves as 'the godly', a minority of genuinely true believers in an otherwise lukewarm or corrupt mass."[13] But the term also might stand for a set of shared values and assumptions about religious worship and practice. Those engaged in advancing or defending ceremonial worship labeled people critical of these practices "puritans" as a term of abuse. As a term of opprobrium, "puritan" came to include Calvinists who had formed the orthodox mainstream of the Elizabethan and Jacobean church, as well as those who wished further reform in the church. While rejecting the hostile intent of the term as used by Laudians, I use "puritan" to refer to those who not only embraced some form of Calvinist theology but wanted a "purer" kind of worship than presently existed in the English church, a worship purified of supposedly idolatrous ceremonies. The term is appropriate in its focus on the concern with purity that marks this religious ideology. To call this ideology "Calvinist" overemphasizes the theological issue of predestination. Moderate Calvinists could support ceremonial worship even though they were unenthusiastic about Laud and his program. The conflicts were not simply doctrinal, between Calvinist predestinarianism and Arminianism, but about matters of worship that themselves sometimes involved doctrinal issues.[14]

I use the term "ceremonialist" to designate the position of those who embraced the English church's rituals and ceremonies, partly because the term "Anglican" has been discredited as anachronistic, perhaps most accurately used to describe those who remained loyal to the Prayer Book and episcopacy after 1642.[15] Though puritans mocked the proponents of ceremony as "formalists," "ceremonialist" more properly points to the centrality of the ceremonies – of worship involving the body – in their religious experience. In designating the anti-puritan position about worship, I prefer "ceremonialist" to "anti-Calvinist" or "Arminian," which (like "Calvinist") focuses on the single issue of predestination, or to "conformist" which emphasizes only the matter of conformity. "Laudian" at times is appropriate, since it encompasses a whole set of attitudes and beliefs.[16] But there were also clergy who shared the ceremonialist values that were part of Laudianism but disliked or distanced themselves from Laud's rigors. Many people unenthusiastic about Laud's program valued the ceremonies of the church and the Prayer Book. These people sought to preserve the worship of the Church of England during the civil wars, and they account for the ease with which the church was reestablished.[17] What matters, of course, is not the labels but the identity of these two ideologies, which should be understood not as logically worked out positions (though for some they were) but as distinctive sets of mental and emotional attitudes, of assumptions and beliefs, that have an internal coherence, representing and shaping human experience and practices. These ideologies were competing for dominance not only in the church but in English culture and society. The ceremonialist ideology in part revived a Catholic mentality, while puritan ideology fostered the religious sects and socially transgressive prophets that appeared in the 1640s and 50s, who were as troubling to conservative puritan orthodoxy as to adherents of the ceremonial worship of the Church of England. A full analysis of radical religion – and of the lingering presence of Catholicism in England – is beyond the scope of this book, as is the relation of women to these religious ideologies. Nevertheless, my discussion of ceremonialism suggests its Catholic affinities and I indicate where radical religion develops features of puritan ideology. Certainly Milton, who is the focus of the last part of this book, bears witness to certain radical implications of puritan ideology.

If one goal of this book is to define the cultural significance of religious conflict in seventeenth-century England, the other is to show how imaginative literature functioned in this conflict. I bring together cultural history, the history of religion, and formalist analysis in the conviction that the better we understand the history and culture of this period, the better readers we are of its literary texts – and perhaps vice versa.

Religious controversies about worship made literature itself contested, for they raised the question of the legitimacy of "human invention." The defensiveness about art that we see in seventeenth-century literature grows out of these concerns, as does the preoccupation with art's role in society, which was particularly intense for poets hoping to create a lasting poetic monument in a culture suspicious of idolatry. But seventeenth-century literature addressed other aspects of the religious conflict, both directly and indirectly, particularly as religious ideologies were not simply a set of theological doctrines, but constitutive of what it meant to be "human" and of a whole range of human and social relations.

This book offers new readings of literary texts by George Herbert, Robert Herrick, Sir Thomas Browne, and John Milton. I also refer to other writers, especially John Donne, whose sermons from the mid- to late 1620s are self-consciously positioned in the escalating conflicts over ceremonial worship. But given the range of Donne's writings, and the interpretive challenges posed by his "conversion" from Roman Catholicism, full examination of his relation to religious conflict must await future study.

Written from the 1620s through the 1660s, these literary texts span devotional and secular poetry, meditative essay, prose polemic, epic, and closet drama, but they are linked by a concern with ceremony and worship. All of these texts confront the conflict over worship in ways that are not always obvious to twentieth-century readers, but that would have been clear to contemporaries. To some extent, these texts embody religious conflict simply as they bear the imprint of the culture. Sometimes, however, they more actively engage these conflicts.[18]

Herbert, Herrick, Browne, and Milton all publicly took stands in relation to the Church of England. Herrick, Browne, and Milton published their most creative works when the religious practices they were committed to had been declared illegal and punishable. A shared sense of religious oppression links writers separated chronologically as well as by religious conviction, in an England that repeatedly saw those in power prohibit the religious practices of others with different beliefs. Perez Zagorin speaks of the strategies of "dissimulation," "equivocation," and "lying" that developed in response to religious persecution in early modern Europe. Zagorin's work, which complements Annabel Patterson's on rhetorical strategies for avoiding censorship, should alert us to the presence of covert religious stances in the "literary" and poetic writing of mid-seventeenth-century England, much of which grows out of an experience of living under conditions where certain forms and expressions of religion were restricted.[19]

Imaginative literature, especially poetry, illuminates the significance and impact of these seventeenth-century religious conflicts, revealing what was at stake in the cultural battles over religion. As cultural artifacts, they are inscribed by the ideologies and socially constructed values of seventeenth-century England; but they also show writers reexamining these cultural values and critically reflecting on changes within English culture and society. Herrick and Browne are not simply spokesmen for a conservative order, any more than Milton is merely a voice for puritan orthodoxy. The impulse to see texts as entirely culturally or ideologically determined seems the modern secular analogue of a Calvinist predestination that takes away human volition and agency – and, as Milton intuited, makes change for the better impossible.

This book focuses on the period of Charles I and the English Revolution, though it extends beyond 1660 to acknowledge the effect of the Restoration and to include Milton's late poetry, the most complex and extended poetic engagement with the issues of religious conflict over worship. I first examine the conflict over ceremonial worship during the reign of Charles I, showing how puritan and ceremonialist ideologies diverged over a range of interrelated issues, defining human identity, experience, and sociopolitical relations in quite different ways. Ceremonialist ideology valued the ties to the past, the submission of the individual to humanly instituted power, and the analogous connection of body and soul within the human being. It privileged ceremony and art as they effect and symbolize these things. In contrast, puritan ideology separated the spiritual from the carnal, the present from the supposedly corrupt, contaminating past, rejecting ceremony and the traditions of the past as pollutions that must be expelled. If ceremonialism, under Laud, was repressive of individual liberty in constraining behavior to conform to and support the established sociopolitical hierarchical order, it might also be argued that in rejecting ritual, which anthropologists believe is essential to social relations, puritan ideology inevitably (if unwittingly) weakened the social fabric. It denied the legitimacy of the power of the past and its traditions to determine the present, and the analogous legitimacy of humanly constituted power to bind the worship of the individual believer, and thus loosened the bonds (both enabling and constricting) that tie the individual to society and to the continuum of history.

The rest of the book shows how such an understanding of religious conflict alters how we read seventeenth-century literary texts and transforms our sense of their significance. I first examine Herbert's *Temple*, published the year Laud was appointed Archbishop of Canterbury. *The Temple* privileges the Eucharist and ceremonial worship, yet a puritan distrust of art and "human invention" shapes the anxieties of Herbert's poetry. Addressing issues already present in the church that were soon to become hotly contested, *The Temple* seeks to contain dissonances within the English church. Yet it is because Herbert's poems so thoroughly inscribe ideological tensions within the church that they have encouraged divergent, contradictory readings, both in the seventeenth century and in our own.

Subsequent chapters deal with literature whose involvement with the issues of religious conflict is often less immediately obvious, more oblique. Concerned with the role and interdependence of art, ritual, and ceremony in human civilization, not just within the church, Herrick's and Browne's writings display a distinctly ceremonialist mentality disturbed by the implications of puritanism. Herrick's *Hesperides* bears an interesting relation to Herbert's *Temple*. At a time when the rituals of the Church of England had been outlawed by acts of Parliament, Herrick turned to poetry as the place where ceremonial worship and its values could be preserved. His "paganism," his impulse to expand the boundaries of religion, and his sacrifice poems – all have a distinctive, polemical religious significance.

Browne's *Religio Medici* embodies, stylistically and conceptually, ceremonialist notions of harmony, order, and integration in the face of disorder and division – ideals that find almost parodic expression in *The Garden of Cyrus*. But *Urn Buriall* provides his most philosophical, complex, and powerful exploration of the value of ceremony as a distinguishing mark of human existence. Browne articulates the feelings that allowed the English people so eagerly to embrace the restoration of the liturgy in 1660, yet his skepticism about the value of ritual shows the impact of puritan ideology on even those most attached to traditional forms.

Just as ceremonialist and puritan ideologies demand to be understood in relation to each other, so "ceremonialist" and "puritan" writers need to be read against each other. Thus Milton occupies the attention of the rest of this book. The cultural values represented by Herrick and Browne are precisely the ones Milton attacked. Though Milton separated from orthodox puritanism, the puritan concern with idolatry shapes all his writing. His major poems reveal both the value and cost of puritan individualism. But *Paradise Lost* also shows Milton's puritan stance complicated by his effort to find a place for the body in worship. We see in him the persistence of desire for ceremony, for a ritual experience that might integrate body and spirit and connect human beings.

Reading these literary texts in terms of the religious conflicts that divided England reveals otherwise unrecognized meanings, solves longstanding cruxes, and clarifies authorial intentions. It not only illuminates the contested function of literature but helps us understand in a more precise and interesting way what it means to say that religion permeated most aspects of English life and culture in the seventeenth century. We see how the aesthetic, the domestic, the political were all charged with religious significance, how religious ideological value was figured in a variety of social, personal, and even erotic relations. Finally, the literature that engages the conflict over worship has relevance to pressing concerns in our own time, when the past is often thought to be irrecoverable, unknowable, irrelevant, and when the role and function of the arts in the culture seem uncertain, contested, and even (to some) on the verge of extinction; when religious ideologies continue to prove a divisive force in the world, and when recognition of various human and cultural differences poses an acute challenge to the survival of any sense of human community.

CHAPTER 2

Reading the conflicts: ceremony, ideology, and the meaning of religion

In 1630, Peter Smart brought charges against Dr. John Cosin and five others at Durham Cathedral, accusing them of bringing in "new and strange rites, and order of ceremonyall service." They "built a payre of gorgius organes, which have cost at least 700ii.," and hired a "popish paynter" to make a "gould and scarlett" "image" of Christ above the bishop's throne. They replaced the old wooden "Communion-table" with a "sumpteous" altar "of stone" that stood upon "6 stone pillers curiously polished" and was adorned with costly "paintings and gildings" and "many massing implements, crucifixes, candlesticks, tapers and basons, and copes."[1] Smart estimated the new altar at Durham cost above £3000 (p. 179). The strange rites included "frequent and profound duckings and prostrations before your most sumpteous Altar" (p. 165), using the sign of the cross, having everyone stand at the *Gloria Patri* and the Nicene Creed (pp. 173, 183), wearing copes "imbroidred with images . . . of God himselfe" (p. 186), burning two to three hundred candles at a time, and having a service with "excessive noyse of musitians" (pp. 187, 193). According to Smart, Cosin harassed those who would not conform. Several men were ejected "by the head and shoulders" (pp. 173–4). On another occasion, Cosin accosted "some gentle-women, sitting quietly when other stood when the Niceen creed is song [*sic*]." "Catching a gentlewoman by the sleeve, you tore her sleeve, with these reprochfull words, 'Can ye not stand ye lazie sowes?' " (p. 174).

Cosin and his accomplices were not punished; Smart was imprisoned for twelve years.

In 1644, William Laud, Archbishop of Canterbury, was tried by Parliament for treason. He was charged with endeavoring "to alter and subvert Gods true Religion, by Law established in this Realme, and in stead thereof to set up Popish superstition, and Idolatrie."[2]

The committee of the House of Commons presented evidence that Laud had "defiled" his own chapel at Lambeth, the chapels at Whitehall, Westminster Abbey, Oxford and Cambridge, and cathedrals and parish churches throughout England "with Popish superstitious Crucifixes, Altars, Bowings, Ceremonies, Tapers, Copes, and other Innovations." They cited his repair of stained glass windows at Lambeth, with their pictures *"in fresh Colours"* of Christ "hanging on the Crosse," *"rising out of his grave,"* and *"ascending up into Heaven"* (*Canterburies Doome*, pp. 59–60). Laud replaced the "ancient Communion Table" with a "new Altar . . . hedged in with a new costly Raile," adorned with "two great Silver *Candlesticks* . . . with the Picture of Christ receiving his last Supper with his Disciples in a peece of *Arras*, hanging just behind the midst of the Altar, and a Crucifix in the Window directly over it" (p. 62). Laud's other criminal activities included consecrating churches, insisting clergy bow towards the altar and wear "Gaudy *Romish* Copes," and having the people bow *"very lowly . . . at every recitall of the name of Jesus"* (pp. 113, 64).

Clearly, a variety of practices were understood to constitute ceremonial worship, though there is a pattern to them as well. Both sets of charges criticize a new emphasis on corporeal images, material objects, and aesthetic formalism; on ritualized, regulated bodily practices and gestures. Whereas the charges against Cosin in 1630 proved ineffectual, Laud was executed in 1645 as a traitor.

Conflict over religious worship had been present earlier in post-Reformation England. Under Elizabeth I, some clergy objected to wearing the surplice, and "puritans" wanted to bring England's worship closer to that of the English exiles in Geneva during the 1550s. At the beginning of James I's reign, ministers in Lincolnshire objected to the 1604 Canons and the king's proclamations requiring conformity; they refused to wear the surplice, make the sign of the cross at baptism, or have communicants kneel at Communion. But under Charles I, the conflicts became persistent and intense between those who wanted a "purer" worship and those who approved of at least a moderately ceremonial worship.

Charles valued ritual and uniformity in worship, and promoted clergy who shared these concerns: Matthew Wren, John Cosin, Richard Neile, and especially William Laud, appointed Bishop of London in 1628 and Archbishop of Canterbury in 1633. Under their influence and that of the king, the Church of England became increasingly ceremonial. Whereas, under James I, conformity had been intermittently enforced, Charles's bishops made efforts to ensure clergy wore the surplice and made the sign of the cross in baptism.[3] Part of the new ceremonialism included attention to material structures and furnishings of churches. In the 1630s, the interiors of churches were transformed.[4] New religious paintings and statues, stained glass windows, ornate chalices, altar cloths, and crucifixes adorned chapels and cathedrals. Stone altars were erected, placed against the east wall, and railed. The 1640 Canons insisted that ministers preach at least twice a year on the virtues of uniformity, and announced that sectaries and nonconformists would be subjected to the same punishments as Catholic recusants – a move that angered many loyal members of the church, because it labeled them dangerous and seditious.

This increased attention to ceremony placed ritual rather than preaching at the center of worship, triggering intense reaction among "hotter" Protestants, who felt that this ceremonial worship was bringing the English church closer to Rome.[5] They feared that the accomplishments of the Protestant Reformation were being reversed, that England was returning to Catholic idolatry. Attempts to enforce conformity polarized attitudes about religious worship, while Laud's persecution of nonconformist clergy and lay critics – especially the much publicized 1637 trial and punishment of John Bastwick, Henry Burton, and William Prynne – fostered a climate conducive to a war in which religion would play an important role.

In the early years of the Revolution, religion preoccupied Parliament, the trial of Laud being but one aspect of their effort to reform religion. Parliament called an "Assembly of Divines" to determine the discipline and government of the church and imposed the "Solemn League and Covenant" on all Englishmen over eighteen. They passed ordinances ordering destruction of all "Monuments of Superstition or Idolatry," outlawing episcopacy, and prohibiting use of the Book of Common Prayer and its liturgy. Priests were ejected from their livings. Altars and images in churches and cathedrals were destroyed in the effort to purify religion.[6]

My concern is to explore the significance of the conflict over worship that so deeply tore England during the seventeenth century. How did people on both sides of the conflict think about religious "ceremony?" What kinds of assumptions or beliefs collided in the increasingly violent disagreements over ceremonial worship? The controverted ceremonies were not simply a peripheral part of religion, but were powerfully symbolic. Disputes over ceremonial worship signified deep cultural conflicts encompassing more than what we now think of as religion.

For all the shared Christian (and specifically Protestant) faith of those either defending or attacking ceremony, the controversy over worship shows the existence of two ideologies at odds on so many issues that there seems little meeting ground.[7] Ceremonialist and puritan ideologies each consisted of a constellation of interrelated beliefs: about the nature and role of art, images, and "human invention"; about the relation between material and spiritual, body and soul, which also entailed a valuation of the feminine insofar as the body and matter were identified with the feminine; and about history – the relation of the past to the present, and more specifically the relation of the pagan, Jewish, and Catholic past to the Protestant present. These assumptions were, for each ideology, radically different and, within each ideology, deeply interconnected. Ceremonies meant different things to people on each side, and the language in which they talked about them reveals different habits of thought – even, one might say, versions of Christianity that constructed human identity and social relations in quite different ways.

"HUMAN INVENTION," IMAGES, AND THE GARMENTS OF WORSHIP

In part, the conflict over ceremony was a struggle for power within the church with political significance. When Thomas Morton in 1618 defended the *"Three Ceremonies"* against the nonconforming Lincoln-shire ministers' recently reprinted objections, he insisted on the church's "authority" to impose religious rites.[8] John Burges saw in the church's God-given "power" to constitute rites an authority analogous to the divine right of kings that Charles I claimed. For William Ames, however, such insistence on the church's "power" revealed that the prelates' true ambition was to "domineere . . . over poore men."[9] Ames's judgment seemed confirmed by developments in the 1630s. Resistance to attempts to enforce conformity was punished in the Star Chamber, and Laudian clergy like William Quelch extolled the archbishop's power: "thou hast power enough to make a *ceremony*" and "power thou hast to presse a *ceremony!*"

Invoking the fifth commandment as a model for obedience, Quelch criticized puritans as disobedient children who "discredit the wombe that brought them forth."[10] For defenders of ceremonial worship, familial, church, and political orders were analogous and inter-dependent; thus public and private behavior, spiritual and secular authorities, were necessarily linked.

Conformists admitted the controverted ceremonies were "indiffer-ent," not "essential" parts of worship. Still, it was necessary to use them since refusing to do so challenged the church's authority – and, by extension, the king's – thus undermining the hierarchy assumed to be necessary to order. Though conscientious objectors accused people like Quelch of creating trouble by exaggerating the dangers of peaceful nonconformity, Quelch recognized the potential inherent in puritan ideology for subverting sociopolitical as well as religious order.

More than matters of political control, however, were involved in the conflict over ceremonial worship. Also at stake was the value of human creativity and art. When conformist clergy defended the use of humanly constituted ceremonies, they asserted the role of "human invention." For orthodox puritans, the only ceremonies allowable were those instituted by Christ: baptism and the Lord's Supper.

Emphasizing the primacy of Scripture, and faith rather than works, early Protestant reformers questioned the usefulness in worship of things done or made by human beings.[11] Still, the Elizabethan church had taken a middle ground between the radical Protestant commitment to *sola Scriptura* and the Roman Catholic view that church traditions share authority with the Bible.[12] Despite periodic recurrences of iconoclasm and desire for further reform, the English church under Elizabeth and James retained much of its former worship while emphasizing Scripture's supreme authority and reforming "popish" errors. But changes in worship in the late 1620s and 1630s placed an unprecedented value on "human inven-tions" in the reformed English church, as Laudians insisted on the importance of ceremonies and the physical, aesthetic condition of churches. This commitment to external, material forms drew sharp criticism from clergy and laity, Prynne even suggesting that Laud and his "Crosse erecting Prelates" were "worthy of no painted, but a reall Crosse themselves."[13]

We have become suspicious of accepting the caricature of the

"Puritan" as an austere person who opposed art and music. Many puritans loved art and music, so long as they did not intrude into religious worship, and Tessa Watt has shown the persistence of the visual and iconic among the godly.[14] Nevertheless, we find strong antipathy to "invention," art, and imagination in the puritan attack on ceremonies – an antipathy that, as we shall see, complicates Herbert's poetry and forces Milton to reconceive poetic invention.

Ames declared, *"no humane inventions are lawfull parts of Gods Worship,"* and condemned men who persist "in fynding out of religious worship, according to [their] owne imagination."[15] Although Morton insisted the ceremonies of the English church were not burdensome, their proliferation in the late 1620s and 1630s reinforced the puritan suspicion that the human creative spirit is dangerous and difficult to restrain. If prelates are allowed to invent some ceremonies, there is nothing to stop them, as William Bradshaw said, from inventing "a Religion & worship of their owne." To critics of Laudian ceremonies, that is just what the English church had done. Despite the Reformation, the English church, as Bastwick vividly put it, "is now as full of ceremonyes, as a Dog is full of fleas."[16]

Rejection of "human invention" in worship would become the hallmark of radical religion. Where presbyterians like Prynne in the 1640s pressed for a general form that all worshipers would follow, the religiously heterodox felt that the very attempt to legislate unity was a wrongful imposition of human authority. Fifth Monarchists disallowed all liturgy, even the simplified prescriptions of the *Directory for Public Worship* (1645) that Parliament ordered to replace the Book of Common Prayer. To Quakers, even the two sacraments retained by the Protestant Reformation (baptism and the Lord's Supper) were mere human inventions and thus should be discarded.[17]

Ceremonies were identified with "images," a special kind of "human invention." As material representations of spiritual devotion, ceremonies shared the nature of images.[18] Ames even pointed out that "ceremony" and "image" are etymologically linked in biblical Hebrew (*Fresh Suit*, p. 35). Thus both fall under the second commandment: "Thou shalt not make unto thee any graven image, or any likeness of any thing that is in heaven above, or that is in the earth beneath, or that is in the water under the earth: Thou shalt not bow down thyself to them, nor serve them" (Exodus 20:4–5).

Puritans believed the second commandment forbade all representations in religious worship, including humanly instituted ceremonies and man-made prayers. For Bradshaw, the sign of the cross in baptism is like the "graven images" explicitly forbidden in the Bible.[19] The liturgy comprised ceremonies and holy days created by man, and "set" prayers. Puritans thus charged that religious worship had been turned into art, and spiritual matters into something possessing a material form and fixity not unlike an idolatrous monument. The liturgical service seemed an idolatrous statue impiously erected in God's temple, and the entire Prayer Book nothing but "human inventions."[20]

Defenders of ceremonies and images did not deny they were "humane inventions." Instead, they interpreted the second commandment in ways that left a space for art, images, and ceremony in worship. Lumping puritans with "the *Turkes*" in their literalist reading of God's commandment, Burges insisted that God "hath left free unto man the picturing, engraving or expression of any visible creature, or history of things done, even by God himselfe."[21] As material representations of spiritual things, ceremonies – like images – work on the memory by means of the senses. Both are "memorialls" pointing, like monuments, to something beyond themselves. To superstitiously adore a ceremony or image is to misread it, to divorce the sign from the signified, matter from spirit, to stop at the sensible representation without recognizing the spiritual meaning it conveys. Behind the insistence that ceremonies add "comelinesse" to the worship of God lay the conviction that art and the senses aid devotion – a conviction closer to Catholicism and the Counter-Reformation than to the suspicion of images characterizing much of English Protestantism.[22] Cathedral music "stir[s] up that grace or melody in the heart in praysing of God." Even the artful construction of temples can "inflame" the "devout soule . . . with pure and holy zeale."[23]

For puritans, ceremonies and beautiful temples were incitements not to devotion, but idolatry. Ames asked whether Christians "ever . . . found themselves truely stirred up to *holinesse* by the Surplice, or to *constancie* by the Crosse."[24] Smart objected to Cosin's ceremonial changes at Durham: "When men's mynds should be occupied about heavenly meditations of Christ's bitter Death and Passion, of their owne sinnes, of faith and repentance, . . . their eares are possest with pleasant tunes and their eyes fed with pompous spectacles of glittering pictures, and histrionicall gestures" (Cosin, *Correspondence*, pp. 166–7). Behind this indictment lies not only the Protestant privileging of the Word but the belief that bodily gestures, pictures, and music are sensuous distractions from spiritual truth.

Puritans considered clerical garments an especially offensive instance of human "invention." Wearing the surplice violated Christ's teaching of the "priesthood of all believers," since it represented a false hierarchical distinction between clergy and laity rather than the proper separation between godly and ungodly. Controversy over the surplice, however, had a broader significance. As ceremonies were thought to be the "garments" of religion,[25] arguments about vestments were also, more generally, about the value of ceremonial worship.

Those defending the surplice insisted the white garment was an image of inward, spiritual purity that served for "comeliness" in worship. Just as the naked body becomes more *"comely" "in the apparelling,"* so ceremonies add "comelinesse" to religious worship.[26] And just as fashions of clothing vary in different ages and countries, so the church has had the liberty to alter her ceremonies. Though defenders of ceremony rejected the supposed excesses of the Roman Catholic church, they assumed that an unadorned service, like a naked body, is less beautiful than a clothed one.

In praising these garments of religion, ceremonialists insisted that art and "human invention" have a civilizing role in human life, indeed define human identity. Quelch asked whether the ceremonies of the church, which were "an ornament to *religion* in the *Apostles* dayes," are in "these latter times" to be thought "a stain and blemish to *religion?*"[27] Rather than seeing clothes as a sign of the Fall, these writers take pride in the material ornaments of civilized life. Samuel Hoard explained, though ceremonies are not the "essence" of worship any "more than a mans *coat* or *skin* is of the *essence* of a man," they are "necessary appurtenances."[28] The rejection of ceremony seemed an attack on civility and human culture that threatened the foundations of human society.

But ceremonies, like clothes, were also signs of class distinction. Ceremonies and vestments serve for "decencie" – for what is appropriate to rank (*OED*, s.v. decency). John Donne observed that "Ecclesiasticall persons in secular habits, lose their respect," as if prestige and power depend on external signs of hierarchical difference.[29] The newly rigorous insistence upon conformity in dress was

an attempt to halt the subversive possibility that "Trades-men and
Mechanical persons" could be ministers of God (Morton, *Defence*,
p. 201). Although, as Patrick Collinson argues, puritanism in the
Jacobean church was conservative, there were disruptive implications to puritan ideology that clergy like Morton and Donne
responded to and that would become clear during the English
Revolution. Once the ceremonies and liturgy were abolished along
with episcopacy, conservative presbyterians were unable to restrain
heterodoxy, and people from the lower social orders began to
preach.[30]

Just as rich clothes distinguished the gentry and nobility, so the
ceremonies represented and reinforced hierarchical order within
society. Donne described a hierarchy among the ceremonial features
of the English church, and insisted that kneeling at the Sacrament
acknowledged the hierarchy of divine presence. Though "God is
present every where," God is, as Donne put it, "otherwise present"
in the "Market" or "street," in a private prayer "Chamber," at
"Publike prayer," but in the "Sacrament, [more] then at any other
act of Divine Service" (*Sermons*, VII, 333). This belief in the unequal
distribution of God's presence upheld a social order constructed
according to fixed, unequal degrees of worth.

Whereas ceremonialists were appalled that religion might be
"stript," puritans wanted an unadorned spiritual worship founded
solely on the word of God. To puritans, the ceremonies were
"indecent," "whoorish" clothes of the "harlot of Rome."[31] Just as
the prelates' fondness for "sumptuous vestments" betrayed excessive
care for the body, so their emphasis on ceremonies betokened a
corresponding neglect of the "soul" of religion – Christ's Word.
True "Religion," as Ames put it, "requireth naked Christ, to bee
p[r]eached, professed, Glorifyed."[32] In the puritan mentality,
"naked" worship is spiritual, founded solely on Scripture, which is
conceived of as essentially spiritual. The worship of God has no need
of the bodily, material garments of ceremony, which threaten to
obscure or contaminate its spiritual purity. As such language
suggests, with its opposition between carnal and spiritual and its
deprecation of the corporeal, the contrast between puritan and
ceremonialist attitudes towards the ceremonies turns on sharply
divergent beliefs about the body and its relation to spirit.

CARNAL KNOWLEDGE: CEREMONY AND THE BODY

Ceremonial worship in the Church of England focused on the role of the body and "sensible" things in religion, including the material structures and furnishings of churches. As the "outward" part of worship, ceremonies were "symbolicall" signs of internal devotion.[33] Behind the defense of bodily gestures lay the belief that the external or corporeal is linked to the inward or spiritual. So interrelated are outward and inward parts of worship that, though the external is inferior and not "essential," inward worship actually *depends* on the external.

Morton, a Calvinist, was doctrinally far removed from Arminian Laudians, yet his warning that, if people "neglect the outward worship of God," "their inward zeale and devotion soone cooleth, and in the end vanisheth away" anticipates Laud (*Defence*, p. 167). Donne claimed that corporeal ceremonies are the life of worship: "these *outward Rituall* and *Ceremoniall solemnities* of a Church . . . are the *breath* of Religion." Donne criticized "super-spirituall" people (that is, puritans) who think they can have a totally pure worship with "no body": "God hath made us of both" body and "soule"; we "understand all things . . . by benefit of the senses."[34] Inward spirituality depends on material worship just as the soul depends on the body in this life. Even the sacraments work through the body.[35]

Precisely these beliefs underlay Laud's dedication to ceremonial worship. Laud believed that both priest and people must use "*bodily Reverence*, and *Worship*, of GOD in his Church": "I take my selfe *bound* to worship with *Body*, as well as in *Soule*, whenever I come where GOD is worshipped." Though "the *Inward Worship* of the Heart" is essential, the "*Externall*," bodily worship of God in the church is "the *Great Witnesse* to the World, that Our heart stands right in that *Service of God*." There is an intimate correspondence between outer and inner, physical and spiritual in worship. If "Contempt of the Outward Worship of God" precipitates the decline of the "Inward" or spiritual, then the repair of outward worship should produce a renewal of spiritual holiness.[36] And since outward, visible acts are the "*Witnesse*" of inner devotion, enforcing right external behavior should lead to proper inner worship.

Laud's concern to discipline the body in worship and produce ceremonial conformity served a useful sociopolitical purpose. With its focus on the body, which bears the marks of class, gender, and wealth, ceremonial religion perhaps inevitably reinforces social hierarchy. Intertwined with absolutist politics, the increased attention to ceremony in the earlier seventeenth century was a conservative response to a sense that the sociopolitical order was under stress. Obedience and order in worship, reverence and submission, could encourage those qualities in the political and socioeconomic spheres. Moreover, the body disciplined in prescribed gestures of worship symbolized the subjection of "lower," unruly orders in society, while the insistence on interdependence of body and soul in worship mirrored an idealized social order in which all parts were bound together. Since rites of reverence and subordination gave visible expression to social relations, Charles I and the prelates saw the puritan rejection of these rituals as subverting the structure of the social relations they embodied.

Nevertheless, the significance of Laud's attention to the body in worship cannot be understood solely in terms of power politics. Laudian worship integrated the individual worshiper into the larger Christian community. The goal was not only confirmation of a particular political order but reconstruction of a communal, "corporate Christianity" such as had existed in England before the Reformation.[37] Bodily, corporeal aspects of religious experience were integral to its reestablishment. Participation in ceremonial practices such as kneeling at Communion or bowing at the mention of Jesus was to foster a sense that the personal was part of the communal. Both the controverted ceremonies and the notion of community to which they were tied looked back to the traditional religion that predated the Reformation. Laud's understanding of the necessary role of the corporeal in spiritual matters preserved the Catholic sacramental vision of life and the related notion that human beings are composite creatures of body and soul whose knowledge comes through the senses.[38] Laud believed one could be committed both to the Reformation and to a ceremonial, communal worship that was being destroyed by those aspects of Protestantism that privileged interiority and the individual. But given the close connection between Catholicism and Laud's assumptions, it is not surprising that he privileged the Sacrament over the sermon,[39] or that Laudians, like Catholics, insisted on the "real [corporeal] presence" of Christ in the Sacrament.

The importance Laud placed on the body and the Sacrament is nowhere clearer than in his speech at the censure of Burton,

Bastwick, and Prynne, as he explained why the altar and sacraments should be more important than the pulpit and preaching: the altar is "the greatest *place* of Gods *Residence* upon earth . . . yea greater then the *Pulpit*. For *there* 'tis *Hoc est Corpus meum*, This is my Body. But in the *Pulpit*, tis at most, but; *Hoc est Verbum meum*, This is my Word. And a *greater Reverence* (no doubt) is *due* to the *Body*, then to the *Word* of our *Lord*."[40] Laud here defies not only the word-centered worship of puritans (and of the Elizabethan and Jacobean church), but also the reformed concept of a physically "absent" God. Though for Calvin the Sacrament was an efficacious seal of grace to believers who receive it in faith, he insisted that Christ was only *spiritually* present in the Eucharist, his glorified body having withdrawn to heaven, where it would reside until the Second Coming. Bastwick echoed Calvin when he proclaimed "*the Reall Absence of Christ in the Sacrament of the Lords Supper.*"[41] Laud's sacramental sense of God's continuing presence in the world surely would have seemed to Bastwick clear evidence of popish "carnality."

Convinced to the end that he was a true Protestant, Laud asserted at his trial:

I laboured nothing more, than that the External Publick Worship of God . . . might be preserved . . . the Publick neglect of God's Service in the outward Face of it, and the nasty lying of many Places Dedicated to that Service, had almost cast a Damp upon the true and inward Worship of God; which while we live in the Body, needs External helps.[42]

What for Laud was an obvious, reasonable defense of his actions was for his opponents irrefutable evidence that he overvalued the body. With their conflicting notions of the relation of soul and body, and of the physical and spiritual aspects of worship and human experience, Laudians and puritans were incapable of understanding each other's point of view. Any consensus that might have existed in the Jacobean church had been left behind.

Behind puritan attacks on ceremonial worship as carnal was a dualistic understanding of the relation of body and soul, which contrasts with the ceremonialist and Laudian emphasis on their interdependence. Certain passages in the New Testament support the ceremonialist view of the body's role in spirituality. The Incarnation encourages a positive valuing of the body. Paul asks: "know ye not that your body is the temple of the Holy Ghost which is in you?"

(1 Corinthians 6:19). Nevertheless, a deep sense of conflict between soul and body characterized Christianity from the beginning, particularly as it diverged from the values of Jewish and Roman society.[43] The body and its affections were believed to have dangerous power to contaminate the soul, to distract it from God and matters of the spirit.

The Pauline epistles describe an opposition between body and soul, flesh and spirit. For Paul, the body threatens to pollute the spirit and must be kept in "subjection" (1 Corinthians 9:27). Expanding on pronouncements of Jesus like the one John records ("Except a man be born of water and of the Spirit, he cannot enter into the kingdom of God. That which is born of the flesh is flesh; and that which is born of the Spirit is spirit" [John 3:5–6]), Paul insists that those who "are in Christ Jesus . . . walk not after the flesh, but after the Spirit" (Romans 8:1). While Paul's dualism does not reject the body as wholly without value, it devalues the body in relation to the spirit (the essence of the human being), defines an oppositional relation between them, and insists that "flesh" and "deeds of the body" (Romans 8:13) must be rejected for the spirit to thrive.[44] In Pauline Christianity, the "flesh" describes a sinful, carnal disposition that affects the soul as well, but the term was often interchangeable with "body" in English translations. Moreover, the fact that the carnal person is ruled by bodily appetites and drawn to the material world reveals a deep suspicion of corporeality. "Walk in the Spirit, and ye shall not fulfil the lust of the flesh. For the flesh lusteth against the Spirit, and the Spirit against the flesh; and these are contrary the one to the other" (Galatians 5:16–17).

Pauline dualism was embraced by the early church fathers. Augustine was convinced that the conflict between flesh and spirit determines all aspects of Christian life.[45] Despite the sacramentalism of pre-Reformation Christianity – especially the medieval emphasis on the incarnate Christ – distrust of the body and a sense of conflict between flesh and spirit had a place in Catholicism. Nevertheless, by the early seventeenth century, Pauline dualism had become more strongly characteristic of reformed Christian thinking than of Roman Catholicism. Calvin insisted that the "flesh" must be mortified, since the "flesh is the residence of that depravity of concupiscence"; and he quoted Augustine's comment that "sin" exists "in your [bodily] members" "As long as you live."[46] The sense that Christian experience is structured by necessary oppositions gained a new historically specific meaning as Protestant reformers attacking the Roman church insisted on firmly separating true spiritual worship from the fleshly idolatry of Rome.[47] True worship was defined as inward and spiritual. This oppositional rhetoric, founded on a Pauline body/soul dualism, drives the seventeenth-century puritan attack on ceremonial worship, only now England as well as Rome is the dangerous site of carnal idolatry.

The dualism of puritan ideology involved a devaluation of the "feminine," as the body had long been conventionally identified with woman and the feminine.[48] Natural philosophy had linked the feminine with the corporeal matter of nature and the masculine with spirit. But Paul gave religious significance to this gendered distinction between body and spirit, as he defined Christian life as a conflict between the two (Romans 8) in which the body must be subjected, and constructed marriage as exemplifying the proper subjection of body to spirit: "Wives, submit yourselves unto your own husbands, as unto the Lord. For the husband is the head of the wife, even as Christ is the head of the church: and he is the saviour of the body. Therefore as the church is subject unto Christ, so let the wives be to their own husbands in every thing" (Ephesians 5:22-4). As the wife is identified with the body and the husband with the spirit/Christ, the orderly submission of wife to husband symbolically enacts the proper order of Christian life – a domestic formation that will prove important for Milton.

Just this suspicion of the body and the feminine marks the puritan attack on ceremony. Identified with the body, ceremonies were constructed as feminine and criticized for their seductive power. Sensuous images and bodily ceremonies are "snares and allurements to sinne," a "provocation to . . . spirituall whordome."[49] Puritan discourse defined the true Christian in terms of a spirituality associated with masculine, virginal purity, which could only be retained by guarding against contamination by carnal ceremonies. The pollution of ceremonial idolatry is a feminine presence which must be cast out. Echoing Isaiah 30:22, Cornelius Burges advised the Long Parliament as they began their work of reformation: "cast away (as *a Menstruous cloth*) all Idols and Idolatry."[50] Though puritan ideology could empower women spiritually as it elevated the individual believer and emphasized the primacy of the presumably ungendered spirit, puritan anti-ceremonial discourse was strongly masculinist in gendering idolatry as feminine. If puritan ideology was potentially egalitarian in lessening distinctions between clergy and laity and emphasizing the spirit (which bore no marks of class or gender), its body/spirit dualism reinforced gender and domestic hierarchy. In the 1630s and 1640s, it is, as we shall see with Herrick, defenders of ceremony who affirmed the place of the feminine in the worship of God.

Though puritan writers often denied their thinking was dualistic, sin is regularly imaged in terms of corporeality, as in John Preston's "I am a lumpe, a body of sinne," and the true self is understood as the spirit of God.[51] If to be unregenerate is to be "carnally minded," to be regenerate is to expel the carnal and give dominion to the spirit.[52] Furthermore, the "joy and pleasure" which every Christian should strive for in this life are not only spiritual, but often depend on a martyrdom of the body in the cause of the spirit. Our models, says Downame, are "the Apostles [who] rejoyced, because they were counted worthy to suffer rebuke for Christ; and *Paul* and *Silas* when they were sore whipped, and put into a cruel prison." Thus Bastwick describes Burton's spiritual ecstasy when the executioner chopped his ears so close that he cut the artery: "his spirits were carried aloft as it were upon Eagles wings (as himselfe said)."[53] True joy seems not so much independent of as inversely related to bodily comfort.

Bodily delights threaten to lure the spirit from God, and herein lies the problem with ceremonies. Whereas defenders of ceremonial worship, especially Laudians, believed that the soul works through the body and thus bodily ceremonies perform an integrative, spiritual function, puritans saw ceremonies as inevitably in conflict with religious worship, which is a matter of the spirit. Like other more obviously sensual pleasures, carnal ceremonies distract us from God.

In the puritan mentality, carnal ceremonies are marks of a carnal person. Prynne indicts the Laudian prelates as *"voluptuous"* and proud.[54] Their inordinate concern with the body seemed evident even in their predilection for corporal punishment. Anti-ceremonialists mocked the bodily gestures of the clergy who performed these rites. Peter Smart ridiculed Cosin's "upstartings, downe-squattings, east-turnings, crossings and kissings [of] altar-clothes, and the elements of bread and wine; with your frequent and profound duckings and prostrations before your most sumpteous Altar." Bastwick described Laud's entrance into the Star Chamber, attended by many gentlemen waiting on him: "some of them cariyng [*sic*] up his tayle, for the better breaking and venting of his wind & easing of his holy body." The perverse transformation of spiritual things into carnal is symbolized by the flatulent prelate, ceremoniously breaking wind rather than preaching the word, polluting the space he thinks he has consecrated.[55]

One sees the connection between carnality and ceremonial worship in *The First Century of Scandalous, Malignant Priests*, where carnal transgressions share the stage with spiritual negligence and idolatrous worship as John White describes the sins of one hundred ministers whose benefices were sequestered by Parliament. Vicar Griffith Roberts "practised the late Innovations" and was "a common drunkard." Edward Alston "hath attempted the chastity of some women . . . and was a forward maintainer and practicer of the late illegal innovations." Vicar John Wilson was indicted for buggering his male petitioners and even a mare.[56] It is impossible to tell how much truth there was in these charges, but the common thread is a violation of purity in life as in worship. Spiritual transgression is analogous to and thus representable by sexual transgressions and other bodily pollutions. A carnal life is the counterpart of a carnal religion.

The conflict between external forms and inward worship that characterizes puritan ideology became intensified in radical religion, which was, above all, religion of the spirit, self-consciously defined in opposition to ceremonial carnality. Puritans dissociated themselves from religious radicals. Nevertheless, in an important sense radical religion extended certain assumptions of puritan ideology, albeit further than puritans could countenance. Cromwell was an anti-formalist, committed to "a religion of conscience, rather than ritual," but he was disturbed by the radicalism of the sects.[57] Sectarians and heterodox individuals objected to efforts in the 1640s and 50s to construct a national church and control "blasphemy" as attempts to constrain the free spirit with external, material forms. Religious radicals thought extempore prayer and preaching more spiritual than set prayers and sermons, which presumably hardened worship into external, fixed patterns, hindering the motions of God. The Ranters even justified their sexual promiscuity, "lascivious songs, . . . downright baudry, and dancing" as anti-worldly expressions of the spirit, liberated from carnal laws of men.[58] When sectarians held meetings in domestic dwellings, taverns, warehouses, or the open fields, they symbolically enacted their disdain for material churches. As Anna Trapnel, Fifth Monarchist prophet, proclaimed, "The Lord is building his Temple, it is no time now for them to build Tabernacles."[59] The belief that worship must be inward and spiritual reached its ultimate expression with the Quakers, for whom inward illumination superseded the material text of Scripture and who practiced "silent worship" in their meetings, avoiding the materiality of the spoken, audible word.[60]

One consequence of the puritan emphasis on inwardness and interiority was the large number of people during the mid-seventeenth century who claimed to possess God entirely within themselves – a phenomenon disturbing to conservative Calvinist puritans who sought to restrain such heterodoxy. Margaret Fell proclaimed that the "true Prophet" Christ is now "risen" within our conscience: everyone with Christ inside can prophesy.[61] The privileging of the inward spirit and the dismissal of bodily forms as irrelevant to spirituality could suggest that possession of a female body was no longer an obstacle to full religious service.

Some took the belief that Christ is within the believer literally, claiming actually to *be* Christ. Evan Price, on January 10, 1647, stood up in the middle of a sermon in Butolph's Church and declared that he was Christ. Though he admitted to the examining magistrates that he had yet to perform miracles, he said "he had suffered upon the Crosse, and had the print of the Nailes on his hands."[62] James Nayler rode into Bristol in October 1656 in imitation of Christ's entry into Jerusalem, accompanied by three men and three women singing "*Holy, holy, holy, Lord God of Sabbath.*" Modern commentators have suggested Nayler was only claiming to be a "son of God" like any other person possessed of grace, but he did not discourage those who believed he was really the Messiah, and may have believed it himself. Nayler suffered a brutal punishment at the hands of the puritan Parliament that more than rivaled Laud's punishment of Bastwick, Burton, and Prynne.[63]

Nayler's case may have been most spectacular, but there were others who made similar claims to divinity. *A List of some of the Grand Blasphemers and Blasphemies, Which was given in to The Committee for Religion* (1654) [Thomason Tracts 669.f.17 (80)] includes John Robbins, who "said, *That he was God Almighty.*" Robbins's pregnant wife asserted (with a certain logic) that "*the childe in her Womb was the Lord Jesus Christ.*" Mary Adams claimed to have "*conceived with childe of the Holy Ghost*" but supposedly delivered a "Monster" and killed herself in despair. All these people were imprisoned by puritans for their transgressive "blasphemy" which, in destroying the distinctions between God and the creature, was the logical, if paradoxical, extension of the puritan privileging of the spirit within.

CONTINUITY VERSUS DISCONTINUITY: THE STANCE TOWARDS THE JEWISH, PAGAN, AND CATHOLIC PAST

Defenders of ceremony and their puritan critics had distinctly different historical perspectives, which parallel their divergent attitudes towards the body. Laudians argued for the antiquity of ceremonies, believing that tradition and precedent legitimized them. From a puritan perspective, tradition was merely "human invention," of no authority in religion.

From the late 1620s to the early 1640s, puritans charged that the prelates were introducing "innovations." The charge of "innovation" was leveled by both sides, and historians are still trying to determine the guilt – Nicholas Tyacke and others reacting against the notion that puritanism was the progressive force and finding Laudians the real innovators. I would argue that, though Laudianism marks a "destabilizing, even revolutionary" departure from the dominant Calvinism of English Protestantism and in its alliance with royal absolutism was dangerously innovatory,[64] the Laudian argument from tradition was a deeply conservative commitment to preserving ties to the past in the face of the revolutionary implications of the Reformation.

Responding to the accusation that they were "Novellists,"[65] Laudian apologists insisted their practices were ancient, venerable customs. What the puritan opposition criticized as innovations, Laudians defended as traditions extending back to the apostles, in some cases even earlier. Christopher Dow argued that bowing at the name of Jesus, railing the altar, and praying towards the east were common practices in the primitive Christian church. Heylyn examined the records of early history to prove the antiquity of altars, sacrifices, and priests, concluding that the example of Cain and Abel shows sacrifice "almost co-aevall with the world."[66] Heylyn and the other defenders of ceremony treated both the Bible and the writings of the church fathers as historical documents giving evidence about human practices. Pocklington found evidence in the fathers that communicants kneeled towards the altar and that the altar stood in a separate place that only priests could approach. For Pocklington, the Old Testament showed the antiquity of the name "altar." The removal of the word "altar" from the Book of Common Prayer in the sixteenth century was actually, Heylyn argued, Calvin's innovation.[67] From this perspective, Laud was simply restoring the traditional name in revising the rubrics of the Prayer Book.

This search into the records of history was to show that Laud and his supporters were restoring old, legitimate practices. Defenses of ceremonial worship valued historical inquiry and privileged the historical past as a model for present behavior. "Successionall tradition" and "continuall custome" in the church, as in the state, were signs of legitimacy and ensured order and stability.[68]

When puritans attacked the Laudian "innovations," they contrasted, not new worship with old, but "humane inventions" with Scripture, the commandments of God. Though both critics and defenders of ceremonies used "innovation" as a label of contempt, the word had different meanings for each side. Whereas in ceremonialist discourse "innovation" meant a break from the past and tradition, in the puritan view tradition paradoxically *was* innovation insofar as it represented a departure from Scripture. Hence, the seemingly contradictory charges that the Laudian changes in worship were at once "Innovations" and "backslidings" that would bring England back to the "Popery, and superstition" supposedly cast out of the church at the Reformation.[69]

Insisting on the rule of Scripture alone, puritan ideology dismissed the value of precedent, tradition, and historical continuity, refusing to privilege any historical time. Antiquity is no infallible sign of purity or truth, Burton suggested. When Dow defended "traditions" as "*subservient*" to Scripture, he presumed an interdependent, harmonious, yet hierarchical relation between them analogous to the relation between body and soul.[70] In contrast, puritan opposition between tradition and Scripture mirrored the sense of conflict between carnal and spiritual. Following the word of God necessitates breaking with corrupt traditions, much as devotion to the spirit means rejecting everything carnal.

Both Laudians and those who valued ceremonial worship but drew back from Laud's rigors felt a sense of identity and meaning in their connections with the past, viewed as an unbroken continuum extending into the present. Ceremony, with its commemorative function and repetitive nature, was a way of preserving these connections, as it incorporated the individual worshiper within the community and the continuum of history. Anti-ceremonial puritans, however, assumed a radically different stance towards history. Their contrast between tradition and Scripture implied that the individual's sense of Christian identity involved a separation from the past. Though the Reformation was initially conceived of as a return to the purity of the early Christian church, the felt need to reject corrupt human tradition fostered a sense of discontinuity between present experience and the historical past that became more intense for later reformers, some of whom, like Milton, saw no time in the past that possessed the desired purity of worship.[71] Just as puritan discourse represented human experience as a struggle between spirit and flesh, so it encouraged a sense of conflict between the regenerate individual, identified with God's spirit, and past human history, characterized by "carnal" "traditions" and preserved through material, idolatrous "monuments." The past, thus, was identified with a carnality that threatened to pollute and contaminate both the individual Christian and church worship. Ceremony, with its assimilation of the individual into the corporate, communal group, was inappropriate for a religion of the spirit that emphasized an unmediated relationship between the individual and God, and that assumed sharp divisions between the godly few and the corrupt majority. But ceremony, as a commemorative act tying the experience of the individual to the past, was also inappropriate for those who believed that salvation requires that corrupt traditions be destroyed just as the "old" person must die for the "regenerate" person to be born.

The ceremonialist emphasis on continuity contrasts with the puritan sense of historical discontinuity. These two historical perspectives yielded different understandings of the relation of present Christian worship – and contemporary experience – to the pagan and Jewish past and to the Roman Catholic church. Since the controverted ceremonies were thought to derive from ancient pagan and/or Jewish customs as well as from the Roman Catholic service, controversy over ceremony involved assessing not only the relevance of the past but the value of "other" religions and cultures.

Puritans rejected the ceremonies of the English church in part because they believed these ceremonies were actually Jewish or pagan. It was charged that the white surplice was originally worn by priests in pagan Rome; later, Jewish ornaments were added. Incense, candles, consecration of churches, and the ceremonies surrounding the altar continued pagan practices and ancient Jewish ceremonial worship. The very terms "priest," "altar," and "sacrifice" were suspect. Prynne and Ames objected that many of the festival days celebrated by the church derived from pagan holidays or had Jewish counterparts.[72]

Puritan attacks on the Jewish and "heathen" elements in English worship were based on a vision of Christianity as a religion whose identity depends on excluding elements of other religions and cultures that might contaminate it. Puritan ideology insists on Christianity's separateness, and finds biblical sanction in New Testament passages that present Christianity as breaking with the values of Jewish and Roman society and departing from the religion inscribed in the Old Testament. Contrasts in the New Testament between Gospel and Law encouraged a sense of opposition between Jewish and Christian religion. As a religion of the spirit, Christianity stood in contrast to the "carnal" religion of the Jews as well as to the idolatry of the pagans. As interpreted by the apostles, the coming of Christ offered a new dispensation whereby people would be justified by faith. Paul admonished the Corinthians to "Behold Israel after the flesh" (1 Corinthians 10:18), associating the religion of the Jews with the flesh or body. In Paul's reading, Christian faith frees believers from a carnal worship under the Law which cannot save (Galatians 2–4).[73]

This understanding of Christianity as a religion of the spirit, requiring a break from earlier, supposedly carnal religions, influenced Protestant reformers who objected to Roman Catholic worship and, later, puritans who criticized the ceremonial worship of the English church. Jesus' pronouncements could support the view of Christianity as a revolutionary, historically discontinuous religion demanding an oppositional stance. Jesus suggested that old forms were inadequate and inappropriate to his new gospel: "No man putteth a piece of new cloth unto an old garment . . . Neither do men put new wine into old bottles" (Matthew 9: 16–17). One statement in particular encouraged divisiveness as a mark of true faith:

Think not that I am come to send peace on earth: I came not to send peace, but a sword. For I am come to set a man at variance against his father, and the daughter against her mother, and the daughter in law against her mother in law. And a man's foes shall be they of his own household. (Matthew 10: 34–6).

Embracing this oppositional spirit along with the Pauline dualism between carnal and spiritual worship, Calvin and Luther argued that the Roman church had put Christians under bondage to the ceremonial worship from which Christ had freed them. Echoing Calvin and Luther, puritan critics of the ceremonies of the English church insisted that Christians no longer needed "significant," material ceremonies because Christ fulfilled the promises contained in the Jewish ceremonies.[74] Freeing Christians from the burden of the past, with its ceremonies and traditions – a past identified with the body and "flesh" – Christ enacts a decisive break from the past, which Christians reenact when they flee from idolatry and refuse to perform the ceremonies.

When puritans insisted that Christians must separate from idolatry, they lumped together Jewish and pagan worship as "carnal" and therefore worthy of being despised. The conventional Calvinist and puritan formulation was that the Jewish "Law stood in carnal Rites," which were further corrupted by the "grosse and carnall" Israelites. Where the Christian religion is *"pure"* and *"spirituall,"* the religion of the Old Testament was *"sensible"* and *"earthy."*[75] In the puritan mentality, the carnality of the Jewish religion, with its altars and sacrifices, made it more like the religion of the gentiles than like Christianity.

With their "carnal" ceremonies and priestly clothes, the prelates were reverting to carnal Jewish as well as pagan idolatry and corrupting Christianity's true spiritual worship. Burton charged that Laud was "a setter up of Judaisme or Heathenisme in your *Altars* . . . which are so many damnable *Idols.*" Prynne drew a lengthy parallel between the "Jewish High-Priests" and the prelates, who have reinstituted the carnal priesthood and betrayed Christ by persecuting his apostles.[76]

Attacks on the "Judaizing" Laudian prelates, with their ceremonial worship, should make us rethink assertions that the puritans were favorably disposed to Jews (the evidence usually cited is the 1655 Whitehall Conference considering a proposal to allow Jews to reenter England). True, puritan saints identified with the Jews as God's chosen, taking their pattern from the Jews in destroying the altars of idolatry,[77] and their concern with purity recalls the purity codes of Mosaic law. English puritanism revives the ethos of the

Hebrew Bible, in which the religious identity of Israel was based on an understanding of the "holy" as "set apart." Nevertheless, this sense of identification was crossed by opposition to all things Jewish as carnal and hence idolatrous. Godly Christians are the *"true Israel,"* replacing the Jews, who are seen as the false Israel, Israel "according to the flesh."[78] The Jews and their worship have come to signify in puritan discourse the pollution of idolatry from which Christians must separate. Despite the fact that both Testaments were considered the word of God, puritans stressed the discontinuity between them. Just as regenerate Christians must reject everything carnal distracting the spirit from God, so they must renounce all Jewish and pagan customs comprising much of English religious worship in a transformed but recognizable state.

In contrast to this "pure" notion of Christianity, Laud dedicated himself to restoring and preserving an ancient, continuous tradition of worship. English ceremonialists saw the very connections with Jewish and ancient Roman ceremonies as validating the service of the Church of England. Laud drew analogies between the English church and "the ancient Church of the *Jewes*." Pocklington defended the Laudian altars as continuing the tradition begun when Noah erected the first altar.[79] Supporters of episcopacy derived prelacy from the Jewish high priests. The conformist and Laudian insistence on an inclusive religious worship that embraces past traditions was the counterpart of the belief that the whole person, body and soul, be involved in worship.

Ceremonialists stressed the continuity between the Old Testament types and their antitypes, where puritan discourse emphasized difference and distinction. Pocklington saw the entire Old Testament as a record of the Christian church.[80] If the puritan sense of Christianity as a religion of discontinuity could find biblical support, so too could the idea of Christianity as a religion growing out of the past. Although in many respects Christ's Gospel was revolutionary, the New Testament also insists that Jesus came not to destroy but to fulfil the Law. Attacking the Pharisees' literalized interpretations of God's commandments, Jesus offers his teachings as truly interpreting God's commandments to the Jews (Matthew 15, 23; Mark 7). His rejection of the dietary laws that distinguished not only between clean and unclean foods but also between observant Jews and the supposedly unclean heathens, his inclusion of all who believe as "sons" of God, the very fact that Jesus was a Jew – all these things could support an understanding of Christianity as an expansive, inclusive religion, incorporating Judaism while welcoming the gentiles within its embrace.

In defending continuity of worship, proponents of ceremony pointed out that early Christians observed the festivals and ceremonies of the Jews and even some pagan ones. The church retained the name of "the Paschall Feast," and Easter was long kept on the day the Jews observed Passover.[81] Just as Jewish traditions were "converted" to Christian uses, so pagan ones were similarly appropriated. Defending the celebration of Candlemas, Anthony Stafford insisted that "*a Heathenish custome may be converted into a Christian Right or Ordinance.*" It was often pointed out that in early Christianity, pagan temples were "converted into *Christian* Churches."[82]

Whereas puritans insisted on sharp distinctions between Christianity, on the one hand, and pagan and Jewish traditions on the other, writers defending the ceremonies stressed conversion. The notion of "conversion" was powerful. It not only constructed Christian religion as unitary and evolving; it also suggested a model that incorporated and subordinated difference, controlling potentially discordant, disruptive elements. Thus this reading of Christian history, and this understanding of English ceremonial worship as a composite of Jewish and pagan ceremonies as well as specifically Christian ones, offered a strategy of taming religious differences in the past that was also a model for dealing with potentially dangerous dissent in the volatile present. But just as Jews who converted to Christianity were never free from the suspicion that they were not real Christians,[83] so the "Jewish" ceremonies of the English church were always suspected by zealous Protestants of retaining the taint of their origins.

Puritans and defenders of ceremonial worship divided in similar ways over the relationship of the English church to the Church of Rome. Roman Catholicism constituted a major part of the past towards which the present had to define its relation. Under Elizabeth, Catholicism had been identified with political treason, and the church took an aggressively anti-Catholic stand. Though the Jacobean church retained the mainline Protestant anti-Catholic stance, some clergy adopted the conciliatory position of Hooker, and James late in his reign softened towards Rome. It was under Charles, however, married to a practicing Catholic, that conflict over England's relation to Rome erupted, particularly as the worship of the English church seemed to be moving closer to Rome.[84]

Puritans and Laudians had different ideas of the Reformation. Just as puritans drew a line between Christianity, on the one hand, and Jewish and pagan traditions, on the other, so they believed that true Christian faith and worship were unalterably opposed to Roman Catholicism. In contrast, Laudians emphasized an unbroken continuity of religious worship.

Puritans objected that the controverted ceremonies derived not only from ancient pagan and Jewish ones but more immediately from Roman Catholicism. The surplice may have been first instituted by Numa, but it was also worn by Roman Catholic priests. Laud and his prelates seemed to have turned Christ's "supper" into a "*sacrifice of the masse*," virtually indistinguishable from the Roman Catholic one.[85] Because Laudians acknowledged a "real presence" of Christ in the Sacrament, puritans feared that the Catholic doctrine of transubstantiation would be reintroduced. Bastwick saw a "correspondency" between prelates and Roman Catholic priests, while Prynne believed the Arminianism favored by Laud and others revived popish doctrine. Bastwick and Burton claimed the entire Book of Common Prayer was "taken out of the Masse booke and other Popish pamphlets." Even the calendar of the English church preserved Rome's holy days. Continuity between the pre- and post-Reformation church and the process of translation or "conversion," essential to the ceremonialist notion of Christian worship, were thus for puritans evidence of the popish idolatry of Laud's church. By 1640, Burton could say that the English and Roman churches were "*one and the Same.*"[86]

The Roman Catholic church had persecuted Protestants in an attempt to quell the Reformation, as Foxe's *Book of Martyrs* vividly recounted. But Catholic hatred of Protestant heresy was matched in England by intense Protestant hatred of Catholicism. Antipathy to Rome was expressed in disturbingly vivid language. Bishop Parker told "faithfull" Christians to "burne the very flesh it selfe of the Harlot with fire; that so no foot step, no remnant, no relike of her may remaine . . . make your swords drunken with the blood of her slaine."[87] The sense that Catholicism must be exterminated underlies the first book of Spenser's *The Faerie Queene*, in which the battle of good and evil is located in the conflict between the true Protestant church and the false Catholic one, whose allegorical representatives

in the poem must be bound or killed. One should not underestimate
the power of such language to inflame hatred, to encourage people
to persecute those who hold different beliefs. Parker's language, with
its focus on the violent destruction of Catholic bodies (not just the
abstract "Church"), reveals the human cost of the belief that clear
lines separate the true Protestant faith from Roman Catholic idolatry
and that Christians are obligated to destroy idolatry.

Not all Protestants were so extreme. But as efforts were made to
establish more cordial relations with the Church of Rome during
Charles's reign, puritans found new inspiration for anti-Catholic
rhetoric, now also deployed against the established English church.
Prynne spoke of "our Romish Adversaries," opposing the "*beleeving
world*" of "*Saints and perfect men*" (the true Christians) to the "*unbeleeving world*" of "*wicked men*," which includes the prelates and all
Roman Catholics (*Anti-Arminianisme*, sig. A2r, pp. 163–7). Richard
Sibbes said that the best way to thank God for our deliverance from
the Gunpowder Plot is to "stirre up our selves to a greater hatred" of
Roman Catholicism. As Francis Cheynell told Parliament in 1643,
papists are "Monsters," "Excrements" that must be "expelled" from
England: "wee must hate the Whore, and burn her flesh."[88] For
those who believed it was a holy war in which there could be no
truce, the supposed "popery" of Laud and Charles would require
their death. So fierce was puritan opposition to popery that nonconformists after the Restoration opposed efforts to pass a toleration
act because Catholicism too would be tolerated. Better that presbyterians, Baptists, and Quakers be persecuted than that popery be
allowed.

Puritan ideology insisted on absolute separation from Roman
Catholicism as it was supposedly the repository of Jewish and pagan
idolatry. *The Originall of Popish Idolatrie* traced the Mass to the ancient
religion of Rome, when, after the end of the Missall Sacrifice, men
ate small round loaves consecrated to the gods. According to
Perkins, the "carnall service" of Catholics is "borrowed partly from
the Jewes, & partly from the heathen." Conversions cannot disguise
the idolatrous nature of this worship. Behind the puritan linking of
Catholicism-Judaism-Heathenism lies the assumption that they are
"for substance all one," "pleasing to flesh," luring the spirit away
from God.[89]

Thus whereas Montagu, Heylyn, and Laud saw the Reformation
as removing the abuses of Roman Catholic idolatry while retaining

the essential Christianity that had continued for centuries, puritans saw the Reformation as a radical break with the past. Continuity becomes the mark of idolatry. Although the 1641 Root and Branch Petition to Parliament insisted that all idolatry be "rooted out," puritan discourse often implies that the "roote" of idolatry remains present in all ages, requiring unremitting vigilance.[90]

Critics of Laud's ceremonies discerned alarming parallels between England's worship and the pagan-Jewish service of the Church of Rome. Prynne spoke of the "HEATHENISH & JEWISH ABUSES" of the "*Innovating Romish spirits*" in the English church. Laud had added two new saints days. He substituted "*Church*" or "*Holy* Church" for "*Congregation*" in the Book of Common Prayer, and added the word "sacrifice" in the directions for Communion.[91]

Furthermore, Laud made a small but significant change in the prayer commemorating England's deliverance from the Gunpowder Plot in the 1635 Prayer Book: "cut off these workers of iniquity, whose religion is rebellion, whose faith is faction" became "cut off these workers of iniquity, who turne religion into rebellion, and faith into faction." With the change of a few words, the prayer now implied that puritans, not Catholics, were the principal enemies of religion and the state.[92] When Laud was formally charged with having "traiterously and wickedly endeavoured to reconcile the Church of England with the Church of *Rome*," it was the culmination of repeated charges in sermons and pamphlets. Even after his execution, the notion of a "*secret plotted Conspiracy*" followed him, for in a bogus pamphlet he "confessed" that he had all along aimed at "advancing Popery and the Catholicke faith."[93]

That puritans saw "reconciliation" with Rome as treason reflects a disposition to see the world in terms of perpetual conflict between irreconcilable opposites. Repeatedly one finds insistence on clear and sharp distinctions – between truth and error, light and darkness, spirit and flesh, Christian and pagan/Jewish, Protestant and popish. Ideological emphasis on separation, discontinuity, and division finds its appropriate expression in oppositional titles (*Babel no Bethel*, or *Anti-Arminianisme*) and in a style that works in terms of contrasts and distinctions. When puritan writers draw parallels and show harmonies, it is inevitably to prove idolatry and error.

In the puritan mentality all experience – not just religious worship – tends to be interpreted in terms of binary patterns that emphasize conflict rather than harmony and continuity. God is understood to practice and require firm separations. The Pauline epistles were a rich source of support for puritan thinking and were invoked in anti-ceremonial polemics. One frequently quoted passage was 1 Corinthians 10: 14, 21: "flee from idolatry. . . Ye cannot drink the cup of the Lord, and the cup of devils; ye cannot be partakers of the Lord's table and of the table of devils." Similarly, Paul advised in 2 Corinthians 6:14–16: "Be ye not unequally yoked together with unbelievers: for what fellowship hath righteousness with unrighteousness? and what communion hath light with darkness? And what concord hath Christ with Belial? or what part hath he that believeth with an infidel? And what agreement hath the temple of God with idols?"[94] As the echo of Genesis 1:4 suggests, the creation of the world seemed to establish this paradigm of distinction and discontinuity as God divided light from darkness.

Given such views, it is not surprising that the very notions of harmony, continuity, and mixture were fraught with danger, for they threatened a sense of identity founded on "purity" and difference. Though some religious radicals during the revolutionary years adopted a version of Arminianism, I suspect orthodox puritans were hostile to Arminianism in part because the ideas of free will and universal grace mingle rather than separate human beings. As Prynne observed, Arminian doctrine "makes the Pagan and the Christian; the godly and the ungodly; the Elect and Reprobate, all alike." Many puritans wanted formal communion and community with the established church, but concern with purity and the distinction between the godly and ungodly could ultimately encourage separatism.[95] If the Church of England had become a "member" of Rome's idolatrous "Synagogue," then, as Burton insisted in 1641, Christians should follow the advice of 2 Corinthians 6:17 and separate: "Gods people must be seperatists from the world, and from false Churches, to become a pure and holy people unto the Lord."[96]

Separatism was a logical extension of puritan ideology, but many puritans wanted rather to purify the national church. Edmund Calamy warned the House of Commons, "*Do something to purge out all the defilements that are in the pure worship of God*, that the *pure and holy God* may be worshipped with *pure worship, purely, by pure worshippers.*" Calamy and others preached before Parliament at monthly fasts – the puritan ritual that replaced church festivals. The puritan fast symbolically enacted an ideology of purification as the human body refused meat (most carnal of foods), the individual believer becoming a model of the church which excluded all carnality.[97]

With their insistence on firm separations and their commitment to wage perpetual war against carnal idolatry in the cause of Christian "purity," it is not surprising that opponents of ceremony were viewed as people of "Faction," "intractable," "incompliable," though some like Morton and Joseph Hall strove to reconcile them to the church.[98] From 1627 on, Donne warned of the dangers of the godly who "in an over-valuation of their owne *purity,* condemne, and contemne other men, as unpardonable *Reprobates*" (*Sermons,* IX, 110). Fostering divisions within the church and the human community, these people draw sharp lines between themselves and the supposedly corrupt multitude included in the Church of England, refusing to participate in communal ceremonial worship. A sharper tone was taken by Roger Maynwaring, who proposed that puritan dissidents be disciplined with force: "if the hand of *Discipline* bee not held more streightly, over this late and stif-necked *Broode,* that is now growing to Maturitie in the world; nothing is more to bee expected, then that the comming-*Generation* will bring in such a Torrent of *Vice* and *Corruption,* as will over-runne the *World,* with *Rudenesse, Lewdnesse,* and extreme *Barbaritie.*"[99] Many objectors to ceremonial worship were peace-loving and conservative; it was Laudian persecution that radicalized them. But there was some truth in the fear that in their unwillingness to display "subjection," to "subordinate" the "outward man . . . to the inward" in ceremonial worship, they posed a subversive threat to the sociopolitical order.[100]

In the years of the Commonwealth and Protectorate and beyond, the puritan sense of the separateness of the godly would characterize those churches of believers "gathered" from the rest of the world. Though "puritans" began by wanting to reform the Church of England, the concern with purity and separateness worked against the notion of an inclusive national church (how could one restrict membership to the godly? or agree who was godly?), and made it impossible in the 1640s and 50s to construct a church or service to replace what Parliament had dissolved. The foundational principles of separation and division inevitably fragmented "puritanism."

Where puritans saw separations and distinctions as necessary, Laudians and supporters of ceremonial worship promoted an idea of (comm)unity symbolized by the harmonious yet hierarchical relation

of body and soul in worship and by a syncretic, "catholic" ceremonial worship, with deep ties to the past. It was because of the links
between England's worship and the Roman Catholic church – and
ultimately the ancient Christian church as it had converted Jewish
and pagan worship – that the English church could claim to be
universal. The Arminian emphasis on the universal offer of grace
neatly complemented the function of ceremony to bind people
within a community.

Montagu and Laud wanted a unified Christian faith, but not only
Laudians were attracted to the idea of an inclusive church.[101] John
Hales, who disliked Laud's rigorous enforcement of conformity but
abandoned Calvinism as inhumane, insisted that we take God as our
model in dealing with other Christians: though God originally gave
his laws only to the Jewish nation, afterward he "enlarged himself,
and instituted an order of serving him promiscuously capable of all
the world. As therefore our religion is, so must our compassion be,
catholick."[102] Hales's "promiscuously" loving God is a far cry from
the puritan God who divides light from darkness, the elect from the
reprobate.

It would be a mistake to privilege ceremonialist, conformist
ideology simply on the basis of this language of harmony and unity.
Harmony depended on subjection. For all the talk of charity, those
who tried to enforce ceremonial worship were as uncharitable and
divisive as they accused the puritans of being. Laud's critics charged
that he wooed the Church of Rome while persecuting conscientious
Protestants at home. Moreover, the Laudian notion of unity, conformity, and continuity suppressed differences and dissent rather
than accepting them. As Milton observed, Laud's use of the High
Commission and Star Chamber to enforce religious conformity had
its parallel in the Catholic Inquisition. Not only was there disjunc-
tion between the ideal of unity and the actual divisions created,
between the ideal of inclusiveness and the practice of persecution;
but the Laudian language of charity and harmony sometimes seems
a duplicitous mask for ungenerous aims.

Still, it is worth recognizing the articulation, however imperfect,
of a positive ideal of harmony and inclusiveness. The ceremonialist
and specifically Laudian emphasis on universality and continuity, on
the things that bind people rather than separate them, prepared the
way conceptually (if not in practice) for the development of latitudi-
narianism and deism as well as for James II's Declaration of

Indulgence in 1687 which suspended the penal laws against non-conformity. Perhaps most important, a few people like Hales seem to have been able to imagine, at least momentarily, a more universal human community, tolerant of difference. Thus it is not only the radical sects of the civil war period or the nonconformists after the Restoration who, in their desire for liberty of conscience, might be credited with envisioning religious tolerance.

CEREMONIAL CONFLICT AND TENSIONS WITHIN THE REFORMED ENGLISH CHURCH

The Laudian emphasis on ceremonies, sacraments, and the material accoutrements of worship exalted the clergy, for the material lavishness and glory of the churches as well as the gestures of reverence symbolically represented the prelates' power as well as the honor due to God. But the Laudian program also was a culturally significant attempt to reassert the interrelation of body and spirit, of material and spiritual things, and the unity of the Christian community – to reassert, that is, a "Catholic" understanding of existence as well as worship – at a moment in history when these beliefs and values were most seriously challenged and eroded.

Though the antecedents of Laudianism are to be found in Andrewes and Buckeridge, and before that in Hooker,[103] the violent conflicts between ceremonialist and puritan ideologies during this period are the culmination of tensions that had existed within the English church – and within English society, with which it was officially coterminous – since the Reformation. From the beginning, the reforming spirit of Protestants wanting a decisive separation from Rome's "idolatrous" religion was at odds with the English church's retention of much of its pre-Reformation service and ceremonies and its efforts to include those who had formerly been Catholic within its institution. The early priests and bishops in the Elizabethan church had been Catholic clergy, and many laity had been raised Catholics. Hooker's argument for a sacrament-based worship and for historical continuity with the Roman Catholic church surely spoke to a feeling of continuity that others experienced using a Prayer Book that had retained much of the earlier "Catholic" worship. Traditional Catholic practices and sensibilities, as well as ritualist culture, persisted in England, where the process of Protestant reformation was gradual and far from thorough.[104]

Intensifying a ceremonialism that had never entirely disappeared from England, Laudianism sought to revive and preserve a sacramental vision of worship and human experience and a belief in the hierarchically unified interdependence of body, soul, and affections in the human person. Though Montagu, Cosin, and Laud considered themselves real Protestants, there was some truth in the charges of popery that were brought against them, first in pamphlets and then by Parliament, for the structures of thought and feeling that grounded the ceremonial practices they sought to enforce had much in common with the assumptions of the pre-Reformation Catholic church with which they acknowledged continuity. While attention to ceremonial worship under Charles and Laud reflected the personal values of these two men,[105] it was also, I would argue, a culturally broader effort to maintain a vision not just of worship but of human nature and human relations that was challenged by the divisive, dualist assumptions driving Calvin's and Luther's writings and the beliefs of thoroughly reformed Protestants in sixteenth- and seventeenth-century England. It is inadequate to an understanding of these older traditional values and their cultural significance simply to dismiss them as vestiges of superstition firmly displaced by a rationalist, progressive reformist ideology.[106] As Laudian and puritan positions defined themselves in terms of their differences from each other, tensions and contradictory values that had long existed in the English church – and that to some extent were indigenous to Christianity – became irreparably polarized. The seventeenth-century conflict over worship thus reflects fundamental tensions within Christianity that had intensified with the Reformation but reached a state of crisis in England only during the middle decades of the seventeenth century.

At stake in the disagreements over religion in seventeenth-century England were conflicting ideas about human nature, the relation between the individual and the social community, and the relation of the present to the past. It was not just the Protestant reformers' sense of the individual's direct relation with God that, if pursued to its practical implications, threatened to dismantle a sense of community that was psychologically as well as socially and politically useful. As Laudians recognized, the radical Protestant sense of unyielding distinctions between the spiritual and the carnal, between true and false religion, had the potential to destroy the sense of an integrated, inclusive community and severed the individual from the larger society and the past – though it could justly be said that puritan ideology actually intensified and contracted the boundaries Christianity (or even monotheism) has always drawn between itself and the world of non-believers.[107] By its very nature, puritan ideology was exclusive and oppositional, as it defined the godly as a minority whose identity and purity necessitated the expulsion of all contaminating pollutions and of the ungodly masses of humanity, who were viewed as not sharing the spiritual nature of Christ and thus not fully human. Perhaps some might say that puritans were only concerned with religion, not with secular affairs. True, those calling for reform in the late 1630s and early 1640s attacked the prelates for meddling in secular, temporal affairs, and insisted on the separation of church and state in order to justify following one's conscience in religion. But, like Bacon in his separation of science and theology, religious reformers wanted to separate religious and secular realms only so they could be eventually reunited, for the vision was of a godly England, fully transformed into a new Jerusalem. The process and effects of reformation were to pervade society. Like Laudian ceremonialism, puritan ideology expressed a structure of experience and social relations that extended beyond the confines of the church.

Despite the fact that the battles over ceremonial worship seem to a (post)modern, secular mind to have been fought over small matters, the religious views in conflict were not merely about details of worship or doctrine. If Laudian ideology figured a social model of hierarchical, unified order, to which ceremonies contributed as they embodied reverence and submission and incorporated the individual into communal, public worship, puritan ideology figured a social order fragmented and divided – not only by its emphasis on the individual's responsibility to follow God rather than human traditions but by its sense of necessary divisions between the godly and the reprobate, the spiritual and the carnal. In this sense, Laudians were right to find in puritan rhetoric as well as acts of nonconformity a threat to unified social order. But Laudian ideology was inadequate for solving problems facing England, for it dealt with difference and dissent by trying to contain it. It hoped to purchase unity at the price of individual liberty of conscience and behavior.

CHAPTER 3

George Herbert: devotion in The Temple and the art of contradiction

Ever since its publication in 1633, Herbert's poetry has appealed to people from a remarkably diverse range of religious persuasions, yet the work of few poets has been so sharply contested, as readers have sought to identify his poetry with particular religious positions. In the seventeenth century, Izaak Walton, Henry Vaughan, and Christopher Harvey claimed Herbert as the true son of the ceremonial English church, who had preserved in poetry the rituals prohibited during the civil war and Interregnum. Walton and Harvey identified *The Temple* with Laudian ritual, Walton claiming that Laud persuaded Herbert to take orders, Harvey appropriating Herbert to the polemical cause of the Laudian church in successive editions of *The Synagogue*, his imitation of *The Temple*. For Vaughan in the early 1650s, Herbert's *Temple* took the place of the disestablished church, providing the forms and inspiration for worship.[1]

Those on the other side of the religious divide also claimed Herbert as one of their own. Puritans in the 1650s and dissenters after the Restoration found in Herbert a kindred spirit whose poetry expressed the personal, interior experience of grace. Richard Baxter praised Herbert's *"Heart-work,"* Robert Overton transcribed and adapted Herbert's poems while in prison, and the compiler of *Select Hymns Taken Out of Mr. Herbert's Temple* (1697), used by dissenters, embraced Herbert as "Our Divine Poet."[2]

In the twentieth century, similar appropriations have taken place as critics have seen Herbert, variously, as Anglo-Catholic, as representing the *via media* between Geneva and Rome, even as having affinities with puritan spirituality.[3] Recent critical battles over Herbert are part of larger battles being fought over the interpretation of "Protestant" religious poets. But Herbert has been particularly susceptible to interpretive conflict – both in the seventeenth century and now – because his poetry so perfectly expresses the

ideologically contradictory impulses of the English church, dissonances that would lead to the Revolution and the permanent
rupture of England's Protestant religious community.

As we have seen, the religious conflicts troubling seventeenth-
century England involved a clash between two fundamentally
different ways of understanding human identity and experience as
well as between two different kinds of worship – between, on the one
hand, a ceremonialist ideology that integrates inner and outer,
spiritual and corporeal, and the individual within the community
through ceremonial worship, and, on the other, a puritan ideology
that is suspicious of ritual forms, rejects "human invention," and
sees experience in terms of oppositions between spiritual and carnal,
inward and external, as it focuses on the individual believer rather
than the corporate religious community. Herbert's poetry was
written before it became necessary to choose sides in the escalating
conflicts, and published just as Laud became Archbishop of Canterbury. But conflicts between "ceremonialist" and "puritan" ideologies
were already sharply politicized in the 1620s and early 1630s;
Laudians were assuming greater power and "puritans" were vocal in
criticizing the increasingly ceremonial church. Though *The Country
Parson* shows Herbert distancing himself from Laudian and nonconformist extremes, *The Temple*, I would argue, expresses not a
harmonious, peaceful middle way, but rather the deeply conflicted
via media of the seventeenth-century English church, a *via media* that
would not fully survive either the Revolution or the Restoration
settlement, when puritan dissent was excluded from the established
church by law.[4]

Herbert's withdrawal from the court to Bemerton suggests a move
away from the political world, perhaps even a disgust for the
politicization of religion.[5] Yet contemporary religious conflict left a
deep mark on his poetry. Though personal, meditative poems like
"The Flower" seem far removed from struggles in the church, "The
Familie," "Church-rents and schismes," and "Divinitie" are more
public, less meditative, more directly concerned with dissension
within the church. Herbert's poetry ranges from clearly devotional
meditations to polemically engaged poems. But even his concern
with personal, poetic devotion partakes of the contemporary conflict
over worship.

"The Dedication" of *The Temple* offers Herbert's "first fruits" to
God.[6] The echo of Exodus – "The first of the first fruits of thy land

thou shalt bring unto the house of the Lord thy God" (34:26) – locus
of instruction about the Jewish ceremonial law, immediately raises
the contested issue of ceremonial worship. In *The Temple*, Herbert
struggles with the question of what is proper devotion – precisely the
issue in the conflict over worship. As praise and prayers offered to
God,[7] the lyrics of "The Church" are the work of a poet instinctively
moved to create devotional art in a reformed English church that
questioned the legitimacy of humanly fashioned worship. That
Herbert looks forward *both* to Milton's iconoclasm *and* to Herrick's
celebration of art and ceremony in *Hesperides* suggests the complex
relation of his poetry to the conflict over ceremony.

"THE ALTAR" AND THE PROBLEM OF "INVENTED" WORSHIP

The lyrics of *The Temple* proper begin with "The Altar," followed by
"The Sacrifice," and conclude with a series of eucharistic poems.
This focus on the altar rather than the pulpit, the Sacrament rather
than the sermon, aligns Herbert with defenders of ceremony and
ritual within the church. It resonates with his special attention to the
east end in his renovation of his church at Leighton Bromswold, and
with Walton's remark that Herbert's burial under the altar of his
parish church was a fitting conclusion to a life spent serving God "at
his Altar."[8] Later poems in *The Temple* criticizing puritan nonconformity reinforce this ceremonial emphasis. Yet a persistent "puritan"
distrust of invention and formalism complicates the volume.

The conflicting impulses that mark *The Temple* are evident in the
first poem of "The Church." "The Altar" announces commitment
to ceremonial worship while voicing the deep suspicion of human
invention in worship that characterized puritan opposition to the
ceremonies. It is often assumed that "The Altar" was written too
early for the altar controversy that erupted in 1637 to be an
appropriate context.[9] But by the mid-1620s, the altar was already a
controversial symbol of ceremonial worship.[10] In the summer of
1627, the vicar of Grantham moved the communion table and
declared his intention to build a stone altar; Mr. Wheatley, the
alderman, complained to John Williams, Bishop of Lincoln, sparking
conflicts that would eventually be played out in pamphlets. Williams
was an influential figure in Herbert's life, facilitating his ordination
as deacon at the end of 1624, and presenting him with the positions
of canon of Lincoln Cathedral and prebend of Leighton Ecclesia in

July 1626.[11] Given Herbert's connection with Williams, Herbert may have known of the incident with the vicar of Grantham, which was but one of several disturbances over ceremonial worship in the late 1620s. In 1628, Cosin's reverence towards the altar in Durham Cathedral incited Peter Smart's charges of altar worship. Francis Burgoyne, whom Prynne called Cosin's "Disciple," erected a controversial altar in the east end of his parish church.[12] Though the controversy over altars would not erupt in pamphlets for almost ten years, by the late 1620s the "altar" had become a symbolic focus of conflict over worship.

Herbert's poem "The Altar" is ideologically charged. He capitalizes the very words ("ALTAR," "SACRIFICE") puritans objected to as evoking both the Jewish ceremonial worship and the sacrificial Mass of Roman Catholicism.[13] Williams, no puritan but sympathetic to puritan scruples, pointed out in his 1627 letter to the vicar of Grantham that the word "table" rather than "Altar" had long been used in England's reformed liturgy and canons, and thus was preferred. In his Articles against Cosin in 1630, Smart denounced "preist," "sacrifyce," and "altar" as idolatrous words – he feared that such Jewish and Roman Catholic language would lead to reinstitution of the Mass.[14] With its provocative title and language, its altar shape and placement as the first of the devotional lyrics of "The Church," "The Altar" asserts the importance of ceremonial worship, particularly as Herbert draws an analogy between his poem (an altar for his devotion to God) and the place in the church where Holy Communion is celebrated.[15]

"The Altar," however, substitutes the spiritual altar of Herbert's heart for material altars, and calls into question human invention in ways that echo puritan iconoclasm.[16] The altar he "reares" (line 1), both heart and poem, is "frame[d]" (line 3) and "cut" (line 8) by God, who is its "maker" – the poet contributing only tears to cement it. It is "broken" (line 1), imperfect as well as afflicted and contrite.[17] That proclaimed imperfection, the lack of art, keeps the poem from being an idolatrous monument of human pride. Herbert claims he has avoided the craft that is the mark of idolatrous pride – "no workmans tool hath touch'd the same" (line 4). This line recalls God's instructions in Deuteronomy 27:2,5, that "when ye shall pass over Jordan . . . thou shalt build an altar unto the Lord thy God, an altar of stones; thou shalt not lift up any iron tool upon them." Once in the promised land, Joshua builds "an altar of whole stones, over which no man hath lift up any iron" (Joshua 8:31). Both biblical passages echo the injunction in Exodus 20:25: "And if thou wilt make me an altar of stone, thou shalt not build it of hewn stone: for if thou lift up thy tool upon it, thou hast polluted it." Like these verses, Herbert's poem identifies artifice with the pollution of idolatry.

In the 1620s and 1630s, the church was divided over whether "human invention" had a legitimate place in the worship of God. This is precisely the problem that preoccupies "The Altar" and *The Temple* more generally.[18] William Bradshaw had explained, no human being has "authoritie to frame . . . any forme or fashion of Gods service and worship." Once men think they have "power to make peculiar formes of Religion & worship," their next step will be to "invent" their own religion, substituting their idolatrous "false" worship for the "prescript rule of Gods word." Thus Smart objected to Cosin's gestures of adoration towards the altar, and Burton condemned the proliferation of "invented" forms of worship in the late 1620s and 1630s.[19]

Herbert shares this puritan fear of framing or fashioning an idol. Yet his suspicion of art and invention in worship is at odds with his hopes for the poem's legitimacy and his claims for its devotional function.[20] Pulled between distrust and belief in art, "The Altar" reenacts the tensions involved in the contemporary religious conflict over worship.

Such tensions are evident in the Hebrew Bible as well. Though Deuteronomy 27:2, 5 and Exodus 20:25 warn against art ("tools") as a pollution of worship, God's directions to the Israelites to erect an altar indicate the necessity of humanly fashioned acts of devotion. Moreover, if these biblical passages bespeak a distrust of art as idolatry, as does the second commandment forbidding "graven image[s]" (Exodus 20:4–5), the Hebrew scripture also indicates approval of art in the service of God. In Exodus 25–8, Moses receives meticulous instructions for building the tabernacle, its altars and furniture, and making the special clothing of Aaron and the priests. Exodus 36–9 describes the construction of the sanctuary and everything that will be part of its service. God chooses Bezaleel and Aholiab, and others who later will be "called" by God, as "workmen" to fashion everything required for the service of the sanctuary (Exodus 31:1–11; 35: 30–5). Herbert's repeated claim that he has been "called" to God's service not only signifies his Christian calling to the priesthood but also evokes the calling of sacred artists described in the Hebrew Bible.

And the Lord spake unto Moses, saying, See I have called by name Bezaleel the son of Uri, the son of Hur, of the tribe of Judah: And I have filled him with the spirit of God, in wisdom, and in understanding, and in knowledge, and in all manner of workmanship, To devise cunning works, to work in gold, and in silver, and in brass. And in cutting of stones, to set them, and in carving of timber, to work in all manner of workmanship. And I, behold, I have given with him Aholiab, the son of Ahisamach, of the tribe of Dan: and in the hearts of all that are wise hearted I have put wisdom, that they may make all that I have commanded thee. (Exodus 31:1–6)

So important is this passage in defining and justifying sacred art that Moses repeats it to the Israelites at the end of chapter 35. These "makers," the true artists or workmen, are filled by God's spirit. Although it is well known that Herbert found in David's Psalms inspiration and biblical sanction for his poetry,[21] the holy work of Bezaleel and Aholiab, devoted to God's service, also represents an ideal towards which Herbert strives. Herbert's particularly visual and formal sense of his poems as artifacts distinguishes them from the Psalms, making them more like the special ceremonial vessels fashioned by these makers of the sanctuary. The work of Bezaleel and Aholiab contrasts with the idol-making "workmen" castigated in the prophets,[22] but also with the episode of the golden calf (Exodus 32–4), the most infamous example of idolatry. That Aaron, high priest (and pattern for the English episcopacy), made the golden calf, that he "fashioned it with a graving tool, after he had made it a molten calf" (Exodus 32:4), speaks to the fears of Herbert, priest and poet, who anxiously disclaims the use of any tool and recognizes how easily worship slides into idolatry.

With its conflicting views of human art and its effort to discriminate between making idols and making beautiful things that might serve in the worship of God, Exodus became the locus both for a puritan suspicion of invention in devotion and for the ceremonialist commitment to art in the service of God. The biblical description of Jewish ceremonial worship, which defenders of ceremony believed provided the pattern for Christian worship, gives special attention to the divinely appointed artists and the careful crafting of things for God's worship. To puritans, however, the altar of uncut stones erected after the Israelites crossed Jordan signified the necessary abandonment of art in the promised land of the Christian dispensation.

"The Altar" seeks to avoid the worship of the self, or "*will-worship*," as puritans called it.[23] In claiming that God has "cut" his altar/heart, or engraved, as it were, his poem, Herbert disclaims poetic agency, implicitly identifying his poem with the stone tablets Moses took up to mount Sinai while Aaron was making the golden calf: "And the tables were the work of God, and the writing was the writing of God, graven upon the tables" (Exodus 32:16). Like Moses, Herbert receives God's words rather than fashioning an idol; but, hardened by sin, he is also the stone upon which God works. Yet Herbert also wants to be a "chief artificer," filled with the divine spirit and appointed by the Lord to make things for the "service" of God. He raises a devotional "frame" (line 11) he hopes God will "sanctifie" (line 16), a frame that functions like a sanctuary or place of worship where God can be praised. Herbert's altar will be constructed not from "wood" (Exodus 38:1) or stone but from Scripture, formed into something that might serve for devotion.[24] He hopes that "if I chance to hold my peace" (line 13) (if he stops writing poems, if he dies), "These stones to praise thee may not cease" (line 14) – the poem and the entire volume becoming an altar of living stones, continuously speaking God's praise as a perpetual poetic liturgy.

"The Altar" defines tensions about poetry-writing that run throughout Herbert's volume and grow out of the seventeenth-century conflict over worship. Herbert's personal, poetic concerns take shape within the context of the contested public worship of the English church. His anxious attempt to legitimize and find a place for human invention in devotion has implications that extend beyond the poetic temple to the actual English church.

THE MATERIAL CHURCH, CEREMONY, AND SPIRITUAL WORSHIP

There had long been tension within the reformed English church between those who valued the liturgy and "forms" of the church and those who wanted a "purer," fully spiritual worship of God. But in Charles I's reign, this tension increased with the growing attention to the architecture and furnishings of the church, along with its rites, liturgy, and calendar. From the mid-1620s on, the Laudian program to enforce conformity to the ceremonies, repair decaying churches, and amplify the "beauty of holiness" provoked intense puritan opposition. With its many references to the physical structure and rites of the church, Herbert's poetry calls attention to the very features of the church that were becoming sharply contested.[25] It is not accidental that one of the critical questions about *The Temple* is how we are to understand the importance of church architecture, liturgy, and rites in Herbert's volume.

Herbert frequently points to the material structure and ceremonies of the church, whereas puritans insisted that the place of worship is unimportant and that bodily ceremonies distract the spirit. Herbert's titles draw a continuing analogy between his volume of poetry and the actual, visible church, thus reconfirming the importance of the material, institutional church. Such attention to the material church accords with his friend Nicolas Ferrar's remark that Herbert spent considerable money repairing his church.[26]

Herbert invites the reader to pass through "The Church-porch" before entering "The Church." The subtitle of "The Church-porch," *Perirrhanterium*, refers to the instrument for sprinkling holy water before entering the church, as if the poet's preparatory instructions are a ceremonial sprinkling. After the "Church-porch," we encounter "Superliminare," the lintel over the entrance to the church. These two Latin titles suggest continuity with pre-Reformation Roman Catholic worship. Once in "The Church" proper, we see "The Altar," much as in English churches the sight-lines focused on the altar.[27] Subsequent titles evoke the inner architecture of the church ("Church-monuments," "The Church-floore," "The Windows"), the church calendar ("Easter," "Whitsunday," "Trinitie Sunday," "Christmas," "Lent"), and church rituals and ceremonial worship ("H. Baptisme," "The H. Communion," "Mattens," "Evensong," "Church-musick," "Antiphon"). Through titles, Herbert ties his volume to the liturgy of the Church of England; and the lyrics of "The Church," in imagery and organization, ending with a series of eucharistic poems, emphasize sacrament-centered worship.[28]

Herbert's attention to the liturgy, rites, and physical aspects of the church focuses on exactly those things puritans attacked as evidence of idolatrous worship, the substitution of human inventions for the purely scriptural worship of God. But the clearest indication of Herbert's commitment to ceremonial worship is "The British Church," one of his most partisan poems. In the face of puritan criticism of England's ceremonies, "The British Church" praises the

established church as the mean between the excesses of an overly
ceremonial Rome and a plain, thoroughly reformed Geneva:

> I Joy, deare Mother, when I view
> Thy perfect lineaments and hue
>   Both sweet and bright.
> Beautie in thee takes up her place,
> And dates her letters from thy face,
>   When she doth write.
>
> A fine aspect in fit aray,
> Neither too mean, nor yet too gay,
>   Shows who is best.
> Outlandish looks may not compare:
> For all they either painted are,
>   Or else undrest.
>
> She on the hills, which wantonly
> Allureth all in hope to be
>   By her preferr'd,
> Hath kiss'd so long her painted shrines,
> That ev'n her face by kissing shines,
>   For her reward.
>
> She in the valley is so shie
> Of dressing, that her hair doth lie
>   About her eares:
> While she avoids her neighbours pride,
> She wholly goes on th' other side,
>   And nothing wears.
>
> But, dearest Mother, what those misse,
> The mean, thy praise and glorie is,
>   And long may be.
> Blessed be God, whose love it was
> To double-moat thee with his grace,
>   And none but thee.

As in Donne's holy sonnet "Show me deare Christ," the female
figure of the church derives from the biblical image of the church as
spouse of Christ. But where Donne's poem seems uncertain where
or if on earth the true church resides, Herbert is sure of its British
identity. Addressing the church as "mother," Herbert signals obedience to its authority, his complete conformity to its ceremonial order.
Morton had accused the nonconforming ministers of rebelling
against their *"Mother"* when they should be "obsequious and

dutifull" in accordance with the fifth commandment to honor one's parents.[29] Nonconformists, however, rejected the metaphor of the church as mother. Ames told Morton that the episcopal "Hierarchie" of the church was no "mother" but "a Step-dame, usurping this title and authoritie . . . Shee is a creature of mans making" (*Reply*, "The Preface"). Like *The Country Parson* and the early *Musae Responsoriae* – Herbert's one explicit foray into theological controversy – "The British Church" takes a firm stand against such nonconformist objections to the official ceremonial worship.

Herbert insists that the "lineaments" and "hue" of the British church, the externals of ceremonial worship, are "perfect," "fine," and "fit," the appropriate "dressing" of devotion. Morton and Burges, too, had defended the "decent," "comely" "garments" of the English church against puritans like Ames, who wanted a plain, unadorned service in which "naked Christ" was preached.[30] Whereas Ames saw England's "Popish ceremonies" as garments of "that harlot of Rome," inappropriate for a chaste, reformed, purely spiritual church (*Reply*, p. 104), Herbert distinguishes the British church from the "painted" looks of the Catholic church "on the hills" of Rome, "wantonly" alluring worshipers, but also from the equally distasteful, erring appearance of the church in "the valley" of Geneva, who "nothing wears" and allows "her hair" to "lie / About her eares," taking no care of her appearance. While not necessarily Laudian, this anti-puritan poem presents a view of the church with which Laud could have agreed.[31]

The conformist stance of "The British Church" becomes more polemical in other poems. "Church-rents and schismes" laments the destruction of the beauty, health, and wholeness of the church. The "rose" (line 1) has been fouled by the "worm" of schism (line 3), a schism identified with the "rude and unhallow'd steps" of puritans that "crush and grinde" the "beauteous glories" of the ceremonial church (lines 8–9). "The Familie" draws a double analogy between the controversies in the British church, the internal dissensions of a family, and the conflicts within the heart of the individual believer, but the emphasis shifts to the public concerns of the church.[32] The "noise of thoughts within my heart" (line 1) is like "complaints" by puritan "wranglers" (lines 3, 7) within the family of the church. Although the poem initially seems tolerant of dissenters – "Lord, the house and familie are thine, / Though some of them repine" (lines 5–6) – it quickly takes a sharper turn: "Turn out these wranglers, which defile thy seat: / For where thou dwellest all is neat" (lines 7–8). The advice to expel disorderly thoughts from the heart implies that disorderly members of the church, too, should be expelled. Strictly conformist, "The Familie" praises neatness and "Order" (line 10), which gives "all things their set forms and houres" (line 11). Far from opposing private to public, or the individual conscience to institutional authority, the poem presumes their connectedness as it elaborates an analogy that finds ceremonial order the solution to internal disorder, whether of the individual or of the church. Although "griefs" as well as "joyes" will always exist in God's "house" (lines 18, 17, 21), they must be "without a noise" (line 18), unexpressed or even suppressed. "Peace," "Silence," and "Humble Obedience" must "abound" (lines 9, 13, 21) – "obedience" being the code word for submission to ceremonial worship:

> And where these are not found,
> Perhaps thou com'st sometimes, and for a day;
> But not to make a constant stay.   (lines 22–4)

This warning that God might choose another church if the English one remains a place of dissension might illuminate the controversial lines of "The Church Militant" that almost cost the volume its publication in 1633: "Religion stands on tip-toe in our land, / Readie to passe to the *American* strand" (lines 235–6). These lines bothered the Laudian censor in 1633, and several recent readers have seen in them sympathy for the puritan conscience constrained by conformity. Herbert's attitude in "The Familie," however, suggests that religion may be ready to pass to America, not because of a mistaken emphasis on conformity, but because dissension caused by puritans has made the Church of England a "distemper'd" place where the God who wants all things "neat" will refuse to dwell ("The Familie," lines 19, 8).

Herbert's celebration in "The British Church" of an "Anglican" mean in ceremonial worship bespeaks his own effort to find a middle ground for his poetry between idolatrous artifice and an unacceptable nakedness, to practice a devotional poetry that would avoid proud invention while allowing a place for form and beauty. His attention to poetic form is analogous to the English church's concern to maintain formal worship. Though the ceremonial aspects of the church are "indifferent" things not essential to salvation,[33] "The British Church" makes it clear that they are *important* not just to

Herbert but to God, who, the last lines suggest, has chosen the British church as his only true bride because of her beauty. Insofar as this celebration of the moderately ceremonial church justifies art in the service of God – and hence, Herbert's own poetic endeavor – this poem should make us wary of thinking Herbert was firmly, consistently iconoclastic.[34]

The position of "The British Church" in the middle of the volume evinces the centrality of that church and its ceremonies to Herbert's *Temple*, but "The Church" also exhibits a sharply anti-ceremonial impulse. Committed to ceremonial worship, Herbert nevertheless betrays a suspicion of external, corporeal forms of worship. He focuses on the heart, on the interior spaces and motions of worship. In spite of the many references to the communal worship of the church, the devotional lyrics of "The Church" often focus on personal, private communions with God that, as in "The Glance," might seem to take place outside the institution and its sacraments, particularly if the lyrics are read singly.[35] Herbert's poems personalize and spiritualize the church festivals and ceremonies and even the physical building in a way that deemphasizes the material, ceremonial, and outward aspects of worship. "The H. Communion" deprecates the external, aesthetic aspects of the rite, those associated with human art, invention, and finery, as he insists that God is not "convey[ed]" (line 14) "in rich furniture, or fine aray, / Nor in a wedge of gold" (lines 1–2). Herbert stresses the communicant's *experience* of communion with God rather than the ritualistic aspects or the priest's role. The narrative movement of many poems is away from the materiality of the church, which by the end of poems like "The Windows" or "The Church-floore" is absorbed into the spiritual and figurative meaning.[36]

The deprecation, even dissolution of the material aspects of worship is most striking in "Church-monuments." As Herbert contemplates the tombs and memorials commonly found within English churches – monuments that honored the dead, commemorating their individuality through inscriptions and statues or effigies – he imagines these monuments dissolving like flesh, "crumbled into dust" (line 22). Under his ironic gaze, the monuments meant to preserve individual identity become emblems of human anonymity and insignificance. But "Church-monuments" suggests, not simply the absurdity of class distinctions and earthly titles in the face of death, but the vanity of all humanly created artifacts including religious ceremonies, which were understood to be *"memoratives"* or memorials reminding us of spiritual truths.[37] Herbert's association of the church monuments with ceremonial worship seems inescapable as his monuments enact the very gestures of worship puritans objected to: "they shall bow, and kneel, and fall down flat / To kisse those heaps, which now they have in trust" (lines 15–16). Further, if Herbert's poems are in part monuments that are memorials of the self – as the "Altar" suggests, with its "I" shape, its stones that will continue to praise God, in Herbert's twist on the topos of immortal verse – then they, too, are futile as they attempt to give a distinctive, individual identity to the self.

If "The British Church" defends the traditional ceremonies of the Church of England, "Sion" presents an explicitly anti-ceremonial position. As both poems occur only in the Bodleian manuscript, they are presumably both later ones, so one cannot argue that Herbert moved either towards or away from the ceremonialism of the church. That both poems appear in the exact middle of *The Temple* aptly symbolizes how contradictory religious impulses lie at the center of Herbert's poetry.

> LOrd, with what glorie wast thou serv'd of old,
> When Solomons temple stood and flourished!
>   Where most things were of purest gold;
>   The wood was all embellished
> With flowers and carvings, mysticall and rare:
> All show'd the builders, crav'd the seers care.
>
> Yet all this glorie, all this pomp and state
> Did not affect thee much, was not thy aim;
>   Something there was, that sow'd debate:
>   Wherefore thou quitt'st thy ancient claim:
> And now thy Architecture meets with sinne;
> For all thy frame and fabrick is within.
>
> There thou art struggling with a peevish heart,
> Which sometimes crosseth thee, thou sometimes it:
>   The fight is hard on either part.
>   Great God doth fight, he doth submit.
> All Solomons sea of brasse and world of stone
> Is not so deare to thee as one good grone.
>
> And truly brasse and stones are heavie things,
> Tombes for the dead, not temples fit for thee:

But grones are quick, and full of wings,
And all their motions upward be;
And ever as they mount, like larks they sing;
The note is sad, yet musick for a King.

Where "The British Church" celebrated a moderate ceremonial beauty as most pleasing to God, "Sion" depicts a Christian service stripped of ceremony and material beauty. This poem charts the move from the Jews' worship in Solomon's temple to Christian worship under the new dispensation, in the process also describing the more recent change from the ceremonial beauty of Roman Catholicism, believed to be patterned on Jewish ceremonial law, to the reformed service. The seductions of art, for Herbert, are associated not just with Catholic worship but ultimately with Jewish. "Sion" recounts the change from the times of "old," when God was "serv'd" with "glorie" in a beautiful temple, to the Christian era, with its spiritual, difficult, even painful service in the temple of the individual soul or heart. Though there is nostalgia for the older temple worship – and for the beautiful worship of the Roman Catholic church – an attraction to the beauty of its architecture and furnishings (the "purest gold," the "flowers and carvings, mysticall and rare"), the Jewish temple and spectacular ceremonial worship are dismissed as things of the past that God no longer inhabits or takes pleasure in.

In "Affliction (1)" personal history repeats the ecclesiastical history "Sion" records. When he first entered God's "service" (line 2), he found it "brave" (line 2), beautiful, seductive, with its "furniture so fine" (line 7), its "glorious household-stuffe" (line 9) – language that recalls Smart's description of Cosin's gloriously appointed service at Durham Cathedral. But whereas Cosin unrepentantly continued his devotion to a beautiful, ceremonial service, Herbert's speaker is reformed, forced by God's relentless afflictions to embrace a plain devotion defined in terms of loss.

"Sion" draws a sharp line between Christian worship (understood to be of the spirit and heart) and Jewish, which is renounced for its supposed materiality, its appeal to the senses – the pure gold and rare carvings affect the eye, the music enters the ear. Defenders of England's ceremonial worship stressed the connection between Jewish worship and Christian, seeing in the unbroken line of historical continuity a validation of their own worship, finding a pattern even for a reformed Christian ceremonialism in "the church" of the Jews.[38] Puritan opponents of ceremony, however, contrasted Christian worship with Jewish ceremonialism. Though they sometimes invoked Old Testament types, suggesting an ambivalent relation to the Judaic past, they insisted that Christians (living according to the Gospel not the Law, the spirit not the letter) must abandon corporeal, bodily ceremonies in order to have a "pure" Christian worship, stripped of all remnants of Jewish and Catholic carnality. In his sermon attacking Cosin's ceremonial worship, Smart insisted that the "Jewish types and fygurs" were "long since dead and buried": to "revive" and "rayse" them up again is "an apostasy."[39] Like critics of the increasing ceremonialism of the English church, Herbert's "Sion" contrasts the Christian and Jewish, spiritual and carnal, inward and external devotion. Temples have been replaced by the heart; the communal worship and priestly service of the Solomonic temple by the personal, intimate, solitary confrontation of the individual with God; the brass, visual ornaments, and ceremonial music of the Jewish temple (and Catholic churches) by "grones" that now are our "musick." There is no place here for the beautiful "workmanship" (Exodus 35:31) of Bezaleel, or of the artist who made the brass furnishings of Solomon's temple (1 Kings 7:14) – all "Architecture" now being tinged by sin.

"Sion" leaves behind ceremonial worship as if all material temples, all "human invention" and corporeal worship have been abrogated by Christ's crucifixion. The anti-ceremonial impulse of the poem recalls Ames's claim that all ceremonial worship is "*carnall*," "destitute of . . . spirit," and thus inappropriate for Christians. Such a belief would lead Burton, Prynne, and Bastwick in the 1630s, and Milton in the 1640s, to attack the service and beauty of the Laudian church as a return to a popish idolatry identified with Jewish ceremonialism.[40] Herbert's poem betrays an unpuritan nostalgia for Solomon's temple and even for the beauty of the Catholic church, but its understanding of the purely spiritual nature of Christian worship is strikingly close to Burton, Prynne, and Milton. Herbert's claim that Christian devotion takes place exclusively in the interior recesses of the heart would seem to make the ceremonial worship of the English church not just indifferent but idolatrous.

"Sion" jars with much of *The Temple* in its anti-ceremonialism, its rejection of invention and beauty in the service of God. The suggestion that the only music now fit for God is "grones" is at odds with Herbert's love of David's Psalms (sung in Solomon's temple, and newly transformed in Herbert's), with his well-known love of devotional music, and with his insistence in "Church-musick" that music is an instrument of grace that allows him to "travell . . . to heavens doore" (lines 11–12).

The paired poems, "Sion" and "The British Church," most explicitly define the contradictory attitudes towards worship that characterized the early Stuart English church and that shape *The Temple*, with its concern with form and ritual, on the one hand, and its radical privileging of the heart and spirit, on the other. If the church had retained a liturgy and ceremonial worship with ties to pre-Reformation Catholicism and an earlier Jewish worship, it had also embraced a distinctly Protestant sense of historical discontinuity and of opposition between exterior and interior, carnal and spiritual worship. These distinctive Protestant assumptions, at the heart of puritan ideology, conflict with the sense of historical continuity and connection between body and spirit that underlay the ceremonial worship of the Church of England.

CEREMONIAL WORSHIP AND HERBERT'S POETICS

The unsettling impact of puritan ideology, with its suspicion of invented, external forms of worship, is felt most deeply in Herbert's poems about poetry. As they worry about the idolatrous potential of poetry-writing, these poems express anxiety about ceremonial worship, an anxiety displaced from the arena of the public church onto personal, poetic devotion. For all his love of the ceremonies of the church, these poems indicate that Herbert may not have been as complacent about the increasing ceremonialism of the English church as "The British Church" (and certain of his interpreters) would have us believe.

Many of Herbert's poems ("The Altar," the "Jordan" poems, "Frailtie," "Vanitie (II)," "Gratefulness," "A true Hymne," "The Posie," "Sinnes round," and "The Forerunners") suggest the vanity of art in devotional matters. Suspicious of art's idolatrous potential, they identify "invention" with sin.[41] These beautifully crafted poems argue that beautiful phrases and well-made devotional objects are irrelevant to God's worship – perhaps even opposed to it, as they result from pride in human creativity and are potentially objects of idolatry for both poet and audience. What Herbert says about

Solomon's temple suggests his worries about the motives and effects of his own artistic invention: "All show'd the builders, crav'd the seers care" ("Sion," line 6).

"Jordan (II)" renounces art, poetic invention, and human creativity as Herbert's speaker narrates his conversion to a plain poetic devotion.

> WHen first my lines of heav'nly joyes made mention,
> Such was their lustre, they did so excell,
> That I sought out quaint words, and trim invention;
> My thoughts began to burnish, sprout, and swell,
> Curling with metaphors a plain intention,
> Decking the sense, as if it were to sell.
>
> Thousands of notions in my brain did runne,
> Off'ring their service, if I were not sped:
> I often blotted what I had begunne;
> This was not quick enough, and that was dead.
> Nothing could seem too rich to clothe the sunne,
> Much lesse those joyes which trample on his head.
>
> As flames do work and winde, when they ascend,
> So did I weave my self into the sense.
> But while I bustled, I might heare a friend
> Whisper, *How wide is all this long pretence!*
> *There is in love a sweetnesse readie penn'd:*
> *Copie out onely that, and save expense.*

The tone at first seems mild, as if former poetic efforts were more foolish than sinful. But invention is cast aside by the end as his "friend" declares, "*How wide is all this long pretence!*" All his earlier linguistic creativity is exposed as ostentatious, parading under a false profession of purpose, as God sees that Herbert was really concerned with his own achievement. His art is "wide" in the sense of missing the mark as well as excessive (*OED*) – Herbert's interlinguistic pun on the Hebrew word for sin (*chet*, to miss the mark) firmly identifying art and invention with sin, despite the delicacy of tone.

This witty poem abjuring "invention" revises Sidney's first sonnet in *Astrophil and Stella*, where Sidney rejects "Studying inventions fine" (line 6) and decides instead to "look in [his] heart and write" (line 14).[42] Where Sidney turns to the self for inspiration, Herbert's divine "friend" sends him to something already "penn'd" (the Word?), advising him simply to "copie," adding nothing from the self – like Moses, who when he received the second set of tablets was told by

God, "Write thou these words . . . And he wrote upon the tables the words of the Covenant" (Exodus 34:27–8). For Herbert, secular love poetry like Sidney's is idolatrous invention; its carnal language must be cleansed in the waters of Jordan, converted into something spiritual before it can serve a sacred function.

Not only secular love poetry is rejected. The craft of invention itself comes under suspicion, implicating the ceremonial worship of the church in the process. Herbert's description of the "lustre" of his poetic lines, his "curling" metaphors, the richness of the work he "weave[s]," attributes a striking materiality to his poetry, and recalls the care of the builders of Solomon's temple in "Sion" and the description in Exodus of the careful, beautiful work of the divinely appointed artisans who made the Tabernacle and all its furniture and adornments. The Lord

filled them with the spirit of God . . . to devise curious works, to work in gold, and in silver, and in brass, And in the cutting of stones, to set them, and in carving of wood, to make any manner of cunning work . . . Them hath he filled with wisdom of heart, to work all manner of work, of the engraver, and of the cunning workman, and of the embroiderer, in blue, and in purple, in scarlet, and in fine linen, and of the weaver, even of them that do any work, and of those that devise cunning work. (Exodus 35:31–5)

The images of "Jordan (II)" echo this biblical passage and subsequent chapters in Exodus (36–9) detailing the work of these artists, as well as I Kings 7, which describes the work for Solomon's temple. Herbert links the aesthetic, sensual beauty of poetry with ancient Jewish ceremonial worship, not only with the aestheticized ritual of Roman Catholicism that Protestants distrusted.

Herbert recounts how – like these architects of the Tabernacle and Solomon, who employed the most "cunning" "worker in brass" and spared no expense, making all the vessels and even the door hinges of the "house of the Lord" out of gold (I Kings 7: 14, 47–50) – he began wanting to create the best for God, to "clothe" his devotion so it would match its object. But good intentions became twisted with pride as he "did weave my self into the sense," increasingly delighted in the process and materials of his creation, admiring his own work, losing sight of its end. Defenders of ceremonial worship, looking back to the worship of the Jews, had argued that God must be approached with properly reverent, ceremonious forms.[43] The belief that no expense should be spared led to expensive gifts and purchases of altar-cloths, chalices, and other furnishings for the cathedrals. Puritans, however, thought that such attention to material aspects of the service was suspicously Jewish and "popish." In the charges against Cosin and others at Durham Cathedral, Smart indignantly described their concern with choosing the proper colors for the "images" of angels and Christ that they "sett up . . . about the quire." Smart mentions how they took counsel of a particular "painter, a popish recusant, who told you that nothing can be too good for the church" – precisely the sentiment Herbert recalls having in his pre-reformed artistic life.[44] For all Herbert's attraction to beauty, "Jordan (II)" is strikingly close to Smart in suggesting that the attempt to create a suitably glorious worship inevitably turns into idolatry – a suggestion that distances Herbert significantly from the Laudians.

The ornate, seductive quality of the "quaint words" and "trim invention" (line 3) he abjures recalls the "curious," "cunning work" of Bezaleel and Aholiab (Exodus 35:32, 33, 35; 39:8) and the builders of Solomon's temple (1 Kings 6–7), but also the charges puritans made against the ceremonial Roman and English churches. A reformed devotion would be plain, stripped of the supposed carnality of Jewish ceremonialism. Herbert defines a personal conversion from ceremonial devotion, seen as idolatrous, to a plain one, which has its own beauty. Yet "Jordan (II)" questions whether *any* invention is appropriate in the worship of God. A poem that simply "copie[s]" the "sweetnesse readie penn'd" is like worship founded solely on Scripture, specifically Christ's gospel. The difficulty of imagining what such a poem might be like is analogous to the difficulty of imagining a purely scriptural worship, which was precisely the problem puritans faced once the Book of Common Prayer was outlawed in the 1640s. The very existence of Herbert's poem, with its undeniable art – indeed, the existence of the entire volume of poetry with its distinctive, well-crafted identity, which is never completely subsumed into the Bible that constitutes its materials – attests to his reluctance to embrace the extreme puritan position that the poem inscribes.

Still, Herbert's recurrent fear that his poetic devotions are contaminated by idolatrous invention echoes puritan fears about the English church. In "Sinnes round," Herbert's description of the generation and working of sin sounds suspiciously like the process of writing. His thoughts "work" until they "hatch" an idea (lines 3–4). Once his thoughts "have perfected their draughts" (line 5), they give "fire" to "words" (lines 6–7). "Hands" "joyn" the "intentions" of words to give them form (lines 12–13). Poetic creation that begins in the mind seems a self-centered pleasure – quite different from the work of the inspired artisans of the sanctuary in Exodus, who are called "wise-hearted" (35:25; 36:1–2), as if to specify that the heart (not mind) is the seat of wisdom and holy art. The form of Herbert's finished inventions (the poem) is, not a part of God's sanctuary, but his "Babel" (line 15) – the word puritans used to denote idolatrous ceremonial worship.[45] In "Frailtie," the attractions of poetic creativity are identified with the "Regiment" of the world (lines 9–10), that seductive realm of flesh. God's regiment, "clad with simplenesse, and sad events" (line 11), seems to have no place for artistic invention. "In [his] silence" – when he isn't writing poetry – it is easy to "despise" (line 1) the attractions of the world. But once he begins to write, "glorie and gay weeds, / Brave language, braver deeds" (lines 13–14) become a temptation.

With their distrust of imagination and invention, Herbert's anxious meditations about poetry-writing show how poetry as well as visual images was implicated in the conflict over worship. "*In the worship of God*," Ames explained, "*wee are to devise nothing of our owne braine.*" "The very *phantasies*, or *images* of the minde, not prescribed by God, are . . . as well forbidden, as outward reall images."[46] As "*images* of the minde," devotional poems could seem as idolatrous as religious paintings or the ceremonies that were "images" of spiritual things.

Herbert's worry that the very impulse to create poetry is sinful receives its most eloquent, disturbing expression in "The Forerunners," which rationalizes an anticipated loss of poetic ability as a necessary, painful letting go of the seductive beauties of language that threaten to distract him from God:

> Farewell sweet phrases, lovely metaphors.
> But will ye leave me thus? when ye before
> Of stews and brothels onely knew the doores,
> Then did I wash you with my tears, and more,
>   Brought you to Church well drest and clad:
> My God must have my best, ev'n all I had.
>
> Lovely enchanting language, sugar-cane,
> Hony of roses, whither wilt thou flie?
> Hath some fond lover tic'd thee to thy bane?
> And wilt thou leave the Church, and love a stie? (lines 13– 22)

In this, one of the most beautiful of Herbert's poems, "sweet phrases" and "lovely metaphors" are a deeply loved, deeply feared source of temptation. Herbert's description of the dangerously seductive, promiscuous nature of language recalls Jeremiah and Ezekiel, who represented Israel's idolatry in terms of sexual betrayal (Jeremiah 3, Ezekiel 23), and Hosea, who took a wife from idolatry and whoredom but saw her return to her former ways.[47] Herbert's biblical allusions suggest that "metaphors" and "sweet phrases," like the contested ceremonies, have idolatrous origins and that they continue to be seductive instruments of idolatry.

Herbert claims he has purified and converted the formerly profane language of secular poetry, much as the English church claimed to have reformed the controversial ceremonies. Though ceremonies like wearing the surplice came from Roman Catholicism, and even the pagan or Jewish religions before, it was argued that they had been reformed and converted to good Christian use. Morton claimed the English church had removed the "abuses" and "superstitions" from the Roman ceremonies they retained, and quoted Calvin's comment that *"We may lawfully use the Temples or Churches, which have bin defiled and abused with Idols, and apply them to a better vse"* (*Defence*, pp. 134, 101). The Jews themselves provided a precedent, since the gold used for the sanctuary and its furnishings came from the jewelry the Israelites took from the Egyptians (Exodus 35:22, 24; 12:35–6).

The key trope for the defense of the English ceremonies, as for "The Forerunners" and much of Herbert's poetry, was conversion. Conversion was a powerful argument for those who would legitimize the retention of pre-Christian things. Just as Herbert has washed and reformed his beautiful borrowed language, redeeming it from its former polluted life in the "stews," so Morton recalls how in the early history of the church pagan temples were "converted" to "holy houses of God," how the church fathers took the verses of pagan poets addressed to heathen gods and applied them to God's worship (*Defence*, p. 139). This process of "conversion," long practiced by Christianity, supposedly legitimized the ceremonies the English reformed church retained from Roman Catholic, Jewish, and pagan worship, much as Herbert hoped his purification of language made it acceptable to God.

But it was exactly this notion of conversion that puritans rejected, insisting Christians must separate from all forms of carnal idolatry.

Bradshaw argued that Christians must completely abandon the "Idolatrous ceremonies of that whorish sinagogue" of Rome – a phrase that captures the identification of Catholic and Jewish that we have also seen in "Sion" and "Jordan (ii)." Ames insisted that the taint of idolatry always clings to anything taken from idolaters. Thus the church must "put of from her, all that dressing [that is, ceremonies], which they know to be whorish in the sayd stewes" of Rome, the Whore of Babylon.[48] If Herbert's attempt to convert and baptize poetic language, which was also the project of the "Jordan" poems, recalls the ceremonialist dedication to converting the pre-Reformation ceremonies, his fear that language remains inherently idolatrous, ready to return to its promiscuous ways, echoes the puritan distrust of conversion. The impending loss of the ability to write poetry is made to seem a wilful betrayal by language, which returns to its former carnal nature, much like converted Jews or Catholics, who were always suspected of loyalty to their original, supposedly carnal religion. Thus Herbert, despite his belief that "Beautie and beauteous words should go together" (line 30), at the end turns to a plain, unadorned worship, the equivalent of the church stripped of ceremony, hoping that the "bleak palenesse" of its appearance (reminiscent of the whitewashed walls of reformed churches) will be compensated by the "livelier" spiritual presence of Christ "within" (lines 34–5).

For all the obvious love of language and poetry, Herbert implies not only that tropes converted from secular love poetry to sacred use always remain suspect, ready to relapse into impurity, but also that humanly invented words are inherently idolatrous, carnal, only temporarily redeemable. Though his "sparkling notions" (line 4) and "sweet phrases" (line 13) may be his "best" (line 18) efforts, they must be surrendered as idolatrous distractions. All that counts is that "*Thou art still my God*" (line 32) – the plain declaration of continual, eternal dependence on God – remain in his heart. If that is all poetry can "say," "Perhaps with more embellishment" (line 33), then poetic creativity is finally superfluous.

Though the puritan distrust of invention in worship affects Herbert's devotional poetry, his attitude is more complex than those who see only his "radical devaluations of poetry" admit.[49] For other poems in *The Temple* find poetry and human creation appropriate and necessary expressions of worship. "The Altar" claims his poems are the work of God, an effect of grace. God's grace often seems a condition of writing, as in "The Flower," with its sense of poetic and spiritual renewal, or "Deniall" or "The Collar," where the speaker's spiritual disorder is mirrored in the disorder of the poetic verse. "The Quidditie" claims, "verse . . . is that which while I use / I am with thee" (lines 1, 11–12) – as if it were an instrument or means of communion with God. Poetry seems the proper, harmonious expression of a soul "in tune" with God.[50]

Moreover, shaped poems such as "Easter-wings," "The Altar," and "Paradise" insist on the appropriateness of their form to their content, materially embodying the ceremonialist belief that corporeal things in worship can represent immaterial, spiritual truths, reaching the soul through the senses. Whereas sometimes Herbert worries that his inventions compete with God, in "Paradise" his art seems a proper reflection of God's; he imitates God's pruning by paring away the letters of the words constituting the rhymes of each stanza. The analogy between human art and God's suggests a mode of continuity and connection that also characterizes the relation of material, poetic forms to the spiritual truths they convey. His shaped poems are like the bodily ceremonies of worship that symbolically "represent" spiritual things and whose outward form should match their inward meaning.[51]

Herbert's pattern poems are poetic analogues of the "set forms" of worship that puritans disliked.[52] Whereas puritans objected to set forms as mere external, "outward" worship devoid of spirit, "The Altar" insists that Herbert's set form is "made of a heart" (line 2). For all its announced distrust of invention, the material form of the poem expresses his heart much as bodily ceremonies like kneeling at Communion were understood by defenders of ceremony to express inward devotion and humility.[53] Although "The Altar" contrasts the physical and the spiritual, preferring the heart to material, external forms,[54] its very use of visual form suggests the analogy between material and spiritual aspects of worship, exemplifying their integration rather than opposition. Art and invention, at their best, express the spirit.

Even seemingly "anti-ceremonial," anti-"formalist" poems use poetic form symbolically and hieroglyphically. In the Bodleian manuscript, "Church-monuments" appears as a single unbroken verse paragraph of iambic pentameter lines, full of enjambment. Visually, the solid, rectangular block of lines represents the form of a monument, but the sense of a solid, fixed pattern comes undone in the process of reading the lines, as each spills over into the next, enacting the process of dissolution. Herbert thus reaffirms the representational powers of "set forms" in a poem that calls them into question.[55] Similarly, "Sinnes round," which identifies the "invention" of the creative intellect with sin, is, paradoxically, a poem whose inventive form represents its spiritual meaning: the round (with the last line of each stanza becoming the first line of the next) offers an image of the endless, involuted circularity of sin. The fact that formally the poem embodies the ceremonialist belief that humanly invented forms can represent spiritual truth compromises the poem's stand against art and ceremonial worship. For Herbert's shaped poems are all grounded on the assumption that human invention *can* properly represent religious truths in forms that express and aid devotion.

"Providence" most fully justifies religious art and devotional poetry. The longest poem in "The Church" except for "The Sacrifice," this one sharply counters the anti-ceremonial, anti-poetic stance of "Jordan (ii)" and "The Forerunners." That "Providence" appears in only the Bodleian manuscript suggests it is a relatively late poem, probably later than the "Jordan" poems, which should dispel any suspicion that he abandoned an earlier devotion to ceremonial forms. "Providence" begins:

> O Sacred Providence, who from end to end
> Strongly and sweetly movest, shall I write,
> And not of thee, through whom my fingers bend
> To hold my quill? shall they not do thee right?
>
> Of all the creatures both in sea and land
> Onely to Man thou hast made known thy wayes,
> And put the penne alone into his hand,
> And made him Secretarie of thy praise.
>
> Beasts fain would sing; birds dittie to their notes;
> Trees would be tuning on their native lute
> To thy renown: but all their hands and throats
> Are brought to Man, while they are lame and mute.
>
> Man is the worlds high Priest: he doth present
> The sacrifice for all; while they below
> Unto the service mutter an assent,
> Such as springs use that fall, and windes that blow.   (lines 1–16)

Declaring that the subject of his poetry will be God, this poem defends devotional poetry. Its meticulous elaboration of God's providence in the natural world, where God's "curious art" (line 94) gives order to everything, is framed by a defence of the poetic art of praise. Herbert insists human beings have an obligation to praise God. As the only creatures possessing language and knowledge of God's ways, they must offer the praise that others would if they were not "lame and mute," as if humans were the priests of a well-meaning but inarticulate congregation. Herbert revises David's Psalms 150 ("Let every thing that hath breath praise the Lord") and 148 ("Praise the Lord from the earth, ye dragons, and all deeps / . . . Mountains, and all hills; fruitful trees, and all cedars: / Beasts, and all cattle; creeping things and flying fowl," lines 7, 9–10) as he insists that only "man" can create hymns, though "All [living] things" "honour" God "in their being" (lines 145–7). In contrast to "Jordan (II)", linguistic creativity here is positive, its role not limited to copying. As the image of God, the human creative spirit derives from God, who "put[s] the penne" into "Man['s]" hand, expecting human creative energies to be focused on Him in praise. The body as well as mind ("fingers," "hands," "throats") must be involved. Clearly responding to the puritan charge that ceremonial worship is idolatrous invention, the poem's argument that God has ordained human devotion defends liturgy and the body's role in worship.

Within this defense of ceremonial devotion, Herbert places not just this poem but all his devotional lyrics: "most sacred Spirit, I here present / For me and all my fellows praise to thee" (lines 25–6). While admitting that human praise and devotional poetry are insufficient ("But who hath praise enough? nay, who hath any? / None can express thy works," lines 141–2), the poem concludes proclaiming its function as a "hymne" (line 151), as personal poetic devotion becomes interconnected with public, corporate worship. Herbert condemns the nonconformist who refuses participation in the ceremonial worship that is the necessary sacrifice of praise to God.[56]

> He that to praise and laud thee doth refrain,
> Doth not refrain unto himself alone,
> But robs a thousand who would praise thee fain,
> And doth commit a world of sinne in one.   (lines 17–20)

To create devotional art is to "invent" hymns of praise – that is, to engage in ceremonial worship. Though human creations are imperfect and thus superfluous in comparison with God's, *not* to write devotional poetry – and, analogously, not to perform ceremonial worship – is to omit something God expects.

The challenge Herbert repeatedly confronts in his poetry – how to create a non-idolatrous devotion, how to achieve the right style of worship – is exactly the problem confronting the Church of England in the late 1620s and early 1630s. Hence, though his conversations with God would seem to turn away from contemporary political concerns and from the world of religious strife, his poetry necessarily engages the highly contested issue of appropriate religious worship that was dividing the English church. Herbert inhabits a position between those like Ames who wanted a "naked" worship and those like Cosin and Laud devoted to beautifying the churches and service, between those who would deny any role or value to human invention and agency and those who would extol their powers. Yet, the multiple, contradictory, and dissonant notes of *The Temple* – its unresolved dilemmas – show how this middle position, like the *via media* of the English church in the late 1620s and early 1630s, was marked by conflict and contradiction. They also show how Herbert made poetry out of religious conflict, even as these conflicts made poetry itself suspect, aware of its own threatened irrelevance.

EQUIVOCAL POEMS

Tensions about ceremonial worship not only result in a mix of poems in *The Temple* variously questioning or celebrating art and ceremony; they make individual poems open to contradictory interpretations. The critical tension between ceremonial and anti-ceremonial impulses in Herbert creates a distinctive ambiguity, particularly in poems whose titles explicitly invoke ceremonial worship. Part of the fabric of these poems is an ideological "indeterminacy" that explains why his poetry has elicited "Anglo-Catholic" and "puritan" readings that are to varying degrees persuasive. Many of Herbert's poems allow very different readings that derive from conflicting beliefs about what constitutes true religious worship – conflicting beliefs we have seen voiced in *The Temple*.

This indeterminacy is evident in "The Altar," the first, foundational "stone" (line 6) of Herbert's "The Church." "The Altar" permits both a distinctly "puritan" and an authentically ceremonialist reading. In one sense, Herbert privileges the spiritual altar of the heart, contrasting the external and internal modes of worship, the literal sacrifices in the Jewish ceremonial worship with the figurative, spiritual sacrifices of Christians. It seems to inscribe the puritan belief that, with Christ's crucifixion, all material altars and sacrifices were abolished, that Christian altars are now only "metaphorical," and that the only proper sacrifices are praise and thanksgiving.[57]

Yet as a shaped poem, a "visual" representation of the altar of his heart, "The Altar" displays the intimate connection between external form and interior devotion, expressing precisely the union of physical and spiritual that informs ceremonial worship. Morton and Burges defended ceremony, the "externall" or "outward" part of worship, as symbolic "expressions of internall devotion."[58] Whereas puritans objected to bodily gestures in worship as merely external or carnal, Cosin explained that the "outward gesture" of kneeling at receiving Communion "is ordained . . . to testify and express the inward reverence and devotion of our souls towards our blessed Saviour." It is this belief that external forms and inward devotion are inextricably linked that lies behind Laud's assertion that "the *Externall worship of God* in his Church is the *Great Witness* to the World, that Our heart stands right," and that Herbert's shaped poem enacts as his poetic altar becomes the visible image of his spiritual devotion to God.[59]

"The Church-floore" and "The Windows" are similarly equivocal in their treatment of the materiality of the church. These poems have been interpreted both as evidence of Herbert's high-church "Anglicanism" or "Anglo-Catholicism" and as evidence of his distinctly puritan and anti-ceremonial spirituality.

"The Church-floore"

MArk you the floore? that square & speckled stone,
    Which looks so firm and strong,
        Is *Patience*:

And th'other black and grave, wherewith each one
    Is checker'd all along,
        Humilitie:

The gentle rising, which on either hand
    Leads to the Quire above,
        Is *Confidence*:

> But the sweet cement, which in one sure band
>   Ties the whole frame, is *Love*
>   And *Charitie*.
>
> Hither sometimes Sinne steals, and stains
> The marbles neat and curious veins:
> But all is cleansed when the marble weeps.
> Sometimes Death, puffing at the doore,
> Blows all the dust about the floore:
> But while he thinks to spoil the room, he sweeps.
>   Blest be the *Architect*, whose art
>   Could build so strong in a weak heart.

Identifying the spiritual, figurative meaning of various aspects of the church floor, the poem moves from the outward physical architecture of the church to the inward design of the heart, suggesting that the heart (rather than a physical building) is Herbert's concern. With its emphasis on the interiority and spirituality of worship, the poem distances itself from the growing attention by Cosin, Laud, and others in the late 1620s to the physical aspects of the church. It certainly allows a puritan reading whereby the material aspect of the church vanishes, replaced by the heart which is the true temple.[60] But though the poem seems to leave behind – thus devalue – the literal, material church, one could also see the poem as insisting on the *connection* between the physical church and the temple of the heart, between the external objects of contemplation and their spiritual significance, and between the institutional and the personal. Indeed, the poem's movement from the external to the internal, from physical to spiritual, fits the ceremonial insistence that the architecture and ceremonies of the church are corporeal representations or "images" of spiritual truths, and that contemplation of these outward, material things can lead the observer to spiritual truth. That is precisely what Herbert is doing as he offers the reader lessons on the significance of the material place of worship.

An indeterminate meaning also inheres in "The Windows," the fourth poem whose title refers to ceremonial aspects of the physical church ("Church-musick," "Church-lock and key," "The Church-floore," and "The Windows"). Describing the person who preaches "thy eternall word" (line 1) as "a brittle crazie glasse" (line 2), this poem could be read both as embracing the symbolic significance of the stained glass windows that were a controversial feature of English churches and as privileging the preacher as "the true 'stained glass' of the church."[61] The poem has puritan affinities in emphasizing the power of the minister preaching the sermon rather than the priest performing the sacraments. Yet Herbert's insistence that "doctrine and life" must "combine" (lines 11–12), that "speech" (line 13) must join a holy life "within" (line 7), does not so much endorse the puritan tradition of preaching as express the ceremonialist belief that outward and inward must be in harmony, that the externals of ceremonial worship – and of beautiful church windows – are worthy because they express an internal, spiritual holiness and devotion.[62]

"Lent" and "Aaron" concern ceremonial behavior rather than architecture. "Lent" argues for the importance of observing the church-appointed ceremony. "Aaron" enacts the ceremonial dressing of the priest, thus confirming the propriety of priestly vestments, which Ames and other puritans vigorously rejected as seductive garments of the Whore of Babylon. "Lent" begins supporting the authority of the church and advises dissenters simply to conform to the church when "doctrines disagree":

> WElcome deare feast of Lent: who loves not thee,
> He loves not Temperance, or Authoritie,
>   But is compos'd of passion.
> The Scriptures bid us *fast*; the Church sayes, *now*:
> Give to thy Mother, what thou wouldst allow
>   To ev'ry Corporation.   (lines 1–6)

"Aaron" describes the "holy garments" of the Jewish high priest (Exodus 28:28–43; 39:1–31), which were believed by defenders of ceremony to authorize the clergy to wear the surplice.

> HOlinesse on the head,
> Light and perfections on the breast,
> Harmonious bells below, raising the dead
>   To leade them unto life and rest:
>   Thus are true Aarons drest.   (lines 1–5)

Herbert's use of "priest" (line 10) rather than "minister" reveals his episcopal bent, as does the fact that "The Priesthood" precedes "Aaron."

Yet both "Aaron" and "Lent" have been read as strongly anti-ceremonial because their endings emphasize a spiritual understanding of these ceremonies. "Lent" concludes with a prayer that we may "starv[e] sinne" and charitably feed the "poore" (lines 44, 47).

The poem departs from a strict, literal sense of bodily fasting to describe an attitude of the spirit. "Aaron" contrasts the perfection of the priestly garments with the imperfection and unworthiness of the "Poore priest" (line 10) conscious of his sinfulness, and moves from the physical aspects of Aaron's priestly clothing to the spiritual qualities the priest must possess – holiness and purity, light and harmony "in" his "breast" (line 22). In progressing from the physical ornaments worn by Jewish priests to the inner qualities of the Christian priest "drest" by Christ (line 20), the poem echoes the puritan argument that the "garments and ornaments of Aarons high Priest" were "types" of the "true ornaments" of humility and holiness, types which having been fulfilled by Christ are now abrogated.[63] "Aaron" was one of thirty-two poems included in *Select Hymns Taken Out of Mr. Herbert's Temple,* used by dissenters in their worship. No longer preceded by the poem "Priesthood" that exalted the "BLest Order" of the clergy (line 1), "Aaron" in this new context becomes a celebration of the priesthood of all believers.

The spiritual or internal turn in these poems has recently led some critics to claim that "Aaron" "could have been written by an antivestiarian" and that "Lent" undermines the church's authority, replacing the literal, bodily fast with a "spiritual" feast.[64] But where these readings presume a *necessary* contrast between ceremony and spirituality, Herbert's poems merely allow this as a possible but hardly inevitable position. Both poems assume an ideal harmony between the outer, corporeal forms and the spiritual essence of worship – that is the point of their dismissal of merely external forms. "Lent" never rejects the ceremonial observance of fasting, but rather, like Isaiah 58:3–7 to which it alludes, insists that a true fast requires *both* the physical and the spiritual.

> Yet Lord instruct us to improve our fast
> By starving sinne and taking such repast
> > As may our faults controll:
> That ev'ry man may revell at his doore,
> Not in his parlour; banquetting the poore,
> > And among those his soul.　　　(lines 43–8)

This movement from the church-mandated fast to personal, spiritual regeneration could appeal to puritans who contrasted supposedly carnal Jewish or Roman Catholic practices with spiritual Christian ones, but it entirely accords with Isaiah, who criticizes the wicked for performing a fast of atonement while continuing the wickedness of their lives, Isaiah's point being not that fasting should be abandoned but that a fast is worthless unless accompanied by a reformation of the heart that issues in generous acts.[65]

In rejecting excessive attention to elaborate clothing or mortification of the flesh, "Aaron" and "Lent" assume, like Morton, Andrewes, and even Laud, that religious ceremonies properly represent internal, spiritual devotion, though Herbert has a far keener sense of the potential for ceremonial devotion to degenerate into idolatry. To say that Herbert in "The Church-floore" or "The Windows," or "Lent" or "Aaron" is concerned *only* with the spiritual and inward aspect of religious worship is to accept a puritan perspective that sees the outward and inward, material and spiritual, as necessarily divided and opposed. It is also to misinterpret ceremonialist ideology by seeing it as merely concerned with external forms of religion, whereas the defense of ceremony was based on a conviction that material and spiritual aspects of worship, like the body and soul, are interconnected and interdependent. Similarly, to see Herbert's poems as radically privileging individual, spiritual devotion is to see the personal and institutional, the individual and communal, like the spiritual and physical, as distinctly opposed, whereas Herbert often assumes their connection. Such an essentially puritan perspective simplifies Herbert's poems at least as much as "Catholic" readings that would deny his concern with a distinctly Protestant interiority or iconoclasm, and both minimize the problems *The Temple* confronts, as Herbert presents his devotion, variously, as integrated into the communal worship of the church and as a private, even solitary encounter with God.

THE MEANING OF THE "TEMPLE"

To some extent, how one interprets individual poems depends on how one understands the "temple" that is the controlling metaphor of the volume. Biblically, the word is richly resonant: in the Hebrew Bible, it primarily designates the Solomonic temple, the principal place of worship for the Jews; in the New Testament, Christ and the individual believer or the heart constitute the temple where God dwells and is worshiped.[66] Defenders of ceremony emphasized the continuity between the Jewish temple, with its priestly service, and the ecclesiastical order and worship of the English church. Puritan critics of the ceremonies, however, drew a sharp line between the supposedly "carnal" Jewish worship, with its material altars and sacrifices, and the spiritual Christian worship in the temple of the heart. Ames attacked the "delusion" that "we are heard, *not because of the prayer that is made, but because of the place in which it is made.*" Bastwick contrasted the physical church – idolatrous buildings of human "invention," founded on the instructions in the Mosaic law – with the individual, regenerate Christians, made anew by God, who are "the true temples and Churches of God."[67] The controversy over England's ceremonial worship thus, in part, turned on conflicting attitudes towards the Jewish origins of Christianity. These conflicting attitudes towards the Jewish past intensified dissonances in the New Testament – Jesus proclaiming that he came, not to destroy, but to fulfil the Law (Matthew 5:17); Paul insisting that the Gospel superseded the Law (abrogated with the Crucifixion), and identifying Jewish ceremonial Law with the "flesh" that must be abandoned if Christians are to live in Christ according to the "spirit" (Romans 3–8). Where ceremonialism emphasized continuity with the Hebrew Bible and the Judaic past, puritan ideology emphasized the Pauline notion of supersession.

Herbert's *Temple* is poised between a deep sense of connection with the Jewish temple, with its ceremonial worship, and an equally firm sense of irrevocable separation – between a desire to create, like the artists of the Jewish sanctuary or temple, beautiful, useful things in God's service and a belief that in the new dispensation there is no place for art in Christ's service. Insofar as the craft of poetry is for Herbert identified with the divinely ordained yet suspiciously material Jewish sanctuary and temple worship (and not simply with Roman Catholic art), his ambivalence about creating poetry is intertwined with a deep ambivalence about the relation of the Judaic past to his present Christian identity. "The Altar" and "Aaron" insist on the Jewish connection not only in their titles but also in recalling the woodcuts in the Geneva Bible depicting the incense altar of the temple and the garments of the high priest described in Exodus 28.[68] Both poems, however, also define an opposition between Christian and Jewish, spiritual and material, thus emphasizing the Christian distance from the Jews – much like "Sion" and Herbert's poem "The Jews," which describes that "Poore nation" as like a dead or dying plant, whose sap has dried up, though Herbert looks to its regeneration at the final conversion of the Jews. The ambivalence about the Judaic is part of the equivocal meaning of the "temple" which speaks to divisions within the English church about what constitutes true Christianity and, hence, Christian worship.

If Herbert's temple is "really" the individual, or the spirit or the heart, then his poems renounce continuity with the Jewish and Catholic past and focus on the ultimately separate Protestant believer and are "about" interior, spiritual worship. In this case, Herbert's references to external features of the church or its worship actually spiritualize them, substituting the inward and spiritual for the outward.[69] But if Herbert's temple also signifies the physical, material church, then his volume of poetry *connects* individual devotion to the institution of the church, places it within the framework of corporate, communal, ongoing ceremonial worship rather than in opposition to it.[70] With its repeated references to physical structures and corporeal forms of devotion *and* its description of the heart as God's temple and the spirit as the essence of worship, *The Temple* allows readers to understand Herbert *either* as assuming the connection between physical and spiritual, past and present, outer and inner temples – thus reaffirming the ceremonial worship of the Church of England – *or* as presuming a contrast between these temples – thus representing a distinctly anti-ceremonial Protestantism. His poetry could speak both to those who deeply valued the historical continuity with the past that ritual provided and to those whose puritan sense of Christianity demanded a sharp break from a Jewish and Catholic past identified with bodily, material worship.

"Prayer (I)," for example, might be thought to stress the interiority of worship in valuing the spiritual motions of the heart and soul focused on God – that is, as Herbert's temple is the individual believer. It might even allow for the extempore prayer puritans favored. This was certainly the interpretation of the compiler of *Select Hymns Taken Out of Mr. Herbert's Temple*, which included "Prayer (I)" among the poems set into common meter for use in the "Devotion of Private Christians."[71] In the context of this non-conformist hymnal, Herbert's "Prayer" celebrates the individual's ability to communicate with God without any ritual or institutional intervention.

However, as Herbert's poem defines the function of "Prayer" within the "Church" – and as "the temple" refers also to the actual, material English church – it praises the holiness of the "set forms" of worship to which puritans objected. The distinctively ceremonial significance of "Prayer (I)" was grasped by Harvey, whose poem "Church Festivals" – a series of metaphorical appositives in close imitation of "Prayer (I)" – celebrated the church holidays banned by puritans.[72] In Herbert's poem, filled with eucharistic images, the prayers praised as the "churches banquet" (line 1) are the liturgical prayers of the Church of England. In the 1620s and 30s, Laudians gave public prayer special importance, praising it as a daily "sacrifice" uniting Christians. This emphasis on the communal "read" prayers of the church was intended to counter the supposedly divisive effects of puritanism.[73] In the context of the newly charged significance of common prayer and its close link with ceremonial worship, Herbert's poem on the redemptive effects of prayer celebrates public, liturgical worship. It places prayer (rather than the sermon) at the center of divine worship.[74] Nevertheless, Herbert stops short of contentiously expressing an ideological position, making it possible for later dissenters to embrace this poem as consonant with puritan spirituality.

Even the final poem of "The Church" could be appreciated by ceremonialist and puritan alike. With its sense of eucharistic experience as symbolizing the soul's final communion with God in heaven, "Love (III)" is the culmination of *The Temple*'s attention to ritual. Yet the plainness and simplicity of the poem, the focus on an unmediated, personal experience of grace could appeal to puritans. The final line (18), "So I did sit and eat," with its allusion to Luke 22:27, assumes the posture puritans preferred at Communion, avoiding the gesture of kneeling that was a sharp point of contention.[75] But, as the poem describes the ultimate communion in heaven, Herbert may imply that only in heaven (not on earth, in the church) is the egalitarian posture of sitting appropriate. Lest we think he has abandoned the ceremonialism of the church, this final lyric of "The Church" is followed by his poetic arrangement of the words (translating the Roman Catholic *Gloria in Excelsis*) that concluded the rite of Holy Communion in the Book of Common Prayer service:

> *"Glorie be to God on high*
> *And on earth peace*
> *Good will towards men."*[76]

Herbert thus *allows* readers of different ideological bents to find his poetry expressive of their view of worship.[77] It is not that all readings are inevitably subjective or equally valid, or that his poetry is so "generally" religious that it transcends religious differences. Rather, it is because Herbert's poetry so fully inscribes the ideological dissonances of the early seventeenth-century Church of England that it became accessible to a wide range of readers. In his desire for harmony in a church increasingly "rent" with schism, his poetry focuses on the *experience* of devotional worship as something that can unite people, rather than on divisive topics of controversy.[78] Notably absent from Herbert is the distinction between the elect and reprobate, the puritan preoccupation with the exclusive community of the godly.[79] Rather than worrying about who is fit for Communion, Herbert "invite[s] all" to participate ("The Invitation"). Within his church is a place for both the corporate or communal and the personal or individual. In its devotion to the established liturgical order yet inclusion of what might be called "puritan" perspectives, *The Temple* enacts Herbert's hope for a moderately ceremonial church, conducive to communal worship, that would find a place for the conscience of an individual, upset by the increased ceremonialism of the church, to cultivate interior spirituality while conforming.[80]

I would suggest that it is the very accessibility of *The Temple* and its ambiguous ceremonial "position" that have allowed readers on both sides of the puritan/ceremonialist divide – both in the seventeenth century and now – to appropriate Herbert's work. Though a few poems come down clearly on one side or the other of the religious conflicts, *The Temple* is more mixed and ambiguous in its relation to these conflicts than these single poems suggest. Both "Anglo-Catholic" and "reformed" readings distort Herbert's *Temple* in erasing entire poems or elements of poems that do not fit the presumed model of devotion, in the process constructing different canons. We are closest to the spirit of his poetry when we recognize its contradictory impulses. Its apparent serenity is achieved in the face of an ongoing struggle (personal as well as cultural) between formalist and iconoclastic, communal and private impulses that would produce violent conflicts over worship in the years after Herbert's death.

CHAPTER 4

Robert Herrick: religious experience in the "Temple" of Hesperides

Herrick's modern readers have suspected that he was not deeply religious, despite the fact that he was a priest. His playfully erotic poetry and carpe diem poems encourage these suspicions. As if to dispel them, Herrick appended to *Hesperides* an epigram suggesting that the occasional licentiousness of his poetry contrasted with the propriety of his life: "To his Book's end this last line he'd have plac't, / *Jocond his Muse was; but his Life was chast*" (H-1130).[1] Though this epitaph seems to suggest a sharp division between Herrick's poetry and his life, between imagination and actual experience, there is a close relationship between his poetry and his life as a priest, for *Hesperides* is deeply concerned with issues that were the subject of intense religious controversy in mid-seventeenth-century England. A surprisingly large number of poems are involved with these controversies, and respond to them with varying degrees of explicitness and intensity.

Much valuable scholarship has placed Herrick historically but there remains uncertainty about where he stands in the conflicts of his time. The politics of his poetry, his royalism, and his connections with the ceremonialism of the Laudian church have been emphasized by Leah Marcus, Claude Summers, Thomas Corns, and others.[2] But recently, there has been resistance to "political" readings of his poetry, even a tendency to question Herrick's commitment to Stuart royalism and the Laudian church.[3] Most telling is Marcus's effort to distance herself from her argument in *The Politics of Mirth* that "Herrick was performing [in *Hesperides*] a deliberate act of cultural revival not unlike the political program of the *Book of Sports* itself" promoted by Charles and Laud. Marcus not only insists that in "matters of political and ecclesiastical allegiance, Herrick now appears far from univocal," but she claims that "Herrick criticism today appears most vital . . . in its dismantling and decentering of

79

the previous Laudian line."[4] Such a comment praising the "dismantling" of a supposed "Laudian" line of Herrick criticism betrays "puritan" sympathies, echoing the old puritan/Anglican battles of the seventeenth century as it values iconoclastic criticism for deconstructing Herrick. Associating recent attempts to destabilize his poetry with the postmodern rejection of an earlier twentieth-century idolatrous "reverence" of seventeenth-century lyric poetry, Marcus makes postmodernism – with its removal of "art from its pedestal" (p. 176) – the admired heir of the puritan distrust of "art." Valuable as recent work has been in reminding us of the complexity and variety of Herrick's poetry, there is at work a discomfort with his high-church and monarchist conservatism, a distrust of the "art" of "high culture," and an effort to make him acceptable to those whose sympathies are more with subversion and who find uncongenial Herrick's association with "dominant" and "repressive" ideologies. Such an effort distorts Herrick and implies that only the Laudian ideology was repressive – that the puritan one was liberating. Puritan ideology was also in many ways repressive, and in 1648 it was the puritan rather than the Laudian ideology that was dominant in England. Moreover, we will understand the issues at stake in the conflicts over religion, and the relation of Herrick's poetry to ceremonialist and Laudian ideology, only if we move beyond seeing these religious conflicts exclusively in terms of politics. Disagreements were not simply over who would control the church, or over the power of the clergy, but involved conflicting, culturally powerful notions about the nature of human identity and experience, about community, and about the relevance of the past.

Published in 1648, soon after Herrick was ejected from his parish as part of Parliament's program for removing clergy too closely associated with the Laudian church, *Hesperides* demands to be read within the context of the conflict over worship that was part of the Revolution. Herrick's artistic imagination was stirred by contemporary religious controversies as they challenged basic cultural values, including the legitimacy of art. George Herbert had drawn back from the escalating ideological conflicts within the English church, but those conflicts nevertheless shaped *The Temple*'s anxieties about art. Herrick's understanding and practice of his art was no less profoundly affected. Language that had become charged with specifically religious polemical meaning is part of the very texture of his poetry. Recovering the meaning of that language not only shows how fully Herrick's celebration of ceremonial experience is connected with the ideology and practices of the Laudian church; it also allows us to hear the religious resonance of his seemingly "secular" verse.

Laud had been dead for three years when *Hesperides* appeared, and the battle over worship seemed largely won by puritan forces. On June 12, 1643, Parliament had passed a bill abolishing episcopacy. On January 4, 1645, the use of the Book of Common Prayer was banned "in any Church, Chappel, or place of public Worship."

> The Lords and Commons assembled in Parliament . . . resolving, according to their Covenant, to reform Religion according to the Word of God, and the Example of the best Reformed Churches . . . do judge it necessary that the said Book of Common Prayer be Abolished . . . [and that the many statutes for uniformity of prayer, service, and administration of sacraments from Edward VI on] be and stand from henceforth repealed, void and of none effect.[5]

Seven months later, Parliament extended the ban to private worship, enumerating punishments for violating the ordinance: £5 for the first offence, £10 for the second, and a year in prison for the third. All prayer books remaining in parish churches and chapels were to be carried to committees of respective counties where they were to be disposed of "as the Parliament shall direct."[6]

The issue of ceremonial worship was far from dead in 1648. Though Parliament had ordered the use of the *Directory for Public Worship*, it had yet to replace the governance and worship of the English church with a new model. Some people continued to use the Prayer Book,[7] but the parliamentary orders and the ejection of clergy created a repressive, persecutory atmosphere for those committed to the now illegal forms of worship of the Church of England. Herrick's volume preserves ceremonial worship at a time when it had been outlawed by Parliament. While the Laudian thrust of *Noble Numbers* has received attention, we need a better understanding of how the "secular" *Hesperides* engages the contested issues of religious worship.[8] With its allusive, charged language, *Hesperides* constitutes an elegant expression – at once defiant and elegaic – of a generally ceremonialist, and probably specifically Laudian, mentality. Herrick's deceptively simple poems offer an imaginative, sophisticated, and eloquent assessment of what was at stake.

Herrick was anxious about how he would be read. The opening

poems of *Hesperides* defend the holiness of his verse, but worry about a hostile reception. He curses those who hate the book (H-6) or use it to "wipe . . . The place, where swelling *Piles* do breed" (H-5, lines 1–2). The reader who thus defiles Herrick's poetry will be punished much as a person who desecrates a holy place or thing: "May every Ill, that bites, or smarts, / Perplexe him in his hinder-parts" (H-5, lines 3–4). In "*When he would have his verses read*" (H-8), Herrick speaks of his verse as "holy incantation" (line 2), as if it were both magically powerful and sacred. If "rigid *Cato*" (line 10) reads Herrick in the right spirit, even he will lose his inflexibility. His reference to the Roman censor in a poem addressed to his contemporaries implies that in seventeenth-century England, too, there are rigid, intolerant people. His readers are asked to rethink what is "holy." Herrick curses only those who cannot be converted – those who, having read the whole volume, persist in detesting it:

> IF thou dislik'st the Piece thou light'st on first;
> Thinke that of All, that I have writ, the worst:
> But if thou read'st my Booke unto the end,
> And still do'st this, and that verse, reprehend:
> O Perverse man! If All disgustfull be,
> The Extreame Scabbe take thee, and thine, for me.   (H-6)

The hostile readers Herrick curses, I would argue, are "puritanical" in several senses. The anti-puritanism of his volume is multifaceted, subtly coded, and more thoroughly intertwined with its ceremonialism than has been recognized.[9] Herrick opposes puritanism not only in satirical epigrams mocking "zelots" and in his celebration of pleasure but also in his "paganism" and his recurrent concern with various "mixtures" and "minglings." These notable characteristics of his poetry are aspects of a self-conscious effort to reassert a particular cultural and religious vision of life and experience at a time when he felt it threatened with extinction. Herrick's effort parallels the Laudian attempt to reinvigorate a communal, ceremonial worship in the face of puritan opposition. But he is not just reactionary in his effort at preservation, for at its most engaging his poetry enlarges our sense of what is religious, expanding the boundaries of religion and of the human community far beyond what the Laudians envisioned.

PAGANISM, ROME, AND THE "RELIGION" OF *HESPERIDES*

Although we think of Herrick as a secular poet, he repeatedly draws analogies between his poetry and religion. He calls his book a *"Sacred Grove"* (H-265, line 3). But *Hesperides* is not only a garden. It is also a *"Temple"* (H-496, line 1; 445) in which Herrick enacts a "Poetick Liturgie" (H-510, line 4), performing "ceremonies" and "rites" and urging others to perform them. In styling himself a "priest" of poetry, he follows Ben Jonson.[10] But Herrick's position as an ordained priest gives the title added resonance and invites comparison with Herbert, another priest who constructed a poetic temple. Herrick makes this analogy between poetry and religion central to his volume, and appropriates to his poetry exactly the words – *ceremonies, rites, liturgy* – that figured prominently in the controversy over ceremonial worship.

The "religion" of *Hesperides* is decidedly mixed. With its classical name and its frontispiece depicting the hill of Parnassus, the spring of Helicon, Pegasus, and the poet about to be crowned with wreaths, the volume flaunts its classical, "pagan" appearance. The emphasis on the classical, the pagan, is everywhere evident in *Hesperides*, and has led some readers to think he is not a very Christian poet. But in *Hesperides* the pagan shares space with the Christian. The volume includes, within the physical compass of the bound book, the decidedly Christian, sacred *Noble Numbers*. Within the "secular" part of *Hesperides*, there are hymns and vows to pagan gods linked to the natural world and sensual pleasures, but also poems on *"Mattens, or morning Prayer"* and *"Evensong"* (H-320, 321), whose titles refer to the Church of England's liturgy. Indeed, the Christian and pagan are often intermingled, as in the poem near the end of *Hesperides*, where Herrick anticipates receiving the "incorruptible" crown promised in the New Testament (1 Corinthians 9:25) to those faithful to Christ:

> AFter thy labour take thine ease,
> Here with the sweet *Pierides*.
> But if so be that men will not
> Give thee the Laurell Crowne for lot;
> Be yet assur'd, thou shalt have one
> Not subject to corruption.
>
> ("*The mount of the Muses*," H-1123)

His Christian God will not punish him for including the seemingly "pagan" and "secular" within his "temple" of poetry.

Herrick announces his intimacy with the ancient pagan world and mingles the pagan with the Christian at a time when puritans in England were attacking all things that smacked of paganism. Hostility to the pagan runs through earlier writers like William Perkins, who sought to define and defend Protestant Christianity from various forms of contaminating idolatry, but it also characterizes the writings of puritans in the mid-seventeenth century who attacked the increasingly ceremonial worship of the Church of England. Puritan hostility to the pagan found particularly vivid expression in Prynne, who aroused the anger of Laud and the king with his inflammatory pamphlets. Underlying Prynne's more than one-thousand-page attack in *Histrio-Mastix* (1633) on stage plays, court entertainments, and other "lewd" or "prophane" recreations or practices is his violent dislike of all "pagan" customs, and his sense that English culture is riddled with them. In his exhaustive catalogue, Prynne points out that many customs and practices current in seventeenth-century England are of pagan origin. For Prynne and other puritans, such "pagan" customs are "carnal," concerned with the body and its pleasures, and thus not fitting for godly Christians, who must be of the spirit not the "flesh."[11]

Herrick celebrates the "pagan" practices Prynne attacks. *Hesperides*, and to a lesser extent *Noble Numbers*, offer a virtual catalogue of Prynne's forbidden delights. Where Prynne finds it "unlawfull" for Christians "*to decke up their Houses with Laurell, Yvie, and greene boughes,* (as we use to doe in the Christmas season)," Herrick encourages the tradition in poems like "*Ceremonies for Candlemasse Eve*" (H-892) and "*Corinna's going a Maying*" (H-178). Like other puritans, Prynne rejected "Grand Christmasses" as pagan celebrations, but Herrick records folk traditions connected with Christmas (H-319, 784–7, 892–4, 980). If Christmas celebrations seemed suspiciously pagan to puritans – Parliament in the 1640s outlawed its celebration – so did the traditional celebration of New Year's Day, with its custom of exchanging gifts. Prynne condemned these observances as "reliques" of the pagans who consecrated the day to "*Janus their Devill-God*" and exchanged gifts with friends. Herrick, however, not only sends poems as "*New-yeares gift*[s]" to a friend and to Charles I (H-319, N-97–8), but, reminding readers that January first is also the festival of Christ's circumcision (N-97–8), exchanges a New Year's gift with Christ (N-125). Prynne insisted that it is sinful for Christians to wear a "Laurell Crowne or flowrie Garland" "*because those Crownes, and*

Garlands, were first invented by the Devill, and worne by his Minions, to his honour."[12] But garlands and laurel crowns abound in *Hesperides* (H-111, 197, 224, 319, 1062).

Prynne's attack on these customs is based on the belief that there is a clear distinction between the "Christian" and "pagan," which is irredeemably associated with the carnal realm of the body. Christians are obligated to keep absolute separations between them. Prynne quotes 2 Corinthians 6:14–16, a foundational passage for many puritans: "*what fellowship hath Righteousnesse, with Unrighteousnesse? What communion hath Light with Darkenese? What concorde hath Christ with Belial? what part hath hee that Beleeveth with an Infidell? or what agreement hath the Temple of God with Idoles?*"[13] Throughout Prynne, as in this biblical passage, runs a rhetoric of division and opposition, an insistence on a purity that is understood as necessitating the exclusion of polluting, contaminating elements.

How far this is from Herrick's preoccupation with minglings, his eclecticism, and what often seems a blatant "paganism." Not only does *Hesperides* bring together rituals from various pagan, folk, and Christian practices, but individual poems themselves effect such a mixture. "Corinna's *going a Maying*" (H-178) is the most obvious, famous example. Whereas puritans rejected May Day rites as pagan and therefore profane, in Herrick's poem the joyous celebration of May becomes a sacred act of "Devotion" (line 32). Corinna is invited to participate in a May ritual that embraces all of nature, which is seen as instinctively alive with devotional impulses. The poem assimilates the rituals and language of folk and pagan traditions, classical mythology, the Hebrew Bible, and Christianity. In the world of "Corinna's *going a Maying*," "Mattens," beads, and Christian priests keep company with Titan and Aurora; the carpe diem motif blends with the urgings of the lover in the Song of Songs, "Rise up, my love, my fair one, and come away. For, lo, the winter is past" (2:10–11). The point and effect of "Corinna's *going a Maying*," and *Hesperides* more generally, are that we cannot neatly divide the sacred from the secular, the Christian from the pagan or Jewish.

Herrick not only mingles the Christian and pagan; he highlights the pagan aspect of his poetry in ways that seem calculated to arouse delight in some readers but outrage in others. Prynne, anticipating the first books of Milton's *Paradise Lost* where the fallen angels are identified with the pagan deities, insists that the deities of classical mythology are mere "Devill-gods, or Goddesses, which the Idolatrous

Pagans did adore" (*Histrio-Mastix*, p. 28). According to Prynne, "the Scriptures doe expressely condemne all Imprecations, all Adjurations, all Admirations by, all Invocations of, all Heathen Gods . . . How then can it bee lawfull, to Invocate, or Implore the aide, or helpe of *Jove*, of *Juno*, *Apollo*, *Minerva*, *Neptune*, *Bacchus*, or such like Heathen Idoles"? (p. 81). These are exactly the gods that Herrick invokes, asking them for various kinds of aid and protection.

> MIghty *Neptune*, may it please
> Thee, the *Rector* of the Seas,
> That my Barque may safely runne
> Through thy watrie-region;
> ("*Another* [short poem] *to* Neptune," H-325, lines 1–4)

Rather than keeping the ancient past and its classical gods in their distant place, Herrick insists on their connections with the present, as when he asks Æsculapius to help Pru Baldwin recover from sickness (H-302). Priding himself on knowing the appropriate offering for each classical god,[14] he even promises to offer a "gallant Cock" to Æsculapius (H-302, line 5), swans to Apollo (H-303), an owl to Minerva (H-530), "*Tunnie-fish*" to Neptune (H-325, line 5).

To some extent, Herrick's "paganism" is conventional. Deeply indebted to classical lyric poetry, he shares Jonson's sense of literary tradition, but Herrick's classicism is more polemically charged, as he insists on the place of the pagan in his "temple" of poetry. Herrick's eclectic mixture of traditions, rituals, and ceremonies does not simply (as is often assumed) reflect the unexceptional eclecticism of English culture; that eclecticism had become hotly contested. His self-conscious preoccupation with mixtures embodies a distinctively ceremonialist sense of the continuity and community of worship and of human experience.

Pagan customs not only persisted in England but had invaded the church. The English church seemed contaminated with practices of the Church of Rome, which "hotter" Protestants associated with ancient Rome as the locus of carnal and heathen idolatry.[15] The author of *The Originall of Popish Idolatrie* traced the Roman Catholic Mass to "the auncient Ethnicke Religion, Instituted by *Numa*, more then seaven hundred yeares before the Incarnation of Jesus Christ," even deriving the etymology of the word "Mass" from "the ancient Romane Idolaters" who at the end of their sacrifices pronounced the words "I licet Missa est." Various customs of the Roman Catholic church such as the wearing of white vestments, the procession of the priest, and the use of tapers, incense, and holy water were believed to be taken from Numa's religion.[16] Thomas Jackson simply stated a commonplace view when he declared "the Identitie or aequivalencie of superstition in Rome-Heathen and Rome-Christian."[17]

The identification of contemporary Rome with ancient heathen Rome, as well as the sense that true Christians must be forever at war with all forms of idolatry, encouraged intense hatred of Roman Catholicism. Perkins wrote anti-Catholic diatribes in the hope of kindling in Englishmen "a further detestation and loathing of the Romish religion."[18] In sermons on the anniversary of the Gunpowder Plot, Richard Sibbes suggested that the best way to thank God for our "deliverances" is to "stirre up our selves to a greater hatred" of Rome. It is impossible, Prynne insisted, to have cordial relations with "our Romish Adversaries": the *"beleeving world"* of *"Saints and perfect men"* must always oppose the *"unbeleeving world"* of *"wicked men,"* "polluted," "damned," and unredeemed.[19]

It is within this highly charged context of puritan hostility to Rome and all things "Romish" that Herrick's fascination with Roman customs and ceremonial practices, and his identification with Rome, needs to be read. The potentially inflammatory power of his "classical" poetry becomes clearer when we recognize that terms like "Rome" and "Roman" were for puritans synonyms for carnal idolatry and false worship, and were associated with contemporary, Catholic Rome, seen as the counterpart of pagan Rome.

Herrick proudly insists on his "Roman" identity in the poem *"Upon himself"* (H-456) which, echoing one of Jonson's odes, begins, "COme, leave this loathed Country-life, and then / Grow up to be a Roman *Citizen"* (lines 1–2). In *"His returne to London"* (H-713) he claims, "I am a free-born *Roman*; suffer then, / That I amongst you live a Citizen" (lines 11–12). Herrick's identification of England with Rome seems to confirm the deepest puritan fears. But whereas in the puritan mentality Rome was the embodiment of idolatry and false religion, Herrick insists that London's intimate, longstanding ties with Rome make her a "blest place" (line 4), full of gifts for the spirit. Indeed, because of these ties, London is not narrowly provincial but "fram'd to please / All *Nations, Customes, Kindreds, Languages!"* (lines 9–10). Herrick is doing more than recalling his participation as a "son of Ben" in a classical tradition of poetry. Insisting on his Roman connection midway in the volume he called a "temple", probably with a glance at Herbert, this impassioned poem acquires polemical resonance when one considers that a main dispute during Herrick's day – and one over which blood was shed – was about the proper relationship between England and Rome.

Believing that the English church was contaminated with "Roman" practices, puritans wanted to "purify" what they saw as the mixed, and therefore polluted worship in the English church. As Prynne insisted: "God, and the Devil, Christ, and Belial, are contrary, are inconsistent: therefore the service, and ceremonies of the one, are altogether incompatible with the other." Burton declared that Christians must "utterly renounce all *communion*" and "*seperate* themselves" from all "Heathenisme," even if that meant leaving the Church of England.[20] The Long Parliament in the 1640s was encouraged by puritan preachers to restore the "purity" of the Gospel by casting out what Stephen Marshall called the "rubbish and filth" defiling "Gods house."[21] It is precisely this obsession with purity that led their opponents to label them "puritans,"[22] and that Herrick rejects in his complex interminglings of Christian and classical, his incorporation of "pagan" rites into the temple and liturgy of *Hesperides*. With its "mixed" religion, *Hesperides* is a poetic counterpart of the Laudian church.

HESPERIDES AND THE LAUDIAN CHURCH

Changes in worship during the reign of Charles struck more rigorous, anti-Catholic Protestants as evidence that Laud and his prelates were undoing the Reformation and moving the Church of England dangerously close to Rome. On June 11, 1628, a remonstrance delivered by the House of Commons to King Charles noted a "generall feare" that there was "some secret working and combination to introduce [Popery] into this Kingdome."[23] Through the 1630s and early 40s, puritan clergy like Burton and Marshall and lay people like Prynne and Milton exposed what they believed were the dangerous similarities between England, the Church of Rome, and ancient Rome. Burton's sermons *For God, and the King* (1636) warned that Laud and his clerical cohorts were "setting up Popery againe," and he encouraged "Gods children" to "hinder and stop the beginning and creeping in of Idolatry and Superstition." By 1640, Burton was convinced that the English and Roman churches had become *"one and the same."*[24] In Laud's 1644 trial for treason in subverting the Protestant religion, his supposedly seditious "Popish" practices in worship were viewed as part of *"a secret plotted Conspiracy"* to bring England back to Rome.[25]

There are fascinating parallels between *Hesperides* and the popish, heathen "innovations" in the English church with which Laud was charged – too many to be coincidental. Prynne's account of the trial described in detail Laud's supposed *"endeavours to set up and introduce all kind of Popish superstitious Idolatrous ornaments, furniture, ceremonies in our church formerly cast out of it upon the reformation."*[26] Laud did not act alone, but as Archbishop of Canterbury he bore major responsibility. In cathedrals, universities, parishes, and private chapels, Laud, it was charged, brought in the "superstitious *Rites and Ceremonies*" of Rome (*Canterburies Doome*, p. 70). Is not this what Herrick is doing in his own way in *Hesperides*, importing the practices of both pagan and ecclesiastical Rome into a volume of poetry which is, he insists, both a *"Temple"* and a "Liturgie" (H-496, 510)? That he draws attention to these controversial matters is evident not only in the particularity with which many poems describe classical rituals but also in the fact that the words "rites" or "ceremonies" appear even in the titles of poems that do not actually include liturgical rites, such as *"The Funerall Rites of the Rose"* (H-686), *"Ceremonies for Candlemasse Eve"* and Candlemasse Day (H-892–4), and *"Ceremonies for Christmasse"* (H-784–7).

Puritans criticized Laudian bishops for their "curious formality, and punctuall observance of their holy rites,"[27] – a charge that Herrick lays himself open to when he instructs Julia in the exact order of the church "Rites" for purification after childbirth:

> PUt on thy *Holy Fillitings*, and so
> To th' Temple with the sober *Midwife* go.
> Attended thus (in a most solemn wise)
> By those who serve the Child-bed misteries.
> Burn first thine incense; next, when as thou see'st
> The candid Stole thrown ore the *Pious Priest*;
> With reverend Curtsies come, and to him bring
> Thy free (and not decurted) offering.
> All Rites well ended, with faire Auspice come
> (As to the breaking of a Bride-Cake) home:
> Where ceremonious *Hymen* shall for thee
> Provide a second *Epithalamie*.
>
> ("Julia's *Churching, or Purification*," H-898, lines 1–12)

The rites must be properly, fully performed – with no details omitted and in the correct sequence. Bishop John Cosin's Visitation Articles for evaluating clergy reflect a similar obsession with order, including some of the same details that appear in Herrick:

> Cap. XI. *Touching the Churching of Women.*
> Doth your Minister duly observe the order and forme prescribed in churching of women after childbirth? Is the same done publikely and reverently in the Church, the woman comming in that decent and grave attire which hath bin accustomed, and the Minister attending in his surplice, causing her to kneele neere the place where God's Table standeth, and to make her thanksgiving and her offring, as is prescribed?[28]

Such careful attention to ceremonial detail is evident in many of Herrick's poems:

> Dead when I am, first cast in salt, and bring
> Part of the creame from that *Religious Spring*;
> With which (*Perilla*) wash my hands and feet;
> That done, then wind me in that very sheet
> Which wrapt thy smooth limbs (when thou didst implore
> The Gods protection, but the night before)
>
> ("*To* Perilla," H-14, lines 7–12)

> Cut off thy haires; and let thy Teares be shed
> Over my Turfe, when I am buried.
> Then for *effusions*, let none wanting be,
> Or other Rites that doe belong to me;
>
> ("*His charge to* Julia *at his death*," H-627, lines 3–6)

Herrick's insistence throughout *Hesperides* on the importance of following prescribed ceremonies is more deeply serious than individual poems might suggest – indeed, it gains strength from the sheer number of poems concerned with proper ceremonial order. All these poems inscribe the Laudian position that it is necessary to observe ceremonies in worship, but they also express the psychological importance of ceremony in linking the personal and communal. Ceremony cements human bonds. Herrick's personal sense of the necessity of ceremonies is nowhere more apparent than when he laments that for "seven *Lusters*" (thirty-five years) he has been unable to perform the proper "*Rites*" for his dead father ("*To the reverend shade of his religious Father*," H-82, lines 1–2).

Aware that performance of ceremonies and rites could degenerate into a superficial observance of externals, he asks his reader:

3   Is it to fast an houre,
      Or rag'd to go,
      Or show
    A down-cast look, and sowre?

4   No; 'tis a Fast, to dole
      Thy sheaf of wheat,
      And meat,
    Unto the hungry Soule.

5   It is to fast from strife,
      From old debate
      And hate;
    To circumcise thy life.   *("To keep a true Lent," N-228)*

Like Herbert's poem of the same title, the point of these questions is to insist that ritual practices are only valuable where the spirit gives life to the literal observance.[29]

Many ceremonies like Lent that puritans objected to were associated with Roman Catholicism. Whereas Herbert firmly breaks with Catholicism in poems like "Sion," Herrick provocatively flirts with the religion of Rome. Throughout *Hesperides* are recurrent allusions either to Roman Catholicism or to practices in the English church, encouraged by Laud, that Puritans condemned as "Popish." "Beads" appear in "Corinna's *going a Maying*"; Herrick prays to free Lucia's soul from purgatory (H-814); he tells Perenna that Monks, Friars, and Nuns will sing dirges and trentals and perform a candlemass for them (H-976). Laud was accused of importing "Popish" things into the English church (though most indeed had existed previously) – the wearing of surplices and other clerical vestments; the use of incense, candles, and holy water; making the sign of the cross; kneeling at the Sacrament and bowing before the altar.[30] In Herrick's volume of poetry, tapers burn (H-604, 976), and holy water and incense abound (H-957, 974, 1069, 898). Julia is instructed to wear "the white Vestures" when she burns the "Mornings Incense" (H-539, lines 2, 4), and both Julia and Herrick don "pure Surplices" according to the "commands" of "Old Religion" (H-870, lines 14, 3). These ceremonial poems, typically combining the light and the solemn, inscribe the ceremonialist assumption that the physical can be used in the service of the spiritual – an assumption especially evident in Herrick's poem *"Mattens, or morning Prayer"* (H-320):

WHen with the Virgin morning thou do'st rise,
Crossing thy selfe; come thus to sacrifice:
First wash thy heart in innocence, then bring
Pure hands, pure habits, pure, pure every thing.
Next to the Altar humbly kneele, and thence,
Give up thy soule in clouds of frankinsence.
Thy golden Censors fil'd with odours sweet,
Shall make thy actions with their ends to meet.

The specific ritual sequence is given attention here, as is the importance of physical acts of reverence, including kneeling "to the Altar" – a Laudian practice puritans criticized as idolatrous worship. Herrick's instruction, "First wash thy heart in innocence, then bring / Pure hands," makes clear that outward acts of the body are the valuable representation of the inward or spiritual, not its substitute. Similarly, the offer of incense symbolizes and thus properly accompanies the sweet offer of the soul to God.

Herrick values ceremony because of its presumed ability to engage body and soul, and to reach the spirit through physical, external means. Whereas puritan ideology, with its spirit/flesh dualism, criticized the "carnality" of ceremony, the English defenders of ceremony insisted that ceremonies such as kneeling or bowing are outward "expressions of internall devotion," intimately connected to the spiritual.[31] The corporeal, outward aspects of worship can represent and even sustain the inward because, in the ceremonialist mentality, the physical and spiritual planes of existence, like the body and soul of the human being, are interconnected. Inward worship actually depends upon the external. As Morton put it, though he was no Laudian, if people "neglect the outward worship of God," "their inward zeale and devotion soone cooleth, and in the end vanisheth away." Laud, defending his program for the repair of ceremonial worship, echoed Morton's sentiments: "I found that with the Contempt of the Outward Worship of God, the Inward fell away apace, and Profaneness began boldly to shew it self."[32] Precisely this sense of the interdependence of bodily ceremonial worship and inward devotion, of ceremony as a means of integrating body and spirit, shapes Herrick's understanding of ceremony and his poetic representations of it.

If Herrick, like Laud, introduces ceremonies involving the body, he also fills his "*Temple*" with "*eternall Images*" and "*Statues*" (H-496, lines 1, 10, 7) – much as Laud did the English churches. Images were an important part of ceremonial worship. Burton was one of many who expressed outrage at the "setting up of Images" and statues in many churches and cathedrals, and at Laud's trial much was made of these images as well as his repairing the stained glass windows at Lambeth and other chapels. To Laud's puritan opponents, it was "against Gods law & commandment" for Christians to "make Images, and publickly to set them up in the Temples and Churches."[33]

When Herrick announces his role as a maker of images, his language evokes these contemporary controversies about the legitimacy of images and monuments in the church:

> TO this *white Temple* of my *Heroes*, here
> Beset with stately Figures (every where)
> Of such rare *Saint-ships*, who did here consume
> Their lives in sweets, and left in death perfume.
> Come thou *Brave man*!
> ("*To his Honoured Kinsman, Sir* Richard Stone," H-496, lines 1–5)

Encouraged by puritan ministers like Stephen Marshall who urged they follow Josiah's example of reformation, "breaking down all the *Images and relicks of Idolatry*," Parliament passed ordinances in 1643 and 1644 for destroying altars, monuments, and other relics of "Idolatry and Superstition." The second, in May 1644, closely speaks to the subject of Herrick's poem to Richard Stone, for it declared that "all Representations of any of the Persons of the Trinity, or of any Angel or Saint, in or about any Cathedral, Collegiate or Parish Church, or Chappel, or in any open place within this Kingdome, shall be taken away, defaced, and utterly demolished; And that no such shall hereafter be set up."[34] William Dowsing and others were commissioned to purge churches and cathedrals.[35] Churches were ransacked by parliamentary soldiers. Not only Dowsing's journal but outraged Royalist publications described the iconoclasm. *Antidotum Culmerianum* attacked the activities of the fanatic minister Richard Culmer, who destroyed painted glass in Canterbury Cathedral with his own hands and, by the account of an "eye-witnesse," urinated "in the open Church, and at noon-day," "converting" God's "house of prayer" to "an Augean stable."[36] *Mercurius Rusticus* noted that the soldiers would sometimes, as a final insult, "defile each part and corner both of Church and Chancell with their owne excrements."[37] These transgressive acts of desecration not only bear witness to the brutal residue of human nature; they mock the notion of consecrated space and things.

Such iconoclasm provides an essential context for understanding Herrick's poem to Stone and *Hesperides* more generally. At a time when churches, altars, and images were being destroyed, Herrick publishes *Hesperides*, in which he consecrates its holy space and objects, performs rites, and erects altars and images. In *"To his Honoured Kinsman, Sir* Richard Stone" (H-496), almost certainly written during the 1640s when puritan iconoclasm was at its height, Herrick claims that his "Statues" are "High" and "no lesse / Strong then the Heavens for everlastingnesse" (lines 7–9). He follows Jonson in celebrating the immortalizing power of poetry, but once again literary conventions take on political significance. Herrick's invocation of the commonplace of poetic immortality is heavily charged with anti-puritan meaning. His language insists on the very things puritans were attacking as he erects his *"eternall Images"* of virtue (H-496).

Laud's puritan opponents were upset by attempts to revive Roman Catholic practices of preserving the "Reliques of Saints" and, even worse, commemorating and praying to these saints.[38] And what is Herrick doing but insisting that his worthies should be reverenced as he preserves their relics in his poetry? Laud was sharply criticized for adding two new saints days. Herrick adds his own new saints, inscribing Stephen Soame in his "eternall Calender" of saints (H-545, line 10), and making Penelope Wheeler "a Saint . . . In Chiefe" (H-510, lines 3–4). He prays to his special patron saint, Ben Jonson.

[1.] WHen I a Verse shall make,
      Know I have praid thee,
      For old *Religions* sake,
      Saint *Ben* to aide me.

2.   Make the way smooth for me,
      When I, thy *Herrick*,
      Honouring thee, on my knee
      Offer my *Lyrick*.

3.   Candles Ile give to thee,
      And a new Altar;
      And thou Saint *Ben*, shalt be
      Writ in my *Psalter*.

("*His Prayer to* Ben. Johnson," H-604)

Herrick was no more a secret Roman Catholic than Laud (up to the moment of execution Laud insisted he was a true Protestant),[39] though there was much in his poetry to encourage the charge. In its witty adaptation of the Roman Catholic practice of praying to saints, this poem pays tribute to Herrick's poetic mentor, himself a convert to Roman Catholicism for part of his life. But the poem goes beyond compliment as Herrick prays to Jonson for "old *Religions* sake," a term which may refer not only to "the ancient form of *pietas*" (as Patrick observes in his notes to the poem) and to the religion of poetry to which Jonson, too, was dedicated, but also to the ancient Roman Catholic religion. I can think of no better gloss for Herrick's poem than William Perkins's comment that Roman Catholicism

makes the Saints in heaven idols. For it teacheth men to kneele downe to them, and to make prayer to them, beeing absent from us, as farre as heaven is from earth. And by praying to them, men doe acknowledge, that they have power to heare and help in all places, & at all times, and that they know the secret mindes and hearts of men.[40]

Herrick credits Jonson with the power to "heare and help" him; his "honouring thee, on my knee" insists on the physical demonstration of spiritual reverence that puritans abhorred; and he promises to give "Candles" and "a new Altar" to Ben.

ALTARS, SACRIFICES, AND THE CONTINUITY OF CEREMONIAL WORSHIP

Herrick's preoccupation with altars and sacrifices is tied to one of the most controversial features of ceremonial worship. Herbert's "The Altar" ambiguously pointed to this symbol of ceremonial worship, at once evoking the materiality of the altar and insisting on its interior, spiritual identity for the reformed Christian. Herrick's persistent attention to altars, however, is far from equivocal; it sharply challenges puritan sensibilities and beliefs.

Throughout *Hesperides* "altars" appear with striking frequency.[41] Some are associated with Cupid and the religion of erotic love – as in *"An Hymne to Cupid"* (H-874) where he promises that if he prospers in love he will "raise" "Altars" to Cupid "Unto the end of daies" (lines 14–15) – but many are associated with a kind of religious worship that conventions of love poetry cannot adequately explain. As in *"Mattens, or Morning Prayer"* (H-320), the altars are often the site of a religious, ritual performance of sacrifice. He tells Julia in *"The Perfume"* (H-251) that "the Altar's ready" for him to "offer" a sacrifice "for some small fault" (lines 2–3), and in "*The Sacrifice, by way of Discourse betwixt himselfe and* Julia" (H-870) explains the ritual order for making their "offering" (line 12) upon the "Altar" (line 6). Herrick's many altars, with their sacrifices, which are interspersed throughout *Hesperides* from poem H-63 to H-974, gain added significance when we remember the antagonism Laud aroused with his attention to the centrality of the altar in worship.

Laudian "innovations" in ceremonial worship gave special attention to the altar, privileging the priest's performance of Holy Communion over preaching the word.[42] As we have seen, by the early 1630s, when Herbert's *Temple* was published, the altar had become a powerful symbol for the conflict over ceremonial worship. But in the mid-1630s, the pamphlet wars over the altar broke out. At Laud's request, Heylyn published *A Coale from the Altar* (1636). Heylyn was answered by Williams's anonymous *The Holy Table, Name and Thing* (1637), which was answered in turn by Heylyn's *Antidotum Lincolniense* (1637) and John Pocklington's *Altare Christianum* (1637). Prynne, who could not stay out of the fray, responded with *A Quench-Coale* (1637). The argument over altars continued into the 1640s with Henry Parker's anti-Laudian *The Altar Dispute* and William Bray's *Sermon on the Blessed Sacrament of the Lords Supper* attacking Pocklington, both published in 1641. When Parliament tried to destroy all "Monuments of Superstition or Idolatry" in churches, altars were a main object of violence. On August 26, 1643, Parliament ordered that all altars in English churches "be utterly taken away and demolished."[43]

When Herbert's *Temple* was published in 1633, the poet may well have felt that his work could still speak to diverse positions within the church. But by the time Herrick published his "temple" of poetry, it was another matter entirely.[44]

A number of issues in the altar controversy have relevance for Herrick's poetry. Under Laud, the old Communion "Tables" were replaced by new stone "Altars." In contrast to the movable table placed in the midst of the congregation during Communion, the "*fixed*" altar of stone "that stirs not an ynch" took on the qualities of an idolatrous monument.[45] Conferring on altars a special holiness, Laudian prelates shifted the meaning of the Sacrament away from the puritan understanding of it as a communion of the faithful, in which the minister as well as the communicants were all "brethren" in Christ. By fixing the altar in a higher place in the church, farther from communicants, setting it off with rails, and adding steps by which one approached it, these priests emphasized hierarchical distinctions between the priest and the lay congregation (rather than between the godly and the ungodly), placing additional barriers or mediations between the individual believer and Christ. In contrast to Calvin's notion of the priesthood of all believers, Heylyn and Pocklington insisted that only the priest could enter where the altar stood or touch it.[46] Laudians considered the altar the most holy place of the church, as if there were even within its consecrated walls degrees of holiness. Laud declared, the altar is "the greatest *place* of Gods *Residence* upon earth."[47] The fact that priest and congregation were to bow towards the altar seemed to encourage "Altar-Worship." To puritans, Laud's whole "altar-service" seemed an idol, "devised" by men and "set up" in the house of God.[48]

Puritans objected to the very name "altar," insisting it was another of Laud's dangerous changes in the liturgy. It was a mere "Nick-name," "the invention of man, "more proper to Jews than Christians," but others defended the use of the word.[49] Joseph Mede wrote an entire pamphlet defending the propriety of calling the holy table "an altar" on the basis of historical records about the primitive Christian church.[50] The fact that so much of the pamphlet controversy focused on what was the appropriate word (both sides believed that the choice of word involved a whole set of theological positions) should alert us to the inflammatory potential of Herrick's repeated insistence on the word "altar." Puritans feared that using the word would encourage a belief in sacrifices,[51] thus opening the way for reviving the Mass as a reenactment of Christ's sacrifice in which Christ was believed to be really, materially present. Like Calvin, they insisted that Christ is our only "altar": Christ's coming fulfilled and abrogated all previous physical altars and sacrifices, and made unnecessary all subsequent ones. Thus the Sacrament of the Lord's Supper is properly a "Communion."[52] "Altars" and "sacrifices" seemed a reversion to what they understood as heathen, Jewish, and Catholic carnal idolatry.

Within his poetry, Herrick sets up "*Altars*, with all their *Service* and *Ceremonies*," much as Burton had charged Laud with doing.[53] Unlike Herbert, who insists his altar is made of his heart, Herrick emphasizes the materiality of his altars – mentioning their holiness, describing acts of reverence towards them. What is even worse, he focuses on the sacrifices performed on these altars, playing to puritan fears that England was reverting to the carnal modes of worship that Christ had supposedly abolished.

Within *Hesperides* are poems about offering sacrifices – at least twenty-six that are separate from the poems on funeral rites or the poems that simply mention altars. Some are to pagan gods like Juno or Mars. But there are poems that cannot simply be described as recreations of distant, classical things. Some, like *"The Frankincense"* (H-417), wittily transfer ceremonial worship to the practice of love:

> When my off'ring next I make,
> Be thy hand the hallowed Cake:
> And thy brest the Altar, whence
> Love may smell the *Frankincense*.   (cf. H-874, 946)

In *"To* Julia, *The* Flaminica Dialis, *or* Queen-Priest" (H-539), where Julia is told to offer a sacrifice "t'appease / Love for our very-many Trespasses" (lines 5–6), Herrick blurs the secular realm of love with the sacred realm of religious worship, allowing the verse to invoke the contested issues of religious worship. Still other poems describe sacrifices (H-957, 974) that are not secular rites of "Love" but fully religious rituals.

Many poems highlight the materiality and physicality of the sacrifices. Herrick mentions "a thousand Bullocks thies" (H-63, line 1), *"Tunnie-fish"* (H-325, line 5), a "Cock" (H-302, line 5), all of which are sacrificed to the gods. When the king comes to Hampton Court to "re-possess" his home, "A thousand Altars smoake; a thousand thighes / Of Beeves here ready stand for Sacrifice" (H-961, lines 7–8). Such focus on the physical sacrifice of animals encourages the perception that Herrick is a "pagan" poet, more interested in ancient Roman religion than in Christianity, but it also shows the place of material things and physical acts in worship. Behind Herrick's sacrifice poems lies the ceremonialist belief in the materiality of worship. Rejecting the puritan notion that all we now need are spiritual sacrifices, Heylyn insisted that God still requires real sacrifices of praise and thanksgiving, which have a material component. The Sacrament of the Lord's Supper is, for Heylyn, a real, *"materiall"* "sacrifice," not simply spiritual; thus we need priests and altars to perform it.[54] Just such an understanding of the materiality of worship informs Herrick's poems, with their emphasis on the necessity of sacrifice and the importance of exactly following the prescribed ritual.

If some of Herrick's poems seem grossly carnal in their emphasis on the physicality of sacrificial worship, others offer a spiritual understanding of sacrifice.

> . . . come thus to sacrifice:
> First wash thy heart in innocence, then bring
> Pure hands, pure habits, pure, pure every thing.
> Next to the Altar humbly kneele, and thence,
> Give up thy soule in clouds of frankinsence.
>
> *("Mattens, or morning Prayer,"* H-320, lines 2–6)

Purifying the heart must precede and parallel purifying the body; the offer of incense must include the sacrifice of the soul. The ritual is deeply spiritual, but its spirituality is inseparable from the physical. Even some of Herrick's most "pagan" poems emphasize the inward, spiritual component of sacrifice as essential, inscribing the ceremonialist and Laudian position that outward, material ceremonial acts involve the spirit.

> 'TIs not a thousand Bullocks thies
> Can please those Heav'nly Deities,
> If the Vower don't express
> In his Offering, Cheerfulness.
>
> *("Cheerfulnesse in Charitie: or, The sweet Sacrifice,"* H-63; cf. H-65)

Herrick's sacrifice poems assimilate ceremonial worship from different times and cultures. They show a deep and precise familiarity with Roman pagan religion and thus are thought to have a classical, "pagan" flavor.[55] What has not been recognized, however, is that his sacrifice poems often allude to the Hebrew Bible, incorporating Jewish practices recorded there.

Herrick's "pagan" sacrifice poems echo the sacrificial worship described in Numbers and Leviticus. Herrick comments on the *"Sweetnesse in Sacrifice"* (H-65) and the special appeal of the aroma of sacrifice to the gods.

> THe Gods require the thighes
> Of Beeves for sacrifice;
> Which rosted, we the steam
> Must sacrifice to them:
> Who though they do not eat,
> Yet love the smell of meat.
>
> *("The smell of the Sacrifice,"* H-736)

This focus on the sweet smell of sacrifice is not simply "pagan" or a mark of his sensuality; it also recalls the biblical instructions for sacrificial worship, which repeatedly mention the "sweet savour" of sacrifice by fire as pleasing to God: "And the Lord spake unto Moses, saying, Command the children of Israel, and say unto them . . . And the other lamb shalt thou offer at even: as the meat offering of the morning, and as the drink offering thereof, thou shalt offer it, a sacrifice made by fire, of a sweet savour unto the Lord" (Numbers 28: 1–2, 8; cf. Leviticus 2:2, 9; 3:16; 4:31). Behind Herrick's observation that the Gods, though they love the smell of meat, "do not eat" (H-736, line 5) are the instructions in Leviticus that for some offerings only the fat and kidneys were to be burned, leaving the rest for the people. After the priest had burnt part of the "meal offering" (made of fine flour, oil, and frankincense) on the altar to God, the rest was to be left for Aaron and his sons (Leviticus 2:10; cf. Numbers 18:18). The protocol of Leviticus thus allows Herrick, the priest, to justify keeping the "roast" for himself:

> IF meat the Gods give, I the steame
> High-towring wil devote to them:
> Whose easie natures like it well,
> If we the roste have, they the smell.
>
> ("*Steame in Sacrifice*," H-66)

Performed in the right spirit, even our common, daily cooking becomes a significant reenactment of the required sacrifices to God. Herrick shares the Jewish belief that God should be worshiped in one's everyday acts, that all aspects of human life are holy and should be performed in recognition of the divine Creator. The humor of the poem does not disguise its serious conviction – shared with Leviticus – that the gifts of God that nourish us require acts of repayment that, however inadequate, are necessary acknowledgments of debt and dependence.

Leviticus is crucial for understanding Herrick's sense of the importance of sacrifice and ceremony in life. The instructions for sacrifice in Leviticus are meticulous, defining different sacrifices for different occasions – daily offerings, sacrifices for festivals, sin- or trespass-offerings for general atonement and for specific sins or "uncleannesses," peace-offerings, freewill offerings. Throughout, there is an unswerving sense that sacrifice is necessary to life, that the proper order must be exactly followed. Sacrifice was central to the life of the Israelites. And God insists that these laws for sacrifice are given to his people "by a statute for ever" (Leviticus 7:36). At the end of Leviticus, the Lord warns the Israelites what will happen if

they "will not hearken unto me" (26:21), "if ye shall despise my
statutes" and "will not do all my commandments" (26:15):

And I will make your cities waste, and bring your sanctuaries unto
desolation, and I will not smell the savour of your sweet odours. And I will
bring the land into desolation: and your enemies which dwell therein shall
be astonished at it . . . and your land shall be desolate, and your cities
waste . . . And upon them that are left alive of you I will send a faintness
into their hearts in the land of their enemies. (Leviticus 26: 31–3, 36)

I think Herrick believed that this is just what had happened to
England. He is not suggesting that Christians should have continued
to sacrifice animals; but he does share Cosin's view that "The true
and proper nature of a sacrifice is, *To be an oblation of some real and
sensible thing, made only to God*, for the acknowledging of man's
subjection to God, and of God's supreme dominion over man," and
that such sacrifices are still required.[56] Having refused to perform
the proper ceremonies of worship, the sacrificial devotion that God
requires, England was being laid waste, made desolate, just as God
had warned.

For Herrick, Leviticus provided the frame for understanding the
civil wars. The land is "Sick . . . to th'heart" (*"The bad season makes
the Poet sad,"* H-612, line 5). "This War . . . tempest-like doth spoil /
Our salt, our Corn, our Honie, Wine, and Oile" (H-642, lines
17–18)), fulfilling God's warning to the Israelites of what would
happen if they abandoned Him (cf. Deuteronomy 11: 13–14, 16–17).
Herrick pours out his lamentation for England, mourning a loss
both personal and larger:

> PLay I co'd once; but (gentle friend) you see
> My Harp hung up, here on the Willow tree.
> Sing I co'd once; and bravely too enspire
> (With luscious Numbers) my melodious Lyre.
> Draw I co'd once (although not stocks or stones,
> *Amphion*-like) men made of flesh and bones,
> Whether I wo'd; but (ah!) I know not how,
> I feele in me, this transmutation now.
> Griefe, (my dear friend) has first my Harp unstrung;
> Wither'd my hand, and palsie-struck my tongue.
> (*"To his Friend, on the untuneable Times,"* H-210)

Behind the image of the harp, abandoned and unstrung, stands
David's Psalm lamenting the destruction of Jerusalem: "By the rivers
of Babylon, there we sat down, yea, we wept, when we remembered

Zion. We hanged our harps upon the willows in the midst thereof"(Psalm 137:1–2). The devastation of England is like Israel's, a
punishment for having fallen away from God's commandments.
Turning against the puritans both their identification of the English
church with idolatry and their sense that their suffering under
Laudian rule was like that of the Jews in Babylon after the
destruction of the temple, Herrick suggests instead that it is those
faithful to the disestablished, desecrated Church of England who are
suffering a Babylonian captivity under parliamentary and puritan
rule.[57]

Leviticus was the principal locus of the Jewish ceremonial law and
worship that Calvin and English puritans insisted had been abrogated by Christ. The belief that Christ had fulfilled the Law and thus
ended the Jewish ceremonies grounded both the reformers' rejection
of Roman Catholic ceremonies and the puritan attack, from Ames to
Milton, on the "idolatrous" bodily ceremonies of the Church of
England. With its emphasis on material, physical sacrifices of
animals and other things, Leviticus – and by extension, the Jewish
religion – seemed disturbingly "carnal," a religion of the "flesh,"
opposed to the presumably more "spiritual" worship of Christianity.[58] Evoking the sacrifices of Leviticus, *Hesperides*, the work of
an ejected priest, would seem to puritan readers perfect evidence of
the carnality of the Church of England. Herrick's anti-puritan
sacrifice poems suggest, like the Laudians, that God still requires
worship that includes body as well as soul.

Herrick's mingling of pagan and Jewish sacrificial rituals with
Christian elements violates the puritan conception of Christianity as
a "pure" religion," uncontaminated by the "carnal" worship of the
Jews or heathens. This mingling takes an interesting form in several
sacrifice poems involving Julia. In *"To Julia, the Flaminica Dialis, or
Queen-Priest"* (H-539), Julia is to perform a ritual to "appease"
"Love" for "our very-many Trespasses" (lines 5–6). She wears an
"Inarculum" (line 3), which Herrick notes was "a twig of Pomgranat,
which the queen-priest did use to weare on her head at sacrificing"
(Patrick, p. 262n), and she is a devotee of a female goddess of "Love"
– details which define the ceremony as appropriate in heathen
Rome. But she also recalls the high priests in Leviticus 7, who were
instructed to make "trespasse-offerings," and she wears the "white
Vestures" (line 4) of the Roman and English churches. This is a light,
witty poem about the need to attend to the rites of love, but another,

more serious meaning is suggested by the ceremonial language and the plot of the poem, which concerns the need to make atonement for neglecting to perform certain ceremonies. Love's "Temple" was not "drest" with flowers (line 8), "her Altars did not shine / With daily Fyers," and "Wine" was "neglect[ed]" (lines 9–10). These lapses are at once trivial and of great significance. "Love did our Death decree" for these sins of omission, and it is only by Julia's sacrificial act "That we escape" (lines 15–16). Obliquely and deftly, the poem describes the state of the church under the influence of puritanism and presents Herrick's sense that in neglecting ceremonial worship, England has committed a deadly sin for which special atonement is necessary to avert God's wrath.

Perhaps less topical is "*The Sacrifice, by way of Discourse betwixt himselfe and* Julia" (H-870).

> HERR. COme and let's in solemn wise
> Both address to sacrifice:
> Old Religion first commands
> That we wash our hearts, and hands.
> Is the beast exempt from staine,
> Altar cleane, no fire prophane?
> Are the Garlands, Is the Nard
> JUL. Ready here? All well prepar'd,
> With the Wine that must be shed
> (Twixt the hornes) upon the head
> Of the holy Beast we bring
> For our Trespasse-offering.
> HERR. All is well; now next to these
> Put we on pure Surplices;
> And with Chaplets crown'd, we'l rost
> With perfumes the Holocaust:
> And (while we the gods invoke)
> Reade acceptance by the smoake.

Herrick, Anglican priest, and Julia participate in a "Sacrifice" that is clearly material and pre-Christian, as the focus on the sacrificial animal makes clear. The "Chaplets" and the reference to "the gods" seem to identify the ceremony as peculiar to the pagan religion of ancient Rome, as does the detail of pouring wine between the horns of the beast.[59] But the poem also subsumes into its ritual much from the Hebrew Bible. The "Trespasse-offering," as well as the detail that the beast must be "exempt from staine," both derive from Leviticus, which insists that all animals sacrificed to

God must be "without blemish," the purity of the beast signifying not only what God desires but the purity the sacrificing priests seek to achieve for themselves and the people. The "Holocaust" refers not only to pagan sacrifices but also to "burnt offerings" in Leviticus that were wholly consumed.[60] There is no effort to make this poem seem to be about the secular religion of love – rather, Herrick presents himself as cheerfully participating in a carnal, pre-Christian religious ceremony.

The very mixed nature of these sacrifice poems – and of Herrick's ceremonial poetry more generally – reflects, not an ahistorical anachronism, but a historical understanding of Christianity as growing out of and assimilating elements of the Jewish and pagan religions. Following Calvin and other early Protestant reformers, puritans saw Christianity as constituting a radical departure from both Jewish and Roman values and practices, and as involving historical discontinuity. But Laudian defenders of ceremony had a different understanding of Christianity that emphasized historical continuity rather than separation. Finding the entire Old Testament a record of the Christian church, Pocklington claimed that "*Christian Altars came in at* Noahs *Flood*." If the Christian church was "framed by the patterne of the Jewish Church" with divine approval, then episcopacy, altars, and beautiful churches and cathedrals were legitimized by their continuity with Jewish worship, and Leviticus with its ceremonial instructions had not lost its relevance for Christians. As Pocklington argued, though some "Judaicall Ceremonies" were "taken away" by Christ, many others are legitimately kept.[61]

Defenders of ceremonial worship saw Christian worship as incorporating Jewish and pagan traditions. The early Christian church assimilated these traditions when it kept the "Paschall Feast" of the Jews and retained the pagan and Jewish customs of having special feast or fast days.[62] Though some heathen temples were destroyed, the author of *De Templis* observed, many others "in the Apostles times, and in the time of *Constantine* the great, were converted from Idols, to the worship of the true God, yet still reteined their old figure and shape."[63] From this Laudian perspective, the Christian religion is marked by historical continuity and a cultural inclusiveness that "converts" the Jewish and pagan customs.

For puritans, however, continuity between the "carnal" Jewish and pagan religions and Christian worship was a sure sign of idolatry. Sibbes asked: "What is Popery, but a masse of Jewish, and

Heathenish Ceremonies?"[64] Puritans indicted the ceremonies of the Laudian church and even the terms "priest," "altar," and "sacrifice" as pagan and Jewish, suggesting that England was reverting to Catholicism, the repository of both pagan and Jewish "carnal" idolatry.[65] We have seen that Herbert's attitude towards the Jewish and ceremonial past was deeply conflicted: though drawn to the notion of "conversion" of a carnal, idolatrous past, his poetry also bespeaks a fear that whatever is converted to spiritual, Christian uses will revert to its former impurity. Herrick, however, enthusiastically embraces pre-Christian and pre-Reformation bodily ceremonies. His is a "carnal service" of "bodily rites and ceremonies borrowed partly from the Jewes, & partly from the heathen" (to quote Perkins's description of Roman Catholicism).[66]

Whereas puritans would separate the "Christian" from all "heathen," "Jewish," and "Catholic" elements and eliminate all carnal elements from spiritual worship, Herrick's pagan-Jewish-Christian ceremonial poetry insists on the roots of Christianity, on the connection between the physical and spiritual elements of worship, and on the continuity of religion. When he speaks of cutting his hair as part of the rites of grief (H-82), he reenacts the ritual mourning recorded in the Hebrew Bible (for instance, Job 1:20; Jeremiah 7:29). The poem on Julia's churching (H-898) reminds us that the Roman Catholic and Church of England rites for purification of women after childbirth derive from the Jewish ceremony prescribed in Leviticus 12. In his ceremonial eclecticism, Herrick mocks the puritan notion that it is possible to have a "pure" or purely spiritual Christianity.

A UNIVERSAL, "CATHOLIC" RELIGION

Herrick's mingling of pagan, Jewish, and Christian ceremonial practices in his poetic temple suggests that, at some level, all these religions are compatible. Each of them recognizes that life and prosperity depend on God. Hence the various prayers for health and success in undertakings (H-302, 303, 325, 337, 360, 871), the offerings of thanks and praise (H-320, 530, 772, 778), and the trespass-offerings (H-251, 539, 870) atoning for sins in the hope for renewal of God's blessings. The effect of Herrick's eclecticism is to suggest a generally religious worship in which ceremony is central, rather than a narrowly denominational one.

Hesperides describes a "universal" religious spirit. Though this may well have been a personal preoccupation, Herrick was not alone in this concern. In examining the records of the past in order to defend the antiquity of ceremonial worship, Laudian apologists discovered something like a natural, universal religious instinct. Heylyn finds that "*Sacrifices, Priests,* and *Altars,* were from the beginning, by the light of nature; and that not onely amongst the *Patriarchs,* but amongst the *Gentiles.*"[67] Writing in defense of Laud's program to beautify places of worship, the author of *De Templis* insists: "All nations, from the beginning of the World, have beene naturally inclined, to build and adorne Temples, as if it were impossible for a humane life, to be lead here upon earth, without them." In a passage particularly apt for contextualizing *Hesperides,* he cites Plutarch's comment that "you shall never in all your travailes see a City that has no God to worship, no kind of Temples, to serve him in: that offers no sacrifice to avert calamities, or thanksgiving for prosperitie."[68]

What from the puritan perspective is the continuity of idolatry – which is difficult to extirpate and against which Christians must continually wage war – is to Herrick the amazing continuity of the human religious spirit. The thought that it could be extinguished is deeply disturbing. All the rituals and ceremonies Herrick records are linked to the seasonal cycles of nature and of human life – harvest, Christmas, New Year's, springtime; marriage, childbirth, and death. Most involve transitional or liminal moments. Seeking to perpetuate the cycles rather than escape or transcend them, the ceremonies give thanks to the divine spirit and invoke its aid and assistance, in the recognition that God the Creator is the sustainer of life. Herrick's ceremonial poetry suggests that all religions share not only a faith in the divine spirit (no matter how diversely they may name it) but also the belief that it is necessary to connect with God through ceremonial rites.

Herrick's insistence on drawing the boundaries of religion to include the pre-Christian and the Roman Catholic associates him with an ideological perspective within the Church of England identified with Laud and his supporters but not limited to them. Diminishing – sometimes virtually erasing – the divisive features of the Protestant Reformation, defenders of ceremonial worship saw the Church of England as reforming Catholic abuses but preserving "the old religion" – a significant phrase in *Hesperides* (H-604, 870).[69]

Laud's incorporation of Roman Catholic prayers and language into English Protestant worship was one of the crimes with which he was charged at his trial. Prynne brought as evidence a book of private devotions, in which Laud had included passages from "the *Roman Missall, Breviary, and Howers of our Lady.*"[70] For Prynne it was enough that Laud used the words or prayers of Catholics to convict him of being a Papist, a traitor to the English church. Laud's defense, however, makes explicit the historical perspective that shapes Herrick's eclectically religious poetry:

I would have them remember, that we live in a Church *Reformed*; not in one made *New*. Now all *Reformation*, that is good and orderly, takes away nothing from the old, but that which is Faulty and Erroneous. If any thing be good, it leaves that standing. So that if these Changes from the *Book of* England be good, 'tis no matter whence they be taken. For every line in the *Mass-Book*, or other *Popish Rituals*, are not all Evil and Corruptions. There are many good Prayers in them; nor is any thing Evil in them, only because 'tis there. Nay, the less alteration is made in the Publick Ancient *Service* of the Church, the better it is.[71]

For Laud, continuity with earlier practices was a sign that England's church was a true church because it was "catholic" and universal, not divisive and sectarian.

During the time that Herrick was writing his poetry, Arminians in the Church of England were voicing an ideal of a "catholic" or universal church that seems remarkably close to the assumptions about religion underlying *Hesperides*. Criticizing the divisiveness of those "Purer *Brethren*" who identified themselves narrowly as members of a Protestant sect, Montagu emphasized the "Essentials and Fundamentals" that English and Roman Catholic churches share rather than the differences that divide them.[72] Laud took the same position in his *Relation of the Conference Betweene . . . Lawd . . . and Mr. Fisher the Jesuite*, when he declared that his aim was "to lay open those *wider-Gates* of the *Catholike Church*, confined to no *Age, Time*, or *Place*; Nor knowing any *Bounds, but That Faith, which was once* (and but once for all) *deliver'd to the Saints.*"[73] As puritans bitterly noted, Laud was eager to make overtures of friendship to the Roman Catholic church but persecuted puritan consciences at home. But the concern to establish a more inclusive church was also voiced by moderates in the Church of England who did not necessarily endorse Laud's repressive activities. Emphasizing the many "*Prayers, and holy ceremonies*" that the English church has in common with the Church of

Rome, John Hales insisted that "*It is the unity of the Spirit in the bond of peace*, and not *Identitie of conceit*, which the Holy Ghost requires at the hands of Christians." Hales suggested that English Protestants should be "Universally compassionate" to Roman Catholics, and he drew an analogy particularly relevant to Herrick's poetry:

As therefore our religion is, so must our compassion be, catholick. To tye it either to persons or to place, is but a kinde of *moral Judaisme* . . . In some things we agree, as we are men, and thus far the very heathen themselves are to be received . . . St. *Paul* loved the *Jews* because they were *his brethren according to the Flesh*. We that are of the *heathen* by the same analogy ought to be as tenderly affected to the rest [of] our brethren, who though they be not as we are *now*, yet now are that which we sometimes were.[74]

Our human bonds are perhaps more important than our differences. Here is an incipient, glimmering perception of a natural religious sense and of the underlying unity among various religions that could open the space imaginatively for a more tolerant and inclusive attitude.

It would be wrong to think that the emphasis on unity or the perception of a universal religious impulse necessarily entailed a charitable embrace of religious difference. We should not misread a seventeenth-century vocabulary of inclusion as expressing late twentieth-century ideas of tolerance, pluralism, and diversity. The politically useful notions of "conversion" and integration as well as the language of unity and universality in ceremonialist religious discourse were often ways of containing and suppressing dissent. Indeed, it is a sad irony that Laudians were, in their concern with ceremonial conformity, intolerant of dissent. Herrick himself is hardly universally charitable, as the satirical, obscene epigrams in *Hesperides* make clear. He separates those he promises to immortalize from the "bastard Slips" that will die ("*To his Friend, Master J. Jincks*," H-859, line 3). In his "temple," he distinguishes those named men and women whom he canonizes – and the women like Julia, Perenna, or Anthea, whose beauty he celebrates – from the unregenerate, whose physical repulsiveness is made a sign of their lack of grace in more than one sense.

Some epigrams are explicitly directed at puritans. "*Upon* Trigg, *Epigram*" (H-703) mocks a man who claims to be "regenerate" (line 2). "*Upon* Zelot" (H-666) and "*Upon* Peason. *Epigram*" (H-843) satirize a puritan whose zeal has been punished by having his ears cropped.

IS *Zelot* pure? he is: ye see he weares
The signe of *Circumcision* in his eares.

(*"Upon Zelot,"* H-666)

Unperturbed by the violence of corporal punishment, Herrick may refer to the Star Chamber's notorious punishments of Bastwick, Burton, and Prynne, whose ears were chopped off (Prynne's twice, in 1634 and 1637). As the 666th poem in *Hesperides*, *"Upon Zelot"* shares the number traditionally assigned to the Beast in Revelation. Herrick turns against puritans their habit of identifying the Church of Rome and the Pope with the Beast or Antichrist, implying that the proliferation of puritans is a sign the apocalyptic end is near.

Herrick defines his (sub)human objects of derision in terms of religion as well as class, associating puritan schism and nonconformity with the lower socioeconomic classes.[75] His exposure of their physical impurity and deformity overturns the "purer Brethren's" obsession with "purity." These satirical epigrams focus on repulsive bodies and bodily functions, on offensive smells and excretions. The state of spiritless, graceless physicality is, for Herrick, the appropriate condition of those (puritans) who, drawing sharp lines between spirit and flesh, fail to integrate body and soul.[76] Bice farts (H-795); *"SKoles* stinks so deadly, that his Breeches loath / His dampish Buttocks furthermore to cloath" (H-650, lines 1–2); Lungs's breath pollutes his meat (H-637). There is a disgust for the lower classes, an anxiety to keep them in their place, but there is also more at work.

The oozing fluids and physical deformities are presented as marks of uncleanness and evidence of disease. Blanch's husband's eyes are "blear'd" by a "scald" or inflammatory disease (H-99, lines 1–2); Brock's eyes have a "clammie Reume" and his mouth is "furr'd" (H-273, lines 3–4); Skurffe's fingers have been eaten away by disease (H-480). Dundrige has an "Issue" or running sore (H-533, line 2) and Megg a mucous discharge from her nose (H-945). Some women even have "Leprosie" in their teeth (H-738, line 4).

Behind all these poems lies Leviticus with its purity laws. Leviticus describes in detail various unclean and leprous conditions – notably similar to those in Herrick's epigrams – that require that the priest cleanse the affected person and make sacrificial atonement. Sometimes the diseased persons must be excluded from the community until they are whole and healthy. "And the priest shall see the *raw flesh*, and *pronounce* him to be unclean: for the raw flesh is unclean: it is a leprosy . . . All the days wherein the plague shall be in him he shall be defiled; he is unclean: he shall dwell alone; without the camp shall his habitation be" (Leviticus 13:15, 46; italics mine). "When any man hath a *running issue* out of his flesh, because of his issue he is unclean" (Leviticus 15:2; italics mine). "And this is the law for all manner of plague of leprosy, and scall, And for the leprosy of a garment, and of a house, And for a rising, and for a scab, and for a bright spot: To teach when it is unclean, and when it is clean: this is the law of leprosy" (Leviticus 14:54–7). Herrick takes on the function of the priest in Leviticus, making the judgment between the clean and unclean.

Herrick identifies uncleanness both with disease and with lack of "civility" (the laundress washes clothes with piss [H-237]; Craw befouls his pants [H-428]) – itself a key concept in the defense of ceremony as encouraging decency.[77] The puritan refusal to engage in ceremonial worship has produced in Herrick's society a disgusting uncleanness, a perhaps incurable leprosy. His epigram "*Leprosie in houses*" (H-1004; the title comes from Leviticus 14:55) is illuminating, for it describes a house lacking "discipline" as one "spred through" with "*Leprosie*" (line 12). Herrick's image recalls Herbert's description of the English church as a rose whose "health and beautie" are being destroyed by the "worm" of schism ("Church-rents and schismes," lines 1, 3, 20). Herbert condemns those who "crush and grinde" the ceremonial "glories" of the church (lines 8–9). But Herrick is even more sharply anti-puritan. Echoing Laud's lament about the "neglect" of ceremonial service in the house of God,[78] he suggests that neglect of discipline leads to "leprosie" – a condition that as in Leviticus signals spiritual as well as bodily impurity.

Herrick's castigation of these unclean, anti-ceremonial, uncivil people is nasty, full of contempt. It hardly shows a genial, tolerant spirit. Ceremonialists could be just as repressive as puritans, condemning those who believed differently as subhuman and deserving of exclusion. Both could find support in Leviticus for persecutory distinctions. But Herrick's prejudices might seem less disturbing as they are aimed primarily at those who draw the boundaries of religion too narrowly. Puritans objected to the inclusiveness of the Church of England Communion, wanting to restrict it to those judged regenerate.[79] With incisive irony, *Hesperides* suggests that puritans themselves are the "unregenerate," condemned for drawing the circle of salvation so narrowly that they themselves, in retribution, will be excluded.

Blurring distinctions between the pagan-Jewish and the Christian, between Catholic and Christian, and between carnal and spiritual, Herrick seeks to enlarge the boundaries of religion and our sense of what is religious.[80] He is unusually inclusive in his mixtures and his appreciation of the rituals of different cultures. Though the powerful sense of interconnection between nature and grace, body and soul, that informs his poetry inscribes the ceremonialist/Laudian understanding of the interrelation of the material and spiritual domains, Herrick's celebration of the body and its pleasures as well as his representation of the natural world's engagement in religious rites (birds sing matins, roses have funeral rites) pushes that understanding to its limit. He persistently tests the bounds of religion. He virtually implies that the "Faith" necessary to be included in his temple is not strictly the New Testament belief in Christ, but a generic faith in God, available even to pagans.

Herrick is interested in the uncertain place at the very boundaries or limits of religion. He asks Anthea to bury him at the oak tree that marks the parish boundary (H-55), positioning himself at the edge of sacred space. This desire to be at the place where the holy, consecrated ground meets the unconsecrated captures the unique spirit of his poetry. It also suggests his recognition that he is almost beyond the pale – might even be thought so by some. Still, one of the most appealing aspects of *Hesperides* is its emphasis on harmony and inclusiveness at a time when so many of Herrick's contemporaries (on both sides of the controversy over worship) felt driven to draw the boundaries of religion, precisely, authoritatively, in ways that excluded those who did not share either their doctrines or their practice.

Significantly, Herrick includes an important place for women in his religion. Though some readers are disturbed by what they see as his objectification of women in his poems on female beauty, Herrick offers a principal, exalted place to woman in his religion. His emphasis on the purity and place of the feminine in his temple contrasts with the puritan Stephen Marshall's masculine-gendered definition of "the true *Church* of *Christ*" as "a virgin company, *not defiled with women.*"[81] Whereas the Protestant Reformation, in associating carnal idolatry with the feminine and rejecting the adoration of the Virgin Mary, diminished the role of woman and the feminine in the church, Herrick gives woman a powerful presence in his church as he extols the sacredness of the feminine. In this he recalls not only Aemelia Lanyer's *Salve Deus Rex Judaeorum* (1611), with its glorification of women's spirituality and special closeness to Christ, but also more nearly contemporary works such as Anthony Stafford's *The Femall Glory; or, the Life, and Death of our Blessed Lady, the Holy Virgin Mary* (1635), which was condemned by puritans as "popish" Mariolatry, and Richard Crashaw's *Carmen Deo Nostro* (1652), published after his conversion to Catholicism, whose poems on Mary Magdalene and Saint Teresa exalt women as models of sacred devotion. Herrick's Julia is a priest in the temple, a daughter of Aaron, garbed in priestly vestments, worthy of offering the holiest sacrifices (H-870; cf. 539, 974). She is even a figure for divinity. Herrick tells his "Queen-Priest" that *"Redemption comes by Thee"* (H-539, line 16; cf. 350), and he makes Julia the object of his reverence, devotedly following her petticoat as the Israelites followed God, appearing in a "pillar of cloud," out of Egypt (H-175; Exodus 13:21). Witty and sensual as these poems are, they show the capacity to imagine a sacred role for woman that was far beyond what most of his male Protestant contemporaries would have accepted.

CEREMONY, ART, AND THE DEATH OF CIVILIZATION

To Herrick, puritans who tried to outlaw the liturgy and ceremonial worship of the Church of England threatened not only religion but human civilization and human existence. To exterminate ceremony was, for him, not only to violate a natural religious impulse and to cut off the ties to the past, but also to deny human agency, and to obliterate the very acts that allow human beings to connect with God and ensure the Creator's continuing beneficence.

Hesperides' ceremonies and ritualized prayers to God insist on the importance of human effort in continuing the cycles of life and ensuring personal as well as communal well-being. The brief epigram *"Gods Bounty"* (N-76) in *Noble Numbers* expresses what is implicit in the many ceremonial poems of *Hesperides*: "GOds Bounty, that ebbs lesse and lesse, / As men do wane in thankfulnesse." Herrick's God requires human acts, though the acts alone do not save. This sense of the necessity and efficacy – though not the sufficiency – of human acts defies the Calvinist predestinarian belief that human beings are powerless to effect their salvation and perfectly expresses the assumptions of Laudian defenders of ceremony, whose Arminian belief in free will and the universal offer of grace constituted a theological position that implicitly legitimized ceremonial worship as an aid in salvation.[82]

When puritans rejected ceremonial worship, they questioned both the efficacy of human acts and the legitimacy of "art" in ways that had implications beyond the sphere of religious worship, particularly for those who did not believe that the religious sphere was separate from the rest of societal life. Herrick recognized that both art and human agency were at stake in the puritan attack on ceremony. His poems celebrating art and beauty thus have a close relation to his defense of ceremony.

Perhaps the most important poem is "*The Lilly in a Christal*" (H-193). Characteristically blending erotics and aesthetics, Herrick explores the affective power of art. Cream with a strawberry in it "draws the sight," "wantoning with it" (lines 13, 14). Amber partially "conceal'd" in streams "stroaks the sight" and produces "delight" (lines 18–19).

> Thus Lillie, Rose, Grape, Cherry, Creame,
> And Straw-berry do stir
> More love, when they transfer
> A weak, a soft, a broken beame;
> Then if they sho'd discover
> At full their proper excellence;
> Without some Scean cast over,
> To juggle with the sense. (lines 33–40)

All this becomes a rationale for advising a woman that she will "Raise greater fires in men" (line 56) by wearing "Lawns and Silks" (line 52) than by appearing naked. In its defense of the power of art to "stir" love, to move the affections, to raise desire and a kind of reverence, and in its argument for the preference of clothes to nakedness, the poem bears an interesting, provocative relation to the defenses of ceremony. As the "garments" of religion, ceremonies were frequently compared to ornaments and clothes, as the defenders of ceremony rejected the puritan ideal of a "naked" worship.[83] Like Herrick, who celebrates the appeal of a little clothing but rejects rich and immodest clothes ("*Leprosie in Cloathes*," H-1010) and extreme artifice ("*Delight in Disorder*," H-83), they saw the ceremonial garments of the English church as a mean between the plain worship of Geneva and the excessive, ornate ceremonies of the Church of Rome. The "*apparelling*" of worship adds to its "comelinesse" just as it does in the "*naturall*" bodies of men."[84] Whereas puritans condemned the seductive power of art as a dangerous incitement to "spirituall fornication" and carnal idolatry,[85] ceremonialists extolled ceremonial worship precisely *because* of its ability to "worke upon the affections" and "stir up . . . the heart." "The man who enters the West doore from farre beholding the Altar where he seriously intends to offer his devotions to his God and Saviour, shall find his devout soule, more rapt with divine awe and reverence, more inflamed with pure and holy zeale, in the delay and late approach unto it than if at first he had entered upon it."[86] This language describing the effect of beautiful churches – the proper setting for ceremonial worship – focuses on their erotic power, a power seen as desirable and ultimately serving God and moving the spirit. The perspective is not dissimilar from Herrick's, as is the recognition that delay and distance excite desire. I am not arguing that Herrick's poem – or, for that matter, his other meditations on beauty and art – is "really" about religion or ceremony, but rather that Herrick's poems and the Laudian defenses of ceremonial beauty share an understanding of the erotic yet spiritual power of art to move, and both feel the need to defend art because puritans had called its legitimacy into question. In its assertion of the importance and power of art, and of the power of material things to affect the spirit through the senses, Herrick's poem "*The Lilly in a Christal*" expresses a quintessentially ceremonialist, even Laudian mentality, though his emphasis on the erotic characteristically pushes it towards its limits.

The notion that material, sensual beauty has a spiritual dimension and the power to move the spirit is everywhere evident in Herrick's celebration of female beauty. Even Julia's clothes are animated, full of a motion dependent upon spirit ("*Upon* Julia's *Clothes*," H-779). The physical beauty of his mistresses typically possesses a spirituality and moves him to an eroticized state of devotion. He smells "the most sincere / Altar of Incense" at Anthea's lip ("*Love perfumes all parts*," H-155, lines 3–4). If Julia will let him stay with her, she will be "my endless Tabernacle" ("*To* Julia," H-156). In "*The Transfiguration*" (H-819), Julia seems almost divine, "Cloth'd all with incorrupted light" (line 5). He falls into a "swoone" (line 16) watching her petticoat:

> And all confus'd, I there did lie
> Drown'd in Delights; but co'd not die.
> That Leading Cloud, I follow'd still,
> Hoping t'ave seene of it my fill;

> But ah! I co'd not: sho'd it move
> To Life Eternal, I co'd love.   (H-175, lines 17–22)

Much of this is amusing. Nevertheless, one of the great perceptions of Herrick's poetry is that the truly erotic is never separate or separable from the soul. Desire necessarily involves both body and soul, and imagination is the work of the spirit. His highly developed imagination is made to seem a sign of his exalted spirit, willing to humble itself in the presence of a divine beauty.

The very conjunction of the sensual and devotional, the erotic and the reverent, reenacts the ceremonialist sense of interconnection and harmony between body and spirit. But where Laud was committed to "the beauty of holiness" in his program for ceremonial worship, Herrick promotes "the holiness of beauty." The beauty of his mistresses such as Julia, whose very sweat is the "oyle of Blossomes" and whose breath is "rich spices" ("*Upon* Julia's *sweat*," H-719, lines 1, 6), whose teeth are perfectly "white" (H-741, line 1), contrasts with the repulsive corporeality of the women in Herrick's obscene satirical epigrams, with their leprous teeth (H-738), stinking breath (H-659), and unredeemed bodies. If the ugliness and physical uncleanness of the puritan objects of his scorn symbolically represent their moral and spiritual uncleanness, the perfection and beauty of his celebrated mistresses are symbolic of a spiritual grace. "COnformity gives comelinesse to things" ("*Conformity is comely*," H-1040, line 1), and is "A foe to Dissolution" ("*Conformitie*," H-76, line 2). Equivocating on the meaning of religious "conformity," these epigrams confirm the link between beauty and ceremonial worship and imply that lack of "Conformity" – that is, the absence of ceremonial worship – will bring about "Dissolution," which is one of the deepest fears in *Hesperides*.[87]

Herrick sees puritanism – with its belief that oppositions and dichotomies structure human nature, religious experience, and social relations – as a fatal threat to the sense of community, to the connectedness of past and present, nature and grace, the physical and spiritual, and to art as it enacts, expresses, and sustains all these connections. His ominous poems about the "bad" times combine with his sense of his own impending death, present from early on in the volume but increasing towards the end, to produce a fearful awareness in *Hesperides* that civilization may be coming to an end.

> O! Times most bad,
> Without the scope
>   Of hope
> Of better to be had!
> . . . .
> Some storms w'ave past;
> Yet we must all
>   Down fall,
> And perish at the last.
>
> ("*Upon the troublesome times*," H-596, lines 1–4, 13–16)

There is a strong sense of impending, irreversible doom. Of all the many ceremony poems in *Hesperides*, by far the largest number concern funeral rites, for Herrick is obsessed with a sense that the life and civilization he knows are ending.

Facing the prospect that the apparently triumphant forces of puritanism will extinguish both ceremonial religious experience and the sense of interconnection between physical and spiritual, sacred and "prophane," Herrick records that ceremonial mentality and way of life. He offers his poetry as preserving religion in perhaps the broadest sense, preserving a culture and sensibility in which ceremonial behavior is at the heart of an integrated sense of life and experience, at a time when that culture seemed threatened with extinction. Perhaps the very fact that religion is preserved in art – like the lily, "Tomb'd in a *Christal* stone" (H-193, line 5) – means it has lost its vitality. Hence, the sense of triviality and frivolity in his ceremony poems. Nevertheless, Herrick insists on the importance of his project. Where puritans warned that Christians should "flie from Idolatry" – the very "*memory of Idolatry is totally to be wiped out*"[88] – he preserves the supposedly idolatrous ceremonies. His poetry reveals his understanding that the puritan ban on ceremonial worship, and the desire for a "pure Christianity" uncontaminated by human traditions, involved wiping out the past, making history as the knowledge of the past irrelevant, and obliterating the memory of those who have lived before us. But if ceremonial worship and experience will die with his civilization, Herrick is determined they will live in his poetry, which in several senses becomes a monument – it preserves memory, is a tribute to the worth of human acts, and will last when people are gone. As his "*Pyramides*" ("*His Poetrie his Pillar*," H-211, line 24), *Hesperides* is his personal monument, giving him fame after death, and the mem-

orial of his civilization, which may soon meet the fate of ancient
Egypt or Rome.

> FAmes pillar here, at last, we set,
> Out-during *Marble, Brasse,* or *Jet,*
> Charm'd and enchanted so,
> As to withstand the blow
> Of overthrow:
> Nor shall the seas,
> Or O U T R A G E S
> Of storms orebear
> What we up-rear,
> Tho Kingdoms fal,
> This pillar never shall
> Decline or waste at all;
> But stand for ever by his owne
> Firme and well fixt foundation.
>
> (*"The pillar of Fame,"* H-1129)

Hesperides ends with this shaped poem, visually recalling Herbert's
"The Altar" but expressing none of the earlier poet's anxiety about
the idolatrous potential of art. Unlike Herbert's equivocal poetry,
Herrick's "standing image" is proudly "up-rear[ed]." As the
allusion to Herbert suggests, this is not simply the secular, neo-
classical poem most readers have assumed. Rather, it is grounded
in contemporary religious conflict over worship. Through his
allusion to "The Altar," Herrick revives the "fixed" stone altars
that had recently been demolished and challenges the puritan
reading of Leviticus 26:1 ("Ye shall make no idols nor graven
image, neither rear you up a standing image, neither shall ye set up
any image of stone in your land to bow down unto it"). By referring
to his poem as a "pillar" (H-1129), Herrick, I think, expects us to
remember the stone Jacob "set up for a pillar, [to] be God's
house," after having been visited by God in a dream (Genesis
28:22) – an important biblical episode invoked by those defending
ceremonial worship.[89] If indeed he has this biblical passage in
mind, then his pillar – both poem and volume – is constructed as a
sacred monument and a place of devotion to God, not just a
memorial for Herrick and his civilization.

"*The pillar of Fame*" is the culmination of Herrick's celebration of
imagination and his claims for the value of human art and its
magical powers of endurance in the face of the puritan attack on
"human invention." Asserting the privilege of art, the power of the

"author," and the efficacy of human agency despite historical contingencies, Herrick hopes that his poems – the seemingly fragile exhalation of the spirit – will last when stone altars and even funeral monuments of marble or brass are gone. Poetry may be the place where the religious spirit will survive.

CHAPTER 5

Sir Thomas Browne: the promiscuous embrace of ritual order

Browne has not been much in fashion these days, in part because his sensibilities and political stance are so at odds with the current interest in puritanism and social activism. Michael Wilding's exposure of Browne's conservative elitism damaged his reputation, but even earlier Stanley Fish made him his example of the "bad physician," all the good ones being either puritans or receptive to reformist readings that privilege struggle, introspection, and spiritual conversion.[1] Historians of the seventeenth century are now giving religious conformity the same kind of scrutiny nonconformity has commanded. Seventeenth-century literary and cultural studies seem ripe for a similar development.

Browne's conformity with the Church of England and his affection for ritual have long been recognized. It is hard to imagine a more perfect example of the ceremonial mentality. His relation to the ideology of the Laudian church, however, has been the subject of considerable disagreement, and is indeed complicated and shifting. *Religio Medici* seems aligned with the Laudians as it engages key polemical texts in the controversy over worship, but Browne's "singularity" and skepticism distance him from Laudian rigor and threaten to destabilize the Laudian ceremonialist order that Browne would defend. These disruptions are, to some extent, contained in *Religio Medici*, but the case is different in *Urn Buriall* and *The Garden of Cyrus*. Published towards the end of the Interregnum, these curious, antiquarian treatises – one an anthropological discussion of funeral rites, the other a survey of quincuncial order in nature and human culture – affirm the necessity and naturalness of ceremonial order, but show the difficulty of maintaining belief in ceremony and ritual order in the wake of the Revolution. *Urn Buriall* and *The Garden of Cyrus* reveal the unsettling impact of puritan ideology, even on someone as committed to ceremony as Browne. As he pushes ceremonialism to the limit, we may sense its collapse. But these fascinating texts also reveal a persistent desire for ritual bonds that helps explain why the Restoration was greeted by many with enthusiasm. Further, they suggest that the ceremonialist impulse towards universalism could lead, not simply to repression, but to a vision of inclusivity that might, at least momentarily, recognize and tolerate diversity.

THE RELIGIOUS POLITICS OF *RELIGIO MEDICI*

Circulated in manuscript for several years before publication, *Religio Medici* appeared in an unauthorized edition in 1642; Browne published his authorized version in 1643. Parliament had already begun reforming the church – the Root and Branch Petition had been presented to the House of Commons, Laud and Bishop Matthew Wren had been arrested, and in June 1643 Parliament called an "Assembly of Divines" to settle the discipline and government of the church. But Browne claimed he wrote the book "about seven yeares past,"[2] which would place its composition in 1635-7, when Burton, Bastwick, and Prynne were publishing anti-Laudian pamphlets and were brutally, publicly punished for supposed sedition – they lost their ears, were fined £5000, and were condemned to separate prisons indefinitely. *Religio Medici* engages the religious conflicts of the mid-1630s, as well as England's situation in the early 1640s. In the 1630s, Browne's remarks associated him comfortably with the powerful Laudians, but in the 1640s they acquired a far more dangerous edge since they were no longer the opinions of those in the ascendancy.

Though Browne has been described as a "moderate," "the great proponent . . . of a spacious pre-Laudian high church,"[3] his statements of faith are discomfortingly close to the controversial positions of the Laudians. Michael Wilding has linked Browne's anti-sectarian, conservative stance in *Religio Medici* with the Laudians, but there is even more textual evidence of this connection.[4] The opening sections of *Religio Medici* echo one of the most controversial books of the time, Richard Montagu's *Appello Caesarem* (1625) – the notorious work which incensed Calvinists and angered Parliament, who forced the king to call in the book. Identified not simply with Arminianism but with the ceremonial worship promoted by Laud, Montagu's book continued to be a target of puritan attack in the mid-1630s.

Burton's 1636 sermons *For God, and the King*, which occasioned his censure by Laud, denounced *Appello Caesarem* as the book that had opened the way to the current divisions in the English church.[5] Given the notoriety of *Appello Caesarem*, Browne's incorporation of Montagu's text not only suggests his interest in religious controversy (despite his protest that he has no "Genius" for "disputes in religion," 1.6, p. 15) but would have made his Laudian connection clear to contemporary English readers.

Browne assumes a peaceable middle way in "matters of Religion, neither violently defending one, nor with the common ardour of contention opposing another" (1.1, p. 11). As Jonathan Post says, "Browne's whole approach in *Religio* is to minimize the possibility of conflict by minimizing the concept of opposition."[6] But the language of moderation, peace, and charity had become the language of the anti-puritan prelates who promoted the increasing ceremonialism of the English church in the late 1620s and 1630s while attempting to repress puritan dissent. As Browne defines his own "reformed" Christian identity, he avoids the name "Protestant" as unpeaceable and distances himself from more zealous Protestants, insisting he has not severed all relation with "those desperate Resolutions" (the Catholics) who have not reformed (1.3). He presents, that is, exactly the positions that Montagu had in 1625 and that were repeated in Laud's *A Relation of the Conference . . . [with] Mr. Fisher the Jesuite* (1639) and by Laudians like Heylyn and Dow. Even Browne's reluctance to adopt a label for his kind of Christianity recalls Montagu's announcement that "I am not, nor would be accounted willingly ARMINIAN, CALVINIST, or LUTHERAN, (names of Division) but a CHRISTIAN."[7]

Browne refuses "to stand in diameter and swords point with" Catholics; he is "not scrupulous to converse or live with them, to enter their Churches in defect of ours, and either pray with them or for them" (1.3, p. 12). His peaceable language not only criticizes those who in 1642 went to war; it reaffirms the position of Montagu and other Laudians, who claimed that the English and Roman churches agreed on the fundamentals of faith. Montagu outraged zealous Protestants with a statement worth quoting in full because it is so close to the language and sentiments of *Religio Medici*:

I professe my selfe none of those furious ones in point of difference now-a-dayes, whose profession and resolution is, That the farther in anything from communion with the Church of *Rome*, the neerer unto God and Truth: that we ought to have no commerce, society, or accordance with *Papists* in things divine, nor almost humane, upon pain of eternall damnation; but must bid defiance irreconcileable unto them forever. I am absolutely perswaded, and shall bee till I see cause to the contrary, that the Church of *Rome* is a *true*, though not a *sound* Church of CHRIST], as well since, as before the Councell of *Trent*; a part of the Catholick, though not the Catholic Church . . . In Essentials and Fundamentals they agree, holding one Faith, in one Lord. (*Appello Caesarem*, pp. 112–13)

Like Montagu, Browne defines his peaceableness against "furious" puritans, who insist on an irreconcilable opposition between true Protestant Christianity and the Church of Rome, who firmly separate true faith and idolatry and refuse "communion" with the supposed ungodly. Burton, Bastwick, and Prynne had invoked not only 2 Corinthians 6:14 ("Be ye not unequally yoked together with unbelievers . . . what communion hath light with darkness?") but also those places in the Hebrew Bible that insisted that the Jews must firmly separate from the idolatry of their neighbors. But Browne remarks:

I could never perceive any rationall consequence from those many texts which prohibit the children of Israel to pollute themselves with the Temples of the Heathens; we being all Christians, and not divided by such detested impieties as might prophane our prayers, or the place wherein we make them. (I.5, p. 12)

His rhetoric of peaceableness contrasts with the oppositional stance of contemporary puritan discourse, with its images of conflict and war. To Bastwick, Burton, and Prynne, their battle with Laud and his prelates in 1637 was simply one "duel" in the continuing, necessary war between true and false religion.[8]

Browne's "soft" approach to Catholicism, like Herrick's, associates him with Montagu and the Laudians. Browne's suggestion that one can be a Catholic and still be saved would have identified him to many contemporaries not simply as a loyal, conforming member of the Church of England but as a Laudian – as would his admission of being naturally inclined to "superstition," and unoffended at "the sight of a Crosse or Crucifix" or the sound of "the *Ave Maria* bell" (I.3, pp. 12–13). As he explains his desire for a "reconciliation" with Rome, he sounds like Montagu: "there is between us one common name and appellation, one faith, and necessary body of principles common to us both" (I.5, p. 12). Laud, too, insisted that Rome was a

"True" church, sharing the same *"Fundamentalls."* Dow thought that Paul's commandment to live "in peace with all men" should guide English Protestants' relation with Roman Catholics, for though they do not agree in all matters of faith, they do share "those points of *faith* which are *absolutely necessary* to salvation."[9]

Puritans, however, saw the idea that Rome was a "true" church as a dangerous innovation. Burton charged that the prelates were trying to make the English church "a member of that Synagogue of Rome," and that many of the books Laud approved for publication aimed to bring "us back to a reconciliation & union with the Church of *Rome*" (Burton, *For God, and the King*, pp. 69, 122). When Laud remarked that it was acceptable for an English Protestant to worship in a Roman Catholic church, Burton mockingly replied: "your whole Church of *England* is now *at liberty to go to Masse*."[10] The pamphlets by Burton, Bastwick, and Prynne that occasioned their trial in 1637 took a sharply militant stand against this newly conciliatory attitude towards Rome. Bastwick vowed to *"fight"* *"as long as I can stand on my legs."* Prynne urged his readers to "hang up" and "execute justice" on "these Romish Prelates," and suggested that the plague ravaging England would not stop until Laud and his fellow conspirators were executed.[11] That Prynne was advocating violence is clear from his allusion to Numbers 25, and might account for the exceptional severity of his sentence by the Star Chamber: when the Israelites turn to idolatry, the Lord tells Moses, "Take all the heads of the people, and hang them up before the Lord against the sun, that the fierce anger of the Lord may be turned away from Israel" (Numbers 25:4). Once Zimri and the Midianitish woman are slain, "the plague was stayed from the children of Israel" (Numbers 25:8). Laud is Zimri, the Hebrew leader of idolatry, killed by his own people at God's command. Prynne was, indeed, inciting violence.

It is in the context of increasingly violent puritan rhetoric that Browne remarks that "peaceable Spirits doe desire" in their "reformation" of religion an eventual "reconciliation" (1.4). He speaks to like-minded men, with a sense of shared values, dismissing puritan views of reformation as violent, angry, extreme. Indeed, his skeptical comment that not "all those that suffer in matters of Religion" are "Martyrs" (1.26, p. 37) may well refer to the gruesome punishments of Burton, Prynne, and Bastwick, who seemed to court martyrdom and became martyrs in the eyes of many. Prynne said to his executioner: "Come friend, come, burne mee, cut mee, I feare not. I have learn'd to feare the fire of hell, and not what man can doe unto mee: Come, seare mee, seare mee, I shall beare in my body the markes of the Lord Jesus." To Browne, such a posture demonstrated not humble faith, but foolish pride.[12] In the late 1630s, Browne's anti-puritan remarks might have seemed smugly conservative, but they were much more risky in the climate of the early 1640s when Burton, Prynne, and Bastwick were all released from prison and greeted as heroic martyrs, and when Parliament was trying Laudians as traitors for attempting to reconcile England with Rome.

Browne's reasonable moderation in *Religio Medici* echoes Montagu, who seemed far from moderate to people like Burton, Prynne, and Bastwick. Browne appears balanced, flexible, and independent as he proclaims, "I condemne not all things in the Councell of *Trent*, nor approve all in the Synod of *Dort*. In briefe, where Scripture is silent, the Church is my text" (1.5, p. 14). Yet this is precisely the position that got Montagu in trouble with Calvinists, who saw a dangerous Arminianism, a sliding towards Rome, in his insistence that "I nor have, nor ever will subscribe that Synode [of Dort] absolutely, and in all points . . . but so farre forth onely, as their Determinations shall be found and made conformable unto the doctrine of OUR CHURCH" (*Appello Caesarem*, p. 108). Even Browne's objection to calling the Pope Antichrist echoes *Appello Caesarem*.

It is as uncharitable a point in us to fall upon those popular scurrilities and opprobrious scoffes of the Bishop of *Rome*, [to] whom as a temporall Prince, we owe the duty of good language: I confesse there is cause of passion betweene us; by his sentence I stand excommunicated, Heretick is the best language he affords me; yet can no eare witnesse I ever returned to him the name of Antichrist, Man of sin, or whore of *Babylon*. (1.5, p. 14)

One might compare Montagu's refusal to conclude that the Pope is Antichrist: "Who can finde it to be the doctrine of the Church of *England*? What Synod resolved it? Convocation assented to it? . . . I never yet saw proofe or argument brought."[13] For puritans, to deny the Pope is Antichrist was to reject "the resolved Doctrines of our Church," but Montagu skeptically notes there is "diversity of judgements, discrepancie of opinion among Divines" about who is "THE MAN OF SINNE."[14] Montagu refuses to "contest with any man" about mere "*opinions*." "It is an evill disease in the world among Divines in things of indifferency they cannot endure dissentients. Hee is not my friend, I will hold no correspondency with him, that will not *per omnia* and *in omnibus* bee of my minde" (*Appello Caesarem*, p. 160). The similarity between Montagu's statement and Browne's famous declaration, "I could never divide my selfe from any man upon the difference of an opinion" (I. 6, p. 15), must complicate our understanding of Browne's tolerance.

Browne seems the epitome of charity, refusing to insult the Pope with "uncharitable" words even when excommunicated. Even his early "heresies" were charitable: he was inclined to "prayer for the dead" out of "charitable inducements"; he believed that God would eventually "release the damned" (1.7, pp. 16–17). Browne characteristically displays a promiscuous, charitable embrace, not only in his attitude towards Catholics in Part I of *Religio Medici* but in the description of his "Charity" that begins Part II. He claims to have no aversion to anything: "I am of a constitution so generall, that it consorts and sympathizeth with all things" (II.1, p. 70). He has no ethnic prejudices. His tolerance even extends to the lowest animals: "at the sight of a Toad, or Viper, I feel in me no desire to take up a stone to destroy them" (II.1, p. 70).

Browne claims his "charity" is simply part of his nature, but it is also culturally constructed and historically specific. A distinctive emphasis on "charity" characterized the ideology of ceremonialists, especially Laudians, who envisioned a universal, "catholic" English church.[15] Where puritans privileged "chastity," with its rigorously policed boundaries, as symbolic of spiritual purity (as we shall see in Milton's *Comus*), for ceremonialists charity's loving embrace was the symbol of true religion. Not only did "charity" define a gesture of inclusion symbolizing the ideal of a "catholic" English church; it also was carefully constructed to contrast with puritan zeal, which supposedly produced "faction" and division rather than unity. Joseph Hall, for example, criticized the "uncharitablenesse" of the opponents of episcopacy who want to expel the prelates and furiously "spit" in the face of their "Mother" church.[16] Browne's charitableness virtually always entails an implicit criticism of puritans, who are believed to be full of "antipathy" and hate, and who, concerned to maintain purity, draw rigorous distinctions between the saints and the reprobate.

Browne's expressions of charity sound not just like the episcopalian Hall but like Hall's more extreme Laudian contemporaries. Montagu contrasted his own supposedly generous position with the "Faction" of "insociable" "PURITANS," while Dow accused them of an "uncharitable . . . rigor and strictnesse" in excluding Catholics from all hope of salvation. As Laud remarked, "*Salvation* is not shut up" in the "*narrow Conclave*" of either "*Rome*" or a "*Conventicle*."[17] In much the same spirit, Browne attacks the "uncharity" of those "particular Churches and Sects" that "usurpe the gates of heaven, and turne the key against each other" (1.56, p. 67), of those who too narrowly draw the circle of salvation, who are combative in their religion. "Those who doe confine the Church of God, either to particular Nations, Churches, or Families, have made it far narrower than our Saviour ever meant it" (1.55, p. 66) – a statement with which Herrick would have agreed.

Browne's contemporary, Alexander Ross, recognized the Laudian resonance of his language. Ross objected to Browne's comment that English Protestants and Roman Catholics share one faith, his willingness "to pray with *Papists*," and his insistence that we owe the Pope civility. Condemning this "charity" as mere "luke-warmnesse or stupidity," Ross insisted that Christians are obliged to "fight against" their spiritual "enemy," the Church of Rome.[18] Ross saw Browne's very style as a counterpart of Laudian ceremonial worship. Browne's rhetorical flourishes, his "curious dressing," not only violate Bacon's call for a plain style in philosophy but are like the elegant garments of worship that obscure or distract from the truth.[19] Ross criticizes Browne's rhetorical, metaphorical style just as he "suspect[s] . . . that Religion, which is trimmed up with too many *Tropiall pigments*, and *Rhetoricall dresses*" (*Medicus Medicatus*, sig. A3v). A similar distrust of Browne's eloquence has been voiced in our own century by Joan Webber and, especially, Stanley Fish, who disapproves of the way Browne's rhetoric seduces readers to admire its beauty and stylistic effects.[20] Twentieth-century criticisms of Browne's style thus resurrect the puritan suspicions of ceremonial worship, which was dismissed as mere "human invention," and whose beauty was presumed to distract people from spiritual truth.

Puritans persecuted under Laud did not fail to point out that the language of charity and reasonable moderation could be deceptive. The rhetoric of reasonableness, tolerance, peacefulness, and flexibility – which dismisses puritans as rigid, intolerant, dogmatic, and combative – contrasted with the actual practices of Laudian prelates, who punished puritan dissent and insisted on conformity to "indifferent" ceremonies. Writing his *Letany* from jail, deprived of his ability to practice medicine, Bastwick saw himself as an example of

Laudian persecution: the prelates have made it a "crime" to "*discourse about . . . religion*"; they "devoure the Soules, bodyes, and goods" of true Christians. Prynne told how these "persecutors" have silenced preachers. As Burton put it, there is "a pretence of Piety and peace, of unity, and uniformity, preaching peace, peace, when nothing but warre is in their heart & hand."[21] By the mid-1630s and early 1640s, the language of reasonable moderation and peace had become the rhetoric of Laudian repression.[22] The ideal of an English church, unified in ceremonial worship and coterminous with the English nation – or of an enlarged universal, Christian church, confined to no geographical region or nation (1.56) – was in practice repressive of difference. We see a seemingly inclusive tolerance turn to intolerance as Browne, after describing his charity towards all people and creatures, excepts as a proper "object of hatred" the monstrous "multitude," which Michael Wilding quite rightly identifies with the puritan and sectarian populace.[23] Yet the question remains whether the language of peace and moderation could ever signify something more positive, something closer to a genuine tolerance of difference.

We need to recognize the limitations and containment implicit in seemingly liberal seventeenth-century notions of tolerance and in the language of charity. But what is often obscured by those who glorify puritanism while attacking the conservative elitism of the English church is that puritans, too, were repressive and far from egalitarian. The puritan distinction between the saints and the corrupt mass, the elect and the reprobate, also constituted a hierarchy, which – while not based on class or wealth (and thus potentially subversive of the established political and socioeconomic hierarchy) – created deep divisions among human beings. (It should be remembered that opposition to proposed toleration acts after the Restoration came from puritan nonconformists who did not want toleration for Catholics.) Only "true" Christians, the elect, really counted. Much like Herrick, Browne's hostility is not solely towards those who seemed to threaten the privileges of his class; it is also directed at those who would cast out much of humankind in their definition of Christian (and, by implication, human) identity. Browne's anti-puritan stance reflects not merely a conservative satisfaction with the status quo, but a positive desire for a more inclusive community, for strengthening the bonds among human beings that Browne feared had been irreparably damaged.

Thus Browne's text cannot adequately be understood as simply Laudian, authoritarian, and complacent. For all its echoes of Laudian polemic, *Religio Medici* is not narrowly Laudian. First, it is not evident that Browne is Arminian, despite his charitable wish that "all" were saved, including the virtuous pagans who died before Christ (1.55, 54). He never claims that grace is universally offered, or that humans cooperate in that grace. Indeed, his "position" on the highly controversial, divisive issue of salvation seems deliberately obscure; he avoids statements that would identify him with a particular party or faction and thus set him at odds with others. At a time when religious polemic was intense, Browne offers opinions, not dogma.[24] He accepts predestination, believing that there is a limited number of the elect, though his vagueness led Sir Kenelm Digby to observe, "by the short touches our Author giveth of it, I doubt hee quite mistakes."[25] What Browne rejects is not predestination, but the assumption that humans can know whom God has elected – which is the assumption that underlies the puritan insistence that the godly must abjure communion with the ungodly. In one of the sections added in 1643, he remarks: "'Tis true we all hold there is a number of Elect and many to be saved; yet take our opinions together, and from the confusion thereof there will be no such thing as salvation, nor shall any one be saved" (1.56, p. 67). Like Herrick, Browne attacks those who presume to draw the boundaries of salvation narrowly and firmly, destroying Christian community not only by refusing to conform with the ceremonies of the established Church of England but also by refusing communion with those who do not pass their test of godliness.

Browne draws the boundaries of religion generously. He even insists there has never been a "positive Atheist" (1.20, p. 31), virtually all human beings sharing a natural religious instinct. Though he "difference[s]" himself (1.5, p. 14) first as a Christian, then as a reformed Christian, and finally as a member of the Church of England, his boundaries are fluid, far less rigid than puritans', for whom the divisions between the godly and ungodly, light and darkness, truth and falsehood, are fixed and unalterable. Browne's deepest impulse is to emphasize community, the things that bind people. Hence, his hostility to puritan "heads that are disposed unto Schisme" and are "naturally indisposed for a community" (1.8, p. 13) – and his fondness for ceremonies that incorporate people into the community by connecting them through shared physical acts.

So deep is Browne's desire for community that his attempts to make distinctions and describe difference inevitably collapse. This characteristic, which Fish describes with implicit disapproval, might instead be thought Browne's virtue: "Browne makes a great show of distinguishing himself from other men . . . but so generous and assimilative is his nature, that he is finally distinguishable only by a distinction-effacing tolerance . . . Rather than identifying (that is, distinguishing) himself, Browne finally surrenders his identity in an excess of fellowship" (*Self-Consuming Artifacts*, pp. 358–9). In Browne's writing, all sorts of distinctions collapse, as in his discussion of beauty, where ugliness and monstrosity disappear, absorbed into a universal, God-created order in which everything is beautiful because "conformable to his will" – a phrase that suggests conformity produces beauty, and thus implicitly supports religious conformity (1.16, p. 26). Browne makes the conventional distinction between "Nature" and "Art" only to conclude that "all things are artificall, for Nature is the Art of God" (1.16, p. 26). The same integrative impulse compromises his major attempt at a Baconian scientific treatise, *Pseudodoxia Epidemica*. He tries to separate truth from error as he discusses popular opinions, only to discover it is almost as impossible to distinguish certainly between truth and error in science as it is to know who is saved and who reprobate.[26] For all his interest in empirical observation, Browne with his ceremonialist instincts could never be a real Baconian scientist, since he lacks Bacon's reformist, puritan belief in distinctions. By showing that fallible human reason is unable to make firm distinctions, Browne's prose works to "dissolve those false, artificial barriers to religious communion, defusing sectarian antipathies."[27] His unwillingness (or incapacity) to make distinctions not only contrasts with the distinction-making puritan mentality, with its rhetoric of conflict and difference. It takes the ceremonialist concern with integration and unity to the limit, out-doing Laud so that the universalism that had seemed repressive turns into something more flexible. Browne collapses boundaries in a way that subverts Laudian rigor, intimating a more tolerant spirit.[28]

At its most generous, Browne's universalism not only includes but tolerates differences, with a willingness to try out alternative, alien experiences. This, I think, is the point of his comment, "I have no antipathy, or rather Idio-syncrasie, in dyet . . . I wonder not at the *French*, for their dishes of frogges, snailes, and toadstooles, nor at the

Jewes for Locusts and Grasse-hoppers, but being amongst them, make them my common viands; and I find they agree with my stomach as well as theirs" (II.1). His all-embracing diet, in which he gladly shares others' foods, symbolizes a universal religious communion. Browne's personal behavior undogmatically sets the pattern for what he wishes would characterize the practice of all peoples, who would then be able to live in peace despite their differences.

Even his conformity to the English church is remarkably flexible. He insists on the "libertie" of his reason to hold "singular opinions" (I.8, p. 18). In the manuscripts and unauthorized edition, Browne remarks in the very section most indebted to Montagu, "no man shall reach my faith unto another Article, or command my obedience to a Canon more" (I.5, p. 14) – a comment apparently critical of Laud's 1640 Canons, though Browne's omission of this passage in 1643 may indicate an unwillingness to set himself so sharply against Laud. Browne's earliest commentator, Sir Kenelm Digby, acutely perceived that, for all his insistence that he humbly follows "the greet wheele of the [English] Church" (I.6, p. 15), there are too many "Eccentricall and irregular motions" in Browne for him to be wholly conformable, let alone a Laudian. Digby was disturbed that Browne arrogates to himself "a controlling ability in liking or misliking the faith, doctrine and constitutions" of the church. "*If I* mistake not, this author approveth the Church of *England* not absolutely, but comparatively with other reformed Churches."[29] It is, indeed, Browne's independent, inquiring, skeptical mind that sets him apart from Laudians who tried to compel uniformity in worship. Perhaps as a scientist, he had too keen a sense of the variety evident in nature to be a real Laudian. His observation that "even in things alike, there is diversitie, and those that doe seeme to accord, doe manifestly disagree" (II.2, p. 73) obviously has applications in religion, where uniformity would violate God's order in Nature, the other book of his scripture.

Repeatedly, Browne draws attention to his own eccentricity and singularity – the ways in which he has strayed from the confines of church dogma – but he always insists that his home is within the English church. Perhaps one could say that this simply demonstrates how the institution of the English church ultimately contains or silences dissenting views. But one could also conclude that Browne is demonstrating a particularly generous vision of a church that, rather than silencing the individual, allows for his or her eccentric beliefs, so long as they are not made the occasion for dissolving the community. His own early heresies "went out insensibly of themselves" since they were given no external "fuell." In contrast, Browne attacks those who "cannot enjoy a singularity without a Heresie, or be the author of an opinion, without they be of a Sect also; this was the villany of the first Schisme of *Lucifer*, who was not content to erre alone, but drew into his faction many Legions of Spirits" (1.7, p. 17). It is not the differences of religious beliefs (which are, finally, human opinions) that bother Browne; it is rather when individual differences become politicized, organized into warring factions. What appals him is the politicization of religion that had characterized Christianity at least since the Reformation – indeed, that he traces back to the beginning of human history with Lucifer. And surely, Browne could hardly have been unaware that the Laudian prelates were as guilty as the "sects" of reducing religion to politics.

"A RATIONALL OF OLD RITES": *URN BURIALL* AND *THE GARDEN OF CYRUS*

When Browne's *Urn Buriall* and *The Garden of Cyrus* appeared in 1658, two years before the Restoration, the church had been dismantled and its ceremonial worship outlawed by act of Parliament for over thirteen years. Norwich Cathedral was one of many churches desecrated by iconoclasts trying to destroy all remnants of idolatry and superstition. *Urn Buriall* and *The Garden of Cyrus* show Browne still preoccupied with ritual order, but where *Religio Medici* had offered professions of faith, these late texts examine obliquely and more anxiously the value of ceremony and ritual in human life.

Urn Buriall, Browne's treatise on funeral practices, was written and published when the burial rites of the church were forbidden. "The Order for the buriall of the dead" was among the ceremonies in the Book of Common Prayer banned by Parliament. After the ordinance of January 4, 1645, it was illegal to bury a person according to these rites. Parliamentary order replaced the Prayer Book with *A Directory for the Public Worship of God*, which rejected the burial rites along with the other "unprofitable and burdensome Ceremonies":

When any person departeth this life, let the dead body, upon the day of Buriall, be decently attended from the house to the place appointed for publique Buriall, and there immediately interred, without any Ceremony.

And because the customes of kneeling down, and praying by, or towards the dead Corps, and other such usages, in the place where it lies, before it be carried to Buriall, are Superstitious: and for that, praying, reading, and singing both in going to, and at the Grave, have been grosly abused, are no way beneficall to the dead, and have proved many wayes hurtfull to the living, therefore let all such things be laid aside.[30]

One wishes to know what were the burial practices in England after Parliament made the *Directory* legally binding. The *Directory* may not have been widely used, despite the parliamentary order, and Clare Gittings notes that at least a few burials were performed in church with the old rites. But the evidence is sparse and inconclusive.[31]

Browne takes as his subject the controversial issue of humanly ordained ceremony, of which burial rites are a particularly compelling example. As a text examining burial practices in different historical times, countries, and cultures, *Urn Buriall* seems curiously modern in its archaeological, anthropological approach. Its antiquarianism has led modern readers to feel that it is remote from the heated political concerns that absorbed Browne's contemporaries. But seventeenth-century antiquarian studies were not always disinterested; they often had applications for the contemporary politics of religion.[32] Browne suggests the connection between distant past and immediate present when he says that these urns have "voices" that "speak" to the present (p. 131). They have something to tell us which is not just a timeless truth about mortality but particularly timely during the period of the Civil War and Interregnum. For Browne's examination of burial practices is in part a defense of burial rites and, indeed, of ceremony more largely. He begins with a focus on the recently discovered urns and on specific burial customs. But just as he moves from the particular Norfolk urns to the ways humans have ceremoniously treated the dead body, so his concerns broaden from specific rites of burial to large conclusions about the role of religious ceremony. The Norfolk urns become an occasion to explore the ways in which humans have treated death and the place of ceremony in human experience. Implicitly, *Urn Buriall* defends the legitimacy of burial rites, and of ceremony more largely, confirming the arguments of those who had defended ceremony in the Church of England. But it is a paradoxical, difficult work, for another voice in Browne's text speaks of the vanity and absurdity of these rites. The contradictions make *Urn Buriall* a fascinating, peculiarly unstable text, representing the cultural conflicts of seventeenth-century England.

Urn Buriall is not simply a Laudian defense of ceremony. Nevertheless, it is grounded in the ideological assumptions that had shaped the polemical apologies for religious ceremony. Browne approaches his inquiry into the variety of human burial practices assuming that these practices are *significant,* that they have meaning. His discussion in the first three chapters discovers the "reason" or logic underlying burial customs:

Some being of the opinion of *Thales,* that water was the original of all things, thought it most equall to submit unto the principle of putrefaction, and conclude in a moist relentment. Others conceived it most natural to end in fire, as due unto the master principle in composition, according to the doctrine of *Heraclitus.* (p. 137)

In each case, the practice symbolizes an attempt to return to the origin of things in the hope of renewed life. The fact that there is some "reason" behind burial rites is what enables them to function symbolically. The belief that ceremonies are not meaningless but "significant" links Browne's discourse with the earlier defenses of religious ceremony.

Behind his attempt to give a "rationall of old Rites" (p. 158) is the belief that "all customes were founded upon some bottome of Reason" (p. 137) – exactly the argument made by apologists for religious ceremony. Heylyn argued that customs such as the consecration of temples and altars were natural and founded on reason. Speaking of the patriarchs and early Jews, he observed that "Nature informed them . . . that proper and peculiar places were to bee set apart to Gods publick worship."[33] In contrast to the puritan opposition between Scripture and custom or tradition (identified with error), ceremonialists argued that, besides divinely ordained ceremonies, there are rituals and customs that have their "foundation in Nature" and reason and thus can be properly observed.[34] This sense of custom appears, for example, in Cosin's discussion of the Office for the Burial of the Dead, where he defends the customary funeral banquet by saying it is "a custom taken from the Jews, as they took it from natural reason."[35]

Much of Cosin's commentary responds to puritan rejection of ceremony. He criticizes "that unchristian fancy of the puritans, that would have no minister to bury their dead, but the corpse to be brought to the grave and there put in by the clerk, or some other honest neighbour, and so back again without any more ado."[36] For Cosin, ceremony is necessary, and his belief that "custom" is reasonable is closely tied to his strong feeling for historical continuity. He stresses the connection between Jewish and Christian customs, and argues for the antiquity of current practices such as singing psalms at funerals or praying for the dead (*Notes and Collections*, pp. 165, 170). In Cosin's discussion of burial rites, as in other Laudian defenses of ceremonial worship, there is a deep sense of historical continuity, a sense that ceremony is a natural, universal human instinct.

We see in the defenses of ceremony glimmerings of an anthropological interest in human behavior. The author of *De Templis* looks for a common denominator in the practices of various cultures. He observes that wherever temples were built they always looked towards the east; they were consecrated as holy places through rituals that are founded in nature and hence universal. Offering a kind of anthropological survey of various religions, he concludes that "All nations, from the beginning of the World, have been naturally inclined, to build and adorne Temples, as if it were impossible for a humane life, to be lead here upon earth, without them" (R. T., *De Templis*, pp. 139–40).

The anthropological interest we see in *De Templis* is even stronger in Browne. As he surveys the customs for dealing with the dead body, he mentions Christian and Jewish burial practices alongside those of other cultures – Greeks, Chaldeans, Persians, Indians, Egyptians, Scythians, Romans. Whereas puritans insisted on clear separations between Christian and pagan, between the godly and ungodly, the first three and a half chapters of *Urn Buriall* show continuity underlying the diversity of human experience. All cultures have taken special care for the body at death. Ulysses desired a "noble Tomb after death," and even "the rigid Jews were wont to garnish the Sepulchres of the righteous" (p. 147). Though we might expect Christians to care less about the body with their faith that all is "reparable by a resurrection," Browne points out that they too have displayed "careful consideration of the body" at burial (p. 157).

What emerges from his survey of burial customs is a sense that, for all their diversity and particularity, there is a single symbolic significance underlying these rites. All of them represent attempts to continue connections with the living and renew bodily life after death. The pagan custom of burying things which "delighted, or . . .

were dear" to the dead person (p. 144), the burial of the tears of friends in a vial, the inclusion of evergreen bay leaves in the tomb of St. Humbert, the pictures of the holy candlestick in an old Jewish burial cell, or the pictures of cypresses, Lazarus, or Jonas in the cells of ancient Christians and martyrs, all these represent symbolically hopes for another life.

When in chapter IV Browne finally turns to Christian practices, we might expect him to distinguish them from pagan, but instead he insists on the similarity, as he shows that even pagan customs symbolically represented the hope for immortality:

> Christian invention hath chiefly driven at Rites, which speak hopes of another life, and hints of a Resurrection. And if the ancient Gentiles held not the immortality of their better part, and some subsistence after death; in severall rites, customes, actions and expressions, they contradicted their own opinions: wherein *Democritus* went high, even to the thought of a resurrection, as scoffingly recorded by *Pliny* . . . who would expect from *Lucretius* a sentence of *Ecclesiastes?* Before *Plato* could speak, the soul had wings in *Homer*. (p. 158)

If the desire for immortality is universal, so is the function of funeral rites to represent this human desire. All funeral customs, no matter how seemingly bizarre, signify "the natural expection and desire" for some further state to come, "unto which this seemes progression-all, and otherwise made in vaine" (p. 163).

Browne remarks that from ancient times Christians have used ceremonies to "gloss" the deformity of death, to "take off brutall terminations," and to symbolize their faith in resurrection (p. 157). This comment not only links Christian practices with pagan ones, stressing their connection, but defines a norm against which the parliamentary prohibition against burial rites must be evaluated. His reference to the "civil rites" of Christians (p. 157) may be calculated to imply that, in deference to Parliament's prohibition of religious ceremonies, he is only concerned with secular rites (the *Directory* allowed "civill respects" at burial).[37] Yet "civil" also meant "well-ordered," "not barbarous," "civilized," "refined," "humane," all appropriate meanings. In this sense, Christian rites, which "have handsomely glossed" (or given a fair appearance to) the "brutal" deformity of death, are a mark of civility.

Much like Herrick's *Hesperides*, *Urn Buriall* suggests that it is a distinctive mark of human beings to have ceremonies, although Browne observes that some animals perform burials or have "exequies" (p. 140). (One might recall that Herrick gives funeral rites to the rose [H-686], and that his birds say "Mattens" and sing "Hymnes" [H-178].) If even animals have burial rites, to have no rites at all would place humans beneath the animals. The discovered urns remind us of the universality of burial ceremonies, this "universal truth" making it evident that the puritan abolition of burial rites radically disrupts and violates human practices that go back to the earliest recorded antiquity.[38]

Browne was not the only one concerned about burial rites in mid-seventeenth-century England. One might recall Herrick's anxious poem in which he worries that his father (suspected of suicide) never received the proper burial rites (H-82). Herrick presents his poem as a funeral rite to compensate for the *"Rites"* (line 2) he never performed at the grave. *Hesperides* itself contains many poems that offer themselves as funeral rites or that ask people to perform the necessary rites when he dies. It is not surprising that Herrick, with his Laudian sympathies, should be concerned with funeral ceremonies. But far more surprising is Milton, who, as we shall see, devoted so much energy to attacking ceremonial idolatry. Though *Lycidas* attacks the decay of the English church, the poem itself constitutes a poetic funeral rite. Milton implies that such rites are necessary to give significance to human life, to commemorate human identity and affirm communal bonds.

> He must not float upon his wat'ry bier
> Unwept, and welter to the parching wind,
> Without the meed of some melodious tear.   (lines 12–14)[39]

Milton is disturbed by visions of Lycidas' body, lost at sea, his "bones" "hurl'd," perhaps visiting "the bottom of the monstrous world" under the "whelming tide" (lines 155–8). Not only is there empathy for the vulnerable body, but without a body the burial rites cannot be performed. Milton's song will fix the weltering body, giving it a peaceful, proper burial.[40]

For all Browne's concern with burial rites, he never mentions the burial rites of the Church of England in his survey of customs. Perhaps to refer to so many customs except the "Anglican" ones, is "safe," a way of avoiding Parliament's prohibition. But there may be a further significance to the absence of the burial rites of the Church of England. As Browne attempts to date and identify the urns in chapter II, references to ancient customs of Romans, Britons, or

Danes which ceased to be practiced suggest that burial customs are mortal and eventually "expire" (p. 146). Perhaps this is what is happening to the burial customs of the English church. The strong apocalypticism of the final chapter suggests the impending extinction of civilization. From his Royalist perspective, the puritan efforts to destroy English culture disrupt man's long history as a ceremonial creature and may well herald the end of time.[41]

Browne nevertheless includes the burial rites of the Church of England obliquely in his text. Like the rites, he interweaves mortality with the promise of resurrection. He gradually shifts from the universality of death to the availability of another life for faithful Christians, and concludes anticipating the end of the world when there will be the final judgment. Much as the church rite ends with the idea that "whoever believeth" in Jesus Christ shall live, so Browne towards the end of *Urn Buriall* insists that only Christians will have their hopes for an afterlife fulfilled. Chapter v eloquently echoes the passages from 1 Corinthians 15 on the resurrection that form the central part of the burial service. Inscribing the prohibited service in his own text, Browne, like Herrick in *Hesperides*, preserves remnants of his own culture for whatever posterity there may be. Ironically, however, this final chapter serves as a funeral oration for burial rites themselves, as it defines a present in which so little time is left that it seems absurd to expect those rites to fulfil a memorative function. No need for "Monuments" when there will be no generations left to remember us (p. 166).

But if Browne's text is a defense of ceremony, it also points out the vanity of funeral customs, and this pessimism becomes most insistent in the fifth chapter. His discourse on burial customs is contaminated by the puritan attack on ceremony which raised questions that apparently struck a responsive chord in his skeptical mind.

Although Browne shows that the invention of ceremony is an essential impulse of human nature, there is a persistent sense of the ultimate absurdity and futility of these rites, with all their attention to the body. There is an ironic edge in his description of substances buried in the grave that were found "fresh," or the bay leaves in St. Humbert's tomb that were "found green . . . after an hundred and fifty years" (p. 149). Though from one perspective, burial rites are marks of civility, decency, and humanity, from another, all the decorations of tombs and urns, all the ceremonies, seem ways of "glossing" or covering over the brutal "deformity" of death. If

Browne appreciates the art of these "glosses," he also exposes the brutal reality of death and decay that art strives to conceal. By chapter v the urns have become "Emblemes of mortall vanities," since they symbolize the many diverse attempts of human beings to create for themselves an earthly, material immortality: "to subsist in bones, and be but Pyramidally extant, is a fallacy in duration" (p. 165). All the efforts of antiquity to preserve names, to build monuments, to gain an earthly immortality are "vanity, feeding the winde, and folly" (p. 168). "In vain do individuals hope for Immortality, or any patent from oblivion, in preservations below the Moon" (p. 168). Although burial rites and customs elegantly represent the human desire for immortality, they cannot ensure continuation of life, and they are "carnal" in their concern with the body rather than the soul.

The puritan distrust of ceremony as a mark of pride and carnality finds an echo in Browne's mockery of ceremonies concerned with the body:

There is nothing strictly immortall, but immortality . . . the sufficiency of Christian Immortality frustrates all earthly glory, and the quality of either state after death makes a folly of posthumous memory. God who only can destroy our souls, and hath assured our resurrection, either of our bodies or names hath directly promised no duration . . . But man is a Noble Animal, splendid in ashes, and pompous in the grave, solemnizing Nativities and Deaths with equall lustre, nor omitting Ceremonies of bravery, in the infamy of his nature. (p. 169)

The irony is heavy here, and the association of ceremony with infamy as well as splendor is closer to the puritans than to Laud.[42] Seen from this perspective, there is folly even in the Christian concern with the body in death. Indeed, Browne's remark that God has not directly promised resurrection of our bodies or names is startling, especially after he has just detailed all the concern among Christians, Jews, and pagans with the position in which the body is buried.[43] It effectively comments on the emphasis on bodily resurrection not only in the various pagan customs he has described but also in the Prayer Book's rite itself, which invokes (with some changes) Job's words (19:25–7): "I know that my Redeemer liveth, and that I shall rise out of the earth in the last day, and shall be covered again with my skinne, and shall see God in my fleshe yea, and I my self shall behold him, not with other, but with these same eyes." Browne's insistence that we have no way of understanding what our resurrected state will be (possibly only the unindividuated soul will rise) suggests that perhaps even Christian rites such as those in the Common Prayer Book place too much emphasis on the body, on an immortality modeled on earthly life.[44] Certainly, his ironic perspective on all the attention to the body evident in human funeral customs marks his distance from Laud's extraordinary emphasis on the body. Browne shows the human dependence on and attachment to the body, but he finally insists on its limits ("Circles and right lines limit and close all bodies, and the mortall right-lined circle must conclude and shut up all" [p. 166]), and on the limits of bodily ceremonies.

The radically contradictory perspectives in *Urn Buriall* do not admit of any easy resolution. The text both defends ceremony as natural, necessary, and universal, and exposes it as vain, carnal, and ineffective. The balance shifts from the first chapters, with their recognition of the reason behind customs, to the final two chapters, with their insistence on the irrationality of customs; from a ceremonialist, even Laudian emphasis on continuity and universality in human experience, to a puritan sense of firm divisions between Christian and pagan, between the few who will be saved and those multitudes without hope. Yet it is no simple progression.[45] If the anti-ceremonial implications of the final chapter severely compromise the defense of ceremony which animates so much of the work, so also the rather grim, inflexible conclusions of that last chapter seem inadequate to the generosity of spirit and flexibility which characterize Browne's approach to human experience throughout most of the text. Moreover, if the Christian God promises only resurrection of the soul, not the body, then (Browne's protests to the contrary) Christianity itself fails to match the human desire for continued bodily life.

Ultimately, we see here the secularization of ceremony that Keith Thomas has seen as a major consequence of the Protestant Reformation.[46] Rejecting the older belief that ceremony has a material efficacy, the Reformation redefined legitimate ceremony as a "commemorative rite," not a magical one. The puritan rejection of religious ceremony during the period of the English civil war secularized ceremony much further than Calvin and Luther had envisaged, restricting rites to a civil arena. This cultural process of the secularization of ceremony is evident in Browne's tendency to approve of customs which have practical effects – pouring oil upon the pyre facilitates burning; the custom of burying coins helps "posterity" make "historicall discoveries" (p. 160). Once ceremony is secularized, its role is circumscribed. Although Browne suggests that ceremony is necessary (and thus should not be prohibited), he drastically restricts its role and importance in *Urn Buriall*. Ceremony is a legitimate "human invention," but it is a human invention none the less, with no supernatural, magical power to effect any transcendence of the physical. As human art, ceremony can only, with more or less elegance, express human desire.

When Browne published *The Garden of Cyrus* with *Urn Buriall*, he defended the pairing of these seemingly disparate texts: "the delight-full World comes after death, and Paradise succeeds the Grave" (pp. 176–7). The connection between the texts has long been recognized, but I would suggest a further connection: *The Garden*, like *Urn Buriall*, provides a "rationall" of ceremonial order, though a more optimistic one. Where *Urn Buriall* emphasizes death and endings, *The Garden's* focus on life and renewal anticipates an eventual restoration of ceremonial order.

Much as Browne's discussion of specific ancient funeral rituals was a way of talking about the persistence and universality of ceremony, so *The Garden of Cyrus'* discussion of quincuncial order becomes a way of talking about the importance of artful, formal order, of which ceremonial worship was a prime, contested, example. The quincunx is, in a sense, an analogue of the "set forms" puritans detested in worship. As Browne insists on the beauty and usefulness of the quincuncial order, his comments echo the earlier English defenses of religious ceremony and thus have application to worship. He does not *make* this application – he never talks directly about seventeenth-century religious worship, just as in *Urn Buriall* he avoided describing English burial rites – but the link is nevertheless implicit.

Written at a time of extreme political and religious instability, this work seems oddly out of touch with the contemporary cultural upheavals that undermined the older analogical modes of under-standing social, religious, and political relations. Like *Hesperides*, it is deeply nostalgic, finding solace in the exercise of an imagination that can reconstitute order. As *The Garden of Cyrus* asserts the ubiquity of the order represented by the quincunx, this text perfectly exemplifies what Foucault has described as the sixteenth-century *episteme* founded on "resemblance," similitude, and analogy – the *episteme* that he sees replaced by an *episteme* of discontinuity, "identity and difference" in the early seventeenth century.[47] But appearing in 1658, *The Garden* seems immensely belated, almost a parody of the older vision, a desperate reassertion of the validity of analogical, ceremonial order in the face of so much evidence to the contrary.

The Garden of Cyrus is the ultimate ceremonial text – a vision of order endlessly replicated throughout the world, integrating everything. Browne obsessively traces the quincuncial order not only in ancient gardens, but in various "artificial contrivances" (p. 185) and throughout the divinely created natural world. Browne's is an order where everything is, as it were, "conformable," where he manages to make everything fit. He begins the treatise describing the order in which Cyrus planted his gardens, arranging his trees in "regular ordination": "five trees so set together, that a regular angularity, and through prospect, was left on every side. Owing this name [Quincunx] not only unto the Quintuple number of Trees, but the figure declaring that number; which being doubled at the angle, makes up the Letter X, that is the Emphaticall decussation, or fundamental figure" (p. 181). This order is "regular" but flexible and expansive, encompassing number, letter, geometrical figure. Browne will show how the quincunx is "accommodable" (p. 191) and useful, how it is "elegant" (p. 201) and has mystical signficance. All these qualities are, as we have seen, precisely those that had been attributed to ceremonial worship by its defenders.

In the opening chapter, he actually points to religious ceremony by insisting what he will *not* discuss:

Where by the way we shall decline the old Theme, so traced by antiquity, of crosses and crucifixion . . . Nor shall we take in the mysticall *Tau*, or the Crosse of our blessed Saviour . . . We will not revive the mysterious crosses of *Ægypt*, with circles on their heads . . . We shall not call in the Hebrew *Tenupha*, or ceremony of their Oblations, waved by the Priest unto the four quarters of the world, after the form of a cross. (pp. 182–3)

The effect of such disclaimers is actually to bring into mind the connection between quincuncial order and the order of religious ceremony, which (as this list suggests) has united Christian, pagan, and Jewish experience. Further, I think it no coincidence that Browne repeatedly uses the word "ordination," which not only signifies order in general but also commonly refers to the ritual

ordination of priests prohibited when Parliament abolished episcopacy and the Book of Common Prayer.[48]

Having subtly suggested the connection between the quincunx
and the contested ceremonial order of the now disestablished
church, Browne shows the universality of quincuncial order. He
discovers that Babylon, Greece, India, and Rome all used this order
in planting gardens. He traces it into the more distant past, to Noah
who after the Flood planted his "Vineyards" in this order, but even
speculates that it was used by Abraham in his "grove at *Beer-sheba*,"
and by Solomon in his Gardens (p. 184). Browne's attempt to trace a
particular order back to its ancient origins recalls the defenses of
ceremonial worship in the late 1630s. Defending ceremonial worship
from puritan attack, Heylyn's *Antidotum Lincolniense* conducted a
"search into antiquity" to prove there had always been a "general
consent" about its necessity. *De Templis* investigated the antiquity of
temples in order to justify the Laudian renovation of churches and
cathedrals.[49] Like these treatises, Browne's antiquarian text is not
simply a disinterested, fanciful exercise but is intended to prove the
antiquity, universality, and necessity of "order," which also implicitly
encompasses order in religious worship. As he traces the antiquity of
quincuncial order, he ends up at Creation, speculating that God
planted the Garden of Eden in this figure: "since even in Paradise it
self, the tree of knowledge was placed in the middle of the Garden,
whatever was the ambient figure, there wanted not a centre and rule
of decussation" (p. 185). If that is true, then this way of planting trees
(and formal order, more generally), shared by people in many
different cultures and times, takes its pattern from God.

This belief that human invention imitates God's is precisely the
assumption of the defenders of ceremony, who saw humanly
invented ceremonies in worship as a legitimate extension of God's
order. Having traced Cyrus' supposed invention of the quincuncial
garden ultimately to God, Browne in the second chapter shows how
this order has been repeated in various "artificial contrivances" (p.
185). He discovers the quincunx in pyramids, laurel crowns "pleated
after this order" (p. 186), the crowns of Roman and Christian
emperors, the "mitrall Crown" on the high priest Aaron (p. 186), the
"network" construction of ancient beds (p. 187), the glass windows
and stonework of "the Temple of *Solomon*" (p. 187), the "grate
through which the ashes fell in the altar of burnt offerings" (p. 187),
the "Greek expression" in Canticles about Christ "looking through

the nets" or lattice windows (p. 187), Vulcan's famous net, the order of Roman armies, the battle form of the Greek and Parthian cavalries, the cities of Babylon and the New Jerusalem, the Labyrinth of Crete, and the Ark of the Covenant described in the Hebrew Bible, as well as the "stone wherein the names of the twelve Tribes were engraved" and the "Tables of the Law" (p. 191). What is striking in this seemingly miscellaneous list is the juxtaposition of secular and sacred, and of pagan, Jewish, and Christian. That all exemplify quincuncial order shows that such order is universal, all-inclusive – originating with God but evident in human culture throughout history. What is also significant, however, is Browne's recurrent attention to the ceremonial worship of the Jews, in which the seventeenth-century defenders of ceremony found the precedent and justification for the ceremonial order of the English church. Whereas puritans rejected the Jewish ceremonial worship as carnal idolatry, Browne presents its details (the construction of Solomon's temple, the Ark of the Covenant, the sacrificial altar, the mitre of Aaron) as expressing a universal, divinely ordained order – an order, built into the fabric of the world, that was not abrogated by the coming of Christ, though it may have been by the puritan Parliament. Ceremonial order thus becomes, not something confined to temples or churches, but part of all aspects of human experience.

The recreation of artful order is not even limited to human beings. Browne digresses from his human examples to describe the work of "the neat *Retiarie* Spider, which seems to weave without transversion, and by the union of right lines to make out a continued surface" (p. 188). He mentions with wonder that as soon as they are born, spiders will create their webs, so instinctive and natural in God's creatures is the recreation of divine order. Browne's exemplary figure here is the spider – the very creature Bacon had used to symbolize idolatry. For Bacon, the spider creates webs out of itself to entrap others. The spider is Bacon's symbol of pride, of the mind that spins false conceptions of order that, like the inventions of beautiful ceremonial worship, seduce the gullible.[50] For Browne, however, the spider's artful works, far from being idolatrous, are natural, divinely ordained. The instinct to recreate order, which is the impulse behind ceremonial worship, is so basic it extends even into the animal world.

The Garden of Cyrus discovers the presence of quincuncial order throughout the natural world – in the arrangement of stars, in gypsum, thistles, the "prickled Artichoak" (p. 193), sunflowers, "the Rhomboidall protuberances in Pineapples" (p. 194), snakeskin, the "scaly covering of Fishes" (p. 204), "the skin of man" (p. 204), the whole body of man extended, and even the "locall motion" (p. 206) of animals, birds, fish, and man. Browne breaks down the distinction between humans and the animal, vegetable, and mineral world, and between nature and art. Repeatedly, he speaks of how "elegantly" these things are ordered in nature (for example, pp. 192, 193). "The needle of nature delighteth to work, even in low and doubtful vegetations" (p. 193); "with incredible Artifice hath Nature framed the tayl or Oar of the Bever" (pp. 187). As he details nature's artistry, he focuses on observable phenomena, but he always assumes the "needle" or "hand" (pp. 193, 203) of nature is guided by a divine intentionality. If "nature . . . observeth order in all things" (p. 203), it is because she is the creation of an orderly God, recreating his orderly forms throughout the universe. And it is from nature that human beings have learned their arts – the "higher Geometry of nature" becomes "a point of art . . . in *Euclide*" (p. 201). Human arts are thus not idolatrous or evidence of pride, but a natural part of God's order.

Implicitly but insistently, Browne's argument defends ceremonial order in worship – the invention of elegant "forms" is natural and intended by God. If we see *The Garden* (dedicated to Nicholas Bacon, Bacon's kinsman) as simply a "scientific" treatise and judge it in Baconian terms, it seems bad science, discovering more order in the universe than there is, making everything conform to a single order. But if we see *The Garden* as not only an empirical and antiquarian treatise but also an argument for the universality of "form" and "order," then it assumes a rather different meaning. *The Garden of Cyrus'* obsession with "formal order" is ceremonialism taken to the extreme. Formalism is seen to constitute *all* of life – it is inscribed everywhere in the universe. In one sense, this text, written when the formal worship of the Church of England had been banned for years, might show the displacement of religious ceremony onto all experience and nature, much as for Vaughan worship takes place in the temple of nature, religious temples having been desecrated. But in another, *The Garden* expresses an irrepressible ceremonialism that sees religious order as part of the larger, natural, divinely ordered world.

Browne remarks that "the eyes of signal discerners . . . know where to finde . . . *Aarons* Mitre in Henbane" (p. 202). His ideal readers are "signal discerners" who can discover secret meanings in a text. But his observation also implies that if the Hebrew ceremonial figure is inscribed in plants, then ceremonial order is natural, not an idolatrous human invention as puritans would have it. In Browne's universe, in which there is "order in all things" (p. 203), not to have elegant order in religious worship would be unnatural, monstrous, a bizarre and ungodly aberration.

What emerges from the final two chapters describing "the delights, commodities, [and] mysteries" of "this order" (p. 209) is the profound sense that formal order is necessary to life. Whereas *Urn Buriall* admits the ultimate futility of ceremony, its inability to preserve us from mortality, *The Garden of Cyrus* shows that formal order is life-supporting, even conducive to generation. The quincunx constitutes the pattern of sight, whereby "Pyramidal rayes from the object, receive a decussation, and so strike a second base upon the *Retina*," as well as the "law of reflexion" in sounds and the pattern of "intellectual receptions" – "Things entring upon the intellect by a Pyramid from without, and thence into the memory by another from within, the common decussation being in the understanding" (p. 219). Without this order, we could neither see, nor hear, nor learn. The quincuncial arrangement makes trees and plants grow better, allowing proper ventilation and the access of the sun's rays. This order, evident in the wrappings of seeds, protects the seeds and allows them to sprout, keeping the "generative particle" "moist and secured from the injury of Ayre and Sunne."

For Browne, the quincuncial order is thus essential to life – and this insight applies not only to the natural, secular world, but to religious experience, which is for him as for Herrick inseparable from nature. Without order we die. For Browne, formal order is far from rigid and repressive. In his hands, the seemingly precise form of the quincunx comes to include a staggering "variety" (p. 214). It includes, for example, virtually all geometrical figures.

Whilest every inclosure makes a *Rhombus*, the figures obliquely taken a Rhomboides, the intervals bounded with parallell lines, and each intersection built upon a square, affording two Triangles or Pyramids vertically conjoyned; which in the strict Quincunciall order doe oppositely make acute and blunt Angles.

And though therein we meet not with right angles, yet every Rhombus containing four Angles equall unto four right, it virtually contains four right . . . the conversion of a Rhombus . . . maketh two concentricall Circles . . . The Cylindrical figure of Trees is virtually contained and latent in this order. A Cylinder or long round being made by the conversion or turning of a Parallelogram. (pp. 214–15)

Some might say this passage shows how the concept of formal order, at the heart of ceremonial worship, is inevitably repressive, forcing everything to be "contained." And Browne's urge to make everything conform may come from the desperate sense that almost nothing does. But I see a more hopeful significance here. In Browne, order becomes loose, generous, flexible. The sheer variety of particular, individual instances exerts such a powerful force that the order itself must expand, its boundaries dissolving so it can accommodate virtually everything.

Perhaps if order really is all-encompassing and universal, the puritan prohibitions against formal worship are only a transitory, temporary phenomenon. *Urn Buriall*'s deep skepticism about ceremony, and its sense of the approaching end of civilization, give way to *The Garden*'s concluding declaration of faith, which grows out of Browne's inextinguishable desire for ritual order, but which has also been earned by his strenuous search into the records of the past and nature: "All things began in order, so shall they end, and so shall they begin again; according to the ordainer of order and mysticall Mathematicks of the City of Heaven" (p. 226). Though this apocalyptic conclusion has been understood as Browne's impulse to transcend the messiness of human history, it may also be more temporally grounded, anticipating the restoration of ceremonial order in England that would occur two years later, though it would be far less inclusive than his idealistic vision.

CHAPTER 6

John Milton: carnal idolatry and the reconfiguration of worship, part 1, 1634–1660

From the early poetry and controversial prose through the major poems published after the Restoration, Milton's writing is driven by an obsession with idolatry. He recalls both the Hebrew prophets who contrasted the true worship of God with the idolatry of the heathen neighboring tribes, and the revival of this preoccupation among sixteenth-century Protestant reformers and, later, among puritans who wished to separate the spiritual worship of Christ from the carnal idolatry supposedly embodied in the ceremonial forms of the Churches of England and Rome. The oppositional stance, the impulse to make distinctions in the service of "purity," is, as we have seen, essential to puritan ideology, and Milton retained it long after he broke from orthodox puritanism, publishing *Of True Religion* at the end of his life in a last vigilant blast against the threat of false worship posed by the prospect of toleration of Catholicism.

Some readers might think Milton's prose too pragmatic to be considered of a piece with his lofty poetry, but in Milton the distinctions between poet and polemicist blur. Poetic passages enter the prose,[1] and polemic diatribe invades all the major poems. In a sense, religious conflict is the "first matter" of all his creations.

True worship and idolatry "grow up together almost inseparably" (*Areopagitica*, II, 514). Yet, despite their "cunning resemblances," Milton insists on making the arduous distinctions, exposing idolatry in all its guises. The prose of the 1640s and 50s shows idolatry lurking not only in churches but in the bedroom, Parliament, the king's court, and other civic arenas. Milton's analyses of these various forms of idolatry during the revolutionary years reveal a remarkable consistency despite important changes and complications in his thinking. We see how religious values were inscribed in political, domestic, and even sexual relations.

Milton did not simply wage war on idolatry. He also took on the challenge of imagining what true worship might be. This is the burden not simply of the prose urging reform but of the late poems, even as they continue to attack idolatry. Insofar as the true poet is a priest and poetry replaces a corrupt church, iconoclasm is not enough. Milton has to represent true worship in order to guide his fit if small audience.[2] But the religious conflict over worship posed problems that made these representations fraught with tension. How can a religious poet who rejects "human invention" in the worship of God, especially one who had spent almost twenty years smashing idols, authorize his imaginative invention as expressive of true worship without engaging in idolatry? Other dilemmas with wider applications preoccupied Milton. Can one have human bonds without bondage? Can worship be expressed in and by the body, in material forms in one's daily life, without becoming carnal?

Committed to reforming religion from a deadening focus on the externals, Milton nevertheless recognized that religious worship demands an external, material, sensible form. The persistence of desire for a worship that involves body as well as soul complicates his "puritan" concern to separate from carnal idolatry. *Paradise Lost* expresses Milton's desire to find a place for the body in worship. Moreover, though he believed that worship is necessarily an individual rather than corporate experience, his felt need of community in worship and his sense of the alienating as well as the liberating potential of Protestantism led him to imagine true worship in ways that might reestablish human bonds. In domestic love and poetry, he seeks a religious experience that would replace the bonds of community fractured by the puritan insistence on breaking from the past and from traditional forms that bind people.

But for all his efforts to reconfigure true worship, the late poems are almost overwhelmed by a vision of the near-universality of idolatry, which in *Paradise Lost* is present even in heaven, contaminates the relation of Adam and Eve, and threatens to obliterate all forms of true worship, and which makes community almost unimaginable in *Paradise Regained* and *Samson Agonistes*. Recent critics have admiringly described Milton's iconoclasm as "creative," but I see his last poems as revealing the costs of iconoclasm and the difficulty of reconstructing something to take the place of what has been destroyed.[3] For Milton, one of the bitterest lessons of both the Revolution and the Restoration was that idolatry is an ineradicable part of human experience. Much as Bacon said of the "natural though corrupt love of the lie," idolatry seems woven into the very fabric of human nature.[4]

THE FLESHLY SERVICE OF CARNAL PRELATES

With five anti-prelatical pamphlets published between May 1641 and April 1642, Milton officially entered the conflicts over ceremonial worship. Joining those attacking the ceremonial worship of the Church of England and episcopacy and insisting on the need for immediate reform, these tracts locate Milton firmly within a puritan ideology, from which he will in some respects diverge but which he will also pursue to its limits. As Milton's most explicit and extended attack on "carnal idolatry," these tracts are critical to his thinking about religion.

Of Reformation opens with a founding narrative against which the church and all human experience will be measured, and which will remain important for Milton to the end of his life. It is the "story of our Saviour," who suffered "to the lowest bent of weaknesse, in the *Flesh*," but then triumphed "to the highest pitch of *glory*, in the *Spirit*, which drew up his body also." Christ's descent into flesh and triumph in the spirit represent the history of God's church, which under the Jewish priests had been burdened with fleshly ceremonies, but through the work of the apostles was "winnow'd . . . from the chaffe of over-dated Ceremonies, and refin'd to such a Spirituall height" (1, 519). This pattern of decline into the body and ascent to the spirit was repeated in the post-apostolic history of the Christian church, which underwent a "foule and sudden corruption" but then enjoyed a reformation. In the mid-seventeenth century, the English church has experienced yet another carnal corruption. As Milton details that corruption, he is concerned not so much with beliefs, which are internal, as with *"Worship"* as something "perform'd" (1, 519) – acts and deeds that are outward and can be judged, that involve people physically and in relation to each other – with "Discipline," which he calls the *"execution* and *applying* of *Doctrine"* (1, 526). His point is that, even though there may be agreement about the doctrines of Protestant faith (the spiritual essence of the church), the actual practice of worship (the externals, the body) can contaminate the faith, corrupting the religion of the church.

Milton's attack on the ceremonial English church relentlessly focuses on the dangerous, persistent power of the body and corporeality to corrupt the spirit. In its concern with ceremony, the Church of England has turned the religion of Christ into something "outward" and carnal, into a "customary ey-Service of the body" (1, 520). To conform to Christ, the church must be "refin'd" to a "Spirituall height," its "body" must be "purifi'd," rid of material and fleshly elements, just as Christ's was (1, 519). Instead, the ceremonial worship of the Laudian church, like the Roman Catholic church, has "drag[ged]" religion "downwards" into "sensuall Idolatry" (1, 520), into the body. Under Laud, the prelates "began to draw downe all the Divine intercours, betwixt *God*, and the Soule, yea, the very shape of *God* himselfe, into an exterior, and bodily forme, urgently pretending a necessity, and obligement of joyning the body in a formall reverence" (1, 520-1). The church now wallows in the "old cast rudiments" of the Mosaic law and "the new-vomited Paganisme" of the Roman Catholic church (1, 520).

As the church is symbolically the body of Christ (a body which is supposed to have been made spiritual), its corruption is figured in terms of bodily disease. The "disease" of episcopacy lurks under "a fair and juicy fleshinesse of body," a false appearance of health that betrays serious illness (*Animadversions*, 1, 675-6). Milton describes the English church as putrefying – its acts of worship, like the issue of sores, "run out lavishly to the upper skin, and there harden into a crust of Formallitie" (*Of Reformation*, 1, 522), the crust of ceremonial forms being the external sign of internal disease. Parodying the Laudian notion that corporeal forms of ceremonial worship work upon the soul, Milton suggests that these forms have corrupted the spirit. In ceremonial worship, "the Soule . . ., given up justly to fleshly delights," turns from heaven and surrenders to her "sensuous collegue the body" (*Of Reformation*, 1, 522), thus reversing the example of Christ.

Milton exposes the carnality of the prelates and their worship in vivid metaphors that arouse the senses.[5] Prelacy is bred from "a masse of slime and mud" (*Reason of Church Government*, 1, 858). The prelates and ambitious clergy are "fat and fleshy, swoln with high thoughts and big with mischievous designes" (1, 793). "Subject to carnall desires" (*Animadversions*, 1, 666), they are libertines who worship "*Mammon*, and their Belly" (*Of Reformation*, 1, 566, 577). With their "many-benefice-gaping mouth[s]," their "canary-sucking, and swan-eating palat[s]" (*Of Reformation*, 1, 549), their greatest fear is the "losse of [their] Capon, and Whitebroth," their "costly suppers, and drinking banquets" (*Animadversions*, 1, 701).

The image of the carnal prelates was commonplace in the anti-ceremonial puritan discourse. Burton, Bastwick, and Prynne all charged that the Laudian clergy were ruled not by the spirit or the Word of God, but by sensuality and bodily appetites. John White's *The First Century of Scandalous, Malignant Priests* (1643) juxtaposed the "idolatrous" practices of Laudian priests with their supposed carnal transgressions such as adultery, sodomy, and drunkenness. A carnal life is the counterpart and symbol of carnal worship. Thus the pollution of what should be purely "spiritual" religious worship through the use of bodily ceremonies is appropriately figured by dissolute behavior.

Milton explains in *Animadversions* that even the priests' early years predispose them to carnality. Not only have the prelates spent their youth "harlotting" (1, 677), but the training of prospective clergy in the universities encourages a looseness of the body and a disposition to prostitution:

in the Colleges so many of the young Divines, and those in next aptitude to Divinity have bin seene so oft upon the Stage writhing and unboning their Clergie limmes to all the antick and dishonest gestures of Trinculo's, Buffons, and Bawds; prostituting the shame of that ministery which either they had, or were nigh having, to the eyes of Courtiers and Court-Ladies, with their Groomes and *Madamoisellaes*. (1, 887)

The dramatic roles of fool and bawd forecast their roles in Laud's church. In *An Apology*, Milton defends himself against the charge of carnality, insisting that as a youth he spent his time studying rather than "concocting the surfets of an irregular feast" (1, 885), and insisting, especially, that he never visited "Bordelloes" (886–7). Such charges are for Milton hardly trivial, for in the puritan mentality carnality is a sign of spiritual corruption and an attraction to whores signifies an attraction to the Whore of Babylon, the Church of Rome.

It is not surprising that the worship of these "fleshly" clergy – the ceremonies and liturgy of the Laudian church – is thoroughly carnal (*Animadversions*, 1, 703). "Obscene, and surfeted," Laud's priests "paw

. . . the sacramentall bread, as familiarly as [their] Tavern Bisket,"
desecrating the host they falsely venerate by insisting communicants
kneel to receive it (*Of Reformation*, 1, 548). The clergy gratify "the
corrupt desires of men in fleshly doctrines" (*Reason of Church Government*, 1, 802), appealing, as Burton said, to men's "*carnall senses*"
(*Replie*, p. 104). All their concern is with bodily gestures and rites in
worship – bowing, kneeling, making the sign of the cross. Burton
complained that the prelates think God is "some *carnall* Man, whose
senses are delighted with such *service*" (*Replie*, p. 104). Milton similarly
charges that Laud's prelates, like the Roman Catholics, "make *God*
earthly, and fleshly, because they could not make themselves *heavenly*,
and *Spirituall*" (*Of Reformation*, 1, 520). A carnal person can only
imagine a carnal God.

Milton's attack on the carnal prelates and service of the English
church is founded on the belief that worship must be "spiritual" and
inward, not "carnal" or "fleshly." In the prelates' "great designe"
"to turne all Religion into a pompous outside" (*Postscript to Smectymnuus' Answer*, 1, 975), they have lost the soul. "*Christs Kingdome* here on
earth," as Burton said, "is *Spirituall*, and the Laws thereof altogether
spirituall, enacted by his *Spirit*" (*Replie*, p. 93). Worship must be based
solely on the Gospel (understood to be spiritual), not on human
inventions, "fleshly ceremony," and "traditions," which are carnal
both in their preoccupation with material and bodily worship and in
their supposed opposition to the spiritual word of God (1, 830). Not
chapels and cathedrals like St. Paul's, which Laud was renovating,
but the "soule of man, . . . [God's] rationall temple," should be the
object of regeneration (1, 758). Only "the inward beauty and
splendor of the Christian Church" – that is, the individual "soule" –
matters (758).[6] If the religion of the Gospel is "pure" and "spirituall"
(*Reason of Church Government*, 1, 766), whatever is outward rather than
inward, whatever is of the body rather than the soul, is impure and
irredeemably "carnal" and hence pollutes the spirit. Thus Laud's
concern with outward forms, material churches, and bodily rites
seemed an anti-Christian carnal religion, whose attention to the
body threatened to extinguish the spirit.

Like other puritan anti-ceremonial discourse, Milton's attack on
carnal idolatry is rooted in a dualism that recalls Calvin, Augustine,
and ultimately Paul, with their oppositions between spirit and flesh,
"spirituall" and "carnal," Gospel and Law – a set of oppositions
that had been profoundly important to sixteenth-century English

reformers and that we have seen Herrick's poetry insistently dismantle.[7] "Carnal" and "flesh" were not in any simple way equated with the body but encompassed the mind and soul, since the whole of human nature was believed to be polluted by original sin.[8] Nevertheless, from Paul on, the carnal/spiritual binary was grounded on a deep suspicion of the body and its desires, seen as always threatening to pollute the mind and soul. As Milton explains, in ceremonial worship "the Soule," "over-bodying her selfe," sinks, and the worshiper becomes entirely "carnall" in "apprehension" (*Of Reformation*, 1, 522). Just as the Christian religion should be purged of all "carnal" traditions and ceremonies, all outward forms (*Reason of Church Government*, 1, 827–8), so the Christian person must strive to become like Christ – purely spiritual, purified of "carnal" desires. The body must be drawn up by the spirit; otherwise, the spirit is "drag[ged] . . . downwards" by the body (1, 519–20).

For Milton, the Church of England had turned the spiritual, Christian worship of God into a carnal service of exterior forms, engaging eye and body, by continuing the practices of Judaism and Roman Catholicism. Milton identifies the carnal with the pagan, the Catholic, and the Jewish, all of which were believed to share an essential carnality incompatible with the spiritual worship enjoined by Christ. From the puritan perspective, Roman Catholicism was preoccupied with bodily worship and ritual forms, reviving in its practices the religion of pagan Rome, with its material altars, priests, and sacrifices – all supposedly signs of carnality that pollutes the spirit. But Catholic worship also continued Jewish ceremonialism. Defenders of ceremonial worship had looked not only to earlier pre-Reformation Christianity but to Aaron and the ancient Jews to justify their practices. This very continuity – exemplified in the syncretic impulses of Herrick's ceremonial poetry or Browne's prose – was for Milton, as for Burton or Prynne, an indelible mark of idolatry.

The virulently anti-Catholic rhetoric of militant Protestant discourse is well known, but the anti-Judaic rhetoric is less well recognized. Milton's anti-prelatical tracts participate in a puritan discourse that regularly identified the "carnal" worship of the Laudian church not only with "popery" and heathenism but with a suspect Jewishness.[9] Milton compares the "Cathedrall *Prelates*" to the "gowned *Rabbies*" who rejected Christ (*Animadversions*, 1, 690). He mocks his opponent Joseph Hall for appearing in disguise without his "*Phylactery*" (the little box containing biblical inscriptions worn by orthodox Jews in prayer) (*Apology*, 1, 897). With their distinctions between holy clergy and profane laity, their purification rites, and their railing of the altar, the prelates have brought in "dead judaisms" (*Reason of Church Government*, 1, 843). For the Christian, the Jewish religion has taken the place of heathen idolatry. In the Hebrew Bible, the Israelites were to keep themselves separate from heathen idolatry; now Christians must maintain a similar distance from the Jewish religion: "that which was to the Jew but jewish," explains Milton, "is to the Christian no better then Canaanitish," for the Jewish service is a "carnall service" (*Reason of Church Government*, 1, 845, 773). Following Paul's identification of the Law with the flesh and the Gospel with the spirit, Milton opposes Christian to Jew as he attacks the Laudian use of bodily gestures and ceremonies in worship: "our Saviour detested [the] customes [of the Jews] . . . How much more then must these . . . much grosser ceremonies now in force delude the end of Christs comming in the flesh against the flesh" (*Reason of Church Government*, 1, 829). To revive Jewish worship – "the outward carnality of the law" (1, 766) – is to return to the detested "flesh," to fall back into the body. For England to imitate the "ceremonial law" is to fall like the "Papists" "into that irrecoverable superstition, as must needs make void the cov'nant of salvation to them that persist in this blindnesse" (1, 766). Far from being embraced as preparing for the Gospel, the Jewish is cast off as impure, carnal, ever threatening to contaminate spiritual worship, and beyond the pale of redemption.

In much the same way, "custom" and "tradition" are stigmatized as "carnal" elements to be purged from worship. The false God of "Antiquity" must be "throw[n] down" (*Animadversions*, 1, 700). What is custom and tradition but human invention? Reverence for custom, then, is idolatry, setting up something humanly invented to be worshiped. Thus Milton describes custom in terms of idolatry and art. Episcopacy, the product of tradition, has "varnish't over" God's instructions; it is "of mans own carving," a "rare device" of "fleshly wisdome" (*Reason of Church Government*, 1, 757, 776, 781). In patterning their ministry on the priesthood of Aaron, the prelates have "frame[d] of their own heads as it were with wax a kinde of Mimick Bishop limm'd out to the life of a dead Priesthood" (1, 777–8). The idol is at once a fantastic invention and a lifeless imitation of a past model.

The language of pollution traditionally associated with idolatry marks Milton's references to custom and the past. To look to the past and human authors for guidance in worship is like searching for something "spotlesse" and heavenly "among the verminous, and polluted rags" of time (*Of Prelatical Episcopacy*, 1, 639). The past (pagan, Jewish, even Christian) becomes identified with the material, fleshly, and carnal, which must be cast off as a pollution if worship is to be truly spiritual. The spirit's discontinuity with the past even determines the relation between the two Testaments, making the Hebrew Bible "Old" and a potential contaminant.

Milton assumes a clear opposition between truth and error, as he relentlessly attacks the false worship of the Laudian church. His sense of absolute distinctions sets him apart from Herrick, with his ceremonial eclecticism, or Browne, who collapses distinctions so that it is difficult to distinguish true Christian rites from false, super-stitious ones. Whereas Herrick's and Browne's impulse is to enlarge their embrace to encompass a multiplicity of cultural practices, Milton believes that the true Christian must wage war on all forms of carnal idolatry. Accordingly, his rhetoric is relentlessly opposi-tional, combative, violent, founded on a dualism that privileges the spirit while positing conflict as the necessary mode of existence in the world. As he puts it in *An Apology*, a true "Christian" cannot be "a cold neuter in the cause of the Church" (1, 868) – a phrase that identifies religious zeal with an aggressive masculinity. In virtually all of his writing he is engaged in battle, defending either himself or his cause and attacking his opponents.[10] The world is divided into "my friends" and "my enemies" (*Apology*, 1, 870). Reformation necessitates "the fierce encounter of truth and falshood" (*Reason of Church Government*, 1, 796), in which "sharpnesse," the heat of "Zeale," and a "sanctifi'd bitternesse against the enemies of truth" are appropriate (*Apology*, 1, 873, 900–1). Though he lumps the Jewish with the carnal worship that opposes the spirit, Milton identifies with the Jewish prophets who waged war on idolatry and warned the Israelites of retribution for being seduced by idols. Whereas Herbert suggested that the tongue is given to humans to offer God praise (a sentiment that will be echoed in Adam and Eve's prelapsarian morning prayer in Book v of *Paradise Lost*), Milton in *The Reason of Church Government* insists that God gave him his "tongue" to participate in the battle for the reformation of the church: God listens to "heare [his] voice among his zealous servants" (1, 805). He attacks Hall in *Animadversions* as an "enimie to truth," an "enemy to Mankind" (1, 662–3), with an "anger" he believes sanctioned by God (664). He attacks all traces of Catholicism and Judaism in the English church, insisting on a necessary and firm separation between the spiritual/Christian and the carnal/anti-Christian, believing like the parliamentary reformers of the church in the early 1640s that all polluting, carnal elements must be excluded from worship, by violence if necessary. His mission is not to convert his enemies, to convince them by reason, but to vanquish them, to have them "discover'd and laid open" (*Apology*, 1, 874).

Milton's combative stance contrasts sharply with Browne, whose *Religio Medici* appeared at the same time as Milton's anti-prelatical pamphlets. Where Milton insists on division, separation, opposition, and the exclusion of contaminating elements, Browne declares that he could never "divide" himself from someone over matters of belief in religion, that the Jews are not as awful as many people think, and that he could worship without a problem in a Roman Catholic church. Milton, believing in the necessity of firm separations, indicts the "communion" of the English liturgy along with Rome's (*Apology*, 1, 940). Browne's rhetorical method – inclusive, ever-expanding, all-embracing – contrasts with Milton's oppositional, divisive, sometimes violent rhetoric in the polemical tracts. Their rhetorical, stylistic characteristics not only express personality differences but are the counterparts of their radically different religious ideologies – one based on notions of hierarchical integration and an inclusivity that represses difference, the other on notions of opposition and exclusion. Browne's promiscuous stance might well recall Donne's holy sonnet "Show me deare Christ thy spouse," which wittily concludes his search for the true church by comparing her to a woman "embrac'd and open to most men" (line 14)[11] – a conclusion that might point either to support for the emerging Arminian movement within the English church, or to a crypto-Catholicism (with a play on the Protestant term of abuse, "Whore of Babylon"), or even to a disillusioned sense that the ideal church does not exist on earth, where (as Browne said) each church seems ready to excommunicate and damn the others. The promiscuity that attracts both Browne and Donne is anathema to Milton, with his sense that the condition of godliness necessitates separation from the corrupt mass of the ungodly.

"A MASK": CHASTITY AND THE SEDUCTIONS OF IDOLATRY

The anti-prelatical tracts of the early 1640s conduct a holy war against idolatry, but Milton's sense of the danger of idolatry, of the imminent threat to true religion in England, was already clear in the poetry of the 1630s.

With its famous digression, *Lycidas* exposed the corruption of the carnal clergy ruled by their appetites and "bellies" (line 114), who, starving rather than feeding their flock, spread the "contagion" of idolatry (line 127).[12] Like wolves, they "Creep and intrude and climb into the fold" (line 115), revealing their kinship with the Catholic church, the "grim Wolf with privy paw" that "Daily devours apace" (lines 128–9). They pervert Communion, as they "shove away the worthy bidden guest" from the "feast" (lines 117–18), and "Grate on their scrannel Pipes" (line 124) – the instrument of church music – rather than feeding the sheep by preaching the nourishing Word of God.

Lycidas, however, was not Milton's first intervention in the religious conflicts. In 1634, his masque *Comus* clearly announced his concern with the threat to true religion and the danger of carnal idolatry. Revised by Milton and published by Lawes in 1637 – the year Burton, Prynne, and Bastwick were pilloried and mutilated for their criticisms of Laud and his worship, and the year the pamphlet wars began over the altar, the symbol of Laudian ceremonial worship – it was published by Milton himself in 1645, after Parliament had abolished episcopacy and outlawed the ceremonial worship of the Book of Common Prayer. Leah Marcus has shown how the masque is anti-Laudian in its treatment of festivity, and David Norbrook, Cedric Brown, and others have alerted us to the seriously reformist stance of the poem.[13] But still more can be done to define and historicize the religious preoccupations of Milton's poem. In the plot of Comus' attempted seduction of the lady, and its concern with preserving her chastity, Milton's masque represents the spiritual dangers facing England – dangers threatening both the individual Christian and the church. With its pointedly symbolic language and plot, the poem's religious concerns would have been clear to at least some of Milton's contemporaries, which may account for its originally anonymous publication and Lawes's comment in the 1637 dedication that the masque is "not openly acknowledged by the Author" – Milton's anonymity perhaps well justified, given the punishments of Burton, Prynne, and Bastwick. Anticipating Milton's explicitly polemical attack on carnal idolatry in the anti-prelatical prose of the early 1640s, *Comus* shares in the puritan fears about spiritual seduction that, with the increasing ceremonialism of the English church, had been voiced since the late 1620s.

The secular bent of humanist and, more recently, historicist readings of the masque has tended to obscure the point that Comus is a representative and agent of religious idolatry. Spokesman for the festivity promoted by the Book of Sports, the figure of Comus also has distinctly religious significance, and Milton's political concerns in this masque cannot be separated from his religious ones.[14] As the Attendant Spirit's opening speech describes this "pagan" figure from classical mythology, Comus assumes characteristics that had a distinctly Christian resonance relevant to the contemporary conflicts over religious worship. As son of *"Bacchus* that first from out the purple Grape / Crusht the sweet poison of misused Wine" (lines 46–7) and Circe, with her "charmed Cup" (line 51), he is from the first associated with the instruments of Communion. "Misused" suggests that not just wine, but the religious ritual of Communion can be properly used or abused – and that Milton wants to discriminate between true and false, holy and demonic uses. The effects of this unholy wine, which "transform'd" the *"Tuscan* Mariners" (line 48) and made them lose their "upright shape" and fall "downward . . . into a groveling Swine" (lines 52–3), perversely parody the Roman Catholic doctrine of transubstantiation, and anticipate Milton's complaint in *Of Reformation* that the church, rather than having been drawn up to the "Spirit," had been drawn down into the corruption of the body. As the son of Bacchus and Circe, Comus represents the revelry and licentiousness that people like Milton and Prynne associated with the king's court, but with his "Crystal Glass" of "orient liquor" (line 65) he also continues a demonic Communion that is at once explicitly pagan and implicitly Catholic.[15] Comus' temptations are not simply to intemperance and revelry, but to idolatry, to a false religion identified with carnality, paganism, and Catholicism.

Comus' "glass" (lines 65, 652), his "baneful cup" of "pleasing poison" (lines 525–6), with which he tempts others to drink, symbolizes the lure of idolatry. For Milton's vigorously Protestant contemporaries, it would have been identified with the false Communion of Roman Catholicism, as it was for Spenser. The glass recalls not just Circe's but the golden cup of wine that Excesse offers Guyon in Acrasia's Bower of Bliss (*Faerie Queene*, II.xii. 56), and Duessa's "golden cup" whose "secret poyson" she sprinkles on the Redcrosse Knight (I.viii.14).[16] The associations of the cup with idolatry, not just intemperance, are distinctly biblical, Revelation describing "the great whore" of Babylon, with "a golden cup in her hand full of abominations" (17:1, 4). Protestants had identified the Whore of Babylon not only with pagan Rome but especially with the Church of Rome, and the marginal gloss of "cup" in the Geneva Bible is as relevant to Milton as to Spenser: "In profession the nourisher of all, in this verse, . . . but indeed most pernicious besotting miserable men with her cup, & bringeth upon them a deadly giddines."[17]

With its lure of a false, "pagan" Communion, this cup was powerfully symbolic to puritans in the 1630s, when it may have represented a more imminent, local threat than in Spenser's day, given the increasing ceremonialism of the church. The image of the cup appears in Prynne's *Histrio-Mastix* (1633), which cited 1 Corinthians 10: 21 and 2 Corinthians 6: 14, 15, and 16 in attacking what he saw as an alarming influx of pagan idolatry in England:

because Christians cannot drinke the Cup of the Lord, and the Cup of Devills: they cannot be partakers of the Lords Table, and the Table of Devills: for what fellowship hath Righteousnesse, with Unrighteousnesse? What communion hath Light with Darkenesse? What concorde hath Christ with Belial? what part hath hee that Beleeveth with an Infidell? or what agreement hath the Temple of God with Idols?[18]

Prynne attacked not just stage plays or specific pagan customs that had survived but a large-scale, rapidly growing contamination of Christianity in England by a pagan, anti-Christian idolatry. Burton quoted the same passages from 2 Corinthians on the title page of *Truth's Triumph Over Trent* (1629), a pamphlet insisting on the necessary separation of the Church of England from the Church of Rome. Burton believed that the reformed English church had been recontaminated with a Catholic "Idolatry" that had to be "purged."[19] For Burton as for Prynne, these verses signify the absolute distinction between the true Communion of the Christian church and the idolatrous Communion of the Roman Catholic church, identified with the devils, darkness, and Belial.

When the civil war broke out, Francis Cheynell invoked the same ominous "golden Cup" in the hand of the Whore of Revelation,

inciting Parliament to fight against Rome/Babylon, as she had
infiltrated the English church: "those that drink of this amorous
Cup, full of enchantments, are bewitched and drunk, or else they
would never worship the Beast, and the Devill."[20] They are, as it
were, the crew of Comus. With its cup, its richly symbolic language,
and its plot of enchantment and seduction, Milton's *Comus*, both
when first performed in 1634 and when published in 1637 and 1645,
would have had a potent, polemical currency; its religious ideological stance would likely have been clear to John Egerton, first Earl
of Bridgewater, for whom the masque was written and performed.
Despite some uncertainty about his allegiance during the Revolution, Bridgewater has been identified as a moderate puritan or
puritan sympathizer.[21] Even if Bridgewater was not puritan-minded
the distinctly reformist cast of the masque would have been appropriate, for as Michael Wilding observes, "Ludlow [where *Comus* was
performed] and the Marches bordered an especially benighted
district, one of 'the dark corners of the land'" where Catholicism
and pagan superstition survived. Upon becoming archbishop in
1633, Laud had ended the active program for bringing the supposed
enlightenment of reformed religion to Wales. Thus the threat of
Catholicism would have felt particularly imminent in 1634.[22]

The Attendant Spirit's first speech describing Comus' coming to
England is suggestive of Catholic infiltration. Born in the south, off
the coast of Italy, Comus has roved "the *Celtic* and *Iberian* fields" (line
60), and now "At last betakes him to this ominous Wood" (line 61) in
the heart of England. It is telling that the progress of Comus begins
in Italy, the center of Catholicism, and moves through the Catholic
countries of Spain and France. The references to the "*Celtic* and
Iberian fields" recall the common belief that many of the Irish had
migrated from Spain, which explained their Catholicism and supposed barbarity.[23] But we might also recall Christopher Hill's
remark that "There had been alarm about the possibility of a
Spanish [Catholic] landing in Wales in 1587, 1597, 1598, 1599, 1603,
and 1625."[24] Though Comus' genealogy is pagan, Milton assumes
the essential identity of the pagan (particularly the Roman) and
Catholic that figures in so much puritan, anti-Catholic discourse.
Comus has invaded Protestant England, threatening to entice its
people to his religion, already having a "monstrous rout" (line 533)
of followers. The seduction of the Lady is presented as a key
moment that would confirm his hold in England.

The arrival of Comus, armed with his poisonous cup, signifies the renewed threat of pagan-Catholic idolatry in England that obsessed puritans, who believed that changes in the worship of the church in the late 1620s and the 1630s signaled its corruption by Catholic, carnal practices. Comus represents not only a secular misuse of the body and of natural pleasures, but a false, thoroughly carnal religion, replete with "rites" (line 125) and "Priests" (line 136).[25] Here, as in the anti-prelatical tracts, a carnal life symbolizes carnal worship. Comus vows that "none" of Cotytto's rites will be "left out" (lines 128–37), echoing the Laudian insistence that all rites of worship be meticulously performed. In recalling Juvenal's condemnation of Rome for following the orgiastic rites of Cotytto,[26] Milton suggests an ominous parallel between contemporary Engand and degenerate Rome. Moreover, Comus' turning religion into pleasure not only anticipates Milton's explicit attack on the voluptuous clergy in his anti-prelatical tracts but evokes the charges puritans were making about the ceremonial worship of England. Bastwick described Laud and his prelates as "LAZY BELLIGODS," "*Epicures*" who want to rule Christ's church according to their lusts rather than his Word (*Answer*, pp. 18, 19). According to Prynne, the "voluptuous" prelates are interested not in the "Kingdome of Grace" but the "Kingdome of Pleasure," where they "wallow in *ease*" (*Lord Bishops*, pp. 7–8). As early as 1628 Alexander Leighton called the prelates and their supporters "the belly-God crew," "*Lords of Misrule*, and *Great Masters of Ceremonies*" who are bringing the king and state into danger.[27] In the *Animadversions*, Milton would insist that the whole "band" of clergy defending the worship and episcopacy of the Church of England are "subject to carnall desires" (1, 666, 701). To read *Comus* in relation to Milton's anti-prelatical tracts is to recognize his early radicalism, the sharp polemical engagement of the masque. In 1634 Milton was already concerned with the very issue of carnal, "popish" idolatry that would preoccupy him in the early 1640s and that had enraged the critics of Laudian ceremonialism from the late 1620s on.[28]

Through language, image, and narrative, Milton subtly but firmly links Comus with what puritans understood as a carnal, bewitching, seductive presence in the church – originally foreign but now establishing roots in England. Comus is not only a promoter of the "pastimes" encouraged by Charles and the Book of Sports. He is a master of disguise, "blear illusion," "charms," "dazzling Spells" (lines 150–5), spectacle, and magic, who uses the music of "Flute" and "Pipe" to "Stir up" his listeners to "wanton" behavior (lines 172–6) – all of which details were identified in puritan, anti-ceremonial discourse with the increasingly ceremonial religious worship of the English church.

The outrage caused by the ceremonial practices of John Cosin of Durham Cathedral helps us understand the charged resonance of Milton's masque. Warning about the dangers facing the English church, puritan attacks on Cosin reveal a link between carnality, idolatry, seduction, and enchantment that is strikingly similar to the masque. Milton may well echo the puritan attack on Cosin and his clerical cohorts at Durham, but it is unnecessary to identify Comus with a single figure such as Cosin or Laud since he represents the threat of false carnal religion that Milton suggests is ever present in the world, waiting for opportunities to manifest itself.

In 1627, Cosin published *A Collection of Private Devotions*, which struck some readers as suspiciously Catholic. Commonly referred to as his "Cozening Devotions," it was attacked in print by Burton and Prynne. On July 7, 1628, Peter Smart preached an inflammatory sermon in Durham Cathedral reprimanding Cosin's ceremonial practices as superstitious and popish, and calling the bishops Rome's "bastardly brood."[29] Smart was censured, but his sermon was published and he repeatedly attempted to bring charges against Cosin and others in Durham House (including Francis Burgoyne, Richard Hunt, and Augustine Lindsell), finally delivering formal Articles to Archbishop Harsnett and the High Commissioners in August 1630 before being himself deprived of ecclesiastical office and committed to prison, where he would remain for almost twelve years.

Smart's sermon criticized the "Babylonish," popish, "Antichristian" practices at Durham Cathedral. He was especially disturbed by a ceremonial devotion that perverted Holy Communion. His description of "the hallowed Priests [who] daunce about the Altar, making pretty sport, and fyne pastime, with trippings, and turnings, and crossings, and crouchings; while . . . Choristers, and singing-men . . . shout and cry, and make most sweet *Apollinian* harmony" (*Sermon*, pp. 22, 24) sounds very much like Comus and his "curst crew" (line 653), dancing, making an "unruly noise" (stage directions after line 92). "Methought it was the sound / Of Riot and ill-manag'd Merriment," says the Lady, "Such as the jocund Flute or gamesome Pipe / Stirs up" (lines 171–4). In his Articles against Cosin and his ceremonialist clergy, Smart condemned their "horrible profanation" of the sacrament "with all manner of musick, both instrumentall, and vocall, so lowde that the Ministers could not be heard, what they said, as if *Baachanalia*, the feasts of Bacchus . . . with fluits, and bag-pipes; with tymbrells and tabers; and not the Death and Passion of our Saviour Christ were celebrated."[30] Repeatedly mentioned in puritan criticisms of the church's ceremonial "innovations" in worship, the chanting, dancing, and "pipes" with their Bacchanalian associations became familiar symbols of the frivolity and carnality of the ceremonial service of the church.

In puritan polemic, this idolatrous ceremonial worship was associated with magic and enchantment. With his spells, disguises, and magic, Comus recalls the magic Spenser associated with his Roman Catholic sorcerer figures like Archimago, but also contemporary puritan descriptions of Cosin and other prelates who practiced ceremonial worship. Smart asked his congregation: "What . . . Ægyptian Sorcerers have bewitched you, that you should follow so readily such vaine superstitions[?]" (*Sermon*, pp. 27–8; cf. Articles, in *Correspondence of John Cosin*, p. 188). As Prynne warned, the "seducing Spirits" that threaten the church "dare not walke Unmasked"; they use a "cunning" and "inchanting manner" to "insnare" "overcredulous Christians" – an apt description of Comus' attempted seduction of the initially trusting Lady.[31] He offers her his "cordial Julep" (line 672), vaunting its power to "stir up joy" (line 677) and life, whereas it actually would transform her into one of his carnal brutes. Though the ceremonialists, too, defended external, sensible rites of worship for their ability to "stir" devotion, puritans objected that bodily rites pollute worship, turning what should be spiritual into something entirely carnal. Comus' method and intents are like the cunning, seductive idolaters Prynne describes, who sweeten their "bitter Potions, with Lushious, and sweete Ingreedients"; "their venome lurkes in Honie Potions, that so men may swallow it downe with greater greedinesse" (*Briefe Survay*, p. 1). Part of the danger and "perfect . . . misery" (line 73) of those who participate in Comus' rites and drink from his Communion cup is that they "Not once perceive their foul disfigurement" (line 74) – they are steadfast in their perverse religion, believing that a degrading rite (like the Mass) that makes them more carnal has actually made them "more comely than before" (line 75) – perhaps a glancing reference to the ceremonialist defense of the "comeliness" of ceremonies. Comus' followers lose their human visage and their individuality, becoming one of the "herd" (line 152), in Milton's parody of both Laudian conformity and Roman Catholic Communion.

With his spells, disguises, his wand and "enchantments," Comus is a "necromancer" and "foul enchanter" (lines 640, 649, 645). His magical transformation of his victims into disfigured, "brutish form[s]" (line 70) looks forward to Milton's comment in *An Apology* that the prelates "by their sorcerous doctrine of formalities . . . transforme [the people] out of Christian men into *Judaizing* beasts" (I, 932). The effect of Comus' wand, which "can unthread thy joints / And crumble all thy sinews" (lines 614–15), anticipates Milton's descripton in *Animadversions* of those ambitious Laudian clergy at the university, "unboning their Clergie limmes" in their dramatic performances (I, 887). When Comus takes away the Lady's power to move, imprisoning her "fixt and motionless" in his chair (line 819), we might think of Milton's comments in *An Apology* that those who adhere to the liturgy "loose even the legs of their devotion" (I, 938). Though Milton is not yet in 1634 rejecting the liturgy (the masque is deeply indebted to the liturgy for Michaelmas),[32] he is clearly already worried about the immobilizing effects of a ritualistic, idolatrous worship.

Comus is in many ways immensely attractive. Milton gives him the best, most beautiful, richest poetry in the masque. This sensuous attractiveness is a necessary part of Comus as he represents idolatry: idolatry would not be seductive were it not attractive. Yet the sensuousness of Comus' poetry may also suggest Milton's own attraction to the beauty and satisfactions of a ceremonial worship that engages the body – an attraction that will reappear in *Paradise Lost*.

Comus' pastoral disguise, signifying his clerical role, masks a thoroughly corrupt carnality. Like Prynne, who unmasks Cosin's supposedly evil designs, warning his audience "against all *Cozening* underminers" who threaten England's "liberties,"[33] Milton exposes the "cozen[ing]" (line 737) Comus. Milton and Prynne would become enemies in the 1640s, and Milton was probably never the zealot that Prynne was, yet for a while they shared similar concerns. The spelling of the original title, *A Mask* (rather than the more common "masque"), may play on the familiar sense of a dangerous deception that must be unmasked, suggesting the role of both author and audience in deciphering the hidden truth – a role that those attacking Montagu, Cosin, and other proponents of "popery" regularly adopted. All of Comus' actions aim to entice the innocent to his way of life, which is properly a religion as it makes nature, the body, and the appetites into a god, extinguishing the spirit – as Milton would say about the Laudian prelates who in their worship "make *God* earthly, and fleshly, because they could not make themselves *heavenly*, and *Spirituall*" (*Of Reformation*, 1, 520). Comus and his crew have "baits . . . To inveigle and invite th'unwary" who are lured to bestial "rites" (lines 528–38). In *Comus* as in Milton's anti-prelatical pamphlets, carnal rites make worshipers irredeemably carnal. When the Lady's elder brother warns that lust

> Lets in defilement to the inward parts,
> The soul grows clotted by contagion,
> Imbodies and imbrutes, till she quite lose
> The divine property of her first being   (lines 466–9)

what he describes as happening to the individual who succumbs to Comus is exactly what puritans from the late 1620s through the mid-1630s said was happening to the English church and its worshipers, made impure by the "contagion" of popish, pagan, carnal ceremonies. The "unpolluted temple of the mind" (line 461) has the potential to turn "by degrees to the soul's essence" (line 462), just as the church should be "refin'd" to a "Spirituall height" (*Of Reformation*, 1, 519). The alternative is to become polluted and decayed by carnal corruption – to be "drag[ged]" downwards into a "fleshly" "Service of the body" (*Of Reformation*, 1, 519–22). Like the Lady, the church in 1634 – and even more clearly in 1637 – stood in danger of carnal pollution, of losing the spirituality that made it the image of Christ.

It is within this context that we should understand the focus on chastity, seduction, and the threat of rape in *Comus*, all of which have religious and public significance and were not only matters of private, personal concern either to the Egertons, for whom the masque was first performed, or to the audience Milton's *Comus* reached in print.[34] I do not wish to erase the threat of rape and violence to the Lady in the masque, the sense of woman's vulnerability to male violence. But I would argue that here, as in so much seventeenth-century writing and thinking, the "private" or domestic and the public are deeply connected, and that public, religious concerns are inscribed in this seemingly most private encounter.

The plot of sexual seduction, with its threat to chastity, was a commonly recognized, highly charged figure for the temptation to false worship and idolatry. In both the language and plot of the masque, Milton's Lady becomes representative not just of the abstract ideals of Faith or Chastity but of the individual godly Christian and the godly church, as she faces seduction and finally the threat of violence. The Lady is symbolically associated with the Wandering Woman of Revelation 12, which reformers interpreted as the church in the latter days. She is Milton's pure but vulnerable representative of "the visible church of true believers" – a figure with whom Milton would empathize, especially in light of his strong "feminine identification."[35] His concern with the Lady's chastity anticipates his defense of his own personal chastity in *An Apology*, not just because of his own abiding psychological anxieties about purity, but because sexual chastity was in puritan discourse a figure for spiritual purity, which had to be maintained in the threat of a polluting carnal idolatry.[36]

The language of sexual pollution and seduction had long functioned as a trope for spiritual failing. The Hebrew prophets talked about idolatry in terms of whoredom, comparing spiritual unfaithfulness to God and sexual transgression or adultery.[37] Jeremiah castigated Israel for being a "harlot," "polluting" the land with "whoredomes" (3:1, 6, 8). God tells Ezekiel that Israel has committed "fornications" and "playedst the harlot" with her neighbors the Egyptians, the Assyrians, and the entire land of Canaan (16: 15–32). In betraying God, she is like a wife who has broken her covenant with her husband; seeking after false gods is like wanting other men. In the New Testament, Israel's marriage to God is replaced by the marriage between Christ and his spouse – the church and each faithful believer. The threat of unfaithfulness, however, remains and is again figured as sexual fornication, notably in Revelation 17, which describes the Whore of Babylon, "With whom the kings of the earth have committed fornication, and the inhabitants of the earth have been made drunk with the wine of her fornication" (17:2).

With the Protestant Reformation, fear of seduction to the whoredom of idolatry gained new currency as the Church of Rome was identified with the Whore of Babylon, and Christians were warned to resist the seductive allure of Catholicism. Spenser, particularly in the first book of *The Faerie Queene*, represented the danger of Catholic idolatry as a temptation to fornication and sexual pollution. Elizabeth I had made it treason to be a practicing Catholic or to harbor a priest, but Charles I, with his Catholic queen, took a softer stance towards Rome. Thus warnings against the seductions of Catholicism became more urgent, as "popish" ceremonialism seemed to have invaded England's worship.

Idolatry was thought to have a seductive potential. Smart's sermon warned his listeners to beware of those like Cosin who draw them to "spirituall fornication" through ceremonies such as bowing towards the altar: "Is not that woman a whore, who yeelds her body to an adulterer? . . . So say I, They are whores, and whoremongers, they commit spirituall fornication, who bow their bodies, before that Idol the Altar" (p. 26). His Articles detailed the ways in which Cosin and the other priests were corrupting their "seduced obeyers" (*Correspondence*, p. 183). From the late 1620s through the early 1640s, Burton and Prynne relentlessly complained of the "seducing Spirits" in the Church of England who were bringing people to "commit fornication with [the] Idols" of Rome.[38] As prosecuting lawyer in Laud's 1644 trial, Prynne explained the connection between sexual seduction and idolatry, quoting from the *Homily against peril of Idolatrie*: "Be not the Spirituall wickednesses of an Idols inticing, like the flatteries of a wanton Harlot? Be not men and women as prone to spirituall fornication (I mean Idolatry) as to carnall Fornication?"[39] In idolatry as in sexual lust, the soul is captured by a desire for the physical, by carnal appetites, and thus made fleshly.

Because in both Scripture and Christian writings the female body, either chaste and closed or open, had symbolically figured the state of spirituality – in either its purity or its pollution – Milton's Lady provided a ready figure for representing the godly Christian and the church, particularly as the church was in danger of being polluted by a carnal worship that (like Comus) required that the body be used in devotion. Comus' argument for using the body echoes the libertine, carpe diem poetry of Charles's court,[40] but it is also the analogue for a carnal devotion to the body that puritans believed characterized the ceremonial worship of Laudian prelates. Mocking the Lady's commitment to "the sage / And serious doctrine of Virginity" (lines 786–7), Comus tempts her to a sexual promiscuity that symbolizes spiritual adultery, understood as conformity with the Whore of Babylon.

While Laudians and conformists like Herbert insisted that the people owe obedience to the Church of England as to their mother (distinguishing the virtuous English matron from the supposedly wanton Roman whore), many of those who disliked the enforced ceremonial worship rejected the figure of the "Mother" Church of England as a degenerate feminization of Christ's church. In the masque, however, a feminine figure represents the church, and a masculine one idolatry. Milton's gendering here relies on the biblical metaphor of the church as "spouse" or bride, but resists the conventional construction of idolatry as feminine carnality. From one point of view, the masque's concern with the purity and chastity of a woman might seem merely to replicate partriarchal expectations – she will lose her value if "polluted." But from another, Milton in allowing Egerton's daughter Alice (as the Lady) to "represent" the church gives woman a central place in religion. Though Protestantism, in its emphasis on the priesthood of all believers, could encourage spiritual equality for women, it narrowed the possibilities for women's relation to the sacred in eliminating female models of devotion, as it prohibited adoration of the Virgin Mary and female saints and banned their images. Puritan anti-ceremonial discourse in the 1630s and early 1640s characteristically gendered the spirituality of the Gospel as a "masculine" purity: the believer was to keep separate from the pollution of bodily ceremonies identified with the feminine. As Stephen Marshall told Parliament in November 1640, "the true *Church* of *Christ* . . . are a virgin company, *not defiled with women*; that is, they were never guilty of the spirituall pollutions of that Apostaticall Church of *Rome*."[41] Though Milton often voices a similarly "masculinist" view, in *Comus* the Lady stands, not as a figure for idolatry, but as an exemplary model of devotion. Both she and Sabrina have an exalted place, and they look forward to Eve's (intermittent) associations with grace in *Paradise Lost.*

Milton's emphasis on the Lady's virginity is appropriate to the condition of Egerton's fifteen-year-old daughter, who performed that part. But Milton's privileging of virginity and chastity is also religiously significant. Her chastity opposes the decadent luxury of Comus, perhaps representing the Protestant emphasis on faith alone (*sola fide*), or the virginity of faith (*virginitas fidei*).[42] But the constructs of virginity and chastity are especially appropriate to a puritan view of the church as a minority of the godly few, beset with temptations to idolatry that must be resisted. For these virtues depend on exclusion, on maintaining clear boundaries, on resisting the threat of contaminating pollutions. Figured by a female body that must resist polluting invasion, chastity as the defining feature of the church and the godly Christian sharply opposes the Arminian emphasis on charity and on laying "open those *wider-Gates*" of the Christian church, as Laud put it in his *Conference . . . [with] Mr. Fisher the Jesuite* – an image of promiscuity that struck puritans as particularly appropriate to those supposedly in league with the Whore of Rome.[43] Laud's, Montagu's, and Cosin's arguments for an inclusive, "catholike" church seemed dangerous to fiercely anti-Catholic Protestants. Prynne's *Briefe Survay . . . of Mr. Cozens His Couzening Devotions* detailed the many parallels between Cosin's *Devotions* and those of the Roman Catholic church, objecting that both have the same "three Theologicall Vertues. *Faith, Hope, Charity*" (p. 59) – as if that alone could convict Cosin of being a Papist. Milton's substitution of "chastity" for "charity" in the traditional "faith, hope, and charity" – a substitution that has bothered some readers as mean-spirited – is no crypto-Catholic privileging of virginity, but clearly identifies him with the puritan position as it defines virtuous godliness as requiring opposition, resistance, and the exclusion of all contaminating elements. The puritan belief that spiritual purity requires exclusion, the maintenance of boundaries rigorously policed, probably received its most elegant, emblematic expression in Marvell's "On a Drop of Dew," where the vulnerable but resolved dewdrop's efforts are all expended on self-containment: "scarce touching" the beautiful rose "where it lyes" (line 10), the dewdrop (like the soul in the body, or the Christian in the world) excludes "the World" (line 29), trying to "inclose" (line 6) spirit within itself, fearing contamination by the seductive materiality that would impede its ascent.[44] Milton's celebration of chastity in the masque closely connects him with Marvell, whose poetry is intensely preoccupied with chastity and virginal purity.[45] It is indicative of changes in Milton that where the masque privileges the exclusive virtue of chastity, *Paradise Lost*, celebrating the holiness of sex in marriage, will privilege integrative "Love, / By name to come call'd Charity" (xii. 583–4).

In puritan discourse, chastity is not simply a personal virtue but the defining feature of the godly Christian and the church as they remain steadfast, "spotless," untouched by the pollutions of carnal idolatry and hence resisting spiritual fornication. The Lady's famous speech to Comus about chastity and the "serious doctrine of Virginity" (line 787) was added to the masque for the 1637 publication. This addition suggests an even more sharply polemical stance in the poem that aligns Milton with those who felt the purity of the church endangered.[46] The Lady's faith in "the Sun-clad power of Chastity" (line 782) associates chastity with grace and divine illumination, and it echoes the elder brother's praise of the power of chastity to protect her from harm:

> 'Tis chastity, my brother, chastity:
> She that has that, is clad in complete steel,
> And like a quiver'd Nymph with Arrows keen
> May trace huge Forests and unharbor'd Heaths,
> Infamous Hills and sandy perilous wilds,
> Where through the sacred rays of Chastity,
> No savage fierce, Bandit or mountaineer
> Will dare to soil her Virgin purity.   (lines 420–7)

As he offers a chivalric vision of the Lady defended by chastity, he declares a faith in its triumphant spiritual power, which is confirmed by the outcome of the masque despite the threats posed by Comus. This faith might well be glossed by Henry Burton, who recounts the remarkable story that bees will not sting a *"chaste"* person who comes among them. "But if an *adulterous person* come amongst them, they will quickly smell him out, and be all about his eares. And be sure, *Christs Bees* cannot brooke such *Priests*, as smell of the whore of Babels Smocke, and commit *spirituall whoredome* with her, or have any hankering affection after her."[47] For Burton as for Milton, to be chaste is to be untouched by carnal, popish idolatry; to succumb to the lure of idolatry, to be drawn to Rome, is to commit fornication and adultery (to "smell of the whore"). Comus' offer of the perverse cup of Communion (symbol of Roman Catholic idolatry) is thus also appropriately an invitation to embrace sexual pleasure.[48] The slippage in Comus' argument between tasting his potion and having sexual intercourse confirms rhetorically and logically the belief that idolatrous Communion *is* spiritual fornication. Quickly, Comus' temptation to drink becomes an invitation to sex, for fornication is the consummate image of idolatry.

In the puritan attacks on encroaching ceremonialism in the church, seduction was seen to yield to compulsion as the prelates first "seduced" the people to idolatrous worship and then "compell[ed]" them "violently" to perform their rites (Articles, in *Corre-*

spondence of John Cosin, p. 183) – a pattern reenacted in *Comus* as the enchanter first attempts to seduce the Lady and then threatens rape. As objectors to the innovations of ceremonial worship realized, pollution can be "enforced," not willing – a point made in Milton's later poem "On the New Forcers of Conscience Under the Long Parliament." Smart charged that Cosin threatened his worshipers – he "so terrifyed the people of Durham, that for feare of indangering theire salvation, by renouncing theire fayth, and baptisme, now they dare not but daunce after your phantastical pipe in evey idle ceremony" – and suggested that prelates elsewhere in England were similarly persecuting the godly.[49] Prynne told Parliament that the church and the faith "are now beset, and violently assaulted, by troops of forraine and domestique Enemies."[50] Milton's emphasis on the threat of violence and rape, on forced pollution, needs to be read within this contemporary puritan sense of the escalating dangers besetting the godly, while it also recalls the situation of Spenser's Una, who comes very close to being raped by Sansloy as she wanders in the wilderness (*The Faerie Queene*, 1.6.3–6). The elder brother's faith that the Lady's chastity will be protected may be right, but so are the younger brother's fears about her vulnerability to violation, injury, and a polluting "touch" (line 406). The Lady may keep her true faith intact, but her body can still be unwillingly polluted or she may suffer death like Sabrina or the martyrs of the Protestant faith.

For all the connections between Milton's masque and the puritan fears about the seductive dangers of idolatrous ceremony, Milton does not entirely reject ritual worship. He distinguishes between Comus' perverse sacrament of Communion, with its foreign, Italian roots, and the sacred, cleansing, baptismal, liberating waters of Sabrina, a native, English figure. Ceremoniously, the Attendant Spirit "invok[es]" Sabrina with the "power of some adjuring verse," his "warbled Song" (lines 854, 858). Rising from the Severn's water, singing a song, Sabrina "sprinkle[s]" "drops" from her "fountain pure" on the Lady's breast, "Thrice upon thy finger's tip, / Thrice upon thy rubied lip," and touches with her "chaste palms" the "marble venom'd seat / Smear'd with gums of glutinous heat" that hold the Lady fast (lines 911–18). Sabrina's role in freeing the Lady validates ritual, implying that it can be a means of divine grace, if it is performed by "a Virgin pure" (line 826). As Sabrina is associated both with the baptismal sacrament and with song and poetry, her redemptive presence in the masque identifies good ritual with poetry, conferring on poetry – and on Milton's verse – a transformative, liberating, even sacramental function that contrasts with the imprisoning Communion Comus offers.[51]

But Sabrina's role also suggests that the Lady (as representative of the individual Christian, and of the church) cannot of her own power free herself from Comus' power, and neither can her brothers. Though virtuous and resistant to the seductions of carnal idolatry, she has been deprived of the capacity for action. Haemony, which may represent the Word of God,[52] can protect the brothers from Comus' enchantment. It enables the godly to discern idolatry, to see through Comus' disguises (lines 644–9), and to engage in a righteous iconoclasm, "break[ing] his glass" (line 651). But once the Lady is immobilized by the demonic magic of idolatry and the brothers err through human frailty, an act of grace is necessary. The Lady's situation thus may intimate Milton's fears about the vulnerability of the English church, and his sense that it may take divine intervention to release her from enchantment, just as divine grace is necessary to save the individual. Even after the Lady has been freed, Comus, the spirit of idolatry, remains unconfined in England, ready (as the vigilant Attendant Spirit says) to "entice / With some other new device" (lines 940–1).

DIVORCING FROM IDOLATRY

Milton published *Lycidas* and *Comus* at the end of his 1645 *Poems* with the sense that they shared a prophetic quality vindicated by recent events. But while *Lycidas'* prophecy of the fall of prelacy seemed to have been fulfilled, the threats to true religion that preoccupied Milton in the masque had not disappeared. Despite parliamentary efforts to reform the church, idolatry remained rampant in England throughout the 1640s and 50s. In the polemical prose of these years, Milton's analysis of the need for domestic, civil, and political reform offered a fuller, more complicated understanding of idolatry which would have bearing on his late poems. By 1660, it would seem he realized that virtually no arena of life in England was untouched by the pollution of idolatry.

For Milton, religion and worship are implicated in all aspects of life. Religion always, inevitably, inscribes all human activity since all human acts exist in relation to God. Thus the issue of idolatry is not confined to his anti-prelatical pamphlets but informs his writing on domestic, civil, and political issues. Fighting for freedom in these various spheres, Milton represents liberty in distinctly religious terms as freedom from a bondage identified with carnal idolatry.

His divorce tracts extend the puritan ideology of religious reform as separation from impurity to the personal level, while suggesting the symbolic appropriateness of divorce as a remedy in the political sphere. The turn to the private sphere as locus of religious and political value anticipates *Paradise Lost*. The reform of domestic tyranny parallels the reform of religious worship and must precede reformation of the political state. If "houshold unhappines" weighs on a family like "tyranny" on the "Common-wealth" (II, 229) – if the relation of "one man to an ill mariage" is like "a whole people" in relation to "an ill Government" (229) – then the remedy of divorce has political applications. Milton's defense of divorce enables his later justification of the people's right to judge and depose an idolatrous tyrant – a right analogous to the husband's right to put away an "unfit" spouse – and anticipates the symbolic attention divorce will receive in *Samson Agonistes*.

The canon law prohibiting divorce is another instance of "Custome" and carnal human inventions (II, 222) that conflict with the Word of God, the sole authority for marital practices as well as church worship. But whereas puritan discourse, following Paul, identified the "Old Testament" with the flesh that must be abandoned in pursuit of the spirit, Milton seeks to "harmonize" New Testament pronouncements on divorce and marriage with those in the Hebrew Bible, signalling a break from his anti-prelatical tracts and the presbyterians, who argued that on these matters, too, the Gospel abrogated the Mosaic laws.[53] Thus the divorce tracts at once push puritan ideology to a further, personal, domestic application and mark his separation from orthodox puritanism.

In *The Doctrine and Discipline of Divorce* Milton claims to be single-handedly going against the weight of tradition. Separating himself from the presumed carnality of tradition, his own rhetorical stance enacts the divorce from a carnal, "spiritles mate" (II, 251) that he recommends. Rejecting in both writing and marriage a mistaken notion of community, he privileges separation over a false conjunction in a way that mirrors his religious position in the anti-prelatical tracts, where reformation requires separation from the carnal and ungodly so that the godly can follow the demands of the spirit.

Milton suggests that, in following the canon law of the pre-Reformation Catholic church, the English church has actually retained the Catholic notion that marriage is sacramental, despite officially removing marriage from the sacraments. The English Reformation is thus incomplete. The same idolizing impulse lies behind the English prohibition of divorce and remarriage as behind the Catholic sacramentalization of marriage: to make an "unfit" marriage "indissoluble" makes marriage a "transcendent command" (II, 276). Those who prohibit divorce turn marriage, ordained and blessed by God, into an idol, for they have "advanc't" "Matrimony . . . *above all that is called God*" (226) and made it "a goddesse" (277). The inventors of canon law have even turned Christ's words into a fixed, idolatrous statue: "our Saviours words touching divorce, are as it were congeal'd into a stony rigor" (II, 237–8). Scripture, when its spirit is missing, becomes a dead idol.

Conceptually, the divorce tracts are closely bound to the anti-prelatical tracts, as Milton shows how the idolatry of the Laudian church is replicated in the English institution of marriage. He draws a telling analogy between the "superstition" that makes marriage indissoluble and the superstition "of Ceremonies in the Church" (II, 228). Much as these ceremonies degrade religion in their attention to the body, so those who follow canon law have turned marriage into a carnal rather than spiritual bond. The sole criterion for either marriage or divorce is now whether the partners are "suitably weapon'd to the lest possibilitie of sensuall enjoyment" (236). In allowing for divorce only in cases of "naturall frigidity" (242) or impotence or "some unaccomplishment of the bodies delight" (246), the followers of canon law have made "carefull provision against the impediment of carnall performance" (248), but they are unconcerned if "the minde hangs off in an unclosing disproportion" (246) and is "deficient and unable to performe the best duty of mariage," apt conversation (248). They have taken what God ordained and made it fleshly, just as the prelates had degraded God's spiritual worship in the church.

Moreover, the Laudian attempt to prescribe a bodily performance of worship – making what is "indifferent" compulsory – finds its counterpart in the insistence that the performance of sexual intercourse constitutes the essential bond of marriage. Under the traditional, canonical understanding of marriage, "to grind in the mill of an undelighted and servil copulation" becomes the "forc't work of a

Christian mariage" (258) – an ugly image of compulsory sexual labor that glances back to the enforced ceremonial conformity of the Laudian church and looks forward to *Samson Agonistes*, where again bondage, idolatry, and sexual subservience to a woman will meet. When the English reformed church insists that marriage can only be dissolved for adultery or for impotence, they make carnal conjunction of bodies the essence of marriage, much as the ceremonialists had made the performance of bodily ceremonies the essence of religious worship. Even before the explicit indictment of the presbyterians in *Areopagitica*, Milton implies that the presbyters, if they refuse to reform marriage, are no different than the Laudian prelates.

Insisting instead that the mental, inward, and spiritual connection between partners constitutes the essence of marriage, Milton reconstructs marriage as conforming to the "puritan" idea of religious worship as inward and spiritual. His distinction between idolatry and true religion is reinscribed in the domestic sphere of marital relations. He privileges the mental and spiritual component in marriage much as he had in his discussion of religious worship: a "minde" "inaccessible" to "due conversation" is far worse than "a body impenetrable" (II, 250) and thus should be the true grounds of divorce. Milton persistently spiritualizes marriage, revising "due conversation" to refer exclusively to mental and verbal (not sexual) intercourse, reinterpreting the assertion that love "*is stronger then death*" in the Song of Songs to refer only to the "pure . . . desire" of the soul "of joyning to it self in conjugall fellowship a fit conversing soul" (251), and insisting that Paul's advice "*It is better to marry then to burne*" refers not to "fleshly" "burning" but to the "rationall burning" of a soul to join with another soul (251). The primal "lonelinesse" that God ordained marriage to remedy was not physical but the "lonelinesse [of] the mind and spirit of man" (246). Where Donne, with his sacramental sense of the interconnection of body and soul, had suggested in "The Extasie" that souls join *through* sexual intercourse, that the body is necessary for the soul to experience joy in this life, Milton here insists that souls merge without the assistance of bodies, his grotesque images of sexual intercourse implying that conjunction of bodies is repulsive and degrading – a matter of "servil copulation" (258), being joined to "an image of earth and fleam" (254). Though some readers have seen in this tract a monism that anticipates *Paradise Lost*, Milton's discussion of love and marriage in *The Doctrine and Discipline of Divorce* is actually grounded on the same body/soul, outer/inner dualism that undergirds the puritan ideology of worship and that structured his anti-prelatical tracts.[54] Marriage no more exists when its soul is absent than religious worship when the spirit is missing. When there is no love or union of souls in marriage, there is just "the outward formalitie" (II, 269), "the empty husk of an outside matrimony" (256), which like the empty outward form of ceremonies is "no way acceptable to God" (*Tetrachordon*, II, 630) and must be discarded. Just as the ceremonies of the Laudian church enslaved English Christians in worship, so the superstitious idol of matrimony has enslaved the English in their homes. Marriage without possibility of divorce becomes intolerable "bondage" (*Martin Bucer*, II, 431), and without the spirit of love, compulsory sexual intercourse in marriage becomes rape, "the lowest slavery that a human shape can bee put to" (*Tetrachordon*, II, 625–6). The "mis-interpreting of some Scripture" has turned "matrimony . . . into a drooping and disconsolate houshold captivitie" (II, 235) – a captivity analogous to bondage in an idolatrous, ceremonial church, or what Luther had called the *Babylonian Captivity of the Church* (1520). Bondage to a carnal, formalist view of marriage results from a carnal reading of Christ's words, which attends only to the "letter" or the body of Scripture, ignoring its spirit (II, 242, 280). All Christ's pronouncements – including his seemingly absolute prohibition of divorce (Matthew 19:6, "What therefore God hath joyned together, let not man put asunder") – must be read according to the spirit of "charity" (*Tetrachordon*, II, 588), which allows Milton even to revise Christ's sentence to read: what God has "put assunder" (two incompatible people) should not be joined "by compulsion" (II, 651).

The individual must be free to divorce an unfit mate, in part because the quality of marriage affects religious devotion. Anticipating the religious role of marriage in *Paradise Lost*, Milton suggests that the personal, domestic relation of marriage mirrors and influences one's relation to God. In a bad marriage, the inevitable "dejection of spirit" prevents a person from properly serving God since a bad marriage produces "wrath, the canker of devotion" (*Tetrachordon*, II, 259–60). But in a good marriage, the strong bonds of peace and love foster harmony with God. In marriage, Milton stresses the primacy of the (male) individual's need to find the solace of love that will cure radical "loneliness"[55] – and of his need to connect with God – much as the anti-prelatical tracts glorified the individual as the true "temple" of God. Divorce becomes a personal, spiritual right. The completion and happiness of the individual trapped in a carnal marriage require the breaking of communal bonds, much as the salvation of the Protestant individual requires him to leave the community of the ungodly church.

Milton puts puritan ideology – with its notion of the necessity of the godly separating from carnal idolatry – to the task of reforming marriage. *Colasterion* takes the foundational Pauline analogy between the relation of husband and wife and Christ and the church (Ephesians 5:22–5) – the very analogy used by the English and Catholic churches to prohibit divorce – and turns it to argue for divorce:

if the husband must bee as Christ to the Wife, then must the wife bee as the Church to her husband. If ther bee a perpetual contrariety of minde in the Church toward Christ, Christ himselfe threat'ns to divorce such a Spouse, and hath often don it. If they urge, this was no true Church, I urge again, that was no true Wife. (II, 732)[56]

The Reformation is understood as Christ's divorce from a church that was not a "true spouse," and it sanctifies divorce in the service of reconstituting a true marriage. Divorce becomes the logical extension and symbol of the Reformation. It is thus appropriate that Milton quotes in support of marital divorce the same passages that Burton and Prynne quote to incite the English godly to cast off the pollutions of idolatry: "*Mis-yoke not together with Infidels*"; "*What fellowship hath righteousnesse with unrighteousnesse? what communion hath light with darknesse? what concord hath Christ with Beliall?*"; "*come out from among them, and be ye separate*" (2 Corinthians 6:14, 15, 17; II, 262).

Separation and divorce are not ends but the means for achieving true communion in both the church and marriage. The aim is to reconstruct both a true church and the "sweet and gladsome society" of a good marriage (II, 254). Milton imagines a fully integrative marriage that is physical and spiritual, that in integrating the whole person and the two partners brings them closer to God and thus recaptures an originary Edenic condition.[57] Yet it is a far from untroubled monism that asserts that the world began with God's "divorcing command" and will be "renewed" at the end "by the separating of unmeet consorts" (II, 273).

THE IDOL OF LICENSING

When presbyterians condemned Milton's divorce writings as heretical and blasphemous, Herbert Palmer even advising Parliament to burn Milton's book,[58] they proved themselves, in Milton's eyes, defenders of idolatry, despite their professed goal of reforming the church. The hostile reception of his divorce tracts, coupled with Parliament's Licensing Order of June 16, 1643, prompted Milton's *Areopagitica* (November, 1644), which exposed yet another form of idolatry that was part of the fabric of English life.

Modern readers tend to see *Areopagitica*, even more than *The Doctrine and Discipline of Divorce*, as a progressive work concerned with civil liberty, ignoring how thoroughly religion was interwoven with seemingly secular matters. But the obsession with idolatry is as critical to Milton's argument for liberty of printing as it was to his defense of divorce. For if indissoluble marriage was one form of idolatry hindering the Reformation in England, licensing was another. Much like the 1634 masque which began by describing Comus' suspiciously popish genealogy, *Areopagitica* traces the origin of licensing to Catholicism. It, too, is a foreign import. The Council of Trent and the Spanish Inquisition "engendring together brought forth, or perfeted those Catalogues, and expurging Indexes that rake through the entralls of many an old good Author" (II, 503). As a "project" of the Inquisition (II, 493), licensing is an invention of Antichrist, the enemy of God and the Reformation, an instrument of popish idolatry enthusiastically "catcht up by our Prelates" (II, 493). That the very people like Prynne who had been victims of Laud's censorship now want to regulate the press to prevent heresy and schism shows how thoroughly this Catholic practice has infiltrated Protestant England, and proves that "Bishops and Presbyters are the same to us both name and thing" (539).

As in his discussion of marriage, Milton suggests an analogy between the civil sphere and the church, showing how idolatry and false religion pervade areas of social experience we tend to think of as separate from the church and thus free from religious value. For Milton, the licenser or censor assumes the position of the humanly ordained priest, interposing himself between God and the individual conscience. It betrays the divine spirit, implanted within each human being, to submit to the "judgement" of another person, which is precisely what happens when licensers determine what books one will read. Like the Pope, the licenser usurps God's authority in presuming "the grace of infallibility" (521). As a human invention, licensing is an idol that functions precisely like prelacy in the anti-prelatical tracts or divorceless marriage in the divorce tracts. Licensing forces people to bow down to a false God (the licenser), imprisoning their conscience and judgment in yet another form of idolatrous bondage.

In defending the individual's responsibility to seek truth, Milton at once pushes puritan ideology to its extreme and transforms some of its assumptions in ways that paradoxically bring him close to certain emphases of the English Arminians who had supported ceremonial worship. The radical Protestant notion of the priesthood of all believers and the puritan privileging of the inner spirit rather than outward forms enable Milton's claim that each person, guided by the divine spirit within, must seek truth for him- or herself and thus must be free to read all books. But this emphasis on "freedom to choose" (527) rejects the Calvinist determinism of orthodox puritanism for an Arminian belief in free will.[59] Moreover, when Milton asserts that "good and evill . . in the field of this World grow up together almost inseparably" (514), he has moved far from the position of Burton or Prynne, who imply that it is easy to separate truth from error, good from evil, light from darkness – and far, indeed, from the easy oppositions of his own earlier masque. Milton now has a far more complex sense of the difficulty of distinguishing between good and evil, truth and error: "the knowledge of good is so involv'd and interwoven with the knowledge of evill, and in so many cunning resemblances hardly to be discern'd, that those confused seeds which were impos'd on *Psyche* as an incessant labour to cull out, and sort asunder, were not more intermixt" (514). The task is still, as for Prynne or Burton, to "sort asunder" good and evil – and Milton throughout his polemical writing will continue to draw absolute distinctions between himself and his "adversar[ies]," between the cause of truth and the various manifestations of error in his world – but it is an arduous, ongoing task. Milton's insistence that we are "purifie[d]" by "triall" (515) retains the puritan notion that conflict and opposition are a necessary part of the Christian life, but purity is no longer a state or condition (or even a goal) but a *process*, one which is presumably never complete in this life just as the dismembered pieces of "Truth" will not be completely reassembled until the end of time (549). And the separation of good and evil, truth and falsehood, is a labor that each individual must perform for him- or herself. Thus each person must be free to read books "promiscuously" (517) – a key word that departs from the emphasis on chastity and exclusion in *Comus* and evokes the earlier Arminian argument of Montagu and Laud that the church should be "open" to all, only now it is the individual (the true temple) that enlarges its boundaries.

Fearing heresy and "schism" and wanting to preserve a sense of community from the threat posed by the individualist tendencies of Protestantism, the presbyterian Parliament wanted a conformity not entirely unlike that imposed by the prelates. In *The Tenure of Kings and Magistrates* and *Eikonoklastes*, Milton warned that the imposition of the *Directory of Worship* would simply replace the Book of Common Prayer with a different kind of "sett Forms" in worship (III, 508).[60] As the Restoration drew close, Milton continued to argue that the "final judge . . . in matters of religion" can "only" be the individual "conscience" illuminated by the Holy Spirit in reading the Scripture (*Treatise of Civil Power in Ecclesiastical Causes*, VII, 242–3). If idolatry lies in revering human invention rather than God, then legislating religious belief or practice constitutes idolatry. Thus Milton's last published work, *Of True Religion, Haeresie, Schism, Toleration* (1673), would take the final logical step and redefine heresy, not as an individualistic or heterodox belief but as religious conformity: "Heresie . . . is a Religion taken up and believ'd from the traditions of men" (VIII, 421).

But this radical position is already implicit in *Areopagitica*, as Milton rejects any kind of community based on a conformity that binds the individual conscience, erasing difference. Individuals are to be united not by shared dogma or by externally imposed conformity, but by the fact that they all, individually, participate in the same process of discovering truth for themselves. If licensing and civil restrictions are understood in terms of idolatry, freedom of the press and the sociopolitical reform Milton expects are also imagined in religious terms. Rejecting the "outward union of cold . . . and inwardly divided minds" (II, 551) – a phrase which echoes his description of a bad marriage – Milton constructs a different kind of unified community in which separateness and distinctions are part of the fabric, and this community is essentially religious:

there must be many schisms and many dissections made in the quarry and in the timber, ere the house of God can be built. And when every stone is laid artfully together, it cannot be united into a continuity, it can but be contiguous in this world; neither can every peece of the building be of one form; nay rather the perfection consists in this, that out of many moderat varieties and brotherly dissimilitudes that are not vastly disproportionall arises the goodly and the gracefull symmetry that commends the whole pile and structure. (555)[61]

In Milton's hands, Solomon's temple, which Laudians had invoked to support uniformity in ceremonial worship, is made to testify to the importance of individual differences and nonconformity. Milton envisions, replacing the ceremonialists' and the presbyterians' notions of conformity, a community of dissimilar, unique individuals who will always be separate, touching only contiguously, yet in their variety and differences creating a beautiful structure.

MONARCHY AND IDOLATRY

Such a community, however, would be impossible so long as England had a king. From 1649 until the end of Milton's life, despite hopes raised by the execution of Charles I, monarchy – that deeply ingrained institution – was one of the most difficult obstacles to the reconstruction of true religion. For Milton, monarchy was inextricably linked with idolatry: the "dark roots" of "Tyranny and fals Religion" "twine and interweave one another in the Earth, though above ground shooting up in two sever'd Branches" (*Eikonoklastes*, III, 509). In defending the right of the people to have deposed, tried, and executed Charles I, *The Tenure of Kings and Magistrates* distinguished between a good king and an absolute monarch or tyrant, as if Milton was not attacking the institution of monarchy. But eight months later in *Eikonoklastes*, he unconditionally rejected monarchy as a condition in which the people are "a multitude of Vassalls in the Possession and domaine of one absolute Lord" (III, 458). What bothered Milton (who never seriously considered a limited monarchy) was that a king arrogates power to himself, assuming the position of God and making his subjects' desires completely dependent upon his will, much as Calvinist determinism imagines the relation between powerless, meritless human beings and an all-powerful, wilful God.

Like the Pope, Laudian prelates, makers of canon law, and presbyterian licensers, Charles has "with incomparable arrogance" assumed the "abilitie of judging for other men," making "his own will" the rule and standard of everything (*Eikonoklastes*, III, 417, 416).

The absolutist ideology embraced by Charles and his defenders – the notion that kings are above the law – inevitably produces religious idolatry since it encourages the people to "adore" their king (*Tenure*, III, 237). Such idolatry seemed most obvious in the *Eikon Basilike*, which, presenting the dead King Charles as a Christ-like martyr, was idolized by the "vulgar" who "set it next the Bible" (III, 363, 339). In *Eikonoklastes*, Milton exposes the king as an idolater, who in his reign fashioned himself as a god and now even after death presents his image to be worshiped. The idolatrous image of Charles, not only in the famous frontispiece but also inscribed in the text, must be destroyed just as Parliament had ordered the destruction of all monuments of idolatry in all cathedrals and churches.[62] Because "the People . . . are prone ofttimes not to a religious onely, but to a civil kinde of Idolatry in idolizing thir Kings" (III, 343), reform of the church alone is insufficient. Religious and civil forms of idolatry are virtually inseparable and mutually sustaining. In *Eikonoklastes*, Milton dismantles what was thought to be the king's word, chapter by chapter, sentence by sentence, deconstructing the very notion of monarchy, exposing it as a design of arrogant individuals from Nimrod through Caligula and later tyrant-kings to deify themselves and reduce the people to "Slaves" (III, 462). Particularly heinous is hereditary monarchy, as in England, which exalts "one person and his Linage" into "an absolute and unaccountable dominion" over the people and their "posterity" (III, 486–7), reducing the people to property that is "owne[d]" and inherited, like "slaves or cattle" (*Defence of the People of England*, IV, i, 471–2). It amazes Milton that the English, "like men inchanted with the *Circoean* cup of servitude," are drawn to monarchy (*Eikonoklastes*, III, 488). The presbyterians, who earlier had opposed the king, are "againe intoxicated . . . with these royal, and therfore so delicious because royal rudiments of bondage, the Cup of deception" and are surrendering to Charles's "glozing words and illusions" (*Eikonoklastes*, III, 582). In recalling Comus' deceptive attractions and the cup of false Communion in the masque, this language firmly associates monarchy with the seductions of religious idolatry. Under rule by a king, individuals surrender their reason, their free will, their spirit, and thus become a herd, an indistinguishable multitude of carnal creatures, a false community – just as Milton believed happened in the Roman and Laudian churches under the bondage of fleshly ceremonies.

Charles imposed idolatry on the nation, not only by insisting on being worshiped, but also by importing a popish ceremonial worship and persecuting true worship. All the "superstition" of the Laudian church, Milton charged, "issu'd out originally" from the king's "Autority" (*Eikonoklastes*, III, 359). Charles put the people under the "servile yoak of Liturgie," forcing them into "a Pinfold of sett words" (*Eikonoklastes*, III, 505), and turning the Church of England into "his old *Ephesian* Goddess" (III, 571). As an "Uxorious," effeminate king "govern'd" by his Catholic wife (III, 421), Charles in his private, domestic state mirrors the feminization of religion and the people's enslavement by the emasculating seductions of a popish idolatry now clearly identified with the feminine.

Nothing more clearly shows the association of monarchy with idolatry than Milton's increasingly pointed references to 1 Samuel 8, which describes how the Israelites got a king. Having been ruled by prophet-judges (who represent Milton's sense of himself as well as his ideal of the wisest and best men who would constitute a ruling council in the commonwealth described in *The Readie and Easie Way*), the Jews became dissatisfied with Samuel's sons and asked for a king. In *The Tenure*, Milton cites 1 Samuel 8 to explain the origin of monarchy among God's people, suggesting that monarchy is related to the Jews' bondage (III, 202).[63] The first *Defence* (1651) gives fuller atention to the issue of idolatry as he quotes 1 Samuel 8:7–8 to prove that the Jews' desire for a king was not so much a desire for political change as an idolatrous defection from the Hebrew God:

"They have not rejected thee, but they have rejected me, that I should not reign over them, according to all the works which they have done wherewith they have forsaken me, and served other gods." The meaning clearly is that it is a form of idolatry to ask for a king who demands that he be worshipped and granted honors like those of a god. (IV, i, 369)

As Milton reads the biblical history of the Jews, monarchy is from the first implicated in idolatry. "Affecting rather to resemble the heathen" than retain the government of "God's own ordaining," the "gentilizing *Israelites*" wanted a king to be like the neighboring idolaters, who worshiped false gods (*Readie and Easie Way*, VII, 449–50). The desire for a king is an impulse in the chosen or the godly to conform to heathen idolatry, and the book of Samuel shows the Jews in the process of losing their status as God's chosen.

As God was the Jews' only king before Saul, so for Christians the "only King" is Christ (*Tenure*, III, 256). For Milton, politics cannot be thought of apart from religion. He finds that both Deuteronomy 17 (first *Defence*, IV, i, 344) and the New Testament privilege the order of a commonwealth as most conducive to true worship. Christ "forbids" his disciples and followers to have the "heathenish government" of monarchy (*Readie and Easie Way*, VII, 424). A "free Commonwealth" comes nearest the "precept of Christ" (*Readie and Easie Way*, VII, 425) because it encourages each individual's faithfulness to God rather than obedience to the will of a king. Milton's republicanism is indebted not only to republican Rome but to the biblical description of Israel as a commonwealth before their descent into monarchy. But in his Christian Commonwealth, the people would be ruled by the inward illumination of the divine spirit.

Thus though the commonwealth of the Israelites provides Milton with a pattern for political order, the Jews embody the carnality which is a continual temptation to the English. For England to be the true Israel they must become a spiritual Israel, purged of the carnality that is the sign of the Jews' bondage. Jason Rosenblatt has astutely described Milton's rejection of the Hebraism of the divorce tracts in the late *De Doctrina Christiana* and the final books of *Paradise Lost*, observing a change from the "hopeful nationalistic tracts of the 1640s, in which he views England as a second Israel under a benign moral Mosaic law."[64] But the anti-Judaic stance was already present in the anti-prelatical tracts. From 1649 on, Milton firmly distanced himself from the Jews in his prose; his references to them and his comparisons of the English to the Jews are persistently, deeply, and increasingly negative. *The Tenure of Kings and Magistrates* remarks that "the people of Asia, and with them the Jews also, especially since the time they chose a King against the advice and counsel of God, are noted by wise Authors much inclinable to slavery" (III, 202–3). The first *Defence* cites Aristotle's and Cicero's opinion that "the Jews and Syrians were born for" "slavery." Only the "few," "the wise," and "brave" – that is, the elect, the true Christians – can enjoy liberty (IV, i, 343). In order to fulfil their divine potential, to become the spiritual Israel, the English must break not just from the corruptions of Roman Catholicism but from the pattern of the Jewish past and become *unlike* the Jews, who are for Milton associated with the carnal, the unredeemed body, and hence with bondage and slavery.[65]

Perhaps Milton's ugliest image of the idolatrous, bondage-loving

English "rabble" occurs at the end of *Eikonoklastes*, where he remarks that with the *Eikon Basilike* Charles hoped to

catch the worthles approbation of an inconstant, irrational, and Image-doting rabble; that like a credulous and hapless herd, begott'n to servility, and inchanted with these popular institutes of Tyranny, subscrib'd with a new device of the Kings Picture at his praiers, hold out both thir eares with such delight and ravishment to be stigmatiz'd and board through in witness of thir own voluntary and beloved baseness. (III, 601)

The passage recalls Deuteronomy 15:12–17, which, after insisting that "an Hebrew man, or an Hebrew woman" who is a servant must be freed after six years, describes what should be done if a person decides to become a servant for life: "Then thou shalt take an aul, and thrust it through his ear unto the door, and he shall be thy servant for ever. And also unto thy maidservant thou shalt do likewise" (15:17). Amazed that anyone would choose bondage, Milton suggests the English are worse than the Hebrew bondslaves, since they offer "both . . . eares" with "delight" at the prospect of perpetual bondage.

The English people's debased and continued longing for a king, condemned at even greater length in *The Readie and Easie Way*, is a terrible inclination to idolatry that exceeds even that which Milton believed characterized the Jews. At least the Jews, after their Babylonian captivity, returned to their republican government (first *Defence*, IV, i, 354). But the English, having suffered the afflictions that God told the Jews would befall them under kings, and then having fought nobly for liberty and been delivered by God, still "basely and besottedly" want to "run their necks again into the yoke which they have broken" (*Readie and Easie Way*, VII, 427–8), which leads Milton at the end of *The Readie and Easie Way* to cry out with "the Prophet [Jeremiah], *O earth, earth, earth!*" (VII, 462; Jeremiah 22:29). Throughout, Milton echoes Jeremiah's warnings and diatribes against Israel for having forsaken God, for her "backslidings" after God had "broken [her] yoke" (Jeremiah 2: 19–20).[66] As Jeremiah said of the Israelites, the English have gone "backward, and not forward" (Jeremiah 7:24); they "set up altars to . . . burn incense unto Baal" (Jeremiah 11:13). It is crucial to our understanding of Milton's sense of his prophetic role in his later works to recall that for the Hebrew prophets (especially Jeremiah) not hope of reform but disgust and rage at rampant, incurable idolatry dominate their writings. What God tells Jeremiah would have seemed all too fitting to Milton's situation: "thou shalt speak all these words unto them; but they will not hearken to thee: thou shalt also call unto them; but they will not answer thee" (Jeremiah 7:27). Despite his own appropriation of a Hebraic prophetic role, to be like the Jews is, finally, for Milton the worst fate.

The persistent presence of idolatry in England belied the hopes of the early 1640s, expressed by the Root and Branch Petition, that it could be rooted out. Prelates, presbyters, the independent clergy who wanted to be supported by tithes (*Likeliest Means*, VII, 275), Charles I, the Long Parliament, and even Cromwell in his kingly aspirations (*Second Defence*, IV, i, 672–3) – all shared the same appetite for power that turned them into false gods and their subjects into idolatrous slaves. If Milton's representations of those he criticizes sound similar, it is because he presumes the essential identity of all forms of idolatry and all idolaters, who form a kind of satanic community, marked by a "conformity" that erases individuating identity.

In the 1630s and early 1640s, Milton wanted to purify the English church, to save it from the threat of a pagan-Catholic idolatry threatening to infiltrate it from outside. But the polemical prose of the Civil War and Interregnum shows that his understanding of idolatry became more complex as he sought to reform not just the church but the institutions and practices of marriage, the press, and political government. He discovered that idolatry was not simply located in church worship and was not a foreign import; it was part of the very fabric of English social experience, even of human nature – present in the private bed of marriage, the intercourse of print, and the relations between governors and governed. If such was the case, what hope could there be for reconstructing true worship, particularly when England was ready to welcome back a king? This was the difficult question addressed by Milton's final poems.

CHAPTER 7

John Milton: carnal idolatry and the reconfiguration of worship, part II, after the Restoration: the major poems

In May 1660, Charles II returned to the English throne. For Royalists, his return was like a providential Second Coming. It was greeted by bonfires, popular celebrations, and poetic tributes. Dryden's *Astraea Redux* compared the king to Christ as he recalled the star that had appeared at his birth, "Guiding our eyes to find and worship you" (line 291).[1] Eleven months later at his coronation, costly and lavish pageants, processions, and theatrical entertainments were orchestrated to present Charles II as a deified ruler. Paula Backscheider observes, "the coronation celebrations and ceremonies consisted of the rituals and mysteries of king worship." The coronation itself took place on a "stage" in Westminster Abbey.[2] All these proceedings would have confirmed Milton's distaste for a culture addicted to external shows, his conviction that monarchy and idolatry are inextricably linked, and his disillusioned assessment of the idolatrous longings of the English people.

Along with monarchy came a restored national church bent on forcing the consciences of the godly. Despite the king's initial promises of religious toleration and the presbyterian hopes for a church that would accommodate their beliefs, Parliament passed a series of acts that expelled puritan worship, orthodox as well as radical, from the established English church, thereby officially creating the category of religious Nonconformity or Dissent.[3] The Uniformity Act, which received Charles II's assent May 19, 1662, insisted that the Book of Common Prayer, with all rites, ceremonies, sacraments and public prayers, be used throughout England, and that only episcopally ordained clergy be recognized. According to its provisions, all clergy by the Sunday before St. Bartholomew's Day (August 24, 1662) publicly had to read "the morning and evening

187

prayer appointed to be read by and according to the said Book of Common Prayer at the times thereby appointed" and to declare before their congregations their "assent and consent to all and everything contained and prescribed" in the Book of Common Prayer or else lose their ecclesiastical benefices (*Documents*, p. 604). The Uniformity Act tried to force puritan clergy either to humiliate themselves by renouncing their former convictions – proving themselves the hypocrites their enemies thought them – or to leave the church. An estimated two thousand ministers were cast out of the church.[4] In an attempt to prevent ejected nonconformist clergy from establishing alternative churches, Parliament passed a Conventicle Act in 1664, and a second in 1670, prohibiting the religious assembly of "five persons or more assembled together" in nonconformist worship (*Documents*, p. 624). According to the first Conventicle Act, people attending these forbidden meetings were subject to fines or imprisonment – even banishment to the colonies for the third offense. The second Act eliminated prison and banishment, but added fines for offending preachers and for those who failed to inform or prosecute. The Five Mile Act of 1665 made it illegal for unlicensed preachers or clergy who refused to comply with the Uniformity Act to come within five miles of any town or parish where they had exercised "unlawful" religious authority, or within five miles of "any city or town corporate, or borough."[5]

For Milton as for other nonconforming English Protestants, such acts meant that idolatry had again been legislated as an instrument of political order and community. Ceremonialist worship was officially reestablished. The Prayer Book annexed to the Uniformity Act, though modestly revised, retained all the ceremonies, liturgy, and festivals that Milton and others had objected to, added new formal prayers of thanksgiving for the return of Charles II and commemorating the martyrdom of Charles I, and made no allowances for ministers' extempore prayers, which the presbyterian clergy had requested.[6] It has been said that Laudians like Cosin and Wren who were involved with the revision of the Prayer Book were disappointed, but surely the presbyterian clergy and more radical sectarians were more so. For the language of the 1662 Prayer Book clearly endorsed a ceremonial worship (referring to "priests" rather than "ministers"), and the practices of the Restoration church – the use of candlesticks, chancel screens, and bodily gestures of reverence such as making the sign of the cross or bowing – renewed the

Laudian ceremonialism, producing a more highly ceremonial worship than had characterized the Elizabethan and Jacobean churches. Ceremonialism even marked the execution and public display of the bodies of regicides and revolutionaries. As Thomas Corns well says, "Grisly ritual characterized the judicial style of the Restoration."[7]

For Milton, as for other nonconformists, true worship would necessarily be dissenting, private, and persecuted. Keeble has argued that the atmosphere of persecution gave Restoration nonconformity and nonconformist literature its identity, with Milton's Abdiel standing for the cause of nonconformity. Milton's turn to the spirit within is now well recognized as, not passive withdrawal after defeat, but a strongly dissenting and oppositional stance.[8] But still more can be said about the ways Milton's late poems engage the problem of true religion in a persecutory age of idolatry.

Paradise Lost, Paradise Regained, and *Samson Agonistes* all are marked by angry attacks on idolatry – some quite explicit, others more subtle, equivocal, indirect, as might be expected of literature produced during a time of persecution. The various devices nonconformists used to avoid detection in their meetings – trap doors or architectural contrivances, meetings at night, disguises, equivocation – have analogues in Milton's complex, often equivocal poetry, which could seem to support monarchy and ceremonial worship and reject rebellion while it actually remained true to his iconoclastic and subversive religious principles. As encoded histories of idolatry that spoke to the situation of Restoration England, Milton's poetry also constituted a site for true worship in an England polluted by idolatrous forms. All the major poems present characters who (however much we may be critical of them) are intended as models of true devotion, examples for an endangered nation. I would further suggest that Milton's focus on the private, domestic sphere in these poems (Adam and Eve's marital relation; the Son's solitary encounter with Satan and return home to his mother; Samson's confrontation with his estranged wife) is more closely related to religious concerns than has been recognized. His emphasis on the domestic not only shares the general tendency of persecuted nonconformity to cultivate interiority, the private, and the inward (an interiority with a subversive political resonance) but also aligns his poetry with the practices of nonconformist religious worship, which had to take place secretly in forests, fields, caves, barns, and

especially private homes.[9] The private house of the family became
the primary site for dissenting worship. Though we know virtually
nothing about Milton's own religious worship after the Restoration,
it most likely took place within the home – one might recall that *De
Doctrina Christiana* justified Communion in the home (VI, 557; Bk. 1,
chapter xxviii). His focus on the domestic relation in his late poetry
thus needs to be read, not simply as a sign of the move towards the
novel or romance or towards the secular privileging of the private
sphere of love,[10] but as an important marker of nonconformist
identity, bearing powerful religious significance.

PARADISE LOST: TRUE CREATIVITY VERSUS IDOLATROUS INVENTION

As a number of readers have recognized, *Paradise Lost* is an act of
worship. Michael Lieb has shown how the poet-priest celebrates
"the holy" in hymns of "adoration" addressed to God, and Regina
Schwartz has described the epic as a "sacred song" or prayer, a
liturgy commemorating and reenacting Creation. As an act of
worship, the poem seems to reach beyond the local, political
concerns of Milton's moment, echoing Christian rites and liturgy
that had a long history.[11] But its devotional stance is also firmly
grounded in the specific historical, cultural context of seventeenth-
century England, where worship was contested and divisive.

Milton's song to the Creator is intended to ward off a "chaos"
that is identified with the encroaching idolatry of Restoration
England.[12] Prayers, praise of God, and representations of true
devotion are repeatedly set against idolatrous perversions of worship
that had contemporary resonance. The poet, chosen by God,
replaces the priest ordained by the established church, and his
poetry replaces the public worship of England. Born of a sense of
isolation, even persecution ("fall'n on evil days . . . In darkness, and
with dangers compast round, / And solitude" [VII. 25, 27–8]), his
poetry not only is an act of devotion but serves as a safe place of
worship where the godly "fit audience . . . though few" (VII. 31) can
meet.

Conceived of as a temple, *Paradise Lost* is related to Herbert's
Temple, Harvey's *Synagogue,* and Crashaw's *Steps to the Temple.*[13]
Milton's poem, however, bears a quite different relation to the
material and devotional structures of the English church. Harvey's

and Crashaw's volumes poetically restore the forms and devotions abolished by the reforming Parliament of the early 1640s, thus reconfirming the forbidden ceremonial worship of the English church (and the Roman, in the case of Crashaw). The relation of Herbert's *Temple* to the material church is more complicated, the poems in one sense representing the external forms of the Church of England, but in another suggesting that worship is really the work of the heart. Insofar as Herbert privileges interiority and the spirituality of worship, he looks forward to Milton. But Milton's poem takes a self-consciously oppositional relation to the established English church that sets him apart from Herbert. Though *Paradise Lost* may incorporate rituals and echo traditional hymns and rites of the church, it replaces the material, institutional church and its supposedly idolatrous set forms with what Milton claims is inspired, extempore poetry that constitutes the true worship of God.

As a work of art in the service of God, Milton's Protestant poem, like Herbert's *Temple*, must confront the controversial issue of the role of invention in worship. The deep suspicion of "human invention," which underlies the puritan attack on ceremonial worship and pervades Milton's polemical prose, did not disappear when he turned to religious poetry. Herbert's anxieties were in part relieved by his sense of his poetry's place within the established church. But for Milton, the very stability of the Church of England and its forms was a mark of their idolatrous nature. Where Herbert's attention to visible form and shaped poems figures a ceremonialist devotion to the spiritual potential of art, Milton's turn to blank verse in his late poems is religiously as well as politically significant – the "bondage of Riming" (Hughes, ed., p. 210) being a poetic counterpart and symbol not only of political servitude but of the "Pinfold" (*Eikonoklastes*, III, 505) of liturgical, religious forms. His rejection of rhyme bespeaks a distrust of art as idolatry – a distrust that remains in tension with the abundant, generous creativity that produces in *Paradise Lost* what has been called an opulent, "almost Catholic, liturgy"[14] – a description Milton would have found shocking.

If Milton's poem was to be a place and means of worship, how could he avoid the idolatry of invention and justify his creativity? In *Eikonoklastes*, his most iconoclastic pamphlet of the late 1640s, he had already felt his way towards a solution. His attack on the idolatrous art of the king's devotions actually became the occasion for formulating a positive ideal of creativity as he discussed the nature and genesis of true prayer.

Milton's definition of true prayer occurs in the context of an attack on Charles's borrowed prayers. Charles's imitative prayers, stolen from David, Christ, and even Sidney's *Arcadia,* are the counterpart of the idolatrous "set forms" of the church – derivative, bound to the past, lacking in spirit.[15] Milton distinguishes between Charles's lifeless, imitative borrowing and true creativity, which is "a work of grace onely from above" (*Eikonoklastes,* III, 553). Whereas Charles lacks any creative spirit – "it [is] not in him to make a prayer of his own" (367) – Milton describes true prayer as original, artistic creation. Prayer is the "Gift" of God, who "every morning raines down new expressions into our hearts" (III, 505–6). God's participation in the creative process both enables the author's originality and absolves him from pride in his creation. God's "sanctifying spirit" puts "filial words" into us, giving us "plenty" and "variety." These "new expressions" mark a decisive break from the past, and they cannot be "hoarded up" or, like manna, they will "*breed wormes and stink.*"[16] They must not be "imprison[ed] . . . into a Pinfold of sett words," bound to an endless round of repetition, like the liturgy (III, 505–6). True prayers are always new beginnings; thus they avoid the statue-like qualities of permanence and immutability that in puritan ideology characterized the idolatrous image. This model for legitimate creativity privileges originality and individuality (each person should make prayers of "his own," III, 553), while acknowledging dependency on God's creative power. No two authentic prayers or creations will ever be the same; each will have its distinct identity.

The metaphor of reproductive generation appears in Milton's description of prayer, distinguishing true prayer both from servile imitation and from proud invention and anticipating his description of the origin of his own poetry in *Paradise Lost.* Prayer is "conceav'd in the heart" (III, 504; cf. 507), not the head. The heart of the believer, which must be receptive (not stony) when God "raines down new expressions" (505), is like a woman, open to the impregnating spirit but also actively contributing to the creation of prayers with fertile "matter, and good desires" (III, 504). By appropriating the conventionally subservient female role in generation yet infusing that role with an active contribution to conception/generation traditionally denied to the female, the (male) creator of original prayers (or poems of prayer) is absolved of idolatrous pride, for true prayer becomes the product not of solitary invention but of a generous coupling. Without God's inseminating spirit, words are dead images.[17] But prayer, as it contains the spirit of life, is regenerative – like the good books in *Areopagitica*, which as "the dictat of a divine Spirit" are "not absolutely dead things" (II, 534, 492).

One thus sees in the midst of his most explicitly iconoclastic prose – at a time when Milton's change to a plainer prose style suggested an increasing distrust of art and invention[18] – a definition of human creativity that could justify his own poems. *Eikonoklastes* confronts the problem puritan ideology posed for his own artistic ambitions. By discriminating precisely between the idolatrous image and legitimate human creations, Milton tries to find a safe, privileged place for his art, thus provisionally resolving the dilemma created for him as a religious poet by the puritan attack on "graven images" and "human invention" in worship.[19]

Paradise Lost repeatedly makes claims for the non-idolatrous status of its art. Milton needs to assure himself that his poem is true worship, particularly since his desire to write a poem that might live on to later ages could seem what puritans called "will-worship," the epitome of idolatry. Though the initial comparisons between the narrator and Satan suggest, in William Riggs's words, Milton's "recognition of the satanic potential of his poetic act," Milton anxiously separates his poetic work from the idolatrous inventions of Satan and the fallen angels by distinguishing his "song" and his "tell[ing]" of sacred story from the "inventing" and "building" that characterize Satan and the fallen angels – in particular, the building of Pandemonium.[20] Like Charles's borrowed prayers, Pandemonium is a derivative imitation, an attempt to imitate heaven. But it is also monumental, glorious, and embodies Milton's fear that his glorious structure could rival and violate divinity.

When the fallen angels are not imitating heaven, they are "inventing" instruments of destruction. "Invention" – a key term in the conflict over ceremonial worship – is a decidedly negative word in Milton's poem. In the war in heaven, the fallen angels "invent" (VI. 464) gunpowder and weapons; digging up "the Celestial soil," they "mingl'd" and "Concocted" the "originals of Nature" with "subtle Art" (VI. 509–14), turning the elements of life into agents of destruction – providing the pattern and precedent for the perverse, lethal inventions that will mark the history of human civilization.

Milton tries to separate his poetic song from the Satanic "invention" (VI. 498) and "wondrous Art" (I. 703) that might seem its perverse mirror. Like Herbert, he wants to reclaim the holiness of art by insisting that his poetry worships God not the self, and that it is the product of God's grace. Milton's distrust of "invention" recalls Herbert's "Jordan (II)" and "Sinnes Round." But Milton's poetic ambitions are stronger than Herbert's, and his reformist fears of idolatry deeper. Linda Gregerson suggests that Milton's "broken" similes emphasizing unlikeness (for instance, "Not that fair field / Of *Enna*" [IV. 268–9]) are a strategy to make his poem an imperfect, hence non-idolatrous image, thus preserving verbal images "safe for use."[21] There are many other strategies whereby Milton distinguishes his poem from idolatrous inventions. Where Herbert delights in the verbal and visual wit of his poems, Milton tries to dissociate his song, his temple, from material, corporeal features that might make it seem either a "set form" or one of those "Monuments of Fame" (I. 695) that are products and instruments of idolatry. He no longer voices the desire, as in *Lycidas*, to build "the lofty rhyme" (line 11). His conscious dematerialization of his poem contrasts with the physicality of Pandemonium, with its "Doric pillars," "Cornice," "Sculptures," and roof of "fretted Gold" (I. 714–17), which evokes the lavish architecture of St. Peter's in Rome.[22] Where Milton identifies his poem with the "upright heart," which is the "Temple" God prefers (I. 18) – much like Herbert, whose poem made of his "heart" was his "ALTAR" – Pandemonium is the original of "*Babel*" (as in Herbert, the conventional symbol of idolatrous invention in worship) and the Egyptian temples that were "the works of *Memphian* Kings" (I. 694). "Built like a Temple" (I. 713), and the scene of "awful Ceremony" (line 753), Pandemonium rises out of the earth to the music of an "Organ" (line 708), with the sound of "Dulcet Symphonies and voices sweet" (line 712) that later will provide the model for the service of Roman and English churches.[23]

From the first, Milton insists his poem is not "invented" or built but "created" – a crucial distinction. The opening invocation (I. 17–23) asks the spirit of God, who "with mighty wings outspread / Dove-like satst brooding on the vast Abyss / And mad'st it pregnant" (lines 21–3), to inspire his sacred song. Poetic creation is analogous to the original Creation. Like the feminine abyss – or Mary, who will bear the incarnate Word, or the receptive heart in prayer – Milton hopes to be visited by the spirit of God which will make him "pregnant," able to bring forth his vital creation.[24] Echoing *Eikonoklastes'* description of the generation of true prayer, this first invocation claims the essential identity of his poetry and prayer.

Milton thus distinguishes "Creation" (the distinctive, life-giving work of God) from "invention" (a satanic, solitary endeavor, associated with death and destruction). Perhaps the "birth" of Sin springing out of Satan's head (II. 757–8) complicates this distinction and, like Pandemonium, expresses anxiety about poetic creation. But whereas the nightly visitations of the divine Muse legitimate Milton's labors, Satan conceives and brings forth Sin through a parthenogenesis that arrogates to himself all power of creativity, much as when he announces to Raphael that he and the other angels are "self-begot . . . By our own quick'ning power" (V. 860–1). Nevertheless, the history of the poem's reception might be said to have defeated Milton's efforts to avoid idolatry even as it has met his ambitions for fame. For, whatever Milton could claim about its holy genesis, *Paradise Lost* would become an object of reverence, canonized as a monument of English culture, superseding the Bible as the version of "the Fall" and Judaeo-Christian history most familiar to many people.

AN EPIC HISTORY OF IDOLATRY

Paradise Lost is not only presented as a true rite of worship; it is also a history of idolatry. In contrast to Virgilian epic, which celebrates a nation by retelling its founding, or Spenser's epic glorification of England as a stronghold of Protestantism, vanquishing the supposed evils of Catholic idolatry, Milton's poem searches for the origins of idolatry that might explain the failure of the English Revolution.[25] For Milton, political disasters have religious causes. From the first book, with its roll call of devils that would be worshiped later, to the last books with their dismal record of defections from God, he focuses on the various permutations of idolatry and false worship, implicitly evoking and assessing the conditions of contemporary England, bringing the language and issues of the seventeenth-century conflict over worship into his epic portrayal of the sweep of human history.

The Fall begins with Satan's refusal to "serve" – a word with important religious meaning. Modern readers easily recognize the political and military aspects of Satan's role as commander and king.

But all the political images of the poem – tyranny, kingship, submission, bondage, liberty – are religiously charged, as they were in Milton's prose. When Satan declares he would rather "reign in Hell, than serve in Heav'n" (I. 263), he not only rejects political service or obedience to a superior; he refuses to participate in the official rites of God's public worship.[26] When God appoints the Son "Head," insisting that "All knees in Heav'n" shall "bow" to him and "confess him Lord" (V. 606–8), Satan refuses to engage in what seems compulsory worship. Significantly, kneeling at the Sacrament and bowing at the name of Jesus were two bodily gestures particularly offensive to puritans. There is no doubt that Milton intends the reader to be appalled by Satan's refusal to worship God. He distinguishes, as puritans did, between the reverence due to God and reverence to the human authorities enforcing humanly invented ceremonies in the church. But Satan, in his refusal to bow to the Son, his vocal rejection of "Knee-tribute" and "prostration vile" (V. 782), his objection to having to "bend / The supple knee" to both God and the Son (V. 787–8), expresses a disgust for enforced conformity and ceremonial bodily worship that is strikingly similar to that of Milton and others who refused to participate in the compulsory worship of the Church of England. It is hard to think that similarity would have gone unnoticed by at least some contemporary readers. Satan's function is thus complex and equivocal – intentionally so, I believe. Equivocation was the normative strategy for the religiously persecuted in early modern England and Europe.[27] It allows one to survive, even to conform to the expectations of repressive authorities, while remaining true to inner, spiritual convictions. Thus while Satan is Milton's supremely dangerous representative of idolatry, he also offers (particularly in the first books of the poem) a strong, yet safe voice for Milton's subversive opposition to the compulsory, enforced formal worship of the Restoration English church.[28]

As the language of Milton's own earlier attacks on "formal" worship is inscribed in Satan's bitter attacks on God's service, readers might well be suspicious of the worship God requires. God's authoritarian tone at times sounds all too much like those earthly authorities in Milton's England who tried to impose conformity in worship.[29] Such a tone could seem to Royalist readers evidence that Milton had acquiesced to the reigning conformity of the Restoration. Yet he stresses that God's worship is voluntary in order to absolve it of any Laudian or uniformist taint. God claims that he takes pleasure only from "Freely" given "obedience"; he wants active not "passive" (or compulsory) service from both human beings and angelic "Spirits" (III. 101–11). Milton insists the angels' songs and hymns of worship are spontaneous, full of "concord" (III. 371) but not following any prescribed form, their song and "Mystical dance" about the hill of God "Eccentric" and "irregular" (V. 623–4) – in marked contrast to the uniform worship favored by Laud and now legislated by the Uniformity Act. Milton has it both ways in the struggle between Satan and God – he both defines the kind of worship God wants, distinguishing it from idolatry, and registers through Satan's words his protest against conformity to human laws that would prescribe a set, uniform, compulsory worship and persecute dissenters. The problem, though, is that Satan's complaints about conformity retain the potential to contaminate the reader's view of heaven and God.

Yet another problem is that humans and angels are "free" to choose whether to serve God, but there is only one right choice – a condition which hardly seems free to modern readers. As Raphael puts the paradox to Adam, "Our voluntary service he requires" (V. 529). Satan admits that God's "service" is not "hard" (IV. 45). Adam similarly tells Eve that the "service" required – not to eat from the Tree of Knowledge – is easy to "keep" (IV. 420–4). God asked Satan simply "to afford him praise . . . and pay him thanks" (IV. 46–7) – a service the poet has twice given in his invocations and that the unfallen Adam and Eve will soon give (IV. 720–35). But for Satan such praise and thanks are "subjection" (IV. 50) even before the Fall, and afterward he considers it "ignominy and shame" to "bow and sue for grace / With suppliant knee" (I. 115, 111–12), an intolerable admission of courtier-like dependence. To worship or render any service *is* to be a slave. For Satan, all worship of God is forced, compulsory, inherently demeaning. Hence, his refusal to "serve" is not so much an assertion of political freedom, though it could equivocally also function as a rallying call for religious dissenters, as an insistence that he does not depend on any higher power for his existence – that is, that he is his own god.

Satan does not want freedom to worship in his own way; he wants to be god, to "reign" like the tyrants who exalt themselves as gods over their peers. He wants to be served with the perfect obedience that God himself wants. Satan rouses his despondent cohorts by mocking their "abject posture," prone on the flaming sea, as a gesture seeming to "adore the Conqueror" (I. 322–3), but he does not reject such bodily gestures of worship when directed towards himself. Satan and the fallen angels may seem to reject ceremonial worship in refusing to "celebrate [God's] Throne / With warbl'd Hymns, and to his Godhead sing / Forc't Halleluiahs" (II. 241–3). But he sets himself up as the object of ceremonial adoration, and the fallen angels are the image of the ceremonialist worshipers Milton attacked in his prose, as they engage in various forms of idolatrous ceremonial worship. Where heavenly angels play harps, the fallen angels, like Comus' followers, play "Flutes" and "Pipes" (I. 551, 561) evocative of the English cathedral service. For all their supposed rebelliousness, they exemplify the "outward conformity" and "carnall" "Formallitie" Milton attacked in *Of Reformation* (I, 522). At the end of the Council of Hell, they "bend" towards Satan "With awful reverence prone; and as a God / Extol him equal to the highest in Heav'n" (II. 477–79) – imitating the reverence towards God that they abjure and initiating the reverence for false monarchs, political leaders, and tyrants that will be a sign of the human bondage to idolatry.

Satan incorporates the features of the power-hungry men that people Milton's prose. The figures of prelate, military commander, parliamentary leader, and monarch-tyrant all meet in Satan, because they are all kin. Rather than being an allegorical representation of a single historical figure, Satan is the original of all those who throughout history seek to assume the power of gods. He recalls Milton's prelates, with their "insatiate . . . ambition" (*Animadversions*, I, 720), as well as the presbyterian clergy, who ousted the bishops only to usurp their power and become "Tyrants" themselves (*Tenure*, III, 242). When he enters Eden like a "prowling Wolf" (IV. 183), he is like the predatory, greedy clergy of the Catholic and English churches described in *Lycidas*, *Of Reformation* (I, 614), and *The Tenure of Kings and Magistrates* (III, 241). As a political, military leader, manipulating his followers in the council of Pandemonium and organizing them in military order, Satan recalls both the parliamentary leaders during the Revolution and Cromwell, whom Milton had sharply warned in the *Second Defence* not to seek absolute power or the title of king (IV, i, 672–3).[30] But Satan is, above all, a monarch. Aiming "Against the Throne and Monarchy of God" (I. 42), he aspires "To set himself in Glory above his Peers" (I. 39) – like the monarchs who elevate themselves over "thir brethren" (*Readie and Easie Way*, VII, 425).[31] No true revolutionary, Satan, like the defenders of monarchy and prescribed ceremonial worship, insists on custom, tradition, and precedent, objecting that in exalting the Son God has "impos'd" "new Laws" (V. 679). Satan's insistence that he wants to restore the previous order also aligns him with Charles II and Royalists who saw the Restoration as a return to an order that had been interrupted.[32] Milton's depiction of Satan – "exalted" "High on a Throne of Royal State" (II. 5, 1), with Sin as his queen who will "Reign" at his "right hand voluptuous" (II. 868–9), with his "offspring" Death (II. 781), and his "crew" of servile and "lewd" fallen angels (I. 477, 490) – glances at the courts of Charles I and the profligate Charles II, as it echoes Milton's contemptuous remark on the eve of the Restoration that "a king must be ador'd like a Demigod, with a dissolute and haughtie court about him," with a "queen" and "issue" and a "servile crew" (*Readie and Easie Way*, VII, 425). The devils' perfect obedience to Satan exemplifies the "folly" of those who willingly serve a king, ready "to adore and be the slaves of a single person" (*Readie and Easie Way*, VII, 448).

That idolatry originates in heaven, though it flourishes in Hell, suggests how close idolatry is to true worship – a point emphasized by the roll call of devils in Book I of *Paradise Lost* that traces demonic idolatry throughout human history. In the ancient Middle East, the "chief" devils fixed "Thir Seats . . . next the Seat of God, / Thir Altars by his Altar" (I. 375–84). The proximity of heathen idolatry to the true worship of the Israelites suggests the threat of infiltration and contamination. As Milton lists the numerous fallen angels according to the various names by which they were worshiped and the extensive geographical territory each encompassed, we see the fertility of idolatry, which like the vegetation in Eden threatens to take over the world. Idolatry soon seduces Israel from its worship of God in spite of all the codes of purity to keep the Jews separate from idolaters. The chief devils "often plac'd" their "Shrines" within God's "Sanctuary" and "profan'd" God's "Rites" and "Feasts" (I. 387–90). Moloch led "the wisest heart / Of *Solomon*" (lines 400–1) to build a temple to him next to God's temple, and "fair Idolatresses" beguiled him to build a temple to Astoreth (lines 443–6). The "Love-tale" of Thammuz "Infected *Sion's* daughters" with the "heat" of idolatrous desire (lines 452–3). The contagion of idolatry corrupts the whole nation as the Israelites build a golden calf in "*Oreb*" (lines

483–4), the very place that Moses received the Law from God, and that Milton's first invocation identifies as a place of sacred inspiration. Bringing us quickly to the present of Restoration England, Milton remarks that Belial continues to pollute "the house of God" as "Priest / Turns Atheist" (lines 494–6).

In this long section of Book I, Milton presents a devastating picture of idolatry as a contagious "infection" (line 483), capable of seducing even the wisest of men, occasionally driven out of Israel by men like Josiah (line 418), but always returning. Given its power, no wonder Milton so anxiously defends his own poetry, zealously policing the boundaries of true worship.

Thus before we ever glimpse the paradisal life of true worship, the first book offers a grim prospect of "the greatest part / Of Mankind," "corrupted to forsake / God thir Creator" and to transform "th' invisible / Glory of him that made them" into the carnal "Image of a Brute" (I. 367–71). This pessimistic assessment is driven home by the history Michael presents to Adam in the last two books. Here the emphasis shifts from the contagion of idolatry to the persecution of the godly, the few who, like Abdiel, remain loyal to God. Establishing the paradigm for subsequent history, the first scene Adam witnesses presents the issue of worship as divisive. Both Cain and Abel sacrifice on the "Altar," performing "all due Rites" (XI. 432, 440–1), but only Abel's is accepted with "propitious Fire," showing that not outward rites but purity of heart matters to God. In the first sons of Adam, we see the distinction between true "Rites" (in which external and internal devotion are united) and worship which is "not sincere" (line 443) but merely a matter of external forms. Cain kills his brother, showing how "Piety" and "pure Devotion [are] paid" (line 452) on earth. Though Michael assures Adam that Abel's death will be "aveng'd" (line 458) and his faith ultimately rewarded, the rest of Michael's history of the world shows that true faith will always be persecuted by the ungodly majority. Thus the example of Cain and Abel becomes representative of the long struggle between true and false worship, while speaking to the plight of the godly in Restoration England.

Subsequent scenes show men who study "To worship God aright" (line 578) seduced by the daughters of idolaters; Enoch, the defender of "Justice," "Truth," and "Religion," attacked by "old and young" (lines 667–8) but rescued by God; and Noah, the one good man saved when God punishes the earth with the Flood. Even the near-destruction of the human race is not enough to stop idolatry, for Nimrod soon rises to "arrogate Dominion undeserv'd / Over his brethren" (xII. 25, 27–8) and build the tower of Babel, a juxtaposition that tellingly identifies political tyranny with idolatrous religion. As the world goes "from bad to worse," God withdraws his "presence," leaving the people to their "polluted ways" (lines 106–10). Still there seems to be the possibility of a new beginning as God selects "one peculiar Nation" from among the rest to spring from a "faithful man" (Abraham), who had been "Bred up in Idolworship" (lines 111–15) but turned to God, providing a pattern the godly should follow. Milton's account of this select nation, the Israelites, suggests the recent history of contemporary England, singled out by God for the reformation of worship but sliding into idolatry. Israel's experience is ominous for England, for the "foul Idolatries" (line 337) of the kings after Solomon incense God to punish the Jews with bondage. Even after deliverance from Babylon, the priests bring "pollution" upon the "Temple" with their strife (lines 355–6) – a likely reference to the dissensions within puritanism in the aftermath of winning the war against Charles I. Nations and communities seem inevitably idolatrous; faithfulness is only possible at the individual level. The coming of Christ does not change this pattern. Though the Messiah fulfils the Law, triumphs over death, and leaves his Spirit among his believers, idolatry still dominates. The world remains Satan's realm until the Second Coming. And so the "few / His faithful" are encompassed by the "unfaithful herd" (lines 480–1), and the enemies of truth will persecute the faithful as they did the Messiah.

The history of religion after the Crucifixion is if anything worse than before, as Milton exposes an idolatry within the Christian church that surpasses that of the Israelites. After the death of the Apostles, "grievous Wolves" become "teachers" in the church (line 508), seeking "lucre" and titles, forcing conscience by means of "carnal power" (line 521), persecuting true "worship," and "unbuild[ing]" God's "living Temples" (lines 532, 526–7) – in Milton's evocative image for the desecration of the bodies of religious martyrs, including perhaps the regicides who were quartered and publicly displayed after the Restoration.[33] Early Christianity and late are conflated as Michael describes how religion becomes mere "outward Rites and specious forms" (line 534). Much of what he says implicitly indicts the restored English church, whose continuity with earlier forms of worship is for Milton not the guarantee of its authority but the decisive mark of its idolatry. But there is no suggestion that the continental reformed churches are any purer. Milton's vision is unrelenting in its focus on corruption, violence, and idolatry in the communal, institutional church. The only locus of true worship here is the rare faithful individual.

MARRIAGE, TRUE WORSHIP, AND THE HOLY RITE OF SEX

Devastating and sweeping as Milton's sense of the near-universality of idolatry is, *Paradise Lost* also articulates what true worship might be, even in a fallen world, in order (like Michael) to give some hope and direction to those few still struggling, like Adam and Eve, to be faithful. As we have seen, Milton presents his poem as an exemplary act of worship, an acknowledgment of his dependence on God, and a celebration of God's creativity and wisdom. But the most interesting and unusual example of the true rites of worship appears in his depiction of the prelapsarian love of Adam and Eve. In what is arguably his most unconventional move, Milton imagines married sexual love as a rite of true worship, sharply departing from the carnal/spiritual, body/soul dualism that marked his treatment of sex in *The Doctrine and Discipline of Divorce* and that undergirds puritan thinking about worship. Where puritan ideology had insisted that worship must be inward, a matter of the spirit, distrusting all "outward" and bodily forms of worship, Milton's *Paradise Lost* seeks to find a place for the body in worship and to recapture a sense of the wholeness of creation, the connection and interdependence of matter and spirit that Raphael describes (v. 469–505). The poem does this particularly in the representation of the unfallen erotic relation of Adam and Eve. Milton's effort to sanctify sexual love might recall the more radical sects, particularly the Ranters who encouraged sexual promiscuity for men as a sign and privilege of their state of grace. But Milton emphatically dissociates himself from the promiscuous Ranters as he glorifies monogamous marriage.[34]

He turns to marriage to replace the false community of an idolatrous, ceremonial, public worship. That he seeks community in the private, domestic sphere marks a cultural shift whereby private relations and love become the primary source of value.[35] But it also aligns him with the puritan tendency to center religion in the family – and, especially, with the mentality and practices of Restoration nonconformists, whose religious meetings took place in private dwellings. Under conditions of persecution, the private home becomes at once a secret place of refuge and an alternative, oppositional locus of spirituality. In Milton's divorce tracts, the reform of the household was the first step towards reforming the English church, but in *Paradise Lost* marriage replaces the church.

Adam's eloquent expression of his desire not to be alone – of a need for "society" essential to his very nature – echoes Milton's own deep need for a religious community. This longing for community speaks both to Milton's personal sense of isolation in the Restoration and, I think, to the alienating consequences of radical Protestant individualism, with its emphasis on the need for each person to seek truth for him- or herself and to keep separate from all contaminating idolatry. In the primary human relation of marriage, Milton hopes to find bonds without the bondage of idolatry, though as we shall see it is a precarious hope. As marriage is made to fill spiritual as well as psychological and physical needs, Milton places an enormous responsibility on this relation – a responsibility that, given the differences in Adam and Eve as Milton constructs the original man and woman, and their innate tendencies towards different forms of idolatry, seems impossible to fulfil. The erotic relation between man and woman becomes the anxious site for defining the relation between human beings and God. Thus it is inevitably charged with danger.

When we first see Adam and Eve, they present an image of true worship, of a right relation to God, and their connectedness to God is an essential part of their idealized marriage. Adam's first speech to Eve praises the infinite goodness of the "Power / That made us," "rais'd us from the dust and plac't us here /In all this happiness" (IV. 412–17), thus fully acknowledging his dependence on his Creator even as he affirms his bond with Eve. Eve's first speech similarly acknowledges her dependence on *her* source of being, which is Adam, "my Guide / And Head", "for whom / And from whom I was form'd" (lines 440–3). As Adam was made "for God only, shee for God in him" (IV. 299),[36] he is to her as God, which from the first makes the relationship unequal.

But Milton uses this disparity to make the relation between Adam and Eve a model for true worship and for the proper relation of humans to God. Though Eve is Adam's "partner" (line 471), her dependence on him is a model for human dependence on the

Creator; hence her "submissive" (line 498) qualities and humble address to him as "My Author and Disposer" (line 635) figure the proper human attitude towards God.[37] In a significant departure from seventeenth-century marital conduct books, which present the wife's subjection as a model for earthly political order that reinforces the authority of magistrates,[38] Milton makes Eve's subordinate relation to Adam a model only for human beings' relation to God, not for subjects' obedience to magistrates, thus opening up the possibility for egalitarian, non-hierarchical relations among people. But the gendering of subjection to God – not only in Milton's poem but in Paul's pronouncements which lie behind it (for example, "Wives, submit yourselves unto your own husbands, as unto the Lord. For the husband is the head of the wife, even as Christ is the head of the church: and he is the saviour of the body. Therefore as the church is subject unto Christ, so let the wives be to their own husbands in every thing," Ephesians 5:22–4) – inevitably casts women in an inferior position and sanctions domestic gender hierarchy as necessary. Conflicting with Milton's egalitarian sense that man was not made to rule over other men is his conviction that woman's submission and acceptance of her dependent position are required, since this is the supposedly perfect image of true religious worship. Submissive behavior must be adopted by Adam and all men – but not towards women, only towards God. It is indicative of the disparity between Adam and Eve – and of the unnaturalness of woman's subordination to Adam or dependence on an external God – that Eve must be *taught* submission to Adam, whereas Adam instinctively acknowledges dependence on his "Maker" (VIII. 278) in his first act and speech.[39] Eve's obedience, like our "service" to God, is "voluntary" yet "require[d]" (V. 529) – which precisely states the problem of the separation scene, where Eve must be free to go but should decide to stay.

So long as the marriage is perfect, so long as Eve depends on Adam as humans must depend on God, it constitutes for Milton an ideal model of the worship that forms an essential part of their prelapsarian marital lives. Their day is framed by freely given acknowledgment of their dependence on and love for the Creator. In the evening, before they retire, they "ador'd / The God that made both Sky, Air, Earth, and Heav'n" (IV. 721–2). Their prayer is extempore but "unanimous" (line 736), spoken in one voice as a sign that their hearts are one, just like the angels in heaven who all sing the praises of Father and Son ("No voice exempt, no voice but well could join," III. 370). In the morning upon rising, they pray with "prompt eloquence" flowing "from thir lips" (V. 149–50). Their "Unmeditated" (V. 149) words mirror the poetic prayers of Milton, moved by the spirit of God to acknowledge his dependence.

Milton distinguishes Edenic prayers from the "set forms" of the English and Catholic liturgy, with their accompanying music. Adam and Eve pray "In various style" and "holy rapture," either "in Prose" or "Verse" needing no "Lute or Harp" to add sweetness (lines 145–52). Yet Milton's Edenic worship, like its heavenly counterpart, has decidedly ceremonial features and involves external, bodily gestures. Like the angels, both unfallen and fallen, Adam and Eve bow "Lowly . . . adoring" (V. 144), and after the Fall they fall "prostrate" and "reverent" before God (X. 1087–8, 1099–1100). Bowing is a surprisingly frequent bodily gesture in *Paradise Lost*, a sign of "reverence meek" to a "superior Nature" (V. 359–60); and though it can be misdirected (as in Hell, or when Eve bows in "low Reverence" [IX. 835] to the Tree after eating its fruit), Milton retains the gesture in contrast to puritans and religious radicals, who disdained such gestures in worship as carnal, or to revolutionaries like John Lilburne or Gerard Winstanley who refused to display reverence to social "superiors."[40] But Adam bows towards Raphael, and Eve falls humbly at Adam's feet (X. 911–12). Such emphasis on reverent bodily gestures throughout *Paradise Lost* suggests not only acceptance of hierarchy but a dissatisfaction with worship that is "purely" spiritual, a desire to engage body as well as soul in devotion.[41]

Milton's attraction to ceremony strikingly appears at the beginning of Book XI, when the Son as "Intercessor" and "Priest" receives Adam and Eve's prayers of repentance and mixes them "With Incense" in his "Golden Censer" before presenting them to the Father (lines 14–25). Milton may intend this passage to sharply reject ceremonial worship in an earthly, material church: Christ is the only Priest; only in heaven should there be a "Golden Altar," "Censer[s]," and "Incense." Nevertheless, the attentively sensuous description of the scene betrays an attraction to ceremony and ritual also evident in Milton's description of Edenic worship. His lingering affection for the ceremonial is seen in the echoes of the Prayer Book's liturgy for evening and morning prayer in Adam and Eve's bedtime prayer and morning hymn.[42] It also explains why Adam and Eve's morning prayer incorporating Psalm 148, asking all the creatures to worship God (the angels with "choral symphonies," the sun and moon in their rhythmic courses, the elements in their "Circle" of "ceaseless change," mists, fountains, plants, and all of the earth "Made vocal" [v. 160–204]), sounds oddly like Herrick's "Corinna's *going a Maying*" – that consummate expression of the ceremonialism Milton seems to abjure.

Prayer is not the sole act of worship Adam and Eve perform. In one of the most unconventional, powerful moments in the poem, Milton turns their love-making into a holy rite, bringing the body fully into the worship of God and sanctifying sex as a way of connecting with God as he moves far beyond the puritan notion of the "companionate marriage." Although transgressive sexuality was, as we have seen, a common image for carnal idolatry, the Edenic books of *Paradise Lost* take an uncommon turn in using sexual love between the first man and woman to represent true religious worship.

Whereas *Comus*, with its body/spirit dualism, revealed an attraction to virginal purity and the divorce tracts showed disgust for the sexual act, *Paradise Lost* celebrates the erotic and clearly sexual relation of Adam and Eve before the Fall as a mark of their perfection, purity, and innocence. As other readers have recognized, Milton's emphasis on sexual love in paradise gives vigorous, positive recognition to human sexuality and pleasure, even as it excludes other erotic possibilities in privileging heterosexual marriage.[43] But Milton goes to extraordinary lengths to suggest the holiness of Adam and Eve's love-making, framing it with their prayer to God and with his own hymn "Hail wedded Love" (IV. 750).[44] That Adam and Eve pray before turning to "Rites / Mysterious of connubial Love" (IV. 742–3) suggests that one act naturally leads to the other. By juxtaposing prayer and love-making, Milton suggests that in paradise both are equally "befitting [the] holiest place" (IV. 759). Condemning "Hypocrites" who defame "as impure what God declares / Pure" (IV. 744–7), he insists that human heterosexual intercourse and the body are naturally sacred, even in the postlapsarian world.

Milton further suggests the special holiness of sexual intercourse and its religious significance by having it take place inside the nuptial "bower" (IV. 738), within the holy place of paradise, doubly separated from the profane space outside. As the "holiest place" (IV. 759), this "Nuptial Bed" (IV. 710) recalls the "holy of holies" in the

Tabernacle or temple described in the Hebrew Bible (Exodus, Leviticus, Numbers, 1 Kings).[45] No "other Creature . . . / Beast, Bird, Insect, or Worm durst enter" (IV. 703–4). With its "verdant wall" and "inwoven" roof (IV, 697, 693), the bower is like the place in the Jewish sanctuary that was circumscribed by a "vail" of "cunning work" to "divide" the "holy place" from the "most holy" (Exodus 26: 31–3). In the sanctuary, the holy of holies was a place for the most sacred, intimate communion between the high priest and God, between humans and divinity. Only the high priest could enter, for God was presumed to be specially present there. In Milton's erotic revision of Scripture, the bedroom becomes the temple and marital intercourse a rite of worship as Adam and Eve take the place of the Jewish high priests, exemplifying the priesthood of all believers.

Perhaps it seems odd for Milton to privilege the bower as a holy of holies since he rejected the ceremonialist, Laudian idea that one place is more holy than another or that God is specially present in any one place. That holiness – and God – cannot be tied to special places is clear when Michael tells Adam that, though henceforth human beings will be deprived of Eden, God will send "His Spirit" to "dwell" "within them" (XII. 487–8), and that Adam (and the godly) will "possess / A paradise within" (lines 586–7). But Michael is describing the condition of holiness in a postlapsarian world. *After* the Fall there will no longer be a specifically holy place available to Adam and Eve, which implies that before there was.

"Chos'n" by God and "framed" for performing the "delightful" rites of marriage (IV. 690–2), the bower as locus of love conflates the "holy of holies" with the enclosed garden of the Song of Songs. In *The Doctrine and Discipline of Divorce*, Milton had invoked the Song of Songs as expressing a love of souls not bodies (II, 251), but the celebration of married sexual love in *Paradise Lost* presumes a very different reading of the Hebrew text, one that refuses to obliterate its human and sexual significance by imposing an allegorical, spiritual interpretation. A long, powerful tradition of allegorical reading had desexualized the biblical text, insisting that it describes a spiritual relation between God and his people.[46] But as the Song of Songs expresses the mutual erotic desires of Solomon and his bride, their longing to enjoy each other's body, it presents the pleasures of sexual love within marriage as natural and worthy of poetic celebration in the holiest of books, the Bible. With a frank sensuality diluted by subsequent translations and interpretations, the Hebrew text sanctifies sexual love and erotic desire between man and woman, even suggesting that this love is the "flame of God" (Song of Songs 8:7).[47]

The integration of sexual and spiritual, body and soul, that distinguishes the Hebrew Song of Songs above all other books of the Bible, characterizes Milton's description of paradisal life. Departing from dominant Christian traditions,[48] his celebration of the sacredness of sexual love is part of the Hebraic ethos that Rosenblatt has shown characterizes the Edenic books of *Paradise Lost.*

In privileging renunciation and associating sexuality with sin, Christianity from its inception diverged from the Jewish emphasis on marriage and sexuality as divinely created, necessary, and good.[49] Milton revives the emphasis on the sacredness of marriage and the holiness of marital sex that characterized not only the Hebrew Song of Songs but Jewish and Talmudic thinking. Some rabbinic commentators on Genesis had argued that Adam and Eve had sexual relations before the Fall. But Milton's insistence on the potential sanctity of married sexual intercourse in the postlapsarian world could also find support in the distinctive Jewish emphasis on the holiness of marital sex *after* the Fall.[50] A belief in the holiness of sex pervades Jewish marital laws and rabbinic commentary. Like all acts sustaining life, sexual intercourse should be performed "for the sake of worshipping our Creator."[51] Indeed, the special link between marital intercourse (understood as the continuation of life) and God's original Creation of the world makes it in Jewish tradition an appropriate activity for the Sabbath, which commemorates the Creation.[52]

Milton's sense of the ritual holiness of marital sex echoes this Jewish understanding of married sexuality. Before the Fall, Milton's priests of love approach the presence of God through sexual intercourse, the single human, bodily act that most fully connects human beings with each other and with the source of life. Prefaced by their prayer praising God as Creator of the universe and looking forward to their production of a "Race / To fill the Earth" (IV. 732–3), their rites of love pay tribute to the mystery of God's creation, which Milton presents as a conjunction of male and female, those "two great Sexes [that] animate the World" (VIII. 151). Their prayer instinctively acknowledges the connection between God's creative power and the generative power of human love. As a reenactment of original Creation, Adam and Eve's love-making is appropriately linked with a prayer to their Creator – and with Milton's own poetry as it is generated by the holy Spirit that created the world.

The sexual embrace of Adam and Eve which promises offspring echoes Milton's invocation of his "Heav'nly Muse" (I. 6), who at the beginning of the world made the "vast Abyss" "pregnant" (I. 21–2), and anticipates Raphael's account of Creation in Book VII:

> . . . on the wat'ry calm
> His brooding wings the Spirit of God outspread,
> And vital virtue infus'd, and vital warmth
> Throughout the fluid Mass . . .   (lines 234–7)

This account strikingly contrasts with John's dematerialized "In the beginning was the Word" (John 1: 1). Milton's distinctly generative, sexualized understanding of the origin of the world – and therefore his sense of the essential connection between love-making, poetry, and Creation – might well have derived from the Hebrew Bible, in which the same word *toldoth* (from *yalad*, meaning "To bear, bring forth, beget") describes both the "generations" of men (as in Numbers) and the "generations of the heavens and of the earth" (Genesis 2: 4). Biblical Hebrew thus could have suggested to Milton that Creation was the result of the reproductive conjunction of male and female necessary to "conception."[53]

By juxtaposing prayer and the "rites" of love as complementary acts of worship commemorating Creation, Milton links love with devotional poetry and separates it not just from animal copulation but from unholy acts of worship. When the narrator comments that the only "Rites" God "likes" are "adoration pure" (IV. 736–8) such as Adam's and Eve's, Milton implicitly contrasts their spontaneous prayer and instinctive love-making, and his own poetic devotions, with the idolatrous versions of worship, eros, and invention that the epic records. By suggesting that Adam and Eve's nuptial "rites" constitute true religion, Milton privileges the most private and personal experience – and potentially the most integrative – against the public forms and institutions of religion. Poetry and love are parallel rites of true worship, still possible in a fallen world, as the eloquent hymn to married love suggests (IV. 750–70).

LOVE, SEDUCTION, AND THE FALL INTO IDOLATRY

But while Milton idealizes erotic love between man and woman as a site of true worship, giving it supreme value in human experience, erotic love is also the cause of Adam's fall and the various defections of men seduced by women that Michael records in the last two books. Human love becomes the material out of which both worship and idolatry are constructed. Relations between man and woman are, from the first, overfraught, inscribed with religious value, bearing both the potential for representing, even effecting, the harmonious relation between man and God and the responsibility for destroying that relation. Love – and particularly woman – provides both an opportunity for connecting with God in worship (Adam offers prayers only after Eve has been created) and the threat to that connection.

In the Fall, Adam and Eve turn from God, repeating the idolatry of Satan and the fallen angels. After eating the fruit and promising to praise the tree every morning as her new God, Eve bows to the tree (IX. 835) in an idolatrous gesture that will be repeated in Adam's subjection to a lower creature when he takes the fruit from Eve, "fondly overcome with Female charm" (IX. 999). Yet Adam's fall involves a different kind of idolatry than Eve's, and those differences define complementary, gendered forms of idolatry that will thenceforth divide the human race.

Satan tells Eve she should be "seen / A Goddess among Gods, ador'd and serv'd / By Angels numberless" (IX. 546–8). As "Empress of this fair World," she should "command" and be "obey'd" (lines 568, 570). Satan suggests he is the first of her subjects, having come to "gaze" and "worship" her as "Sovran of Creatures" (lines 611–12). Satan's temptation of Eve appeals not only to her insecurity and learned sense of inferiority but to her desire to become a god – a desire that links Eve not just with Satan but with all the monarchs, tyrants, and power-hungry prelates Milton had criticized in his prose for wanting to be exalted over their fellow human beings, to be adored.[54]

If Eve's form of idolatry is the impulse to be worshiped, to be a goddess, Adam's is the debased impulse to serve. Adam is like Milton's English people – besotted, prone to worship monarchs and to embrace a carnal service. As Adam explains to Raphael, when he looks at Eve he is drawn to her fair outside, her spectacular beauty: "when I approach / Her loveliness, so absolute she seems . . . All higher knowledge in her presence falls / Degraded" (VIII. 546–52). Perhaps God "on her bestow'd / Too much of Ornament" (VIII. 537–8). As Milton focuses on the seductive outward appearance of Eve, her potentially overwhelming beauty, his language subtly associates her with the seductive external forms of ceremonial worship (the "ornaments" of religion), distrusted by puritans for their very power to move men.[55] There is nothing inherently wrong with Eve's appearance – created by God, she has inner qualities of grace that harmonize with and indeed shine in her physical beauty – but her corporeal beauty is a distraction to others. Adam's disposition to fall in love with the externals and servilely to abject himself to another person – to submit to Eve as the source of his life ("How can I live without thee," IX. 908) – is as dangerous a form of idolatry as the desire to be a god. The desire to be a god(dess) and the desire to worship the creature are mutually sustaining forms of idolatry.

In an important sense, the Fall confirms Raphael's fear that Adam will be seduced by "outward" things, by the body, and by carnal sexuality. Though it seems to have become a new critical orthodoxy that Milton was a "committed monist" and that *Paradise Lost* embodies a radical monism, his monism is neither unremitting nor untroubled. As Jason Rosenblatt has shown, the Hebraic monism of the Edenic books is at odds with the Pauline dualism of the last books.[56] I would suggest that the tension between monist and dualist attitudes is even at work in the middle, Edenic books of *Paradise Lost*, and contributes to the difficult, conflicted representation of the relation between love and worship – and of Eve – in the poem.[57]

A sense of opposition between inner and outer, body and spirit, crosses and complicates the integrative monism of the descriptions of Edenic worship and sexuality. The narrator's depiction of an Adam and Eve in whom outward grace perfectly embodies inward, the description of their harmonious relation as integrating the sexual and spiritual, is abruptly disturbed by Adam's confession to Raphael that he fears God "bestow'd" on Eve "Too much of Ornament, in outward show/ Elaborate, of inward less exact" (VIII. 537–9) – a formulation that in the midst of paradise suddenly suggests the Pauline opposition between outward and inward, carnal and spiritual, at the heart of the puritan understanding of worship. The tension between integrative and dualist assumptions in the poem is even more strikingly exemplified by Raphael's two speeches to Adam. His speech in Book V is the passage cited by those who argue for the monist materialism of the poem:

> O *Adam*, one Almighty is, from whom
> All things proceed, and up to him return,
> If not deprav'd from good, created all
> Such to perfection, one first matter all,
> Indu'd with various forms, various degrees
> Of substance, and in things that live, of life;
> But more refin'd, more spiritous, and pure,
> As nearer to him plac't or nearer tending
> Each in thir several active Spheres assign'd,
> Till body up to spirit work, in bounds
> Proportion'd to each kind . . .   (lines 469–79)

Body/spirit dualism is here rejected for an ontology that has God as the source of the "first matter," and for a chain of being that is fluid not fixed and has varying degrees of substance and spirit. It is this monist embrace of even sexual desire that moves Raphael to admit that the angels also enjoy a kind of sexual love in heaven. But quite a different sense of the world is expressed in Raphael's speech to Adam in Book VIII, when he responds to Adam's confession that "All [his] higher knowledge" "falls / Degraded" in the "presence" of Eve (lines 551–2):

> . . . be not diffident
> Of Wisdom, she deserts thee not, if thou
> Dismiss not her, when most thou need'st her nigh,
> By attributing overmuch to things
> Less excellent, as thou thyself perceiv'st.
> For what admir'st thou, what transports thee so,
> An outside? fair no doubt, and worthy well
> Thy cherishing, thy honoring, and thy love,
> Not thy subjection: weigh with her thyself;
> Then value: Oft-times nothing profits more
> Than self-esteem, grounded on just and right
> Well manag'd; of that skill the more thou know'st,
> The more she will acknowledge thee her Head,
> And to realities yield all her shows . . .
> But if the sense of touch whereby mankind
> Is propagated seem such dear delight
> Beyond all other, think the same voutsaf't
> To Cattle and each Beast . . .
> What higher in her society thou find'st
> Attractive, human, rational, love still;
> In loving thou dost well, in passion not,
> Wherein true Love consists not; Love refines
> The thoughts, and heart enlarges, hath his seat

In Reason, and is judicious, is the scale
By which to heav'nly Love thou may'st ascend,
Not sunk in carnal pleasure, for which cause
Among the Beasts no Mate for thee was found.   (lines 562–94)

Though Adam insists that there is more than carnality in his powerful feelings for Eve,[58] Raphael expresses a remarkably conventional opposition between sexual passion and reason, between "outside" or "shows" (identified with Eve's physical attractiveness) and the inner "realities" of Adam's "reason" or "Wisdom," between body and mind, and between woman and man – dualistic oppositions that Milton's poem in many ways confirms in spite of its monistic impulse.

The potential separation between inward and external, between mind and body, is at odds with the integration of matter and spirit so important to Milton's celebration of life and love in Eden and even the postlapsarian world. It is ominously inscribed even in the initial descriptions of Adam (with his "fair large Front and Eye sublime" [IV. 300]), and Eve (with her "attractive" beauty and "Dishevell'd" "golden tresses" like the "tendrils" of the "Vine" [IV. 298, 305–7]). Both Adam and Eve are, of course, presented as beings in whom matter and spirit are united; Eve has abundant inner qualities of grace and mind.[59] Yet her relation with God is from her first wakening less direct than Adam's. She hears God's voice directing her, but Adam speaks with God – a distinction that recalls Numbers 12:6–8, where God tells the prophetess Miriam that he makes himself known to a prophet like her "in a vision and will speak to him [or her] in a dream," but to Moses "will I speak mouth to mouth, even apparently . . . and the similitude of the Lord shall he behold." Eve may be blessed with visions, but Milton in alluding to this passage suggests that her relation to God is of a lower order than Adam's. According to Raphael's scale of creation, Eve as Adam's inferior has a heavier proportion of matter, is further "plac't" from God (V. 476), and thus, respective to Adam, is more weighted by the body. The dangerous, potential separation of body and mind is even more pronounced in the "separation scene," when Eve (who has from her first appearance been closely associated with physical nature, the body, and materiality) leaves Adam, suggesting the potential of the body to assume an independent power – a potential associated with the threat of Chaos, the first matter, to take over Creation and erect its standard (II. 982–6). Once the external and internal, the material and spiritual, are separated, the person will become thoroughly carnal as the body pulls down the spirit – which is what happens first to Eve and then to Adam.

In the "seduction" of Adam and Eve, Milton intertwines sexual and religious transgression, making one the image of the other, much as in *Comus*. Because sexual adultery figures unfaithfulness to God ("Thou shalt have no other gods besides me," Exodus 20:30), Satan's first attempt to lure Eve through a dream is erotically charged as, "Squat like a Toad, close at [her] ear," he tries "to reach / The Organs of her Fancy" (IV. 800–2). Working on the reproductive organs of her mind, he seeks to "forge / Illusions," to "raise" "inordinate desires" "ingend'ring pride" (lines 802–3, 805, 808–9), thus enacting a perverse conception and generation, much like his own creation of Sin. The link between erotic seduction and the temptation to idolatry is most fully developed in Book IX. Satan curls his serpentine body in a "wanton wreath . . To lure her Eye" (lines 517–18); he addresses Eve with a combination of boldness and servile fawning that recalls the seductions of courtiers and Petrarchan lovers (lines 523–31); his seductive words win "easy entrance" (line 734) into her vulnerable heart. With her "eager appetite" awakened (lines 739–40), she finally eats the forbidden fruit, wholly lost in self-gratifying pleasure, experiencing greater pleasure alone than she had with Adam: "Intent now wholly on her taste, naught else / Regarded, such delight till then . . she never tasted" (lines 786–8). Though Eve's words inviting Adam to eat are cool, hardly erotic, upon hearing them "all his joints relax'd" (IX, 891) – an image invoking the postlapsarian effects of orgasm as it also recalls the effects of Comus' wand, which "can unthread thy joints, / And crumble all thy sinews" (lines 614–15), or the effects of the prelates' ceremonial worship which "despoile[s] us . . . of *manhood*" (*Of Reformation* I, 588). After Adam has eaten the forbidden fruit, they join in a sexual intercourse that Milton figures as adulterous, a fit image for idolatry, given that their earlier love-making had been a holy rite:

> Carnal desire inflaming, hee on *Eve*
> Began to cast lascivious Eyes, she him
> As wantonly repaid; in Lust they burn . . .   (IX. 1013–15)

Sex is here not an act of worship, a remembering of the Creator, but "the Seal" of "thir mutual guilt" (IX. 1043) in which God is wholly forgotten. The intense "pleasure" Adam says he takes in "things to us forbidden" (lines 1024–5) (the fruit of the tree) is transferred to Eve, who, having been seduced by the serpent, now becomes herself an object of adulterous desire, a forbidden fruit (the "bounty" of this "Tree," he calls her) that "inflame[s]" his "sense" more than when she was just his "wedded" spouse (IX. 1030–3). Sexual intercourse, which before the Fall was a means of integrating body and soul, woman and man, and reenacting Creation, now becomes a merely carnal, transgressive act of self-pleasing idolatry, performed out in the open within sight of the animals rather than in the sacred bower.

Because Milton presents Adam and Eve's relationship as a model of relations between human beings and God, our first parents' relation resonates with the tensions of the seventeenth-century conflict over worship. The desire to integrate external and internal, to connect body and spirit in worship, which characterized ceremonialist ideology and shapes Milton's representation of Edenic love, is at odds with fear that the body will pull down the spirit, distract it from God – the fear that drives the puritan rejection of ceremony. That Milton believed in the virtual inseparability of matter and spirit did not prevent him from feeling that they are nevertheless, at some level, in conflict, as Paul, Augustine, Calvin and so much Christian writing had insisted. If the body is not progressively refined by obedience to the spirit (as Raphael's "one first matter" speech promises, and as the opening sentence in *Of Reformation* declared), the spirit will be pulled down by the body. Insofar as Eve or woman is seen as more weighted by the body, she is most easily tempted and most dangerously tempting to Adam. Though made out of Adam and thus containing visibly what is within him already, Eve embodies the lure of physical beauty, of materiality. So long as internal and external, materiality and spirituality, are united – and so long as Adam and Eve are together in a supposedly properly subordinate relation, their love (and the worship it symbolically represents) is integrated and holy, and the poem can express a monism that idealizes a holy ceremonial worship as well as love between man and woman. But once the two are separated, there is a fall (in the poem, and in Adam and Eve) into various forms of dualism: intercourse which is "just sex"; carnal idolatry in which there is an attachment to mere bodily forms of worship; Adam's misogynous speeches, with their distinctions between good men (of the spirit, devoted to God) and evil women (of the body, distracting men to misery); and empty expressions of devotion at odds with inner thoughts, as when Eve tells Adam of her love for him just after she has admitted privately that she would rather see him die than marry another.[60] The epic does indeed express Milton's passionate ideal of integration and wholeness, but it is precarious, unstable, containing from the first the seeds of its dissolution, as Milton shows how difficult it is to prevent true worship from degenerating into idolatry, how difficult it is to embrace the body and materiality without the spirit being overwhelmed.

I would suggest, then, that Milton's depiction of Edenic love and worship expresses a longing for both the community and the sense of integration that the ceremonialism of the Church of England claimed to provide.[61] Though Milton rejected its worship and structure as idolatrous, seeing in it a bondage to the body and external forms, he seems to have been at some level repelled by the dualism of a puritan ideology that would split inner and outer, body and soul, where he instinctively as well as intellectually felt them inseparable. *Paradise Lost* expresses his desire to replace a lost sense of community, as he imagines an Edenic time and state where life and worship were inseparable and integrated, involving body and soul in harmony. And it is this religious ideal that Adam and Eve, at their happiest, represent. The Fall figures the loss of this integrated ceremonialist order, replacing it with a different order, a puritan ideology that divides a Christian present from the Jewish past, a spiritual from a carnal life, the godly individual from the corrupt mass of humanity, permanently rupturing community. One of the deepest ironies in the poem is that the very bonds that form community and love are the cause of the bondage that is idolatry.

As Adam says as he accepts Eve's offer of the fruit, "I feel / The Link of Nature draw me" (IX. 913–14):

> So forcible within my heart I feel
> The Bond of Nature draw me to my own,
> My own in thee, for what thou art is mine;
> Our State cannot be sever'd, we are one.   (IX. 955–8)

What draws Adam is not just a physical bond (that she is literally made of his flesh and blood), not just carnal lust (as Raphael suspects), but the emotional bond of love that connects people. Adam's love of Eve's "society" (IX. 1007) expresses both Milton's desire for community and his fear that bonds between people almost inevitably degenerate into a form of idolatry.

The problem is suggested by Raphael's explanation that the angels serve God out of love not compulsion: "freely we serve, / Because we freely love" (v. 538–9). His comment is meant to justify God's idea of voluntary worship and free it from the satanic suggestion that worship is bondage, but it also implies that love makes you *want* to "serve" the person you love – which is exactly Adam's dilemma with Eve. In Milton's world, woman's love for man is not a problem since it encourages her to serve her supposedly natural superior, thus imaging man's relation to God. But for Adam to "love" Eve means that inevitably he will wish to "serve" her, that he will submit to her desires, and thus in the very nature of things man's love for woman will always at some point conflict with allegiance to God. Woman is put in an impossible situation since she is at once the means for man's proper worship of God and the agent for his idolatrous defection. Adam is in an impossible bind because while "conjugal attraction" is "unreprov'd" (IV. 493), a sacred rite, divinely ordained, it is also the occasion of carnal idolatry, of the spirit being drawn down by body. So long as woman is imagined to be, in her very nature, more bodily than man, the temple of marriage will always be internally threatened with the pollution of carnal idolatry.

If *Paradise Lost* replaces the church with the domestic sphere as the center of religious life, the Fall shows the failure of even Edenic marriage to be a perfect site of true worship. The instinct to idolatry seems innate, perhaps too strong to be overcome. Adam's longing for society is an essential part of his nature – evident soon after his instinctive gaze towards heaven (VIII. 257) and his search for his "Maker" (277–9).[62] He tells God he cannot bear to be "alone": "In solitude / What happiness" (VIII. 364–5). But no sooner does he get his "wish, exactly to [his] heart's desire" (VIII. 451) than he feels that Eve contains everything "fair in all the World" (line 472). His feeling when he first loses sight of her, even before he wakes, is ominous in that it suggests that she is, as it were, his god, the source of his light, happiness, and even life: "Shee disappear'd, and left me dark, I wak'd / To find her, or for ever to deplore / Her loss, and other pleasures all abjure" (VIII. 478–80). If the impulse to idolatry is primal for Adam, it also is for Eve, who when she first wakes is attracted to her image in the pool – no matter how innocent, it is hard to escape seeing this motion as suggestive of self-love. Both Adam and Eve are educated to embrace a supposedly non-idolatrous kind of love, but they seem nevertheless created by God with a gender-specific idolatrous instinct that finds its full, unrepressed expression at the Fall.

If the couple's prelapsarian concord is an image of their harmonious relation with God, the discord, mutual antipathy, and dissension between Adam and Eve in Books IX and X after the Fall reflect their separation from God and echo Milton's vivid descriptions of a bad marriage in *The Doctrine and Discipline of Divorce*. That they cease to pray recalls his earlier comment in the divorce tract that in an unhappy marriage, a person cannot properly perform the duty of serving God (II, 259). Here as in the divorce tracts, the marital state is understood to determine the quality of religious worship. Hence, the reconstruction of Adam and Eve's marriage, for Milton, precedes and enables their spiritual regeneration.

For all the potential for idolatry, Milton still places some hope for the reconfiguration of human worship not just in the individual, guided by the Spirit of God within, but also within marriage. Despite its contamination, Adam and Eve's marriage is in the process of regeneration by the end of Book X, and this gives hope for the survival of some kind of positive community. But the regeneration of the human being and the reconstruction of both marriage and the relation with God require the divinely legislated *subjection* of woman to man ("to thy Husband's will / Thine shall submit, hee over thee shall rule," X. 195–6), which after the Fall even more firmly represents the individual's subjection to God and the disparity between God and man. The turning point after the Fall comes with the submission of Eve to Adam, marked by her falling "humble" "at his feet" (X. 911–12), which provides a model for their falling "prostrate" before God in prayer and asking forgiveness (X. 1087–9). Woman is implicitly charged with the primary responsibility not only for the Fall but for effecting the right relation of human and God. Eve's "submission" and "subjection" to Adam is, as Maureen Quilligan observes, the "price" of regeneration.[63] At the end of the poem, Milton posits hope that in marriage humans can recapture something of true worship and Edenic happiness. But, given what we have witnessed in Eden and in Michael's lessons, the hopefulness of the concluding image of Adam and Eve holding hands, facing the future together, seems immensely fragile.

PARADISE REGAINED AND SAMSON AGONISTES: THE SOLITARY
INDIVIDUAL, DIVORCE, AND THE REJECTION OF COMMUNITY

Milton's last published poems, *Paradise Regained* and *Samson Agonistes* (1671), are far more despairing of the possibility of religious community. Noticeably absent is the vision of marriage as a site for reconstructing worship. Where *Paradise Lost* contains positive images of ceremonial worship and human love that contrast with the idolatry surveyed in its first and last books, these final, rigorously iconoclastic poems represent the lonely, deconstructive, antisocial, and antihistorical implications of a radical puritan ethos.

In *Paradise Regained*, the Son, who represents a perfect example of devotion to God, is a distinctly solitary figure, alone in the desert, obeying a divine Father who gives no material evidence of his presence until the Son at the end miraculously stands on the pinnacle of the temple. The Son's acts of devotion are all, essentially, rejections. He rejects Satan's temptation to make bread out of stones to feed others as well as himself, and he rejects the banquet "Table richly spread, in regal mode" (II. 340), perhaps signifying Milton's suspicion of the idolatrous potential of the rite of Communion.[64] He rejects the kingdoms of Parthia or Rome, just as he rejects human learning, "Arts," and "Eloquence" (IV. 240–1) as irrelevant to his mission. Satan repeatedly tempts Christ to a "carnal," material understanding of his mission and his kingship, while the Son maintains his spiritual, inward interpretation of these things. Milton's puritan privileging of the interior and inward acts of devotion probably precludes a focus on the Crucifixion, which in its display of the body of Christ might seem too Catholic and carnal. But it is also important that, while *Paradise Regained* begins with the Son "revolving" how to begin his "work" of "Savior to mankind" (I. 185–7) and how to "Publish" (I. 188) his office (concerns that lead us to expect his embracing a public, social role), each one of these temptations involves the dangerous lure of communal, social, and human bonds – a lure perhaps not so much deferred as rejected.[65]

Christ's rejections are, of course, necessary steps before he can assume his role of king, messiah, or savior of his people, but that role is interpreted entirely spiritually and is not imagined (except by Satan) socially or politically. Moreover, as a model for what human religious acts should be, the Son's acts remain disturbingly exclusionary, offering little guidance for how human beings might reconstitute a religious community. Being faithful to God requires breaking from the past and tradition, separating from other people, standing alone upheld only by the spirit of God. Perhaps there is, as in *Paradise Lost*, some suggestion that the home, the private and domestic sphere, can still be the site of religious community, since at the very end the Son "unobserv'd / Home to his Mother's house private return'd" (*Paradise Regained*, IV. 638–9). It is, however, significant of the lonely individualism of his last two poems that, whereas marriage and the symbolic embrace of sexual love had formed the center of *Paradise Lost*, Milton's hero in *Paradise Regained* is the unmarried, celibate Son, and the act of divorce is at the center of *Samson Agonistes*.

Long recognized as speaking to the condition of England after the failure of the Revolution, *Samson Agonistes* is Milton's most radically iconoclastic text. Where the hero of *Paradise Regained* resists acting, *Samson Agonistes* concludes with the destruction of the idol-worshiping Philistines and their Temple.[66] What has not been clearly understood, however, is that Samson's iconoclasm is closely bound up with his divorce from Dalila, which is its necessary precondition and symbol.

Dalila has remained a curiously opaque, "inscrutable" character.[67] Much of the difficulty comes from the tendency to read her in terms of a modern psychological notion of human character and motivation that ignores the religious significance and symbolic value attributed to marriage and gender roles in seventeenth-century England. Though some readers have seen Dalila as the wronged and loving wife, the language and plot of the poem clearly present her as a dangerous figure for idolatry.[68] In Milton's transformation, the biblical character infamous for her treachery becomes identified with the idolatry of a heathen ceremonial worship that posed an ongoing, seductive threat to Samson and the Israelites – and to the English.

The Chorus's first description of Dalila evokes the conventional association of idolatry with seduction.

> But who is this, what thing of Sea or Land?
> Female of sex it seems,
> That so bedeckt, ornate, and gay,
> Comes this way sailing
> Like a stately Ship
> Of *Tarsus*, bound for th'Isles

Of *Javan* or *Gadire*
With all her bravery on, and tackle trim,
Sails fill'd, and streamers waving,
Courted by all the winds that hold them play,
An Amber scent of odorous perfume
Her harbinger . . .   (lines 710–21)

Her attractiveness is at once powerfully sexual and religiously charged. Compared to the ship that was the traditional image of prostitution, Dalila's association with the "whoredom" of idolatry is deepened by her lavish, seductive attire, as well as her having been paid gold by the Philistines (lines 830–1).[69] Spectacular in appearance, she intensifies the dangerous power of Eve's natural attractiveness. Dalila's "ornate" appearance recalls the conventional description of ceremonial worship, and echoes Milton's comment in *Of Reformation* that the prelates who brought in ceremonies have "overlai'd" the "chast and modest vaile" of "*Christs* Gospell" with "wanton *tresses*" and "bespecckl'd her with all the gaudy allurements of a Whore" (I, 557). In *Samson Agonistes*, too, the rich clothes symbolize the pride and allure of idolatry, as Dalila becomes identified with the seductive, idolatrous ceremonies of the Laudian church, newly restored in Restoration England.

Dalila's visit is the turning point for Samson in the poem. The violence of his dismissal of his former wife bespeaks no simple, secular misogyny but an iconoclastic desire to cast off all remnants of idolatry.[70] His anger resonates with the prophets in the Hebrew Bible, with kings like Josiah who destroyed Israel's idols, and also with the words of Protestant reformers that continued to be relevant in the Restoration, when clergy were required to announce their allegiance to the Church of England's rites and liturgy. Samson's sharp language publicly abjures any vestiges of his former attraction to idolatry. I would not deny the human, psychological significance of Milton's presentation of Samson's vulnerability to Dalila's sexual appeal, or the suggestion that masculine identity depends on separation from the feminine.[71] But for Milton as for others in the seventeenth century, domestic and sexual relations had religious and political significance and functions, and probably nowhere do we better see this than in *Samson Agonistes*, where political liberation, religious faith, and domestic relations are intimately intertwined. In Milton's poem, Samson's ability to control his carnal, sexual desires for Dalila mirrors his relation to idolatry. That a woman figures the temptation to idolatry suggests that godliness is (even more than in *Paradise Lost*) a masculine virtue that requires the exclusion of the feminine, which is identified with carnality and a body that tempts the soul to forsake God.

Much as Adam and Eve's marriage represented the changing relation between humans and God in *Paradise Lost*, the history of Samson's and Dalila's relation represents his problematic relation to God. It is crucial that Dalila is identified as idolater, gentile, and *wife* – not his mistress as in Judges. Milton's significant change allows Samson's narrative to parallel that of the prophet Hosea, whose marriage to an adulterous idolater symbolized Israel's unfaithfulness to God. Moreover, for Christians, the woman from an idolatrous tribe, taken by an Israelite in marriage, had become a trope for the contested role of ceremony in worship. Lancelot Andrewes defended the controversial ceremonies of the English church by comparing them to the gentile women married and converted by Jews:

By the judiciall Law of *Moses* expressed in *Deut.* 21. If a strange woman be taken in battel, if her beauty please thee, her nails and hairs being pared and shaven, and her garment of captivity being taken away, thou maist lawfully take her to wife: By the morall of this Law, severally write *Isidore* and *Peter Blessensis*, the Ceremonies of the Gentiles, the deformities thereof being taken away may lawfully be used amongst the Christians.[72]

Andrewes found in the pattern of marriage, conversion, and purification of the alien, unclean woman a symbol of the Christian's relation with pre-Christian and Catholic ceremonial worship. Anti-ceremonialist Protestants, however, insisted that England keep separate from the Church of Rome, resisting her seductive "garments" or ceremonies. Milton criticized Rome's persistent attempts to lure Protestant Englishmen with seductive strategies remarkably similar to Dalila's:

If we have indeed given a bill of divorce to Popery and superstition, why do we not say as to a divors't wife; those things which are yours take them all with you, and they shall sweepe after you? Why were not we thus wise at our parting from Rome? Ah like a crafty adultresse she forgot not all her smooth looks and inticing words at her parting; yet keep these letters, these tokens, and these few ornaments . . . let them preserve with you the memory of what I am? No, but of what I was, once faire and lovely in your eyes. (*An Apology*, 1, 942)

Dalila's temptation of Samson would surely have been recognized in Milton's time as a seduction to idolatry, which is at once unfaithfulness to God and a carnal devotion to the body – a link reinforced by the fact that the scene of betrayal takes place in the midst of "Spousal embraces" (line 389). Dalila's cutting Samson's hair suggests the emasculating effect of an effeminating, seductive idolatry, and recalls *The Reason of Church Government*, where Milton warns that prelacy, like Dalila, has shorn the king of his strength while he slept (1, 858–9).

Dalila declares that she chose "to save / Her country from a fierce destroyer . . . / Above the faith of wedlock bands" (lines 984–6). Milton's attention to her Philistine loyalty suggests, not that there is no difference between loyalty to Dagon and loyalty to the "true" God, but that, like the borrowed ceremonies, Dalila never escapes her idolatrous origins. We might recall Herbert's ambivalence about conversion in "The Forerunners," where the lovely verbal images associated with the beauty of ceremonial worship, images he has purified, threaten to return to the "stews" (line 15). Milton is more emphatic: once a heathen, always a heathen. Rather than cleansing Dalila of her gentile impurity, Samson has been seduced and has lost the power and manhood identified with true worship of God. In this sense, his story parallels that of the Jews, who relapsed into idolatry – and of the English people. Bondage is the apt punishment for an idolatry understood as bondage to the flesh.

That Milton makes Dalila Samson's wife not only emphasizes the strength of Samson's former attachment to the idolatry she represents. It allows Milton to evoke the radical reformist position, at the center of his earlier divorce tracts and now pointedly appropriate in the Restoration, that the godly Christian must permanently separate from all idolatry. Samson embodies the proper stance against idolatry – first in his rejection of Dalila, and then in his destruction of the temple of the Philistines, two closely connected actions with subversive contemporary applications. For just as his former uxoriousness represents idolatry on a personal level, so violent, zealous divorce ("Out, out Hyaena," line 748) becomes a domestic figure for Samson's iconoclastic violence at the end of the drama. In resisting Dalila's seductions, he triumphs over not just his carnal sensuality but the temptations of carnal, idolatrous religious worship. It is thus no accident that Samson's rejection of Dalila's "fair enchanted cup, and warbling charms" and "sorceries" (lines 934, 937) recalls the earlier rejection of Comus' attraction, or that the Chorus's description of her as "a manifest Serpent by her sting / Discover'd in the end" (lines 997–8) echoes Spenser's Error, which was identified with the Roman Catholic Church.

In 1634 chastity was the appropriate figure for a church trying to resist idolatrous pollution and retain its purity, but in 1671 the situation had changed. The restored English church was in Milton's view wholly contaminated, beyond reform. Divorce is now the image of the necessary separation from idolatry. In the symbolic logic of the narrative, Samson must reject Dalila, must publicly renounce his former attraction to idolatry, before he can feel the connectedness with God that he expresses in his encounter with Harapha ("My trust is in the living God," line 1140).[73] He must break from a past identified with carnal idolatry. The violence of divorce prepares for the violence of his final iconoclasm, as it clears a space for the inward working of the spirit of God that can give him the extraordinary strength to destroy the Philistine temple. If, as Michael Lieb argues, Samson at the end of the play becomes both the embodiment and agent of God's "Dread" (the awesome, destructive power inflicted on idolaters), then Samson would seem to be regenerated, having become the image of God.[74] We may dislike the image, but I think Milton intended it to be exemplary for the godly English in the Restoration. Those readers who believe that Samson should have shown more charity and forgiveness to Dalila and given her another chance miss Milton's point: if she represents the idolatry Samson was formerly enslaved to, he has no choice but to reject her completely if he is to do God's work.

Samson's divorce from a woman symbolically identified with a foreign, seductive idolatry enacts the stance of the godly non-conformist in the Restoration, repudiating a restored English church contaminated by popish and heathen idolatry. And much as Milton's theorizing of divorce in the 1640s had been the grounds for regicide, now in Milton's 1671 drama Samson's divorce is but the prelude to the destruction of the Philistines and their temple – an exemplary act full of subversive meaning for the faithful few in Restoration England. Samson's climactic act takes place in the midst of their "solemn Feast" to Dagon, a day of ceremonial "Sacrifices . . . Pomp, and Games" (lines 1311–12) evocative of the festivals of the English church disliked by puritan nonconformists, banned during the Interregnum but now restored as part of the nation's compulsory worship. At first Samson refuses to "prostitut[e]" his "Consecrated gift" to "Idols" (lines 1354, 1358), rejecting the Philistine lords' commands that he perform for them, disdaining like the nonconformists to attend "Temples" where there are "Idolatrous Rites" (line 1378). But he abruptly decides to go, equivocally declaring, "Masters' commands come with a power resistless / To such as owe them absolute subjection" (lines 1404–5). In perhaps his most dangerous move, Milton here suggests that outward conformity to compulsory rites may mask revolutionary impulses that will in time erupt.

Milton presents the violent destruction of idolatry and idolaters as Samson's supreme act of worship. In what Samson sees as a contest "to decide whose god is God" (line 1176), he destroys the temple to Dagon and wipes out the Philistines, who are "Drunk with Idolatry" (line 1670). He is moved by "rousing motions" within (line 1382) that are like those motions that inspire prayer. That Samson's final act is a "Holocaust" (line 1702) – a word describing the "burnt offerings" in Leviticus that were completely consumed by fire, a word also appearing in Herrick's ceremonial lyrics – suggests its ceremonial status as an act of worship. But whereas in Leviticus – and Herrick – sacrifice is meant to ensure the continuation of life, it remains an open question whether Samson's iconoclastic violence is regenerative or simply an act of destruction and vengeance. The brutality of his war against carnal idolatry is part of the biblical story, perhaps supporting the Christian stereotype of the Jews as a "carnal" people, bound to the Law; but it is also a sign of the intensity of Milton's anger at idolatry. In Milton's hands, Samson becomes the embodiment of radical puritan ideology in a time of religious bondage and persecution, with iconoclasm as the only legitimate ceremony imaginable for those who would purify a thoroughly idolatrous world. Samson's rage towards the Philistines expresses not just detestation of heathen idolatry and revenge for his humiliations but anger at the Israelites who have rejected his earlier opportunities for deliverance. This situation precisely parallels Milton's relation with the English, who in this sense are the object of Milton's rage. Much as in the disillusioned prose of the 1650s where the similarity between the English and the Jews provoked his disgust, in *Samson Agonistes* England is implicitly identified with both the Israelites and the Philistines, who as idolaters are finally not all that different.

That Milton intends us to see Samson as regenerated and exemplary does not mean that the dramatic poem is unproblematic. Much here is disturbing. *Samson Agonistes* identifies idolatry with the feminine far more exclusively than his earlier published poems. Further, Samson's supposed spiritual regeneration seems compromised by the intensely physical and destructive form it takes. The greatest problem, however, is the sheer lack of any alternative, reconstructive forms of religious worship, which may be related to the absence of any positive role for the feminine in this configuration of true worship. The expulsion of the feminine leaves a barren world. In marked contrast to *Paradise Lost*, where Eve has a crucial if problematic role in human worship, there is in *Samson Agonistes* no representation of what true worship might be other than iconoclasm. Though the iconoclasm in *Samson* has been called creative and "regenerative,"[75] what is striking is the absence of the creative, lifegiving kinds of worship that had existed in *Paradise Lost*, where conjugal love and poetry could constitute sacred rites. The absence of positive forms of worship in *Samson* represents the difficulty – even the impossibility – of Milton's imagining in 1671 what form true rites of worship might take.

Samson Agonistes and *Paradise Regained* offer images of true worship that are socially less positive and constructive than those in *Paradise Lost*. The emphasis on solitude in these poems contrasts with the "sociable" spirit of *Paradise Lost*. In a sense, Samson perfectly represents an oppositional puritan ideology, founded on exclusions and rejections. The rejection of Dalila and the destruction of the Philistines may be the necessary prelude to freeing the Jews and reconstructing true worship. But that reconstruction never comes in the history of the Jews recorded in the Hebrew Bible and is not envisioned in Milton's poem, with its deep sense of connection between England and "servile" Israel (line 1213). Samson's act not only does not free the Israelites; it becomes an occasion for their further idolatry.[76] In his regeneration, Samson thus remains very much alone. Though some critics identify him with the English people,[77] Samson explicitly distances himself from the idolatrous, treacherous Israelites (lines 256–76) in a way that suggests Milton's own distance from his fellow Englishmen. He is exemplary for the nation in that "each [person] must deliver himself from bondage into freedom,"[78] but this deliverance entails a rupture of social bonds.

The difficulty of imagining a positive community may have been the result of Milton's experience of the English Revolution and its aftermath. But *Samson Agonistes* and *Paradise Regained* also show how the individualism of puritan ideology, as well as its stance of separation from impurity, taken to its limits, made it difficult to imagine a real human community. Given the coordinates of puritan ideology, perhaps devotion to God requires that a person be, as Samson was intended, a *"Nazarite,"* "separate to God" (lines 318, 31). The pollution of idolatry is contagious. True worship, obedience to God, and regeneration can only take place at the level of the individual – and thus Milton speaking through Samson and the Son absolves himself of the responsibility of transforming "the people." In response to the Chorus's reminder that despite Samson's deeds, *"Israel* still serves," Samson says, "That fault I take not on me"; Israel "love[s] Bondage more than Liberty" (lines 240–1, 270). Though Jesus was a Jew, Milton's Son dismisses the "captive Tribes" of Israel as unworthy of being delivered from "servitude" by him since they "wrought their own captivity" through idolatry: "No, let them serve/ Thir enemies, who serve Idols with God" (*Paradise Regained*, III. 414, 381, 415, 431–2). In contrast to the egalitarian pronouncements of Christ within the New Testament, Milton's hero contemptuously refers to the people as merely

> . . . a herd confus'd,
> A miscellaneous rabble, who extol
> Things vulgar. . .   (III. 49–51)

Not only for the Son but for Milton, the regaining of paradise is eminently lonely. The intimate, spiritual connection between the individual and an invisible God, while clearly seen as a blessing, is offset by a loss of communal or social bonds that surely was painful for a poet who imagined his Adam as, from the first, needing more than the company of God.

Notes

I INTRODUCTION

1 Sir Thomas Browne, *Religio Medici*, Part I, section 26, in *The Works of Sir Thomas Browne*, ed. Geoffrey Keynes, 4 vols. (Chicago, 1964), I, 38.

2 For a cogent statement of the importance of recognizing religion as a primary determinant, see Janel Mueller, "Complications of Intertextuality: John Fisher, Katherine Parr, and 'The Book of the Crucifix,'" in *Representing Women in Renaissance England*, ed. Claude J. Summers and Ted-Larry Pebworth (Columbia, 1997), pp. 24–41.

3 See Christopher Hill's *Economic Problems of the Church: From Archbishop Whitgift to the Long Parliament* (Oxford, 1956), *Society and Puritanism in Pre-Revolutionary England*, 2nd edn. (New York, 1967), and *The World Turned Upside Down: Radical Ideas during the English Revolution* (New York, 1972); Kevin Sharpe, *The Personal Rule of Charles I* (New Haven, 1992); J. P. Sommerville, *Politics and Ideology in England 1603–1640* (London, 1986); Brian Manning, *The English People and the English Revolution, 1640–1649* (London, 1976); David Underdown, *Revel, Riot and Rebellion: Popular Politics and Culture in England, 1603–1660* (Oxford, 1985); J. P. Kenyon, *The Civil Wars of England* (New York, 1988); Conrad Russell, *The Causes of the English Civil War* (Oxford, 1990). Particularly valuable on historians' debates about the causes of the war and the issues involved is Ann Hughes, *The Causes of the English Civil War* (New York, 1991).

4 See John Morrill, *The Nature of the English Revolution* (London, 1993); Russell, *Causes*, p. 59; see also Hughes, *Causes*, p. 180.

5 See "Introduction" and "The Church in England, 1642–9," in John Morrill, *Reactions to the English Civil War 1642–49* (New York, 1983), pp. 1–27, 89–114, and *Nature of the English Revolution*. On seventeenth-century religious history, see especially Nicholas Tyacke, *Anti-Calvinists: The Rise of English Arminianism c. 1590–1640* (Oxford, 1987); *The Early Stuart Church, 1603–1642*, ed. Kenneth Fincham (Stanford, 1993); and Peter Lake's essays, "Calvinism and the English Church 1570–1635," *Past and Present*, 114 (February 1987), 32–76, "Lancelot Andrewes, John Buckeridge, and Avant-Garde Conformity at the Court of James I," in *The Mental World of the Jacobean Court*, ed. Linda Levy Peck (Cambridge, 1991), pp. 113–33,

and "The Laudian Style: Order, Uniformity and the Pursuit of the Beauty of Holiness in the 1630s," in *Early Stuart Church*, ed. Fincham, pp. 161–85; and Julian Davies, *The Caroline Captivity of the Church: Charles I and the Remoulding of Anglicanism, 1625–1641* (Oxford, 1992).

On conformity, see especially Judith Maltby's "'By this Book': Parishioners, the Prayer Book, and the Established Church," in *Early Stuart Church*, ed. Fincham, pp. 115–37, and her *Prayer Book and People in Elizabethan and Early Stuart England*, forthcoming from Cambridge University Press.

6 Among the important literary-historicist studies of this period are Leah S. Marcus, *The Politics of Mirth: Jonson, Herrick, Milton, Marvell and the Defense of Old Holiday Pastimes* (Chicago, 1986); Kevin Sharpe, *Criticism and Compliment: The Politics of Literature in the England of Charles I* (Cambridge, 1987); Lois Potter, *Secret Rites and Secret Writing: Royalist Literature, 1641–1660* (Cambridge, 1989); Thomas N. Corns, *Uncloistered Virtue: English Political Literature, 1640–1660* (Oxford, 1992); and Nigel Smith, *Literature and Revolution in England, 1640–1660* (New Haven, 1994).

Recent studies concerned with religion include N. H. Keeble, *The Literary Culture of Nonconformity in Later Seventeenth-century England* (Athens GA, 1987); Nigel Smith, *Perfection Proclaimed: Language and Literature in English Radical Religion 1640–1660* (Oxford, 1989); Debora K. Shuger, *Habits of Thought in the English Renaissance: Religion, Politics, and the Dominant Culture* (Berkeley, 1990); Christopher Hill's *The English Bible and the Seventeenth-century Revolution* (London, 1993); and Debora K. Shuger, *The Renaissance Bible: Scholarship, Sacrifice, and Subjectivity* (Berkeley, 1994).

7 Christopher Haigh, *English Reformations: Religion, Politics, and Society under the Tudors* (Oxford, 1993), pp. 15–16. See also Eamon Duffy's excellent, sympathetic treatment of late medieval (Catholic) Christianity in *The Stripping of the Altars: Traditional Religion in England 1400–1580* (New Haven, 1992).

8 See Clifford Geertz, "Religion as a Cultural System," in *The Interpretation of Cultures* (New York, 1973), pp. 87–125; Mary Douglas, *Purity and Danger: An Analysis of Concepts of Pollution and Taboo* (New York, 1966), especially p. 128; and Emile Durkheim's thesis that religion is "the image" of a society: *The Elementary Forms of the Religious Life*, trans. Joseph Ward Swain (London, 1915), especially pp. 10, 421.

9 On ideology, see Louis Althusser, *Lenin and Philosophy and Other Essays*, trans. Ben Brewster (London, 1971); Clifford Geertz, "Ideology as a Cultural System," in *The Interpretation of Cultures*, pp. 193–233; and Terry Eagleton, "What is Ideology?" in *Ideology: An Introduction* (London, 1991).

10 For an emphasis on this common ground, see particularly Charles H. and Katherine George, *The Protestant Mind of the English Reformation 1570–1640* (Princeton, 1961), and Patrick Collinson, *The Religion of Protestants: The Church in English Society 1559–1625* (Oxford, 1982).

11 Most important are Tyacke, *Anti-Calvinists*; Lake, "Calvinism and the

English Church," Collinson, *Religion of Protestants,* and Fincham, "Introduction," in *Early Stuart Church,* pp. 1–22, which provides a valuable overview.

12 See especially Tyacke's *Anti-Calvinists;* Lake's "Calvinism and the English Church," "Laudian Style," and *Anglicans and Puritans? Presbyterianism and English Conformist Thought from Whitgift to Hooker* (London, 1988); Davies's *Caroline Captivity;* and Anthony Milton, *Catholic and Reformed: The Roman and Protestant Churches in English Protestant Thought 1600–1640* (Cambridge, 1995).

13 Lake, *Anglicans and Puritans?,* p. 7. See also Patrick Collinson, *Godly People: Essays on English Protestantism and Puritanism* (London, 1983), especially pp. 1–18.

14 Tyacke's *Anti-Calvinists* implies that the conflicts centered on the issue of predestination. For a qualification of this position, see Fincham's "Introduction," in *Early Stuart Church,* p. 5.

15 Fincham, "Introduction," *Early Stuart Church,* p. 4. The older definition of Anglican and puritan is to be found in John F. H. New, *Anglican and Puritan: The Basis of their Opposition, 1588–1640* (Stanford, 1964). See also Horton Davies on the differences between "Anglicans" and "Puritans," in *Worship and Theology in England,* vol. II (*From Andrewes to Baxter and Fox, 1603–1690*) (Princeton, 1975), chapter 5. Recently, historians have questioned the idea that under Elizabeth and James the church was the *via media* between Geneva and Rome, and they have shown that Calvinism and the anti-Rome stance that supposedly characterized puritans were central to the church under James as well as Elizabeth (see, e.g., Tyacke's *Anti-Calvinists* and Collinson, *Religion of Protestants*). Lake, in *Anglicans and Puritans?,* argues that Hooker "invented" Anglicanism. But see Peter White, "The *Via Media* in the Early Stuart Church," in *Early Stuart Church,* pp. 211–30, for a vigorous anti-revisionist statement.

16 See Lake, "Laudian Style," pp. 162–3.

17 Maltby, " 'By this Book' "; Morrill, "Church in England, 1642–9."

18 On the polemicization of English literary culture, see Steven N. Zwicker, *Lines of Authority: Politics and English Culture, 1649–1689* (Ithaca, 1993).

19 Perez Zagorin, *Ways of Lying: Dissimulation, Persecution and Conformity in Early Modern Europe* (Cambridge MA, 1990); Annabel Patterson, *Censorship and Interpretation: The Conditions of Writing and Reading in Early Modern England* (Madison, 1984).

2 READING THE CONFLICTS: CEREMONY, IDEOLOGY, AND THE
   MEANING OF RELIGION

1 "Articles, or Instructions for Articles, to be Exhibited by his Majestie's Heigh Commissioners, against Mr. John Cosin, Mr. Francis Burgoine, Mr. Marmaduke Blaxton, Doctor Hunt, Doctor Lindsell, Mr. William

James, all learned clerks of the Cathedreall Church of Durham," in *The Correspondence of John Cosin, D.D.*, publications of the Surtees Society, vol. 52 (Durham, 1869), pp. 166, 167, 169–70.

2 William Prynne, *Canterburies Doome. or the First Part of a Compleat History of the Commitment, Charge, Tryall, Condemnation, Execution of William Laud* (1646), p. 26. See Laud's answers to the charges in *The History of the Troubles and Tryal of . . . William Laud . . . Wrote by Himselfe, during his Imprisonment in the Tower*, ed. Henry Wharton (1695).

3 Sharpe, *Personal Rule*, pp. 366, 369–74, argues that Neile and Wren were more rigid than Laud in their approach to conformity. Sharpe and Julian Davies, *Caroline Captivity*, especially chapters 1 and 2, see Charles as the leading force behind the ceremonialism.

4 Hughes, *Causes*, p. 112; Sharpe, *Personal Rule*, pp. 317–28.

5 Morrill calls them the "hotter sort of protestants" ("The Religious Context of the English Civil War," in *Nature of the English Revolution*, p. 52). On religious developments during Charles's reign, see especially Tyacke, *Anti-Calvinists*; Lake, "Laudian Style"; Hugh Trevor-Roper, "Laudianism and Political Power," in *Catholics, Anglicans and Puritans: Seventeenth-century Essays* (London, 1987), pp. 40–119; J. Sears McGee, "William Laud and the Outward Face of Religion," in *Leaders of the Reformation*, ed. Richard L. DeMolen (London, 1984), pp. 318–44; and R. Malcolm Smuts, *Court Culture and the Origins of a Royalist Tradition in Early Stuart England* (Philadelphia, 1987), chapter 8. On Charles's obsession with order and his role in religion, see Sharpe, *Personal Rule*, especially pp. 275–402.

On the efforts to enforce conformity, see especially the following essays in *Early Stuart Church*, ed. Fincham: Kenneth Fincham and Peter Lake, "The Ecclesiastical Policies of James I and Charles I," pp. 23–49, Nicholas Tyacke, "Archbishop Laud," pp. 51–70, Fincham, "Episcopal Government, 1603–1640," pp. 71–91, and Lake, "Laudian Style," pp. 161–85.

6 *Acts and Ordinances of the Interregnum, 1642–1660*, ed. C. H. Firth and R. S. Rait, vol. 1 (London, 1911), 180–4, 265–6, 582–3, 755–7. Morrill, *Nature of the English Revolution*, p. 86, notes that according to the *Commons Journal* over seventy ministers were dispossessed between February and July 1642. See the ordinances of August 26, 1643 and May 9, 1644 for demolishing monuments of idolatry and superstition in the churches (*Acts and Ordinances*, 1, 265–6, 425–6). On the iconoclasm in the Civil War period, see Margaret Aston's *England's Iconoclasts*, vol. 1 (*Laws Against Images*) (Oxford, 1988), chapter 3, and John Phillips, *The Reformation of Images: Destruction of Art in England, 1535–1660* (Berkeley, 1973), pp. 183–200.

7 Russell, *Causes*, has suggested that "within the church of England there were two churches struggling to get out" (p. 82). Though Sharpe, *Personal Rule*, has warned that the various contested issues in the church

did not "align men neatly into warring camps, nor were all of the measures [of Charles and Laud] widely opposed or contentious," he admits that "liturgical and ceremonial issues . . . divided men more," with the lines drawn most sharply from 1637 on (pp. 360, 362).

8 Thomas Morton, *A Defence of the Innocencie of the Three Ceremonies of the Church of England* (1618), pp. 35, 85–6; *An Abridgment of that Booke which the Ministers of the Lincolne Diocesse delivered to his Majestie* (Amsterdam, 1617).

9 John Burges, *An Answer Reioyned to that Much Applauded Pamphlet of a Namelesse Author* . . . (1631), p. 75; William Ames, *A Reply to Dr. Mortons Generall Defence of Three Nocent Ceremonies* (1622), p. 53. Burges is moderate in affirming the church's power, but Matthew Wren's *A Sermon Preached before the King's Maiestie* (Cambridge, 1627) insists on the link between religious conformity and allegiance to the king.

10 William Quelch, *Church-Customes Vindicated: In Two Sermons* . . . (1636), pp. 44, 54. Cf. Samuel Hoard, *The Churches Authority Asserted: In a Sermon Preached at Chelmsford, at the Metropoliticall Visitation of* . . . *Arch-bishop of Canterbury his Grace* (1637), and Morton, *Defence*, pp. 45, 46. On Laud's use of the Star Chamber, see McGee, "William Laud and the Outward Face of Religion," especially p. 322.

11 John Calvin, *Institutes of the Christian Religion*, trans. John Allen, 2 vols. (Philadelphia, n.d.), II, 248–59 (IV.ii); on images, see I, 97–112 (I.xi). Luther rejects the teachings of men, but takes a less harsh stance on "images," wishing for them to be abolished because of their "abuse," but refusing to condemn them utterly or to destroy them violently. See "That we are to Reject the Doctrines of Men" and the third and fourth of "The Eight Wittenberg Sermons," in *Works of Martin Luther*, vol. II (Philadelphia, 1916), 431–55, 401–11.

12 Peter White, "The *Via Media* in the Early Stuart Church," in *Early Stuart Church*, ed. Fincham, pp. 211–30.

13 Prynne, *A Looking-glasse for all lordly prelates* (1636), p. 44. See also Prynne's account of Laud's trial in *Canterburies Doome*, especially pp. 103, 104.

14 Tessa Watt, *Cheap Print and Popular Piety 1550–1640* (Cambridge, 1991), pp. 136–59, 217–53.

15 Ames, *Reply*, p. 17; William Ames, *A Fresh Suit Against Human Ceremonies in Gods Worship* (1633), p. 17. Cf. John Bastwick's *The Answer of John Bastwick, Doctor of Phisicke, To the exceptions made against his Letany* (1637), p. 19, and *The Vanity and Mischeife of the Old Letany* (1637), p. 18.

16 William Bradshaw, *A Treatise of Divine Worship* (Amsterdam, 1604), pp. 28–9; Bastwick, *The Letany of John Bastwick* (1637), p. 17.

17 See Horton Davies, *Worship and Theology*, pp. 490–521.

18 Morton, *Defence*, pp. 82, 85–8; Burges, *Answer*, pp. 125–7, 291.

19 William Bradshaw, *A Shorte Treatise, Of the cross in Baptisme* (Amsterdam, 1604), p. 4; cf. Ames, *Fresh Suit*, pp. 296–7.

20 Bastwick, *Vanity*, p. 4.

21 John Burges, *The Lawfulnes of Kneeling in the Act of Receiving the Lords Supper* (1631), p. 24.
22 Burges, *Answer*, pp. 278, 281, 78–9. On Laudian worship and the emphasis on external beauty, see McGee, "William Laud and the Outward Face of Religion," pp. 326–7, 330; and Lake, "Laudian Style," especially pp. 164–6. Phillips, *Reformation of Images*, remarks that Puritans could say Laud's attention to images resulted in "the invasion of a 'counter-Reformation'" (p. 182). On the distrust of images, see Aston, *England's Iconoclasts*. Watt, *Cheap Print and Popular Piety*, however, shows that Protestant positions ranged from moderate to radical (p. 132) and that the visual remained important for most English people in the seventeenth century (p. 136).
23 Burges, *Answer*, p. 461; R. T., *De Templis, A Treatise of Temples* (1638), pp. 190–1; cf. Morton, *Defence*, pp. 283–5.
24 Quoted in Burges, *Answer*, pp. 277–8.
25 Morton, *Defence*, p. 3; Burges, *Answer*, pp. 111–12; Ames, *Fresh Suit*, "Alphabeticall Table."
26 Burges, *Answer*, pp. 79, 90; cf. Morton, *Defence*, pp. 27–8.
27 Quelch, *Church-Customes Vindicated*, p. 34.
28 Hoard, *Churches Authority*, p. 15; cf. R. T., *De Templis*, pp. 176–7.
29 *The Sermons of John Donne*, ed. Evelyn M. Simpson and George R. Potter, 10 vols. (Berkeley, 1954), VII, 430, 429–33.
30 Collinson, *Religion of Protestants*, pp. 141–88, argues against the views of Christopher Hill and Michael Walzer (*The Revolution of the Saints: A Study in the Origins of Radical Politics* [Cambridge MA, 1965]) that puritanism was revolutionary. But on the disruptions of the period, see especially Hill, *World Turned Upside Down*.
31 Quelch, *Church-Customes Vindicated*, p. 34; Ames, *Fresh Suit*, dedication "To the renowned King," and *Reply*, p. 104. Cf. Bradshaw, *Treatise of Divine Worship*, p. 37.
32 Ames, *Fresh Suit*, p. 269.
33 Morton, *Defence*, pp. 301, 308; Burges, *Answer*, pp. 125, 263.
34 Donne, *Sermons*, VII, 430–1; IX, 168, 170. Cf. R. T., *De Templis*, pp. 122–3.
35 Peter Heylyn, *Antidotum Lincolniense* (1637), section II, p. 19. Cf. John Cosin's remark that Christ exhibits "his Body and Blood" in "the sacramental Bread and Cup" (*Notes and Collections on the Book of Common Prayer*, vol. v of *The Works of John Cosin* [Oxford, 1855], p. 345). See also Lake, "Andrewes and Buckeridge," pp. 128–9.
36 William Laud, *A Speech Delivered in the Starr-Chamber* (1637), pp. 45–6; *A Relation of the Conference Betweene William Lawd . . . And Mr. Fisher the Jesuite* (1639), "Dedicatory Epistle to King Charles"; *History of the Troubles and Tryal*, p. 156. McGee, "William Laud and the Outward Face of Religion," p. 329.
37 See Duffy, *Stripping of the Altars*, on the experience of "corporate Christianity" in the late middle ages. Duffy argues for the vitality of

fifteenth- and sixteenth-century traditional Christianity; ceremony and ritual helped create a society in which personal and individual identity was understood in terms of the community. See especially chapters 3 ("The Mass") and 4 ("Corporate Christians"), pp. 91–130, 131–54.

38 See St. Thomas Aquinas, *Compendium of Theology*, trans. Cyril Vollert (London, 1952), chapter 82 ("Man's Need of Sense Faculties for Understanding"), pp. 75–6, and chapter 151 ("Reunion with the Body Requisite for the Soul's Perfect Happiness"), pp. 160–1. Julian Davies, *Caroline Captivity*, notes Laud was influenced by Thomist Aristotelianism (p. 58).

39 See Lake, "Laudian Style."

40 Laud, *Speech Delivered in the Starr-Chamber*, p. 47.

41 See Calvin, *Institutes*, II, 552 (IV.xvii); Bastwick, *Answer*, subtitle. On the Reformed (especially Calvin's) rejection of the Roman Catholic and Lutheran doctrines of real presence, see Jaroslav Pelikan, *Reformation of Church and Dogma (1300–1700)*, vol. IV of *The Christian Tradition: A History of the Development of Doctrine* (Chicago, 1984). On eucharistic controversies in seventeenth-century England, see Horton Davies, *Worship and Theology*, pp. 286–325.

42 Laud, *History of the Troubles and Tryal*, p. 224.

43 See Elaine Pagels, *Adam, Eve, and the Serpent* (New York, 1988), and Peter Brown, *The Body and Society: Men, Women and Sexual Renunciation in Early Christianity* (New York, 1988).

44 See Daniel Boyarin's discussion of the flesh/spirit dualism shaping Paul's thinking: "Paul and the Genealogy of Gender," *Representations* 41 (Winter 1993), 1–33, and *A Radical Jew: Paul and the Politics of Identity* (Berkeley, 1994).

45 See St. Augustine, *The City of God*, trans. Marcus Dods, 2 vols. (New York, 1948), especially Book 14; *Confessions*, trans. Henry Chadwick (Oxford, 1991); and Brown's discussion of Augustine, *Body and Society*, pp. 387–427, 428–47.

46 Calvin, *Institutes*, I, 540, 543, 545 (III.iii); cf. William Perkins, *The Combat of the flesh and spirit*, in *Workes* (1616), I, 472, and *Articles of Religion (1562)*, Article IX, in *A Collection of Articles, Injunctions, Canons, Orders . . . of the Church of England* (1661), p. 90.

47 See Calvin, *Institutes*, I.xi and IV.ii. Augustine and other early church fathers anticipate the discourse of Protestant reformers in their polemical writings emphasizing antitheses between Christian and pagan, and between soul and body. See Brown, *Body and Society*, pp. 347–8, 387–427.

48 On the cultural identification of the body with woman, see Genevieve Lloyd, *The Man of Reason: "Male" and "Female" in Western Philosophy* (Minneapolis, 1984); Judith Butler, *Gender Trouble: Feminism and the Subversion of Identity* (London, 1990); and Boyarin, *Radical Jew*, especially pp. 180–200.

49 Bradshaw, *Treatise, Of the crosse*, pp. 5, 4. On the Protestant identification

of Church of Rome with the Whore of Babylon, see Paul Christianson, *Reformers and Babylon* (Toronto, 1978).

50 Cornelius Burges, *Sermon* [preached to the House of Commons at their public fast, November 17, 1640] (1641), p. 47. Cf. Alexander Leighton, *An Appeal to the Parliament; or Sions Plea against the Prelacie* (Amsterdam? 1628), pp. 281–2.

51 John Downame, *The Christian Warfare Against the Devill World and Flesh* (1634), p. 16; John Preston, "The Doctrine of Selfe-deniall," in *Foure Godly and Learned Treatises* (1633), pp. 49–50, quotation p. 49.

52 Preston, "Selfe-deniall," p. 48; Downame, *Christian Warfare*, p. 454. Richard Sibbes frequently opposes the "Christian" or "the Godly" to the "carnall man"; see *Sermon* on 2 Timothy 4:17, 18, in *The Saints Safetie in Evill Times* (1634), p. 115, and *The Churches Visitation* (1634), p. 39.

53 Downame, *Christian Warfare*, p. 454; Sibbes, *Churches Visitation*, p. 129; John Bastwick, *A Briefe Relation of Certaine speciall and most materiall passages, and speeches in the Starre-chamber . . . At the Censure of . . . Dr. Bastwicke, Mr. Burton, and Mr. Prynne* (1638), p. 24.

54 Prynne, *Looking-glasse*, pp. 3, 16–17; Bastwick, *Briefe Relation*, p. 20.

55 *Correspondence of John Cosin*, p. 165; Bastwick, *Letany*, p. 6.

56 John White, *The First Century of Scandalous, Malignant Priests* (1643), pp. 12, 22.

57 J. C. Davis, "Cromwell's Religion," in *Oliver Cromwell and the English Revolution*, ed. John Morrill (London, 1990), pp. 181–208, quotation p. 191.

58 Ephraim Pagitt, *Heresiography* (1654), p. 144. Noam Flinker, "Ranter Sexual Politics: Canticles in the England of 1650," in *Identity and Ethos*, ed. Mark H. Gelber (New York, 1986), pp. 325–41, shows Ranter justification of sexual promiscuity was based on a dualistic opposition between spiritual and carnal.

59 Anna Trapnel, *The Cry of a Stone* (1654), p. 29. On the worship of the sects, see Horton Davies, *Worship and Theology*, pp. 490–521, and Keeble, *Nonconformity*, pp. 25–67.

60 See Horton Davies, *Worship and Theology*, pp. 495–515. On Quaker inwardness, see also Smith, *Perfection Proclaimed*, pp. 66–72.

61 Margaret Fell (Fox), *A Call unto the Seed of Israel That they may come out of Egypt's Darkness, and House of Bondage, unto the Land of Rest* (1668), p. 469. On women prophets, see Phyllis Mack, *Visionary Women: Ecstatic Prophecy in Seventeenth-century England* (Berkeley, 1992).

62 *Strange Newes from New-Gate: Or, A true Relation of the false Prophet that appeared in Butolphs Church* (1647) [Thomason Tracts E. 371 (9)].

63 *The Grand Impostor Examined: or, The Life, Tryal, and Examination of James Nayler* (1656) [Thomason Tracts E. 896 (2)], pp. 2, 9–10; *A True Narrative of The Examination, Tryall, and Sufferings of James Nayler* (1657) [Thomason Tracts E. 899 (6)].

64 On Laudians as innovators, see Tyacke, *Anti-Calvinists*; Hughes, *Causes*,

p. 142; and Lake, "Calvinism and the English Church, 1570–1635," quotation p. 33. Trevor-Roper, "Laudianism and Political Power," finds its alliance with royal absolutism an innovation. On the revolutionary aspects of puritanism, see Walzer, *Revolution of the Saints*; Hill, *World Turned Upside Down*; and Anthony Kemp, *The Estrangement of the Past: A Study in the Origins of Modern Historical Consciousness* (Oxford, 1991).

65 Prynne, *Anti-Arminianisme*, 2nd edn. enlarged (1630), "Epistle Dedicatory," sig. A3r.

66 Christopher Dow, *Innovations Unjustly charged upon the Present Church and State* (1637), pp. 113–20; Heylyn, *Antidotum Lincolniense*, section II, p. 2.

67 John Pocklington, *Altare Christianum: Or, The dead Vicars Plea* (1637), pp. 78–80, 4; Peter Heylyn, *A Coale From The Altar* (1636), pp. 39–40.

68 Heylyn, *Antidotum Lincolniense*, section II, pp. 87–8.

69 See, e.g., Henry Burton, *For God, and the King. The Summe of Two Sermons Preached on the fifth of November* (1636), sig. a4v; Burton, *A Replie to a Relation of the Conference Between William Laude and Mr. Fisher the Jesuite* (1640), "Epistle Dedicatory"; William Prynne, *A Quench-Coale* (1637), pp. 5–6; and article 13 of the charges in Laud's trial (Prynne, *Canterburies Doome*, p. 27).

70 Burton, *Replie*, pp. 94–9; Dow, *Innovations Unjustly charged*, pp. 167–8.

71 Kemp, *Estrangement*, argues that this sense of discontinuity is the revolutionary legacy of the Protestant Reformation, though he does not address the persistence of the older conservative ideology. Walzer, *Revolution of the Saints*, notes that "reform" changes by the 1640s from meaning the restoration of an earlier condition to the idea of change for the better, even revolution.

72 Isaac Casaubon, *The Originall of Popish Idolatrie, or the Birth of Heresies* (1630), pp. 44, 32; William Prynne, *Histrio-Mastix* (1633), p. 21; Ames, *Fresh Suit*, pp. 219, 360–78.

73 See Boyarin, "Paul and the Genealogy of Gender," and *Carnal Israel: Reading Sex in Talmudic Culture* (Berkeley, 1993), especially pp. 1–42, on the characterization of the Jews as "carnal" in Paul and the early Christian church fathers.

74 See Luther, "The Babylonian Captivity of the Church," and "A Treatise on Christian Liberty," in *Works*, vol. II, 170–293, 312–48; Calvin, *Institutes*, IV.xiv.20–26, xviii; Ames, *Fresh Suit*, pp. 36, 209, 255–6.

75 William Bradshaw, *Several Treatises of Worship & Ceremonies* (Cambridge and Oxford, 1660), sig. A3r; Casaubon, *Originall of Popish Idolatrie*, p. 23; Thomas Jackson, *A Treatise Containing the Originall of Unbeliefe* (1625), pp. 305–6; and William Bray, *A Sermon Of The Blessed Sacrament Of The Lords Supper* (1641), p. 14.

76 Burton, *Replie*, p. 37; Prynne, *Looking-glasse*, pp. 53–66.

77 Examples of puritan sermons to Parliament in the 1640s advising the godly to take the pattern from the Jews in dealing with idolatry include

Stephen Marshall's *Reformation and Desolation* (1642), *The Song of Moses* (1643), and *Gods-Masterpiece* (1645).

78 On this Christian view of the Jews, see Boyarin, *Carnal Israel*, pp. 1–60, quotations p. 1.

79 William Laud, *A Sermon Preached On Munday, the sixt of February, At Westminster: At the opening of the Parliament* (1625), p. 22; Pocklington, *Altare Christianum*, chapter 22.

80 Pocklington, *Altare Christianum*, pp. 142–54. See Peter Lake, "The Laudians and the Argument from Authority," in *Court, Country and Culture: Essays on Early Modern British History in Honor of Perez Zagorin*, ed. Bonnelyn Y. Kunze and Dwight D. Brautigam (Rochester, 1992), pp. 149–75, on the Laudian strategy of invoking Old Testament and apostolic authority to legitimate the controverted rites and ceremonies.

81 John Burges, *Answer*, p. 602.

82 Anthony Stafford, *The Femall Glory: Or, The Life, and Death of our Blessed Lady, the holy Virgin Mary* (1635), p. 153; Heylyn, *Antidotum Lincolniense*, section II, p. 80; cf. Morton, *Defence*, p. 139, R. T., *De Templis*, p. 41.

83 See Zagorin, *Ways of Lying*, pp. 38–62.

84 See Anthony Milton, "The Church of England, Rome and the True Church: The Demise of a Jacobean Consensus," in *Early Stuart Church*, ed. Fincham, pp. 187–210; Fincham and Lake, "Ecclesiastical Policies of James I and Charles I," pp. 34–5; Lake, *Anglicans and Puritans?*, pp. 155–60; Caroline Hibbard, *Charles I and the Popish Plot* (Chapel Hill, 1983); and especially Anthony Milton, *Catholic and Reformed: The Roman and Protestant Churches in English Protestant Thought 1600–1640* (Cambridge, 1995), which discusses the shifting, increasingly polarized views of the relation to Rome.

85 Ames, *Reply*, pp. 102–3; Bastwick, *Answer*, p. 15.

86 Bastwick, *A More Full Answer of John Bastwick . . . to the former exceptions . . . against some expressions in his Letany* (1637), p. 2; Prynne, *Anti-Arminianisme*, p. 279; Bastwick, *Vanity*, p. 6; Henry Burton, *The Protestation Protested* (1641), sig. A4r; Burton, *Replie*, p. 66.

87 Quoted in John Burges, *Answer*, pp. 625–6, who is rejecting this attitude. Milton, *Catholic and Reformed*, suggests that the fierce anti-popery which characterized Elizabethan and Jacobean clergy (pp. 31–5) came to distinguish puritanism (p. 36).

88 Richard Sibbes, *The Saints Safetie in Evill Times* (1634), p. 68; Francis Cheynell, *Sions Memento, and Gods Alarum* (1643), pp. 19, 11.

89 Perkins, *Workes*, I, 618, 688; Anthony Burgess, *Romes Cruelty & Apostacie* (1645), p. 15.

90 Thomas Jackson, *A Treatise Containing the Originall of Unbeliefe* (1625), p. 216. See the Petition and the Grand Remonstrance in John Rushworth, *Historical Collections*, IV (1721), 437–51.

91 Prynne, *Quench-Coale*, p. 51; *Hidden Workes of Darkenes Brought to Publike Light* (1645), pp. 156–9.

92 Burton, *For God, and the King*, p. 131; Prynne, *Quench-Coale*, p. 13. Dow, *Innovations Unjustly charged*, defending the alteration of the November 5 prayer, insisted that "such *furious cryers downe of Popery*" as Burton could be considered an "*Antichristian sect.*" We should "pray . . . that God would roote them out of the land" (p. 137).

93 See the charges against Laud, in Prynne's *Canterburies Doome*, p. 27. Prynne, *Hidden Workes*, p. 1; [anon.] *The Bishop of Canterbury His Confession* (1645), p. 6. On conflicts over communion with Rome, see Milton, *Catholic and Reformed*, pp. 31–172, 353–73.

94 1 Corinthians 10:14, 21 appears on the title page of Bradshaw's *A Proposition Concerning Kneeling in the very act of receiving* (Amsterdam? 1605) and is invoked by Ames, Burton, and Prynne. Prynne quotes 2 Corinthians 6:14–16 in *Histrio-Mastix*, p. 33.

95 Prynne, *Anti-Arminianisme*, p. 122; Collinson, *Religion of Protestants*, pp. 242–83, especially p. 275.

96 Burton, *Protestation Protested*, sig. B3v.

97 Edmund Calamy, *Gods free Mercy to England* (1642), p. 49. See also Thomas Goodwin, *Zerubbabels Encouragement to Finish the Temple* (1642), Stephen Marshall, *Reformation and Desolation* (1642), William Greenhill, *The Axe at the Root* (1643).

98 Richard Montagu, *Appello Caesarem* (1625), p. 60; Collinson, *Religion of Protestants*, pp. 82–90.

99 Roger Maynwaring, *Religion and Alegiance: in Two Sermons Preached before the Kings Majestie* (1627), second sermon, p. 6.

100 Giles Widdowes, *The Lawlesse Kneelesse Schismaticall Puritan* (Oxford, 1631), pp. 86–7.

101 Montagu, *Appello Caesarem*, pp. 10, 48. Laud, *History of the Troubles and Tryal*, p. 473. On the blurring of confessional boundaries, see Milton, *Catholic and Reformed*, pp. 63–77.

102 *Golden Remains of the ever Memorable Mr. John Hales* (London, 1659), p. 34. On Hales's divorce from Calvinism in response to his experience at the Synod of Dort, see Trevor-Roper, "Laudianism and Political Power," pp. 59–60. See Lake, *Anglicans and Puritans?*, pp. 13, 160–2, and John Fielding, "Arminianism in the Localities: Peterborough Diocese, 1603–1642," in *Early Stuart Church, 1625–42*, ed. Fincham, p. 100, on conflicting ideas about Christian community.

103 See Lake, *Anglicans and Puritans?*, pp. 145–238, quotation p. 245, and "Andrewes and Buckeridge," pp. 113–33.

104 Haigh, *English Reformations*, quotation p. 290. Underdown, *Revel, Riot, and Rebellion*, especially chapter 5.

105 See Kevin Sharpe, "The Image of Virtue: The Court and Household of Charles I, 1625–1642," in David Starkey, D. A. L. Morgan, John Murphy, Pam Wright, Neil Cuddy, and Kevin Sharpe, *The English Court: From the Wars of the Roses to the Civil War* (London, 1987), pp. 226–60; Tyacke, "Archbishop Laud"; and Smuts, *Court Culture*, chapter 8.

106 See Haigh, *English Reformations*, for his criticism of the "whiggish" version of religious history, whereby progressive Protestantism triumphs over decadent, superstitious Catholicism (pp. 12–21).

107 Collinson, *Religion of Protestants*, disagrees with Hill's position that puritanism logically led to " 'individualist anarchy,' " insisting instead that mainstream puritan piety was corporate not individualist (pp. 250–2), though Collinson admits it is "not easy to define" the "social implications" of the "exclusivism" that was also part of puritan piety (p. 269). On the exclusivity inherent in monotheism, see Regina M. Schwartz, "Monotheism and the Violence of Identities," *Raritan* 14 (1995), 119–40, and *The Curse of Cain: The Violent Legacy of Monotheism* (Chicago, 1997).

3 GEORGE HERBERT: DEVOTION IN *THE TEMPLE* AND THE ART OF CONTRADICTION

1 "The Life of Mr. George Herbert," in Izaak Walton, *Lives*, introd. George Saintsbury (London, 1962), p. 289; Christopher Harvey, *The Synagogue, Or, The Shadow Of The Temple. Sacred Poems, And Private Ejaculations. In imitation of Mr. George Herbert* (1640). From the second edition in 1647 on, *The Synagogue* was bound with *The Temple*; the second and third (1657) editions were substantially enlarged and more insistently high church. On the relation of Vaughan's poetry to Herbert's, see Jonathan F. S. Post, *Henry Vaughan: The Unfolding Vision* (Princeton, 1982), pp. 70–115, 116–56; Claude J. Summers, "Herrick, Vaughan, and the Poetry of Anglican Survivalism," in *New Perspectives on the Seventeenth-century English Religious Lyric*, ed. John R. Roberts (Columbia, 1994), pp. 46–74; John N. Wall, *Transformations of the Word: Spenser, Herbert, Vaughan* (Athens GA, 1988), pp. 273–365; M. Thomas Hester, " 'broken letters scarce remembred': Herbert's *Childhood* in Vaughan," *Christianity and Literature* 40 (1991), 209–22; and Robert Wilcher, " 'The Present Times are not / To Snudge in': Henry Vaughan, *The Temple*, and the Pressure of History," in *George Herbert: Sacred and Profane*, ed. Helen Wilcox and Richard Todd (Amsterdam, 1995), pp. 185–94.

2 Richard Baxter, *Poetical Fragments* (1689), "To the Reader." *Select Hymns Taken Out of Mr. Herbert's Temple* (1697), Augustan Reprint Society, no. 98 (Los Angeles, 1962), "The Preface." On Herbert's influence and broad appeal, see especially Robert H. Ray, "The Herbert Allusion Book: Allusions to George Herbert in the Seventeenth Century," *Studies in Philology* 83 (1986), 1–133; Helen Wilcox, " 'Heaven's Lidger Here': Herbert's *Temple* and Seventeenth-century Devotion," in *Images of Belief in Literature*, ed. David Jasper (London, 1984), pp. 153–68; Sidney Gottlieb, "George Herbert and Robert Overton," and Helen Wilcox, " 'You that Indeared are to Pietie': Herbert and Seventeenth-

century Women," in *George Herbert in the Nineties: Reflections and Reassessments*, ed. Jonathan F. S. Post and Sidney Gottlieb, special issue of the *George Herbert Journal* 18 (1995), 185–200, 201–14.

3 Gene Edward Vieth, Jr., "The Religious Wars in George Herbert Criticism: Reinterpreting Seventeenth-century Anglicanism," *George Herbert Journal*, vol. 11, no. 2 (Spring 1988), 19–35, observes that recent critical battles replay those of the seventeenth century. On Herbert's *via media*, see Gene Edward Veith, Jr., *Reformation Spirituality: The Religion of George Herbert* (Lewisburg, 1985); Christopher Hodgkins, *Authority, Church, and Society in George Herbert: Return to the Middle Way* (Columbia, 1993); and Harold Toliver, *George Herbert's Christian Narrative* (University Park PA, 1993), especially p. 193.

Anglo-Catholic readings of Herbert include Rosemond Tuve, *A Reading of George Herbert* (Chicago, 1952), Louis Martz, *The Poetry of Meditation* (New Haven, 1954), Heather Asals, *Equivocal Predication: George Herbert's Way to God* (Toronto, 1981), Stanley Stewart, *George Herbert* (Boston, 1986), and R. V. Young, "Donne, Herbert, and the Postmodern Muse," in *New Perspectives*, ed. Roberts, pp. 168–87. Firmly Protestant readings include Barbara K. Lewalski, *Protestant Poetics and the Seventeenth-century Religious Lyric* (Princeton, 1979), pp. 283–316; Ilona Bell, "'Setting Foot into Divinity': George Herbert and the English Reformation," *MLQ* 38 (1977), 219–41; Richard Strier, *Love Known: Theology and Experience in George Herbert's Poetry* (Chicago, 1983); Veith, *Reformation Spirituality*; and Hodgkins, *Authority*.

4 On *The Temple* as expressing the *via media*, see particularly Hodgkins, *Authority*; Vieth, "Religious Wars"; and Daniel W. Doerksen, "Recharting the *Via Media* of Spenser and Herbert," *Renaissance and Reformation/ Renaissance et Réforme* n.s. vol. 8, no. 3 (August 1984), 215–25, and "Things Fundamental or Indifferent: Adiaphorism and Herbert's Church Attitudes," *George Herbert Journal* vol. 11, no. 1 (Fall 1987), 15–22. On tensions within English Protestantism, see especially Milton, *Catholic and Reformed*.

5 R. V. Young, "Herbert and Analogy," in *George Herbert: Sacred and Profane*, ed. Wilcox and Todd, pp. 93–102, criticizes new historicists who discuss Herbert's religion in political terms and identify him with a party or platform.

6 All references to Herbert's texts are to *The Works of George Herbert*, ed. F. E. Hutchinson (Oxford, 1941).

7 On Herbert's poems as praise and prayer, see Chana Bloch, *Spelling the Word: George Herbert and the Bible* (Berkeley, 1985), Diana Benet, *Secretary of Praise* (Columbia, 1984), and Terry Sherwood, *Herbert's Prayerful Art* (Toronto, 1989).

8 Izaak Walton, *Lives*, introd. George Saintsbury (London, 1962), p. 296.

9 Kathleen Lynch, "George Herbert's Holy 'Altar,' Name and Thing," *George Herbert Journal* vol. 17, no.1 (Fall 1993), 41–60, sees the altar controversy as relevant to Herbert's poem.

10 See Lake, *Anglicans and Puritans?*, pp. 173–82, and "Andrewes and Buckeridge," p. 128.

11 See Walton, *Lives*, p. 278, and Amy M. Charles, *A Life of George Herbert* (Ithaca, 1977), pp. 113–18.

12 Bishop John Williams discusses the original incident concerning the vicar in *The Holy Table, Name & Thing, More Anciently, properly, and literally used under the New Testament, then that of an ALTAR* (1637), especially pp. 5–8. See also William Prynne, *A Quench-Coale* (1637); Peter Smart, *A Sermon Preached in the Cathedrall Church of Durham July 7.1628* (1628), and Smart's formal charges in *The Correspondence of John Cosin, D.D.*, publications of the Surtees Society, vol. 52 (Durham, 1869), pp. 161–99.

13 See, e.g., Henry Parker, *The Altar Dispute* (1641), pp. 19–28; Prynne, *Quench-Coale*, p. 15; John Bastwick, *The Answer . . . To the exceptions made against his Letany* (1637), p. 17; Henry Burton, *A Replie to a Relation of the Conference . . .* (1640), pp. 35–7. Bloch, *Spelling the Word*, observes that Herbert uses titles (like "The Altar," "The Priesthood," and even *The Temple*) that had a "suspect ring" (pp. 122–3). See Lynch, "Herbert's Holy 'Altar,' " on the provocative stance of "The Altar."

14 See "Articles," in *Correspondence of John Cosin*, pp. 175–7. Williams reprints his earlier letter in his anonymous *Holy Table*; see pp. 17–18 on "table" versus "altar." Cf. Prynne's *Quench-Coale*, p. 15; Williams, *Holy Table*, p. 109.

15 See, e.g., Wall, *Transformations*, pp. 201–6.

16 See Strier's discussion of the poem, *Love Known*, pp. 191–5.

17 See Elizabeth Clarke, "Sacred Singer/Profane Poet: Herbert's Split Poetic Persona," in *George Herbert*, ed. Wilcox and Todd, pp. 23–32, on Herbert's "gestures towards disablement" in his poems (p. 29).

18 Toliver, *Christian Narrative*, notes that questions of "what temporal tropes and what art best express divine beauty. . . begin with "The Altar" and figure in the persistent metapoetic and ecclesiastical concerns of *The Temple* virtually to the end" (p. 149).

19 William Bradshaw, *A Treatise of Divine Worship* (1604), pp. 28–30; Henry Burton, *For God, and the King* (1636), p. 98. For Smart's charges, see *Correspondence of John Cosin*, pp. 161–99.

20 M. Thomas Hester, "Altering the Text of the Self: The Shapes of 'The Altar,' " in *A Fine Tuning: Studies of the Religious Poetry of Herbert and Milton*, ed. Mary A. Maleski (*MRTS* 64) (Binghamton, 1989), pp. 95–116, especially pp. 111–12; and Michael C. Schoenfeldt, *Prayer and Power: George Herbert and Renaissance Courtship* (Chicago, 1991), pp. 165–7, describes the poem's pull between self-effacement and self-assertion.

21 On the importance of the Psalms for Herbert, see Bloch, *Spelling the Word*, pp. 231–305.

22 On "workeman" in the prophets, see ibid., p. 64.

23 Henry Burton, *Jesu-Worship Confuted* (1640), pp. 7, 9.

24 Bloch, *Spelling the Word*, shows how Herbert's poems, not just "The Altar," creatively, intricately collate Scripture.

25 Wall, *Transformations*, observes that "we are never more than a few poems from those which remind us of the church itself" (p. 187). See also Sherwood, *Prayerful Art*, on "Herbert's commitment to the physical church and its furnishings," p. 95, and Stewart, *Herbert*, p. 104, on the importance of the liturgical calendar to *The Temple*'s structure.

26 "The Printers to the Reader," *Works of George Herbert*, ed. Hutchinson, p. 4.

27 See Wall, *Transformations*, p. 198.

28 Wall, ibid., emphasizes connections with the liturgy. See also Claude J. Summers and Ted-Larry Pebworth, "The Politics of *The Temple*: 'The British Church' and 'The Familie,'" *GHJ* 8 (Fall 1984), 1–15. On the importance of the Eucharist, see Stewart, *Herbert*, pp. 49–55; C. A. Patrides, "'A Crown of Praise': The Poetry of George Herbert," in his edition of *The English Poems of George Herbert* (London, 1974), p. 17. On sacrament-centered worship in the English church, see Lake, *Anglicans and Puritans?*, "Lancelot Andrewes and John Buckeridge," in *Mental World*, ed. Peck, pp. 113–33, and "Laudian Style," pp. 161–85.

29 Morton, *A Defence of the Innocencie of the Three Ceremonies of the Church of England* (1618), pp. 45, 169. For Donne's sonnet, see *The Complete Poetry of John Donne*, ed. John T. Shawcross (Garden City, 1967).

30 Morton, *Defence*, pp. 156, 167, 200–1; John Burges, *An Answer Rejoyned to that Much Applauded Pamphlet of a Nameless Author* (1631), pp. 79, 101; William Ames, *A Fresh Suit Against Human Ceremonies in Gods Worship* (1633), pp. 77, 269.

31 Summers and Pebworth, "Politics of *The Temple*," observe that in "The British Church," Herbert finds the "undrest" church of Geneva as objectionable as the Church of Rome (p. 3). See also Sidney Gottlieb, "Herbert's Case of 'Conscience': Public or Private Poem?," *SEL* 25 (1985), 109–26.

32 See Summers and Pebworth, "Politics of *The Temple*," on "The Familie" as a public poem, concerned with the visible church (pp. 1–15).

33 See Doerksen, "Things Fundamental."

34 For Strier, *Love Known*, pp. 174–217, Herbert's suspicions about invention and art express a radical iconoclasm that links him with puritans. Herbert, however, exemplifies the desire for the iconic which Tessa Watt has shown persisted despite the iconoclastic impulses of the Reformation; see *Cheap Print and Popular Piety 1550–1640* (Cambridge, 1991).

35 See Toliver, *Christian Narrative*, p. 34. On Herbert's stress on the inward, personal, and individual, see especially Strier, *Love Known*, pp. 143–73; Vieth, *Reformation Spirituality*, pp. 228–9.

36 Strier, *Love Known*, pp. 149–50, claims that the disappearance of the

physical church from poems like "Church-floore" shows that Herbert's "true locus of significance" is the spiritual meaning. Hodgkins, *Authority*, p. 164, similarly argues that Herbert's "overall thrust is internal, toward building the altar and temple in the heart."

37 See, e.g., John Burges, *Answer*, pp. 101–4, 137.

38 See John Pocklington, *Altare Christianum: Or, The Dead Vicars Plea* (1637), especially chapter 22.

39 Smart's words are quoted in Articles, in *Correspondence of John Cosin*, p. 175.

40 William Ames, *A Reply to Dr. Morton's Generall Defence* . . . (1622), p. 94; John Bastwick, *The Vanity and Mischeife of the Old Letany* (1637), p. 2, and *A More Full Answer* . . . (1637), p. 4. Cf. Burton, *Replie*, p. 37, and *For God, and the King*, p. 14.

41 See Strier, *Love Known*, pp. 29–60, 174–217.

42 *The Poems of Sir Philip Sidney*, ed. William A. Ringler, Jr. (Oxford, 1962).

43 See Horton Davies, *Worship and Theology*, p. 204; Lake, "Laudian Style," p. 165.

44 See Articles, in *Correspondence of John Cosin*, p. 169.

45 See, e.g., Henry Burton, *Babel no Bethel* (1629) and *For God, and the King*, p. 32.

46 Ames, *Fresh Suit*, pp. 370, 302.

47 See Bloch, *Spelling the Word*, pp. 95–7; her excellent discussion does not focus on what these allusions suggest about Herbert's attitudes towards language and poetry.

48 William Bradshaw, *A Shorte Treatise, Of the crosse in Baptisme* (Amsterdam, 1604), pp. 24–5; Ames, *Fresh Suit*, pp. 369–85, quotation from "Dedicatory epistle."

49 The phrase is Strier's, *Love Known*, p. 208.

50 See the argument of Asals, *Equivocal Predication*, that for Herbert poetry is "sacramental" (pp. 18–22, 50–1).

51 Morton, *Defence*, p. 181; John Burges, *Answer*, pp. 125–7.

52 Bradshaw, *Short Treatise*, pp. 27–8; Burton, *For God, and the King*, p. 15. On the poem as hieroglyph, see Joseph H. Summers, *George Herbert: His Religion and Art* (Cambridge, 1968), pp. 123–46.

53 John Burges, *The Lawfulnes Of Kneeling In The Act Of Receiving The Lords Supper* (1631), p. 31; Morton, *Defence*, pp. 272, 301.

54 See, e.g., Cosin, *Correspondence*, pp. 162–3, and Prynne, *Quench-Coale*, p. 10.

55 See George Herbert, *The Temple: A Diplomatic Edition of the Bodleian Manuscript (Tanner 307)*, introd. Mario A. Di Cesare (Binghamton, 1995), pp. 95–6.

56 Psalms 29:8 ("In his Temple doth every man speak of his honour"), which appears on the title page of *The Temple*, proclaims the obligation to engage publicly in ceremonial praise.

57 Henry Burton, *The Sounding of the Two Last Trumpets* (1641), p. 21; Prynne, *Quench-Coale*, subtitle. See also Smart, *Sermon*, pp. 8–9, Isaac Casaubon,

The Originall of Popish Idolatrie (1630), p. 23, and Williams, *Holy Table*, pp. 77, 108–12.

58 John Burges, *Answer*, pp. 125, 158, 127; cf. Morton, *Defence*, pp. 82–5, 90, 181.

59 John Cosin, *Notes . . . on the Book of Common Prayer*, vol. v of *The Works* (Oxford, 1855), p. 345. William Laud, *A Relation of the Conference Betweene William Lawd . . . and Mr. Fisher the Jesuite* (1639), "To His Most Sacred Majesty, Charles."

60 Assuming a necessary opposition between external and internal, Strier, *Love Known*, claims that the poem "entirely eliminates the visual and material from its concerns" as did the religious radicals in their worship (pp. 149, 146–59).

61 Ibid., p. 150.

62 Morton, *Defence*, pp. 300, 308; Laud, *Conference*, "To His Most Sacred Majesty, Charles." Hodgkins, *Authority*, argues that Herbert's idea of preaching follows the puritan Perkins (pp. 87–102). For the ceremonialist interpretation, see Stewart, *Herbert*, p. 45. Judy Z. Kronenfeld, "Probing the Relation between Poetry and Ideology: Herbert's 'The Windows,' " *John Donne Journal* 2 (1983), 55–80, discusses the poem's relation to religious ideology.

63 Ames, *Fresh Suit*, "An Addition," p. 63.

64 Strier, *Love Known*, p. 150; Hodgkins, *Authority*, pp. 81–6. Toliver, *Christian Narrative*, sees "Aaron" as a "point-by-point substitution" of inner qualities "for the vestments of priesthood" (p. 208).

65 For a different interpretation of "Lent" and Isaiah, see Hodgkins, *Authority*, pp. 64–86.

66 See, especially, Bloch, *Spelling the Word*, pp. 117–26.

67 Ames, *Fresh Suit*, pp. 219, 49; Bastwick, *Answer*, p. 20.

68 See Bloch, *Spelling the Word*, pp. 124, 135.

69 Lewalski, *Protestant Poetics*, chapter 9, and Strier, *Love Known*, emphasize Herbert's concern with the temple of the heart and with the spiritual experience of the individual. Hodgkins, *Authority*, argues that "most of Herbert's poetic references to ecclesiastical externals are clearly metaphorical from the beginning" (p. 165).

70 Wall, *Transformations*, p. 198, sees Herbert's collection as "built on analogy with the church as building." Sherwood, *Prayerful Art*, stresses "Herbert's commitment to the physical church and its furnishings," his "Anglican emphasis on the body's role in liturgy" (pp. 95, 97).

71 *Select Hymns*, "The Preface."

72 The poem first appears in the second edition of Harvey's *The Synagogue* (1647).

73 Lake, "Laudian Style," p. 168; see also Lake, "Andrewes and Buckeridge," pp. 125–7, where he uses the term "avant-garde conformists."

74 See Lake, "Andrewes and Buckeridge," p. 126.

75 In *The Country Parson*, chapter 22, Herbert moderately defended the ceremony of kneeling at receiving the Sacrament.

76 Hutchinson, ed., *Works*, p. 189, notes that this final epigraph is not in the Williams manuscript; it thus is a later addition.

77 Wilcox, "'Heaven's Lidger Here,'" remarks that "selective readings and interpretation made *The Temple*, like the Bible, available to justify and enrich a variety of devotional approaches" (p. 160).

78 Doerksen, "Things Fundamental," observes that "By dwelling on the spiritual relationship of God and man . . . Herbert deals with what is of great importance to Catholics as well" (p. 20). On Herbert's conciliatory stance, see also Lynch, "Herbert's Holy 'Altar,'" p. 56, and Vieth, *Reformation Spirituality*, p. 35. Herbert's avoidance of controversy fits his advice in the *Country Parson*, chapter 7, and Charles I's prohibition against preaching on controversial issues. See "A proclamation for the establishing of the peace and quiet of the Church of England, 16 June 1626," in *The Stuart Constitution 1603–1688*, ed. J. P. Kenyon, 2nd edn. (Cambridge, 1986), pp. 138–9.

79 "The Elixir" is implicitly Arminian in suggesting the potential availability of God's grace to all. Debora K. Shuger, *Habits of Thought in the English Renaissance* (Berkeley, 1990), observes that Herbert lacks the puritan sense of "an elect community" (p. 104). His comment in *Country Parson*, chapter 34, that only the "thrusting away of his arme" makes us "not embraced" (Hutchinson, ed., *Works*, p. 283) is close to Richard Montagu's notion of universal grace (*Appello Caesarem* [1625]), attacked by Parliament and puritans like Burton for denying predestination and election (see Henry Burton, *A Plea to An Appeale* [1626], "To the High and Mighty Prince, Charles").

80 Herbert's *The Country Parson* shows respect for the conscience yet insists puritans conform (chapters 8 and 22).

4   ROBERT HERRICK: RELIGIOUS EXPERIENCE IN THE "TEMPLE" OF HESPERIDES

1 All references to Herrick's poetry are to J. Max Patrick's edition of *The Complete Poetry of Robert Herrick* (New York, 1968). Poems are cited by the "H- " (*Hesperides*) and "N- " (*Noble Numbers*) numbers Patrick gives them in this edition.

2 See, especially, Leah S. Marcus's "Herrick's *Hesperides* and the 'Proclamation made for May,'" *SP* 76 (1979), 49–74, "Herrick's *Noble Numbers* and the Politics of Playfulness," *ELR* 7 (1977), 108–26, and *The Politics of Mirth: Jonson, Herrick, Milton, Marvell and the Defense of Old Holiday Pastimes* (Chicago, 1986), chapter 5; Claude J. Summers's "Herrick's Political Poetry: The Strategies of His Art," in *"Trust to Good Verses": Herrick Tercentenary Essays*, ed. Roger B. Rollin and J. Max Patrick (Pittsburgh, 1978), pp. 171–83, "Herrick's Political Counterplots," *SEL* 25 (1985),

165–82, and "Tears for Herrick's Church," *George Herbert Journal* (special issue on Robert Herrick, ed. Ann Baynes Coiro) 14 (Fall 1990/Spring 1991), 51–71; Peter Stallybrass, "'Wee feaste in our Defense': Patrician Carnival in Early Modern England and Robert Herrick's 'Hesperides,'" *ELR* 16 (1986), 234–52; Achsah Guibbory, "The Temple of *Hesperides* and Anglican-Puritan Controversy," in *"The Muses Common-Weale": Poetry and Politics in the Seventeenth Century*, ed. Claude J. Summers and Ted-Larry Pebworth (Columbia, 1988), pp. 135–47; and Thomas N. Corns, *Uncloistered Virtue: English Political Literature, 1640–1660* (Oxford, 1992), pp. 91–128.

3 Ann Baynes Coiro's *Robert Herrick's "Hesperides" and the Epigram Book Tradition* (Baltimore, 1988) interprets the dissonant notes in his poetry as calling Stuart ideals into question. This tendency to see Herrick as less of a committed Royalist or Laudian is evident in the special issue of the *George Herbert Journal* on Herrick (see n. 2 above). Some of these articles devalue "political" readings of Herrick (Jonathan F. S. Post, "Robert Herrick: A Minority Report," 1–20, and William Kerrigan, "Kiss Fancies in Robert Herrick," 155–71). Others question Herrick's commitment to the Stuart and Laudian ideologies (Mary Thomas Crane's "Herrick's Cultural Materialism," 21–50; Janie Caves McCauley, "On the 'Childhood of the Yeare': Herrick's *Hesperides* New Year's Poems," 72–96; Katharine Wallingford, "'Corinna,' Carlomaria, the *Book of Sports* and the Death of Epithalamium on the Field of Genre," 97–112).

4 Marcus, *Politics of Mirth*, p. 145, and "Afterword: Herrick and Historicism," *George Herbert Journal* 14 (1990/91), 174, 176.

5 See John Rushworth, *Historical Collections*, vol. V (London, 1721), 337, 785. See also *Acts and Ordinances of the Interregnum, 1642–1660*, ed. C. H. Firth and R. S. Rait, vol. I (London, 1911), 582.

6 See the August 23, 1645 *Ordinance of the Lords and Commons Assembled in Parliament For the more effectual putting in execution the Directory For public worship* (1646), pp. 5–8.

7 John Morrill, "The Church in England, 1642–9," in *Reactions to the English Civil War, 1642–49* (New York, 1983), pp. 89–114. See also Morrill's "The Attack on the Church of England in the Long Parliament," in *The Nature of the English Revolution* (London, 1993), pp. 69–90.

8 Patrick, ed., *Complete Poetry of Robert Herrick*, p. xii, notes that Anthony Wood said *Hesperides* was admired by Royalists when it appeared. Two excellent discussions of *Noble Numbers* are by Claude Summers, "Tears for Herrick's Church," who argues that it "mourns the desecration of the Established church by the triumphant Parliamentarians" (p. 51), and by Thomas Corns, *Uncloistered Virtue* (pp. 114–28), who argues that Herrick "preserves almost a sanctuary for Laudian practice" (p. 123) in these religious poems. Corns stresses the defiant aspect of Herrick, while Summers emphasizes the sense of persecution.

9 On Herrick's anti-puritan political poetry, see Summers, "Herrick's

Political Poetry," pp. 171–83, and "Herrick's Political Counterplots," pp. 165–82. Leah S. Marcus, *Childhood and Cultural Despair* (Pittsburgh, 1978), pp. 120–39, discusses the political implications of Herrick's anti-puritanism. Roger B. Rollin, *Robert Herrick*, rev. edn. (New York, 1992), has argued that *"The Christian Militant"* is a caricature of puritans (pp. 116–18), though he resists seeing *Hesperides* as an attack on puritanism. Robert H. Deming, *Ceremony and Art: Robert Herrick's Poetry* (The Hague, 1974), discusses the anti-puritanism of Herrick's ceremonies (pp. 141–57) but does not examine contemporary Anglican-puritan controversies over ceremonies.

10 Cf. "Epistle to Katherine, Lady Aubigny" (*Forrest* XIII) and "To the Immortall Memorie . . . of . . . Sir Lucius Cary, and Sir H. Morison" (*Under-wood* 72), in *The Complete Poetry of Ben Jonson*, ed. William B. Hunter, Jr. (New York, 1963). See Rollin, *Robert Herrick*, pp. 175–97, on Herrick's "religion" of poetry.

11 William Prynne, *Histrio-Mastix* (1633), pp. 48, 294, and passim. See also Prynne's *Healthes: Sicknesse, Or, A Compendious and briefe Discourse; proving the drinking, and pledging of Healthes, to be Sinfull and utterly Unlawfull unto Christians* (1628). On the contrast between the "carnal" and the Christian (or spiritual), see also, e.g., Richard Sibbes, *The Saints Safetie in Evill Times* (1634), p. 115, and *The Churches Visitation* (1634), p. 39.

12 Prynne, *Histrio-Mastix*, p. 20.

13 Ibid., p. 33. Cf. also William Perkins, *Workes*, vol. 1 (1616), especially *A Warning Against the Idolatrie of the last times*.

14 On Herrick's debt to the Latin poets and the handbooks of mythology and antiquity, see Deming, *Ceremony and Art*, pp. 61–6.

15 On attitudes towards the Church of Rome, see Lake, *Anglicans and Puritans?*, and Anthony Milton, *Catholic and Reformed: The Roman and Protestant Churches in English Protestant Thought 1600–1640* (Cambridge, 1995). The "hotter sort of Protestants" is Morrill's phrase ("Religious Context of the English Civil War," p. 52).

16 Isaac Casaubon, *The Originall of Popish Idolatrie* (1630), pp. 37, 42–4, 53–4, 58. Cf. Perkins, *A Reformed Catholicke* and *A Warning Against the Idolatrie of the last times*, in *Workes*, I, 556, 688.

17 Thomas Jackson, *A Treatise Containing the Originall of Unbeliefe* (1625), p. 217; cf. Perkins, *Reformed Catholicke*, in *Workes*, I, 557: "Ecclesiasticall Rome . . . is all one with the heathenish Empire."

18 Perkins, "To the Reader," *Warning Against the Idolatrie of the last times*, in *Workes*, I; cf. *Reformed Catholicke*, in ibid., I, 557.

19 Sibbes, *Saints Safetie in Evill Times*, p. 68. Cf. Prynne, *Anti-Arminianisme*, sig. A2r, pp. 164–7.

20 Prynne, *Histrio-Mastix*, p. 33; Henry Burton, *A Replie to a Relation of the Conference* (1640), pp. 36–7; cf. p. 349.

21 Stephen Marshall, *A Sermon Preached to the Two Houses of Parliament . . . Aug. 12, 1647* (1647), pp. 28–9.

22 Robert Sanderson, *Twelve Sermons Preached . . . Whereunto Are now added two Sermons more,* 3rd edn. (1637), remarks that the name is "justly given."

For appropriating to themselves the names of *Brethren, Professors, Good-men,* and otherlike; as differences betwixt them & those they cal *Formalists*; would they not have it thought, that they have a *Brother-hood* and *profession* of their owne, freer and *purer* from Superstition and Idolatry, then others have, that are not of the same stampe? and doing so, why may they not be called *Puritanes?* (p. 34).

23 William Prynne, *Hidden Workes of Darkenes* (1645), pp. 91–2. Cf. the Root and Branch Petition and the Grand Remonstrance presented by the House of Commons to Charles on December 1, 1641; selections in *Documents Illustrative of English Church History,* ed. Henry Gee and William John Hardy (London, 1896), pp. 553–62.

24 Henry Burton, *For God, and the King* (1636), pp. 66–7, 33; *Replie,* sig. C1r. See also puritan sermons preached to the Long Parliament in the early 1640s – e.g., Cornelius Burges, *A Sermon . . . at their publique Fast Novem. 17. 1640* (1641), Stephen Marshall, *Sermon* [on the occasion of the same fast] (1641), pp. 33–4, Thomas Goodwin, *Zerubbabels Encouragement to Finish the Temple* [at the fast, April 27, 1642] (1642), p. 54.

25 Prynne, *Hidden Workes,* p. 1. Milton, *Catholic and Reformed,* argues that moderated perceptions of Rome under Laud made it possible for Montagu to contemplate reunion with Rome, and fueled charges against Laudians of a popish conspiracy (pp. 345–73).

26 William Prynne, *Canterburies Doome* (1646), p. 58.

27 Burton, *For God, and the King,* p. 98; *Replie,* sig. C1v. Cf. also John Milton's *Of Reformation,* in *Complete Prose Works,* vol. 1, ed. Don M. Wolfe (New Haven, 1953), 519–22.

28 *Correspondence of John Cosin,* p. 120.

29 Herrick shares the seeming inconsistency of those like Morton, John Burges, and Heylyn, who recognized that ceremonies were "indifferent" yet insisted they must be performed. On "anglican" attitudes towards "indifferent" ceremonies, see George, *Protestant Mind of the English Reformation,* pp. 348–63, especially p. 355.

30 William Laud, *The History of the Troubles and Tryal* (1695), p. 340.

31 John Burges, *Answer,* p. 158; cf. p. 127. See also Peter Heylyn, *Antidotum Lincolniense* (1637), section II; R. T., *De Templis* (1638), especially pp. 122–4. Cosin, *Notes and Collections on the Book of Common Prayer,* explained that "the outward gesture of humility and reverence in our bodies, is ordained only to testify and express the inward reverence and devotion of our souls towards our blessed Saviour" (p. 345; cf. p. 415). For a puritan statement of the opposition between outward, carnal forms and inward, spiritual worship, see, e.g., Richard Sibbes, *The Ruine of Mysticall Jericho* [bound with *The Beasts Dominion Over Earthly Kings*] (1639), p. 77; and Smectymnuus [Stephen Marshall, Edmund Calamy, Thomas Young, Matthew Newcomen, and William Spurstowe], *An Answer to a Booke Entituled, An Humble Remonstrance* (1641), p. 83.

32 Morton, *Defence*, p. 167; Laud, *History of the Troubles and Tryal*, p. 156.

33 Prynne, *Canterburies Doome*, p. 104. Burton, *For God, and the King*, pp. 159–63; Cornelius Burges, *Sermon* [preached November 17, 1640], pp. 25–6.

34 See *Acts and Ordinances of the Interregnum*, I, 425; Stephen Marshall, *Reformation and Desolation* [preached December 22, 1641] (1642), p. 51. John Phillips, *The Reformation of Images* (Berkeley, 1973), discusses the iconoclastic impulse in England and the Anglican versus puritan attitude towards images; see also Margaret Aston, *England's Iconoclasts* (Oxford, 1988).

35 See William Dowsing, *The Journal of William Dowsing A. D. 1643–44*, ed. J. Charles Wall (London, 1885). Aston, *England's Iconoclasts*, describes the work of iconoclasts in the civil war period, especially Cromwell, Dowsing, and Richard Culmer (pp. 62–95).

36 *Antidotum Culmerianum: or Animadversions Upon A late Pamphlet, entituled Cathedrall Newes from Canterbury, &c. By Richard Culmer* (Oxford, 1644), p. 11.

37 [Bruno Ryves], *Mercurius Rusticus: Or The Countries Complaint of the barbarous Out-rages Committed by the Sectaries of this late flourishing Kingdome* (London, 1646), p. 58.

38 Prynne, *Canterburies Doome*, pp. 211, 213, and *Hidden Workes*, p. 159; Burton, *For God, and the King*, p. 67.

39 See William Laud, *The Archbishop of Canterbury's Speech: Or His Funerall Sermon*, Preacht by himself on the Scaffold on Tower-Hill, on Friday the 10. of January, 1644[/5] (London, 1644[5]).

40 Perkins, *Warning Against . . . Idolatrie*, in *Workes*, I, 679.

41 Corns, *Uncloistered Virtue*, pp. 121–3, discusses the importance of altars in *Noble Numbers*, but not *Hesperides*.

42 Smart accused Cosin of setting up an altar in Durham Cathedral; see *Correspondence of John Cosin*, p. 163. Prynne, *Quench-Coale*, p. 11, says Cosin was "one of the first men that brought *Altars* into our Church."

43 *Acts and Ordinances*, I, 265–6; quotation p. 265. Cf. 1: 425–6.

44 The note on *"Upon Love,"* H-863 in Patrick's edition, p. 367, says "Written in the manner of George Herbert."

45 See [John Williams], *The Holy Table, Name & Thing* (1637), pp. 18–19. Williams recounts the incident that began this controversy and the vicar of Grantham's angry insistence that *"he would build him an Altar of Stone at his own charge, and fix it in the old Altar-place, and would never Officiate upon any other"* (p. 6).

46 Peter Heylyn, *A Coale from the Altar* (1636), p. 52; John Pocklington, *Altare Christianum* (1637), p. 86.

47 William Laud, *A Speech Delivered in the Starr-Chamber . . . At the Censure of John Bastwick, Henry Burton, and William Prinn* (1637), p. 47.

48 See, e.g., John Bastwick, *The Answer of John Bastwick* (1637), p. 26; Burton, *For God, and the King*, p. 15, and *The Sounding of the Two Last*

Trumpets (1641); and Daniel Cawdry, *Superstitio Superstes: Or, the Reliques of Superstition newly Revived* (1641), pp. 22–3.

49 Williams, *Holy Table*, p. 94; see Cosin's discussion of the puritan objections to the names "altar" and "priest," *Notes . . . on the Book of Common Prayer*, p. 88.

50 Joseph Mede, *The Name Altar* (1637). Cf. Pocklington's defense of the term, *Altare Christianum*, pp. 137–46; Heylyn's *Antidotum Lincolniense*, section I, pp. 120–1; and Heylyn, *Coale from the Altar*, pp. 39–40.

51 See, e.g., Williams, *Holy Table*, pp. 109–53; Henry Parker, *The Altar Dispute* (1641), pp. 5–28; William Bray, *A Sermon of the Blessed Sacrament of the Lords Supper* (1641).

52 Note Williams, *Holy Table*, pp. 17–20; Parker, *Altar Dispute*, pp. 3–5.

53 Burton, *Replie*, sig. C2v.

54 Heylyn, *Antidotum Lincolniense*, section II, especially pp. 6, 18–19; also Pocklington, *Altare Christianum*, especially pp. 6–15.

55 Deming, *Ceremony and Art*.

56 See Cosin's discussion "Of the Sacrifice of the Eucharist," in *Notes . . . on the Book of Common Prayer*, p. 115. Heylyn, *Antidotum Lincolniense*, arguing for the continuing necessity of sacrifices, says: "A *Sacrifice* there was among the *Jewes*, shewing forth *Christs* death unto them, before his comming in the flesh: a *Sacrifice* there must bee amongst the *Christians*, to shew *forth the Lords death till he* come in judgement" (section II, p. 6).

57 Francis Cheynell's sermon to the House of Commons, *Sions Memento, And Gods Alarum* [preached 31 May, 1643] (1643), pp. 1–2, also cites Psalm 137, arguing that the puritans are like the Jews in Babylonian captivity, mourning the desolation of the true church under the prelates.

58 Boyarin, *Carnal Israel*, discusses how Augustine and patristic writing stigmatized the Jews as "carnal." See especially pp. 1–60.

59 See Deming, *Ceremony and Art*, on the connections between this poem and the descriptions of Roman sacrifice, pp. 25–6.

60 Bernard J. Bamberger observes that the burnt offering, described in Leviticus 1, "is called *olah*, 'what goes up,' i.e., goes up in smoke, because the entire animal, except for its hide, was burned on the altar." Whereas in the Greek religion only sacrifices to the underground deities were completely burnt, "most required communal sacrifices [of the Jews] were *olot*." See Bamberger's commentary on Leviticus, in *The Torah: A Modern Commentary*, ed. W. Gunther Plaut, vol. I (New York, 1981), p. 756.

61 Pocklington, *Altare Christianum*, chapter 22 and pp. 146, 154; cf. Heylyn, *Antidotum Lincolniense*, section II, especially pp. 22–3, and R. T., *De Templis*.

62 John Burges, *Answer*, p. 602; cf. p. 474.

63 R. T., *De Templis*, pp. 41–2; cf. Heylyn, *Antidotum Lincolniense*, section II, p. 80.

64 Richard Sibbes, *The Unprosperous Builder* [bound with *The Beasts Dominion*] (1639), p. 115.
65 See, e.g., Ames, *Fresh Suit*, pp. 405–6.
66 Perkins, *Reformed Catholicke*, in *Workes*, I, 618.
67 Heylyn, *Antidotum Lincolniense*, section II, p. 1; cf. section II, p. 4, and Pocklington, *Altare Christianum*, pp. 4–5.
68 R. T., *De Templis*, pp. 139–40, 141.
69 See, e.g., Cosin, *Notes . . . on the Book of Common Prayer*, p. 13. Joseph Hall, *The Olde Religion* (London, 1628), insists on the difference between the reformed and Roman churches, but disagrees with those who zealously insist there be no communion. Defending the English church against the charge of novelty, Hall insists it continues "the old Religion" of the Roman church before its corruptions. See also Heylyn's *Antidotum Lincolniense*, especially section II.
70 Prynne, *Canterburies Doome*, p. 67.
71 Laud, *History of the Troubles and Tryal*, p. 113.
72 Richard Montagu, *Appello Caesarem* (1625), pp. 112–13; cf. pp. 6, 10, 49.
73 Laud, *Conference*, "To His Most Sacred Majesty, Charles." See Nicholas Tyacke, *Anti-Calvinists* (Oxford, 1987), on the Arminian movement within the English church.
74 John Hales, *Golden Remaines of the ever Memorable John Hales* (1659), pp. 57, 54, 36, 34–5.
75 See Michael Schoenfeldt on the concern with class and incivility in these epigrams: "The Art of Disgust: Civility and the Social Body in *Hesperides*," *George Herbert Journal* 14 (Fall 1990/Spring 1991), 127–54. On the commonplace identification of puritan nonconformity with the lower classes, see, e.g., R. T., *De Templis*, p. 117.
76 Giles Widdowes, *The Lawlesse Kneelesse Schismaticall Puritan* (Oxford, 1631), observed that the puritans' rejection of bowing at the name of Jesus reflected an "unregenerate" sense that "the soule, and bodie are contraries" (pp. 86–7).
77 John Burges, *Answer*, e.g., pp. 91–2, stresses "decency" in describing the role of ceremonies. Cf. Morton, *Defence*, pp. 46, 87, 203, 220, 251.
78 Laud, *History of the Troubles and Tryal*, p. 224.
79 On restricting Communion and the church to the godly, see Marshall, *Sermon* preached to the House of Commons, November 17, 1640, p. 35, and Sibbes, *Churches Visitation*, p. 7. On attitudes towards Communion, see Lake, *Anglicans and Puritans?*, especially pp. 178–82, and Morrill, "Church in England, 1642–9," p. 106, on parliamentary ordinances attempting to restrict Communion.
80 Virginia Ramey Mollenkott, "Herrick and the Cleansing of Perception," in *"Trust to Good Verses": Herrick Tercentenary Essays*, ed. Roger B. Rollin and J. Max Patrick (Pittsburgh, 1978), pp. 197–209, argues that Herrick finds pleasure sacramental and sees God in everything.

81 Marshall, *Sermon* preached to the House of Commons November 17, 1640, p. 28.
82 On Arminianism and ceremony, see Tyacke, *Anti-Calvinists*, and Lake, "Laudian Style," pp. 161–85.
83 See Morton, *Defence*, pp. 3, 27–8, 156; John Burges, *Answer*, p. 79. On "naked" worship, see, e.g., Ames, *Fresh Suit*, pp. 269. Claude Summers discusses ceremonies as clothes in his reading of "*The Widdowes teares: or, Dirge of* Dorcas" (N-123) in "Tears for Herrick's Church," *George Herbert Journal* 14 (1990/91), 61–2.
84 John Burges, *Answer*, p. 79.
85 Ames, *Fresh Suit*, "An Addition," p. 52. See also Ames's dedication "To the renowned King, Edward the Sixt. And . . . King Charles"; Burton, *For God, and the King*; and William Prynne, *A Looking-glasse for all Lordly Prelates* (1636).
86 John Burges, *Answer*, p. 461; R. T., *De Templis*, pp. 190–1. Cf. Cosin on the need to "stir up" the people to devotion, *Correspondence of John Cosin*, p. 112.
87 On the obsession with death and loss in *Hesperides*, see M. Thomas Hester, "Herrick's Masque of Death," forthcoming in *The English Civil Wars and the Literary Imagination*, ed. Claude J. Summers and Ted-Larry Pebworth.
88 Ames, *Reply*, p. 72; *Fresh Suit*, p. 380.
89 Genesis 28 is cited by John Burges, *Answer*, pp. 423–32, and Morton, *Defence*, p. 99.

5   SIR THOMAS BROWNE: THE PROMISCUOUS EMBRACE OF
RITUAL ORDER

1 Michael Wilding, *Dragons Teeth: Literature in the English Revolution* (Oxford, 1987), pp. 89–113; Stanley Fish, "The Bad Physician: The Case of Sir Thomas Browne," in *Self-Consuming Artifacts: The Experience of Seventeenth-century Literature* (Berkeley, 1972), pp. 353–73. Victoria Silver, "Liberal Theology and Sir Thomas Browne's 'Soft and Flexible' Discourse," *ELR* 20 (1990), 69–105, answers Fish (and to a lesser degree Wilding) and offers a more sympathetic analysis of Browne's religious politics.
2 *The Works of Sir Thomas Browne*, ed. Geoffrey Keynes, 4 vols. (Chicago, 1964), I, 9 ("To the Reader"). Subsequent quotations are from this volume and will be referred to by page number, except for *Religio Medici*, which will be cited by part, section, and page number.
3 Jonathan F. S. Post, *Sir Thomas Browne* (Boston, 1987), p. 44; Post, "Browne's Revisions of *Religio Medici*," *SEL* 25 (1985), 145–63, places Browne at a distance from Laud.
4 On Browne as moderate, see Post, *Browne*, pp. 44–8. Wilding, *Dragons Teeth*, identifies him with the Laudian elitism and hostility to puritanism (pp. 89–113).
5 Burton, *For God, and the King*, pp. 51–2.

6 Post, *Browne*, p. 48.

7 Richard Montagu, *Appello Caesarem* (1625), p. 10.

8 John Bastwick, *A Briefe Relation of certain . . . passages and speeches in the Starre-chamber . . . At the Censure of . . . Dr. Bastwick, Mr. Burton and Mr. Prynne* (1638), especially p. 13. On the increasingly polarized views of the relation of the English church to the Church of Rome, see Anthony Milton, *Catholic and Reformed*, especially chapters 1–4.

9 William Laud, *A Relation of the Conference . . .* (1639), pp. 128–9, Christopher Dow, *Innovations Unjustly charged . . .* (1637), pp. 45–6, 47. Cf. Peter Heylyn, *A Briefe and Moderate Answer to The seditious and scandalous Challenges of Henry Burton* (1637), p. 125.

10 Burton, *Replie*, p. 392. Cf. Henry Burton, *A Plea to An Appeale* (1626), and *For God, and the King*, pp. 14, 121–2; John Bastwick, *The Answer . . . To the exceptions made against his Letany* (1637), pp. 7–8.

11 John Bastwick, *The Letany of John Bastwick, Doctor of Physicke* (1637), p. 12; William Prynne, *Newes from Ipswich* (1636), sig. A3v–A4v.

12 See the account in Bastwick, *Briefe Relation*, quotation p. 21; Kevin Sharpe, *The Personal Rule of Charles I* (New Haven, 1992), pp. 758–65, describes how these three became popular martyrs.

13 Montagu, *Appello Caesarem*, p. 143; Heylyn, *Briefe and Moderate Answer*, pp. 128–9, also rejects the idea that the Pope is Antichrist. Anthony Milton, *Catholic and Reformed*, notes that Montagu's *New Gagg* (1624) was "the first clear assault in print" on the Jacobean Protestant consensus that the Pope was Antichrist (p. 112). Wilding, *Dragons Teeth*, observes that Browne's "anti-millenarianism and scepticism about Antichrist indicate his consistent opposition to the world-view of the radical sects" (p. 96).

14 Bastwick, *Answer*, p. 8; Montagu, *Appello Caesarem*, p. 147.

15 Silver, "Liberal Theology," sees Browne's charity as participating in the "liberal strain" of reformed theology (pp. 69–105, especially pp. 75–6). For Raymond B. Waddington, Browne's emphasis on charity identifies him with "Anglicans," who stress the second table of the ten commandments. See "The Two Tables in *Religio Medici*," in *Approaches to Sir Thomas Browne*, ed. C. A. Patrides (Columbia, 1982), pp. 81–99.

16 Joseph Hall, *An Humble Remonstrance to the High Court of Parliament* (1640), pp. 35, 43; *A Defence of the Humble Remonstrance, Against . . . Smectymnuus* (1641), pp. 132, 155.

17 Montagu, *Appello Caesarem*, p. 60; Dow, *Innovations Unjustly charged . . .* p. 48; Laud, *Conference*, "To His Most Sacred Majesty, Charles," [sig. A4r].

18 Alexander Ross, *Medicus Medicatus: or the Physicians Religion cured . . .* (1645), pp. 2, 3, 6–9.

19 Ibid., sig. A3v.

20 Joan Webber, *The Eloquent "I"* (Madison, 1968), p. 152; Fish, *Self-Consuming Artifacts*, especially pp. 365, 367, 372.

21 Bastwick, *Letany*, pp. 10, 14; Prynne, *Newes from Ipswich*, quotation sig. A2v; Burton, *For God, and the King*, p. 159.

22 Wilding, *Dragons Teeth*, concludes: "Browne's peaceableness is the peaceableness of the conservative who is satisfied with the arrangement of society – an arrangement suiting his own class" (p. 95).

23 Ibid., pp. 100–2.

24 Silver, "Liberal Theology," remarks, "*Religio* operates as a kind of inverse polemic: it does not presume to certain truth, and . . . expounds no positive doctrine" (pp. 96–7).

25 Sir Kenelm Digby, *Observations upon Religio Medici* (1643), p. 18.

26 See Achsah Guibbory, "Sir Thomas Browne's *Pseudodoxia Epidemica* and the Circle of Knowledge," *Texas Studies in Language and Literature* 18 (1976), 486–99.

27 Silver, "Liberal Theology," p. 102.

28 Post, *Browne*, observes: "If he does not defend sectarians, he also does not attempt to forbid them their gatherings, and in this act of toleration, Browne distinguishes himself most clearly from Laud" (p. 48).

29 Digby, *Observations*, pp. 6–7.

30 *A Directory for the Public Worship of God* (1645), pp. 73–4. Cf. "The order for the buriall of the dead" in the 1638 Book of Common Prayer. For an important statement of the puritan position, see the 1572 "Admonition to the Parliament," which objected to having "a prescript kinde of service to burie the dead," reprinted in *Puritan Manifestoes: A Study of the Origin of the Puritan Revolt*, ed. W. H. Frere and C. E. Douglas (London, 1907), quotation p. 28. In 1634, John Canne echoed the *Admonition* and the Scottish *First Book of Discipline* (1560) as he insisted that he and other "nonconformists" wanted the corpse to be buried "without all kind of ceremony heretofore used" (*A Necessitie of Separation from the Church of England* [Amsterdam, 1643], p. 102). Henry Machyn's diary describes an unceremonious Protestant funeral he witnessed in 1559 (*The Diary of Henry Machyn . . . from A.D. 1550 to A.D. 1563*, ed. John Gough Nichols [New York and London, 1848], p. 193). See Dennis Kay's discussion of the diary entry and of changes in funerals precipitated by the Reformation in *Melodious Tears: The English Funeral Elegy from Spenser to Milton* (Oxford, 1990), "Introduction."

31 Clare Gittings, *Death, Burial and the Individual in Early Modern England* (London, 1984), has questioned "just how effective the Puritan insistence on simple burial was even during the Civil War and the Interregnum itself" (p. 54), but her data (in her "Statistical Appendix") show a sharp drop in the number of church burials and funeral doles after 1640. The radical decrease during these years in the number of surviving probate accounts, which are her source of information about funerals, makes it hard to generalize about what actually happened. The church burials are referred to by contemporaries as noteworthy, hence probably exceptions to the usual practice.

32 See, e.g., John Selden's *Historie of Tithes* (1618).
33 Peter Heylyn, *Antidotum Lincolniense* (1637), section II, p. 69; on nature and reason's place in the development of ceremony, see also John Pocklington, *Altare Christianum* (1637), pp. 4–5, 154.
34 R. T., *De Templis* (1638), p. 101.
35 John Cosin, *Notes and Collections on the Book of Common Prayer*, vol. v of *The Works of John Cosin* (Oxford, 1855), p. 171.
36 Ibid., p. 168; this is from the 1619 notes on the Prayer Book.
37 *Directory*, p. 74.
38 David E. Stannard, *The Puritan Way of Death: A Study in Religion, Culture, and Social Change* (Oxford, 1977), shows that, in contrast to their counterparts in England, New England puritans during the mid-seventeenth century developed a heightened concern with funeral ritual: "in virtually every aspect . . . the New England Puritans ritualized death as only the most non-Puritan of pre-Restoration Englishmen would have dared do" (p. 117). See chapter 5, pp. 96–134.
39 John Milton, *Complete Poems and Major Prose*, ed. Merritt Y. Hughes (New York, 1957).
40 Michael Lieb, *Milton and the Culture of Violence* (Ithaca, 1994), pp. 51–8, discusses the drowning of Lycidas as a dis-membering, and Milton's poetry as a re-membering of that body.
41 Post, *Browne*, gives a politically more optimistic interpretation, suggesting that *Urn Buriall*'s message is one of "preservation and continuity," of "survival" by "living underground" during puritan ascendancy (pp. 131–4).
42 Post, ibid., p. 132, sees Browne's rejection of monuments in the final chapter as consonant with a puritan dislike of icons.
43 Cf. Canne's attack on the "superstitious" practice in the Church of England of "laying the dead in the grave, viz. *East* and *West*, that he may rise with his face to the East" (*Necessitie of Separation*, pp. 102–3). Gittings, *Death, Burial and the Individual*, distinguishes the traditional Anglican attention to the dead body, seen as the temple of the spirit, from the extreme puritan "insistence on the simple disposal of the corpse, which they viewed with such disgust" (pp. 46–7). Browne's skepticism about bodily resurrection diverges from the dominant Christian views Caroline Walker Bynum has described in *The Resurrection of the Body in Western Christianity, 200–1336* (New York, 1995).
44 Browne's skepticism about whether individuality will be preserved critically reflects on the "increased personalization" that Philippe Aries sees in the development of funeral art forms from the thirteenth to seventeenth centuries (*Western Attitudes toward Death: From the Middle Ages to the Present*, trans. Patricia M. Ranum [Baltimore, 1974], pp. 47–50).
45 Walter R. Davis, "*Urne Buriall*: A Descent into the Underworld," *Studies in the Literary Imagination* 10 (1977), 73–87, and Leonard Nathanson, *The*

Strategy of Truth (Chicago, 1967), pp. 191–4, emphasize progression and see Christian faith as the culmination of Browne's discourse.

46 Keith Thomas, *Religion and the Decline of Magic* (New York, 1971), chapter 3. Gittings, *Death, Burial and the Individual,* discusses the increasing secularization of post-Reformation funeral rituals (pp. 12, 42, 56–7, 221, 224).

47 Michel Foucault, *The Order of Things: An Archaeology of the Human Sciences* (New York, 1973), chapters 2 ("The Prose of the World") and 3 ("Representing"); quotation p. 54.

48 Heylyn, *Antidotum Lincolniense,* uses the term "Ordination" in defending the special priesthood rejected by puritans (section II, p. 27). See also Hall, *Defence of the Humble Remonstrance,* pp. 50–2, 123–4, 134–5, and *Episcopacie by Divine Right* (1640).

49 Heylyn, *Antidotum Lincolniense,* section II, chapter 5, quotation p. 36; R. T., *De Templis.*

50 See *The Proficience and Advancement of Learning Divine and Humane,* in *The Works of Francis Bacon,* ed. James Spedding, Robert Leslie Ellis, Douglas Denon Heath, 15 vols. (Boston, 1900), VI, 122.

6 JOHN MILTON: CARNAL IDOLATRY AND THE RECONFIGURATION OF WORSHIP, PART I

1 See, e.g., the hymn in *Animadversions,* in John Milton, *Complete Prose Works,* gen. ed. Don M. Wolfe, 8 vols. (New Haven, 1953–82), I, 705–7. Subsequent references to the prose will be to this edition and will be included within the text, by volume and page number. Poetry quotations are from John Milton, *Complete Poems and Major Prose,* ed. Merritt Y. Hughes (New York, 1957).

2 Stephen R. Honeygosky, *Milton's House of God: The Invisible and Visible Church* (Columbia, 1993), recognizes that Milton was concerned not just with religion as an "interior" phenomenon but with reconstructing a "visible" church, and the rites of worship, though Honeygosky focuses only on the prose and does not define these rites. On the concept of holiness and the religious function of the poet, see Michael Lieb's *Poetics of the Holy: A Reading of "Paradise Lost"* (Chapel Hill, 1981).

3 David Loewenstein, *Milton and the Drama of History: Historical Vision, Iconoclasm, and the Literary Imagination* (Cambridge, 1990), stresses iconoclasm as a "profoundly radical, creative, and liberating response" (p. 51); Lana Cable, *Carnal Rhetoric: Milton's Iconoclasm and the Poetics of Desire* (Durham NC, 1995), argues that creative and destructive impulses are almost "indistinguishable" in Milton (pp. 40–1).

4 "Of Truth," *Essays or Counsels,* in *The Works of Francis Bacon,* ed. James Spedding, R. L. Ellis, and D. D. Heath, 15 vols. (Boston, 1861), XII, 81.

5 See Cable, *Carnal Rhetoric,* pp. 64, 66, on the affective qualities of

Milton's sensuous and scurrilous rhetoric in the anti-prelatical pamphlets; she finds Milton seduced by the sensuousness of language.

6 Honeygosky, *House of God*, observes that, for Milton, "the hearts of believers . . . are the real house and church of . . . God" (p. 73).

7 See Galatians 5, Romans 7, 8; Augustine's *City of God*, XIV, XV.i–iii; Calvin's *Institutes*, II.i.6, III.iii.8, 10, 12, 13; William Perkins, *The combat of the flesh and spirit*, in *Workes*, vol. 1 (1616), 469–74. On Paul's dualism, see Daniel Boyarin, "Paul and the Genealogy of Gender," *Representations* 41 (1993), 1–33. See also Jason P. Rosenblatt's discussion of Pauline dualism in *Torah and Law in "Paradise Lost"* (Princeton, 1994), p. 71 and chapters 1 and 7.

8 See, e.g., *Reason of Church Government*, I, 835; cf. Calvin, *Institutes*, I, 230 (II.i.9).

9 Rosenblatt, *Torah and Law*, stresses the Hebraism in the 1643–5 tracts and the middle books of *Paradise Lost* but does not mention the anti-Judaic stance of the earlier anti-prelatical tracts. According to Samuel S. Stollman, "Milton's Dichotomy of 'Judaism' and 'Hebraism,'" *PMLA* 89 (1974), 105–12, Milton disparages "Judaic" as referring to the Jews alone but uses "Hebraic" to designate the universal aspects of the Old Testament.

10 Corns, *Uncloistered Virtue*, especially pp. 13–32, discusses the adversarial strategies of the anti-prelatical tracts. Loewenstein, *Drama of History*, discusses Milton's individualism, his role as iconoclast and "aggressive activist in the drama of history" (p. 22). Cable, *Carnal Rhetoric*, shows how his iconoclasm operates at the level of metaphor and "affective language" (p. 2). On his aggression and activism, see also Janel Mueller, "Embodying Glory: The Apocalyptic Strain in Milton's *Of Reformation*," in *Politics, Poetics, and Hermeneutics in Milton's Prose*, ed. David Loewenstein and James Grantham Turner (Cambridge, 1990), pp. 9–40. Christopher Hill, *Milton and the English Revolution* (New York, 1977), discusses Milton as a "radical Protestant heretic," actively engaged in the Revolution (quotation p. 3). See also Michael Walzer, *The Revolution of the Saints* (Cambridge MA, 1965), on the imagery and concept of warfare in Calvinist and English puritan ideology (pp. 57–65).

11 *The Complete Poetry of John Donne*, ed. John T. Shawcross (Garden City, 1967).

12 See particularly Cedric C. Brown's comments on *Lycidas* as a "polemically intended reformist poem" in *John Milton's Aristocratic Entertainments* (Cambridge, 1985), pp. 157–62, quotation p. 158.

13 See Leah S. Marcus, *The Politics of Mirth* (Chicago, 1986), pp. 169–212; Alice-Lyle Scoufos, "The Mysteries in Milton's *Masque*," *Milton Studies* 6 (1975), 113–42; Georgia B. Christopher, "The Virginity of Faith: *Comus* as a Reformation Conceit," *ELH* 43 (1976), 479–99; Maryann Cale McGuire, *Milton's Puritan Masque* (Athens GA, 1983); David Norbrook, "The Reformation of the Masque," in *The Court Masque*, ed. David

Lindley (Manchester, 1984), pp. 94–110, and "The Politics of Milton's Early Poetry," in *Poetry and Politics in the English Renaissance* (London, 1984), pp. 235–85; and Brown, *Milton's Aristocratic Entertainments*. Marcus has most fully argued an "Anti-Laudian" interpretation of the masque, but her focus is specifically on the Book of Sports controversy and is more on politics than religion.

14 On Comus as spokesman for the Book of Sports, see Marcus, *Politics of Mirth*, especially p. 187. See also Wilding's important reading of the masque's political radicalism, in *Dragons Teeth*, pp. 28–88. Brown, *Milton's Aristocratic Entertainments*, rightly insists that Milton's masque is "religiously determined" (p. 82). See also Christopher, "Virginity of Faith," Scoufos, "Mysteries," and Norbrook, "Politics of Milton's Early Poetry," on the reformist significance of the figure of Comus.

15 Norbrook, "Reformation of the Masque," p. 105, and Scoufos, "Mysteries," p. 131, observe that reformers associated Circe with Roman Catholicism; Brown, *Milton's Aristocratic Entertainments*, sees Comus as a "lively inheritor of Archimagan guile" (p. 76).

16 See Edmund Spenser, *Poetical Works*, ed. J. C. Smith and E. De Selincourt (London, 1965).

17 *The Geneva Bible* (The Annotated New Testament, 1602 edition), ed. Gerald T. Sheppard (New York, 1989), p. 133r. Both Norbrook, *Poetry and Politics*, and Brown, *Milton's Aristocratic Entertainments*, link Milton's reformist poetry with Spenser.

18 William Prynne, *Histrio-Mastix* (1633), p. 33.

19 Henry Burton, *Truth's Triumph Over Trent* (1629), title page; "A Prayer Dedicatory" to Christ.

20 Francis Cheynell, "Sions Memento, and Gods Alarum" (1643), preached 31 May 1643.

21 See Marcus, *Politics of Mirth*, pp. 172–3, and William Riley Parker, *Milton: A Biography*, 2 vols. (Oxford, 1968), II, 792n42.

22 See Michael Wilding, *Dragons Teeth* (Oxford, 1987), pp. 46–9, quotation p. 46; Christopher Hill, *Change and Continuity in Seventeenth-century England* (London, 1974), chapter 1 ("Puritans and 'the Dark Corners of the Land'").

23 Edmund Spenser discusses this belief in *A View of the State of Ireland*, in *Spenser's Prose Works*, ed. Rudolf Gottfried (*The Works of Edmund Spenser: A Variorum Edition*, ed. Edwin Greenlaw, Charles Grosvenor Osgood, Frederick Morgan Padelford, and Ray Heffner) (Baltimore, 1949), pp. 82–90.

24 Hill, *Change and Continuity*, p. 23.

25 Brown, *Milton's Aristocratic Entertainments*, sees Comus as a figure for "luxury," which in the Bible had a religious import (pp. 57–77).

26 Hughes, ed., *Complete Poems*, p. 93n, cites Juvenal, *Satires* II, 91–2.

27 Alexander Leighton, *An Appeal to the Parliament; or Sions Plea against the Prelacie* (Amsterdam? 1628), pp. 192, 205.

28 Arthur Barker, *Milton and the Puritan Dilemma* (Toronto, 1942), notes a connection between *Comus* and the anti-prelatical tracts, suggesting parallels in language and images, but stops short of suggesting that Milton's masque is concerned with idolatry.

29 Peter Smart, *A Sermon Preached in the Cathedrall Church of Durham* (1628), p. 11.

30 Articles, in *The Correspondence of John Cosin, D.D.*, publications of the Surtees Society, vol. 52 (Durham, 1869), p. 165.

31 William Prynne, *A Briefe Survay and Censure of Mr Cozens His Couzening Devotions* (1628), pp. 1–2.

32 William Hunter, Jr., "The Liturgical Context of *Comus*," *ELN* 10 (1972), 11–15.

33 Prynne, *Briefe Survay*, "Epistle."

34 Barbara Breasted argues for the relevance to the masque of a contemporary scandal involving rape, sodomy, and incest which concerned the behavior of the Earl of Castlehaven, whose wife was Egerton's sister-in-law (see *"Comus* and the Castlehaven Scandal," *Milton Studies* 3 [1971], 201–24), and Leah Marcus suggests the relevance of the rape of Margery Evans (see "The Milieu of Milton's *Comus*: Judicial Reform at Ludlow and the Problem of Sexual Assault," *Criticism* 25 [1983], 293–327).

35 Scoufos, "Mysteries," pp. 113–42, quotation p. 121. On Milton's "feminine identification" and his identification with the Lady, see William Kerrigan, *The Sacred Complex* (Cambridge, 1983), chapter 2 (quotation p. 50), and John T. Shawcross, *John Milton: The Self and the World* (Lexington, 1993), chapter 3.

36 Discussing the masque's concern to preserve chastity in the context of Milton's pervasive concern with mutilation and dismemberment, Michael Lieb, *Milton and the Culture of Violence* (Ithaca, 1994), well observes, "the ability to remain chaste in the face of overwhelming odds is at the very center of the *agon*" (p. 100).

37 On the connection between idolatry and adultery in the Bible, see also Regina M. Schwartz, "Nations and Nationalism: Adultery in the House of David," *Critical Inquiry* 19 (1992), 131–50.

38 Prynne, *Briefe Survay*, p. 1. Henry Burton, *Truth's Triumph Over Trent: or the Great Gulfe between Sion and Babylon* (1629), "A Prayer Dedicatory" to Christ.

39 Prynne, *Canterburies Doome* (1646), p. 105. Cf. "Homilie against perill of Idolatrie," in *Certaine Sermons or Homilies Appointed to be Read in Churches in the Time of Queen Elizabeth I*, ed. Mary Ellen Rickey and Thomas B. Stroup, facsimile of 1623 edn. (Gainesville, 1968), Second Tome, pp. 61–2.

40 See Marcus, *Politics of Mirth*, pp. 187–90.

41 Stephen Marshall, *A Sermon*, preached to the House of Commons, Nov. 17, 1640 (1641).

42 On chastity versus luxury, see Brown, *Milton's Aristocratic Entertainments*, p. 82; on virginity or chastity as faith, see Christopher, "Virginity of Faith," pp. 484–5.

43 Laud, *Conference*, "Dedicatory Epistle to King Charles." Cf. Montagu, *Appello Caesarem*, pp. 6, 10, 112–13; John Cosin, *A Collection of Private Devotions* (1627), "The Preface."

44 *The Poems and Letters of Andrew Marvell*, ed. H. M. Margoliouth, 3rd edn. revised by Pierre Legouis with E. E. Duncan-Jones, vol. 1 (Oxford, 1971), pp. 12–13.

45 On Marvell's concern with virginity, see John Rogers, *The Matter of Revolution: Science, Poetry, and Politics in the Age of Milton* (Ithaca, 1996), chapter 3.

46 On this change as signaling Milton's increasingly outspoken polemical stance, see Brown, *Milton's Aristocratic Entertainments*, especially pp. 135–40.

47 Henry Burton, *A Replie to a Relation, of the Conference . . .* (1640), p. 42.

48 Marcus, *Politics of Mirth*, p. 197, notes Comus' ploys to get the Lady to drink are inseparable from the effort to seduce her, but the logic of this connection has not to my knowledge been explained.

49 Articles, in *Correspondence of John Cosin*, p. 174; Smart, *Sermon*, p. 20.

50 Prynne, *Briefe Survay*, "The Epistle."

51 On Sabrina's connection with song and poetry, see Norbrook, *Poetry and Politics*, p. 262; on her connection with song and ritual, see Marcus, *Politics of Mirth*, pp. 199–200.

52 Brown, *Milton's Aristocratic Entertainments*, chapter 5.

53 John Halkett, *Milton and the Idea of Matrimony: A Study of the Divorce Tracts and "Paradise Lost"* (New Haven, 1970), argues that the "theoretical postulates" in the divorce tracts indicate Milton's severance from the presbyterians (p. 1). Rosenblatt, *Torah and Law*, shows how Milton's positive conception of the Mosaic law in the divorce tracts rejects the Pauline formulation that Christ frees Christians from bondage to the Mosaic law (especially pp. 46–7, 97–112).

54 Those who stress the monism of Milton's divorce tracts include Rosenblatt, *Torah and Law*, pp. 75, 97–112; Stephen M. Fallon, "The Metaphysics of Milton's Divorce Tracts," in *Politics, Poetics, and Hermeneutics*, ed. Loewenstein and Turner, pp. 69–83; and Lana Cable, "Coupling Logic and Milton's Doctrine of Divorce," *Milton Studies* 15 (1981), 143–59. My own position is closer to James Grantham Turner, *One Flesh: Paradisal Marriage and Sexual Relations in the Age of Milton* (Oxford, 1987), who sees Milton's separation of body and soul and disgust for sexuality crossed by an occasional "materialist monism" that anticipates *Paradise Lost*, pp. 198–200.

55 See Mary Nyquist's discussion of the paradigmatically masculine individualism of these tracts: "The Genesis of Gendered Subjectivity in the Divorce Tracts and in *Paradise Lost*," in *Re-membering Milton:*

Essays on the Texts and Traditions, ed. Mary Nyquist and Margaret W. Ferguson (New York, 1987), pp. 99–127. Halkett, *Milton and the Idea of Matrimony,* observes that Milton gives only the man the right to divorce (p. 90).

56 Anthony Low, *The Reinvention of Love: Poetry, Politics, and Culture from Sidney to Milton* (Cambridge, 1993), observes how rarely Milton evokes the trope of the church as Bride of Christ (p. 165).

57 Honeygosky, *House of God,* well observes that for Milton separation from a diseased church is "a true rite of communion" (p. 97). On the integrative sensibility of *The Doctrine and Discipline of Divorce,* see Rosenblatt, *Torah and Law,* pp. 98, 82–111.

58 See, e.g., Ephraim Pagit, *Heresiography* (1645), sig. A3v; *An Answer to a Book, Intituled, The Doctrine and Discipline of Divorce* (1644); and William Prynne, *Twelve Considerable Serious Questions* (1644), p. 7. Palmer's sermon, preached in August, was published in November 1644 (*Sermons Preached to the Honourable House of Commons,* vol. III).

59 Hill, *Milton and the English Revolution,* distinguishes "radical Arminianism" from the Arminianism of Laud and Montagu (pp. 268–78). See Rosenblatt's discussion of the Hebraic ethos of *Areopagitica* in *Torah and Law,* pp. 113–22.

60 Milton would have found Cromwell's position more congenial, with his distrust of human institutions and forms in religion, and his commitment to the spirit. On Cromwell's antiformalism, see J. C. Davis, "Cromwell's Religion," in *Oliver Cromwell and the English Revolution,* ed. John Morrill (London, 1990), pp. 181–208.

61 Honeygosky, *House of God,* observes that in this passage Milton makes schism "part of the spiritual architecture" of the house of God (p. 122).

62 Loewenstein, *Drama of History,* sees Milton's demolishing the "fiction" of the king's book, *Eikon Basilike,* in an attempt "to free history from the tyranny of the king's image" (p. 51).

63 Mary Ann Radzinowicz, " 'In those days there was no king in Israel': Milton's Politics and Biblical Narrative," in *Yearbook of English Studies* 21 (1991), 242–52, argues that Milton's interest in "premonarchic" biblical narratives "serve[s] a republican politics" (243).

64 Rosenblatt, *Torah and Law,* p. 15.

65 On the early Christian construction of the identity of the Jews as carnal rather than spiritual, see Daniel Boyarin, *Carnal Israel* (Berkeley, 1993), pp. 1–60.

66 Laura Lunger Knoppers, "Milton's *The Readie and Easie Way* and the English Jeremiad," in *Politics, Poetics, and Hermeneutics,* ed. Loewenstein and Turner, pp. 213–25, discusses Milton's tract as concerned with bringing divine judgment against the people. Corns, *Uncloistered Virtue,* focuses on the element of rational justification as Milton's tract addresses "men's narrower interests" and still tries to effect change (p. 284).

7 JOHN MILTON: CARNAL IDOLATRY AND THE
RECONFIGURATION OF WORSHIP, PART II

1 *The Works of John Dryden*, ed. Edward N. Hooker and H. T. Swedenberg, Jr., vol. 1 (Berkeley, 1956), p. 30.
2 See Paula R. Backscheider, *Spectacular Politics: Theatrical Power and Mass Culture in Early Modern England* (Baltimore, 1993), pp. 3–31; quotations pp. 20, 18.
3 On religion after the Restoration, see N. H. Keeble, *The Literary Culture of Nonconformity in Later Seventeenth-century England* (Athens GA, 1987), especially pp. 1–67; Horton Davies, *Worship and Theology in England*, vol. II, *From Andrewes to Baxter and Fox, 1603–1690* (Princeton, 1975), chapters 10 and 12; John Spurr, *The Restoration Church of England, 1646–1689* (New Haven, 1991).
4 Keeble, *Nonconformity*, p. 31; Horton Davies, *Worship and Theology*, p. 439. For the text of the Uniformity Act, see *Documents Illustrative of English Church History*, ed. Henry Gee and William J. Hardy (London, 1896), pp. 600–19.
5 See the Five Mile Act and the Second Conventicle Act in *Documents*, pp. 620–32; quotations p. 621.
6 On the revised Prayer Book, see Horton Davies, *Worship and Theology*, pp. 363–404.
7 Corns, *Uncloistered Virtue*, p. 296. See also Ronald Hutton, *The Restoration: A Political and Religious History of England and Wales 1658–1667* (Oxford, 1985).
8 See Keeble, *Nonconformity*, and David Quint, *Epic and Empire: Politics and Generic Form from Virgil to Milton* (Princeton, 1993), chapter 7, especially pp. 268–9. David Norbrook's paper, *"Paradise Lost* as Republican Epic," presented at the Fifth Milton Symposium (July 1995), argues for the continued persistence of republican values. See also *Milton and Republicanism*, ed. David Armitage, Armand Himy, and Quentin Skinner (Cambridge, 1995), especially Roger Lejosne, "Milton, Salmasius and Abdiel" (pp. 106–17), Armand Himy, *"Paradise Lost* as a Republican 'tractatus theologico-politicus'" (pp. 118–34), and David Armitage, "John Milton: Poet against Empire" (pp. 206–25).
9 See Keeble, *Nonconformity*, especially pp. 48–9; also Horton Davies, *Worship and Theology*, pp. 444–8, 490–5.
10 Quint, *Epic and Empire*, finds *Paradise Lost* moving towards romance (pp. 13, 309–24). For Low, *Reinvention of Love*, Milton's privileging of the domestic world of love is deeply secular.
11 See Lieb, *Poetics of the Holy*, especially pp. 34, 64, 245, and Regina M. Schwartz, *Remembering and Repeating: Biblical Creation in "Paradise Lost"* (Cambridge, 1988), especially pp. 63, 72–3, 74. On echoes of specific religious ceremonies, see Thomas B. Stroup, *Religious Rite and Ceremony in Milton's Poetry* (Lexington, 1968).

12 On chaos, see Schwartz, *Remembering and Repeating*, chapter 3, though she does not identify chaos specifically with idolatry.

13 See Lieb, *Poetics of the Holy*, pp. 84–5.

14 Schwartz, *Remembering and Repeating*, pp. 74–5.

15 For a fuller discussion, see Achsah Guibbory, "Charles's Prayers, Idolatrous Images, and True Creation in Milton's *Eikonoklastes*," in *Of Poetry and Politics: New Essays on Milton and His World*, ed. P. G. Stanwood (Binghamton, 1995), pp. 283–94.

16 Milton's commitment to originality involves the distinctive sense of discontinuity with the past that Anthony Kemp has argued was the radical legacy of the Protestant Reformation; see *Estrangement of the Past*.

17 Lana Cable, "Milton's Iconoclastic Truth," in *Politics, Poetics, and Hermeneutics in Milton's Prose*, ed. David Loewenstein and James Grantham Turner (Cambridge, 1990), pp. 135–51, observes that Milton criticizes Charles for "spiritual laziness," whereas for Milton the "*effort of original prayer* . . . at least partially constitutes prayer's worth" (pp. 146–7).

18 On the change in Milton's prose style, see Thomas N. Corns, *The Development of Milton's Prose Style* (Oxford, 1982), pp. 83–103, and Corns's discussion of *Eikonoklastes* in *Uncloistered Virtue*, pp. 208–17.

19 Several critics remind us that the iconoclasts' use of images testified to their power. See Ernest B. Gilman, *Iconoclasm and Poetry in the English Reformation: Down Went Dagon* (Chicago, 1986), pp. 161–6; Cable, *Carnal Rhetoric*. Loewenstein, *Drama of History*, sees Milton's iconoclasm as an imaginative act.

20 See William C. Riggs, *The Christian Poet in "Paradise Lost"* (Berkeley, 1972), pp. 15–45, quotation p. 45. Linda Gregerson, *The Reformation of the Subject: Spenser, Milton, and the English Protestant Epic* (Cambridge, 1995), sees Milton attempting to distinguish his poem from an idolatrous image. Gregerson's concern with the problem of idolatry focuses on "image" and "likeness" in the construction of subjectivity.

21 Gregerson, *Reformation of the Subject*, pp. 244–5, quotation p. 258.

22 Lieb, *Poetics of the Holy*, p. 128, describes Pandemonium as a temple where Satan's followers engage in perverted worship. Quint, *Epic and Empire*, sees the echoes of Fletcher's *The Apollyonists* in Milton's council in Pandemonium reinforcing Milton's association of Satan and the fallen angels with Roman Catholicism (pp. 270–8).

23 John Harper, in a paper at the Fifth International Milton Symposium (Bangor, Wales, July 1995), observed that Pandemonium resembles the large organs Milton would have seen in Italy that were built like a temple with pillars.

24 On the gendered, sexual metaphoric import of Milton's description of poetic inspiration in *Paradise Lost*, see especially Stevie Davies, *The Feminine Reclaimed* (Lexington, 1986), pp. 194–6, and Michael Lieb, *The Dialectics of Creation* (Amherst, 1970). Kerrigan, *Sacred Complex*, discusses

Milton's "feminine identification" and his placing himself in the feminine "slot" of the " 'vast Abyss' " (pp. 50, 189). See also Schwartz, *Remembering and Repeating*, on Milton's connecting his poem with the Creation (chapter 3).

25 Quint, *Epic and Empire*, aligns Milton not with the Virgilian epic that celebrates empire, imperialism, and monarchy, but with the anti-monarchical tradition of Lucan. Christopher Hill has argued that Milton's late poems struggle with the failure of the Revolution: see *Milton and the English Revolution* (New York, 1977), pp. 341–478, and *The Experience of Defeat: Milton and Some Contemporaries* (London, 1984).

26 See *OED*, s.v. serve. Lieb, *Poetics of the Holy*, recognizes that the "issue of worship . . . characterizes the entire conflict" between Satan and the rebel angels and God (p. 287). Schwartz, *Remembering and Repeating*, finds Satan's denial of his Maker the key to his fall (pp. 21–2).

27 Perez Zagorin, *Ways of Lying* (Cambridge MA, 1990).

28 Recent critics almost uniformly distance Milton from Satan. An exception is Christopher Kendrick, *Milton: A Study in Ideology and Form* (New York, 1986), who sees Satan as a symbolic "fulfillment of Milton's revolutionary desire" (p. 151).

29 Joan S. Bennett, *Reviving Liberty: Radical Christian Humanism in Milton's Great Poems* (Cambridge MA, 1989), observes that Milton's God is "a voluntarily accountable monarch," not an absolutist king like Charles I or Satan (pp. 58–93, quotation p. 67).

30 Sharon Achinstein, *Milton and the Revolutionary Reader* (Princeton, 1994), pp. 177–223, connects the devils with "the Interregnum political figures," arguing that Satan "closely resembles the parliamentary figures lampooned in the Parliament of hell genre of the Interregnum" (pp. 199–200).

31 See Bennett, *Reviving Liberty*, chapter 2 ("Satan and King Charles: Milton's Royal Portraits").

32 Quint, *Epic and Empire*, sees a "pattern of political reference in *Paradise Lost* that topically links Satan's possession of the earth to the Stuart restoration" (p. 269).

33 On the execution of regicides at the Restoration, see Lieb, *Milton and the Culture of Violence*, pp. 70–7; Laura Lunger Knoppers, *Historicizing Milton: Spectacle, Power, and Poetry in Restoration England* (Athens GA, 1994), pp. 43–53.

34 Noam Flinker, "Milton and the Ranters on Canticles," in *A Fine Tuning: Studies of the Religious Poetry of Herbert and Milton*, ed. Mary A. Maleski (Binghamton, 1989), pp. 273–90, suggests parallels between Milton's prelapsarian Adam and the Ranter use of Canticles.

35 Low, *Reinvention of Love*, pp. 195, 201.

36 Anne Ferry, "Milton's Creation of Eve," *SEL* 28 (1988), 113–32, claims that Milton's wording brings Eve closer to God than Paul's formula in 1 Corinthians 11:7 (p. 117).

37 Cf. Diane Kelsey McColley's argument in *Milton's Eve* (Urbana, 1983), that the relation of Adam and Eve is the "image of the Son's relation to the Father within the Godhead" (p. 51).

38 See, e.g., William Whateley, *A Bride-Bush. Or, A Direction for Married Persons* (1623), pp. 200–1, 204; Robert Cleaver, *A Godly Forme of Houshold Government* (1603), pp. 229–30; and William Gouge, *Of Domesticall Duties* (1622).

39 See Mary Nyquist, "The Genesis of Gendered Subjectivity in the Divorce Tracts and in *Paradise Lost*," in *Re-membering Milton: Essays on the Texts and Traditions*, ed. Mary Nyquist and Margaret Ferguson (New York, 1987), pp. 99–127, on how Milton emphasizes Adam's priority and Eve's education in submissiveness. Gregerson, *Reformation of the Subject*, p. 167, remarks how, in contrast to Adam, Eve "has had to be trained against instinct to recognize the source behind her 'likeness.' "

40 John Lilburne, *Regall Tyrannie Discovered* (1647), p. 64; *The Declaration and Standard of the Levellers in England, Delivered in a Speech to his Excellency the Lord General Fairfax, on Friday last at White-Hall, by Mr. Everard* (April 23, 1649), p. 3.

41 Honeygosky, *House of God*, pp. 62–75, sees Milton opposed not to external worship but to worship that is imposed and limits the freedom of spirit.

42 Stroup, *Religious Rite*, finds in the Son's ceremony before God's altar "an adumbration of the Lord's Supper" (p. 43) and discusses the liturgical echoes of Adam and Eve's morning and evening prayers (pp. 28–32). Kathleen M. Swaim, "The Morning Hymn of Praise in Book 5 of *Paradise Lost*," *Milton Quarterly* 22 (1988), 7–16, sees both Psalm 148 and the morning liturgy as sources for the Miltonic hymn.

43 Peter Lindenbaum, "Lovemaking in Milton's Paradise," *Milton Studies* 6 (1975), 277–306; Turner, *One Flesh*, chapter 7; Halkett, *Milton and the Idea of Matrimony*, pp. 102, 108–9; and McColley, *Milton's Eve*, especially pp. 63–74. For Thomas N. Corns, *Regaining "Paradise Lost"* (London, 1994), Adam's leading Eve to the bower evokes the English ceremony of bedding the bride. Turner discusses the history of exegetical interpretations of Adam and Eve's marriage. Gregerson, *Reformation of the Subject*, observes how Milton vigorously excludes "other erotic and domestic possibilities" (p. 175).

44 Several critics have noticed Milton's emphasis on the holiness of sex. See especially Lindenbaum, "Lovemaking," Turner, *One Flesh*, and G. Stanley Koehler, "Milton and the Art of Landscape," *Milton Studies* 8 (1975), 3–40, especially 21–5.

45 On the significance of the holy place and on the "Holy of Holies," see Lieb, *Poetics of the Holy*, pp. 122–5, 127.

46 On the history of interpreting the Song of Songs, see Stanley Stewart, *The Enclosed Garden: The Tradition and the Image in Seventeenth-century Poetry*

(Madison, 1966), pp. 3–30; and Ann W. Astell, *The Song of Songs in the Middle Ages* (Ithaca, 1990).

47 The 1917 Jewish Publication Society translation of the Masoretic text translates *shalhevetyah* as "the flame of God," taking the suffix *yah* to mean "of God, of the Lord." Christian translations have seen the suffix as simply an intensifier (as in "a most vehement flame" [AV and RSV]; "a vehement flame" [Geneva Bible]) – a position also taken by the commentary in Marvin H. Pope's translation in *The Anchor Bible's "Song of Songs"* (Garden City, 1977), p. 672, and by Ariel Bloch and Chana Bloch, *The Song of Songs: A New Translation* (New York, 1995).

48 Turner, *One Flesh*, discusses Christian attitudes towards sexual love, and Milton's departure from its dominant traditions.

49 Elaine Pagels, *Adam, Eve, and the Serpent* (New York, 1988), pp. 3–31; Peter Brown, *The Body and Society* (New York, 1988). See also Boyarin, "Paul and the Genealogy of Gender" and *Carnal Israel* (Berkeley, 1993).

50 Turner, *One Flesh*, pp. 22–3; J. M. Evans, *Paradise Lost and the Genesis Tradition* (Oxford, 1968), pp. 43–6, and especially Lindenbaum, "Love-making," pp. 278 and 302n, mention the rabbinic emphasis on sexuality before the Fall but do not discuss Jewish views of sex after the Fall. Rosenblatt, *Torah and Law*, notes that "the Talmudic view of sacred carnality" is relevant to Milton's treatment of sexual love in the middle books of *Paradise Lost* (p. 136).

51 Quotation from the annotated revised Ganzfried-Goldin English edition, *Code of Jewish Law*, compiled by Rabbi Solomon Ganzfried, trans. Hyman E. Goldin (New York, 1963), vol. I, chapter 31, p. 100. The *Code of Jewish Law*, or *Shulhan Aruh*, composed by Joseph Karo from the extensive rabbinic commentaries and published in 1555, is repeatedly cited in John Selden's *Uxor Hebraica*, which Rosenblatt, "Milton's Chief Rabbi," *Milton Studies*, 24 (1989), 43–71, argues was probably Milton's chief source of rabbinic commentary.

52 Eugene J. Lipman, ed. and trans. *The Mishnah: Oral Teachings of Judaism* (New York, 1970), p. 168n.

53 Cf. John Rumrich's argument in "Milton's God and the Matter of Chaos," *PMLA* 110 (1995), 1035–46, that Milton's "materialist understanding of the deity," in which "chaos is God's womb," presupposes "a hermaphroditic deity" (1043–4).

54 Albert C. Labriola's essay, "Milton's Eve and the Cult of Elizabeth I," *JEGP* 95 (1996), 38–51, shows how Milton in Book IX surrounds Eve with the iconography of Queen Elizabeth.

55 Gregerson, *Reformation of the Subject*, sees Adam's attraction to Eve as representing the seductive power of images (p. 172), and perceptively argues that "Milton unfolds a doctrine of images" in the "progress of domestic love" (p. 153).

56 On Milton as committed monist, see McColley, *Milton's Eve*, pp. 1–62; Kerrigan, *Sacred Complex*, chapter 5; Schwartz, *Remembering and Repeating*,

chapter 1; Stephen M. Fallon, *Milton among the Philosophers: Poetry and Materialism in Seventeenth-century England* (Ithaca, 1991); and Rumrich, "Matter of Chaos." Rosenblatt, *Torah and Law,* argues that the Hebraic monism of the Edenic books is repudiated by the Pauline ethos of Books XI and XIII.

57 Turner, *One Flesh,* recognizes the "irresolvable doubleness at the heart of Milton's apprehension of wedded love" (p. 286).

58 David Aers and Bob Hodge, " 'Rational Burning': Milton on Sex and Marriage," in David Aers, Bob Hodge, Gunther Kress, *Literature, Language and Society in England, 1580–1680* (Totowa, 1981), pp. 122–51, see Adam as correcting Raphael's mistaken reproach (pp. 145–8).

59 See especially McColley's defense of Eve in *Milton's Eve.* McColley, "Subsequent or Precedent? Eve as Milton's Defense of Poesie," *Milton Quarterly* 20 (1986), 132–6, argues that Eve embodies many qualities and processes that Milton attributes to poetry and to himself as a poet.

60 Schwartz, *Remembering and Repeating,* remarks that "the separation between external and internal worship only occurs after the fall" (p. 76). McColley, *Milton's Eve,* notes the dualism of Adam's misogynous speeches after the Fall, but wants to dissociate them from Milton, whom she sees as unremittingly "monist" (p. 9).

61 Low, *Reinvention of Love,* observes that "Milton looks in marriage for a communality that he does not find either in the Church or in the other social institutions of the fallen world" (p. 188).

62 Gregerson, *Reformation of the Subject,* sees Adam's longing as a sign of the "defect" that makes him a proper "image" of God: the human being must be "imperfect . . . lest he set himself up as deity itself" (p. 168).

63 Maureen Quilligan, *Milton's Spenser: The Politics of Reading* (Ithaca, 1983), p. 237. Gregerson, *Reformation of the Subject,* stresses the "fault lines" in Milton's representation of domestic love but casts Eve's postlapsarian subjection in a more favorable light, finding her now "the normative, postlapsarian human subject," providing a model for the "paths available to humankind" (pp. 196–7).

64 Cf. A. B. Chambers's discussion of this temptation in *Transfigured Rites in Seventeenth-century English Poetry* (Columbia, 1992), pp. 68–70.

65 Arguing that Satan tries to lure the Son "into premature or ill-conceived political action," Hill, *Milton and the English Revolution,* does not see the Son as repudiating "the possibility of an earthly kingdom" (p. 417).

66 See especially Gilman, *Down Went Dagon,* pp. 149–77; Loewenstein, *Drama of History,* pp. 126–51; and Knoppers, *Historicizing Milton,* pp. 53–63.

67 Anthony Low, *The Blaze of Noon: A Reading of "Samson Agonistes"* (New York, 1974), observes, "Dalila . . . baffles certainty – not about her crime, but about the nature of her character and motivations" (p. 158).

68 The best of the sympathetic treatments of Dalila is Stella P. Revard's

"Dalila as Euripidean Heroine," *Papers on Language and Literature* 23 (1987), 291–302, which places her among Euripides' complex women, and illuminates the complex politics of her situation.

69 Laura Lunger Knoppers, " 'Sung and Proverb'd for a Fool': *Samson Agonistes* and Solomon's Harlot," *Milton Studies* 26 (1990), 239–51, identifies Dalila with the harlot of Proverbs 7, but does not make the connection with idolatry.

70 Cf. Cable's argument, *Carnal Rhetoric*, pp. 171–96, that in his encounters with Dalila and Harapha Samson strips away and destroys his self-created idols. She sees Dalila as an icon of Samson's shame.

71 See Jackie Di Salvo, "Intestine Thorn: Samson's Struggle with the Woman Within," in *Milton and the Idea of Woman*, ed. Julia M. Walker (Urbana, 1988), pp. 211–29.

72 Lancelot Andrewes, *A Learned Discourse of Ceremonies Retained and used in Christian Churches* (1653), p. 6.

73 In emphasizing Samson's rejection of idolatry in this pivotal scene, I disagree with those who, emphasizing his flaws, deny any regeneration. See especially Irene Samuels, "*Samson Agonistes* as Tragedy," in *Calm of Mind: Tercentenary Essays on Paradise Regained and Samson Agonistes in Honor of John S. Diekhoff*, ed. Joseph Wittreich (Cleveland, 1971), pp. 235–57, and Joseph Wittreich, *Interpreting Samson Agonistes* (Princeton, 1986). An important recent anti-regenerationist reading, which ignores the pivotal Dalila scene, is by Ashraf H. A. Rushdy, *The Empty Garden: The Subject of Late Milton* (Pittsburgh, 1992), who argues that Samson fails to transform "his 'self' into a subject of God" (p. 281).

74 Michael Lieb, " 'Our Living Dread': The God of *Samson Agonistes*," *Milton Studies* 33 (1996), 3–25.

75 See, e.g., Loewenstein, *Drama of History*, p. 147.

76 See Knoppers, *Historicizing Milton*, p. 61.

77 See Hill's reading of *Samson Agonistes* in *Milton and the English Revolution*, pp. 428–48, and Mary Ann Radzinowicz, *Toward Samson Agonistes: The Growth of Milton's Mind* (Princeton, 1978), pp. 87–108, 167–79. Hill finds Samson a "symbol for the revolutionary cause" (p. 435), and Radzinowicz identifies him with the English puritan party, the elect (p. 92). On Samson's progressive isolation in the poem, see especially Low, *Blaze of Noon*, pp. 38–43.

78 Radzinowicz, *Toward Samson Agonistes*, p. 108. Hill, *Experience of Defeat*, sees Samson as revolutionary and exemplary for Restoration England in overthrowing apostasy (p. 317).

Index